Computer Design
and Architecture

Little, Brown Computer Systems Series

Morrill, Harriet
Mini and Micro BASIC: Introducing Applesoft®, Microsoft®, and BASIC Plus

Mosteller, William S.
Systems Programmer's Problem Solver

Nahigian, J. Victor, and William S. Hodges
Computer Games for Businesses, Schools, and Homes

Nahigian, J. Victor, and William S. Hodges
Computer Games for Business, School, and Home for TRS-80® Level II BASIC

Nickerson, Robert C.
Fundamentals of Structured COBOL

Nickerson, Robert C.
Fundamentals of FORTRAN Programming, Second Edition

Nickerson, Robert C.
Fundamentals of Programming in BASIC

Orwig, Gary W., and William S. Hodges
The Computer Tutor: Learning Activities for Homes and Schools

Parikh, Girish
Techniques of Program and System Maintenance

Parkin, Andrew
Data Processing Management

Parkin, Andrew
Systems Analysis

Plzer, Stephen M., with Victor L. Wallace
To Compute Numerically: Concepts and Strategies

Pooch, Udo W., William H. Greene, and Gary G. Moss
Telecommunications and Networking

Reingold, Edward M., and Wilfred J. Hansen
Data Structures

Savitch, Walter J.
Abstract Machines and Grammars

Shneiderman, Ben
Software Psychology: Human Factors in Computer and Information Systems

Simpson, Tom, and Shaffer & Shaffer Applied Research & Development, Inc.
VisiCalc® Programming: No Experience Necessary

Walker, Henry M.
Problems for Computer Solutions Using FORTRAN

Walker, Henry M.
Problems for Computer Solutions Using BASIC

Weinberg, Gerald M.
Rethinking Systems Analysis and Design

Weinberg, Gerald M.
Understanding the Professional Programmer

Windeknecht, Thomas G.
6502 Systems Programming

Computer Design and Architecture

Sajjan G. Shiva

The University of Alabama in Huntsville

Little, Brown and Company

Boston   Toronto

Library of Congress Cataloging in Publication Data

Shiva, Sajjan G.
    Computer design and architecture.

    (Little, Brown computer systems series)
    Includes bibliographical references and index.
    1. Computer engineering. 2. Computer architecture.
I. Title. II. Series.
TK7885.S525 1984   001.64   84-7159
ISBN 0-316-78714-0

Library of Congress Catalog Card No. 84-7159

ISBN 0-316-78714-0

9 8 7 6 5 4 3

HAL

Published simultaneously in Canada
by Little, Brown & Company (Canada) Limited

Printed in the United States of America

To my Mother
and
in memory of
my Father

Preface

This book is about computer design and architecture. *Architecture* is the "art or science of building; a method or style of building," according to *Webster's*. A computer architect develops the specifications for various blocks of a computer and defines the interconnections between those blocks, in consultation with hardware and software designers. A computer designer, on the other hand, refines these building-block specifications and implements the blocks in hardware or software or both. It is my belief that the capabilities of an architect are greatly enhanced if he is exposed to the design aspects of a computer system. Consequently, the backbone of this book is the organization and complete design of a simple but complete hypothetical computer.

Books on digital systems architecture fall into four categories: logic design books that cover the hardware logic design in detail but fail to provide the details of computer hardware design; books on computer organization that deal with the computer hardware from a programmer's point of view; books on computer hardware design that are suitable for an electrical engineering course in hardware design; and books on computer systems architecture that are very high level treatments of computer architecture with no detailed treatment of hardware design. I have tried to gather the important attributes of the four categories of books to come up with a comprehensive text on hardware and software aspects of digital computers.

This book is a result of my teaching the computer architecture sequence of courses at the senior undergraduate and beginning graduate levels for several years, to both computer science and electrical engineering students. The book does not assume prior knowledge of computers, although exposure to programming in a high-level language makes the reading easier. Exposure to electronics is not required as a prerequisite for this book.

The following method of study is suggested for a single-semester course in computer architecture:

> For computer science students with no logic design background: Chapters 1, 2, and 3 in detail, review of Chapter 4, Chapter 5 in detail, followed by selected topics from Chapters 6, 7, and 8.
>
> For computer engineering students: review of Chapters 1 and 2, Chapters 3 through 7 in detail, followed by selected topics from Chapter 8.

A two-semester course in computer architecture could follow:

> Semester 1: Appendix A, Chapter 1, Appendix B, Chapter 2, Appendix C, Chapters 3 and 4 and parts of Chapter 5.
>
> Semester 2: Chapters 5, 6, 7, and 8 and projects (case studies of practical systems).

The introductory chapter briefly outlines digital computer systems terminology, hardware, and software. Traditionally, a discussion of number systems and computer codes is found in this chapter. I have moved this material to Appendix A, since a majority of students are now familiar with this subject much earlier than college level. Appendix A should be the starting point for those who are not familiar with number systems.

Chapter 1 covers combinational logic analysis and design. I have moved the logic minimization discussion to Appendix B. A mastery of logic minimization aspects is not required for the purposes of this book.

Chapter 2 deals with the analysis and design of sequential logic circuits and register-transfer concepts. The material in this chapter could be augmented with the discussion of hardware description languages given in Appendix C. A simple hardware description language (HDL) is introduced in Chapter 2, but the book is not dependent on that language. Any other HDL available can thus be used. Chapters 1 and 2 also contain information on some commercially available integrated circuits.

Chapter 3 introduces models for commonly used memories and describes various memory organizations and devices.

Chapter 4 provides the programmer's view of a simple hypothetical computer (ASC). The organization, assembly language programming, and details of assembler, loader, and other software support are briefly described in this chapter.

Chapter 5 provides a detailed design of various blocks of ASC. Material from Chapters 1, 2, and 3 is used in developing this detailed design. Although development of such a detailed design may be tedious, it is my belief that each designer, architect, and system programmer should go through the steps of such a design to enhance his understanding of the machine.

Chapter 6 draws upon the attributes of commercially available machines to enhance ASC architecture. The intent of this chapter is to show the possibilities of ASC enhancement through examples of architectural features rather than to provide a complete description of any commercial machine.

Chapter 7 details enhancement of the input/output subsystem of ASC and provides pertinent details of various system structures as examples.

Chapter 8 is an overview of architecture classification and current trends in computer architecture. Architectural features of selected supercomputers are described in this chapter. Impact of software and integrated circuit technologies on computer design and architecture are briefly discussed.

Problems are given at the end of each chapter. References, which are also provided at the end of each chapter, may be consulted by readers interested in further details. Examples are provided within the body of each chapter as needed.

Many colleagues and students have contributed to the development of this book. In particular I would like to thank Dr. H.S. Ranganath and my students in the computer architecture course sequence at the University of Alabama in Huntsville for their comments on the manuscript. Essential to the development of the book was the untiring typing support of Jo Peddycoart. I would like to thank Kalpana, Sruti, and Sweta; Kalpana for her patience and encouragement during the manuscript preparation, Sruti for understanding how busy Daddy was, and Sweta for arriving at a propitious moment. Last, thanks to Tom Casson and Elizabeth Schaaf at Little, Brown; Tom for his encouragement and Elizabeth for her superb support in the production of this book.

S.G.S.

Contents

Computer Design
and Architecture

Introduction

Computer System Components

Recent advances in microelectronic technology have made computers an integral part of our society. Each step in our everyday lives may be influenced by computer technology: we awake to a digital alarm clock's beaming of preselected music at the right time, drive to work in a digital-processor-controlled automobile, work in an extensively automated office, shop for computer-coded grocery items and return to rest in the computer-regulated heating and cooling environment of our homes. It may not be necessary to understand the detailed operating principles of a jet plane or an automobile in order to use and enjoy the benefits of these technical marvels. But a fair understanding of the operating principles, capabilities, and limitations of digital computers *is* necessary, if we would use them in an efficient manner. This book is designed to give such an understanding of the operating principles of digital computers. We will provide the detailed design of a simple hypothetical computer to reinforce knowledge of operating principles and discuss the architectural tradeoffs employed at various stages in the design. We will concentrate on logical-level details of design rather than on details at the more technical electronics level. Hence, no prior electronics exposure is required to understand the material in this book.

The basic objective of this book is to provide comprehensive coverage of both hardware and software aspects of computers with emphasis on hardware design and the architectural tradeoffs required during design. We assume a familiarity with binary, octal, and hexadecimal systems as well as popular computer codes. Appendix A reviews these topics.

This chapter introduces the organization of a general-purpose computer system and briefly traces the evolution of computers. Chapters 1 and 2 cover the basic concepts of digital hardware design. Logic design concepts covered in these chapters are used in later chapters in designing logic circuits that form the components of digital computer hardware. Chapter 3 outlines memory system organization and discusses popular memory devices. A simple hypothetical computer (ASC) is introduced in Chapter 4. The description of ASC in this chapter follows a programmer's (or user's) point of view and includes both hardware and software components of the machine. A detailed logic design of ASC is provided in Chapter 5. Chapters 6 through 8 expand the concepts discussed in earlier chapters relative to the architectures of several commercially available machines. Chapter 6 provides design enhancements to each component of the simple computer to bring it closer to a practical machine. Chapter 7 details input/output mechanisms and devices and their organization. Chapter 8 delineates advanced architectural concepts and machine architectures.

Although logic minimization theory is important, a mastery of it is not required for the purposes of this book. For reference, a summary of logic minimization is provided in Appendix B. Appendix C details one computer hardware description language; a familiarity with this or any other hardware description language, although not essential, enhances our ability to describe architectural features of machines in a nonambiguous manner.

I.1   Computer System Organization

The primary function of a digital computer is to process data input to produce results that can be better used in a specific application environment. For example, consider a digital computer used to control the traffic light at an intersection. The *input* data is the number of cars passing through the intersection during a specified time period, the *processing* consists of the computation of red-yellow-green time periods as a function of the number of cars, and the *output* is the variation of the red-yellow-green time intervals based on the results of processing. In this system, the data input device is a sensor that can detect the passing of a car at the intersection. Traffic lights are the output devices. The electronic device that keeps track of the number of cars and computes the red-yellow-green time periods is the processor. These physical devices constitute the *hardware* components of the system. The processing hardware is *programmed* to compute the red-yellow-green time periods according to some rule. This rule is the *algorithm* used to solve the particular problem. The algorithm (a logical sequence of steps to solve a problem) is translated into a *program* (a set of instructions) for the processor to follow in solving the problem. Programs are written in a language "understandable" by the processing hardware. The collection of such programs constitutes the *software* component of the computer system.

Hardware. The traffic-light controller is a very simple special-purpose computer system requiring only a few of the physical hardware components that constitute a general-purpose computer system (see Figure I.1). The four major hardware blocks of a general-purpose computer system are its memory unit (MU), arithmetic and logic unit (ALU), input/output unit (IOU), and control unit (CU). Programs and data reside in the memory unit. The arithmetic and logic unit processes the data taken from the memory unit and stores the processed data back in the memory unit. Input/output (I/O) devices input and output data (and programs) into and out of the memory unit. In some systems, I/O devices send and receive data into and from the ALU rather than the MU. The control unit coordinates the activities of the other three units. It retrieves instructions from programs resident in the MU, decodes these instructions, and directs the ALU to perform corresponding processing steps. It also oversees I/O operations.

Several I/O devices are shown in Figure I.1. Devices such as the card

Figure I.1 A typical computer system

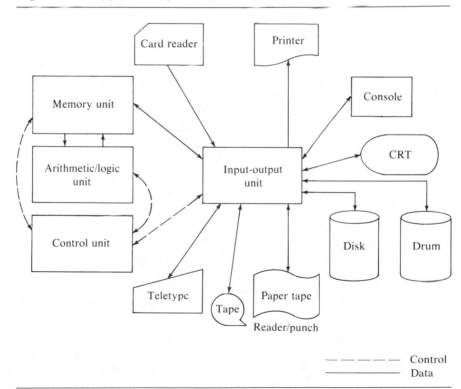

reader and paper tape reader are strictly input devices and others such as the printer and paper-tape punch are used only for output. The other devices shown are used both for input and output. The magnetic tape, disk, and drum are also used as memory devices to increase the capacity of the MU. The console is essentially a special-purpose I/O device that permits the operator to interact with the computer system.

Software. The hardware components of a computer system are electronic devices in which the basic unit of information is either a 0 or a 1, corresponding to two states of an electronic signal. For instance, in one of the popular hardware technologies a 0 is represented by 0 volts while a 1 is represented by +5 volts. Programs and data must therefore be expressed using this binary alphabet consisting of 0 and 1. Programs written using only these binary digits are *machine language* programs. At this level of programming, operations such as ADD and SUBTRACT are each represented by a unique pattern of 0s and 1s, and the computer hardware is designed to interpret these sequences. Programming at this level is tedious since the programmer has to work with sequences of 0s and 1s and needs to have very detailed knowledge of the computer structure.

The tedium of machine language programming is partially alleviated by using symbols such as ADD and SUB rather than patterns of 0 and 1 for these operations. Programming at the symbolic level is called *assembly language* programming. An assembly language programmer also is required to have a detailed knowledge of the machine structure, because the operations permitted in the assembly language are primitive and the instruction format and capabilities depend on the hardware organization of the machine. An *assembler* program is used to translate assembly language programs into machine language.

Use of high-level programming languages such as FORTRAN, COBOL, and Pascal further reduces the requirement of an intimate knowledge of the machine organization. A *compiler* program is needed to translate a high-level language program into the machine language. A separate compiler is needed for each high-level language used in programming the computer system. Note that the assembler and the compiler are also programs written in one of those languages and can translate an assembly or high-level language program, respectively, into the machine language.

Figure I.2 shows the sequence of operations that occurs once a program is developed. A program written in either the assembly language or a high-level language is called a *source* program. An assembly language source program is translated by the assembler into the machine language program. This machine language program is the *object code*. A compiler converts a high-level language source into object code. The object code

Figure I.2 Program translation and execution

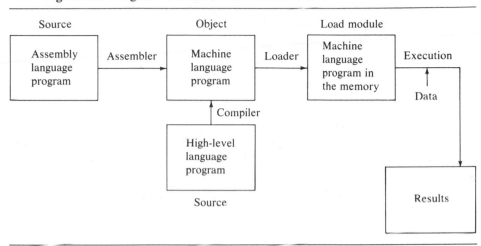

ordinarily resides on an intermediate device such as a magnetic disk or tape. A *loader* program loads the object code from the intermediate device into the memory unit. The data required by the program will be either available in the memory or supplied by an input device during the *execution* of the program. The effect of program execution is the production of processed data or results.

Operations such as selecting the appropriate compiler for translating the source into object code; loading the object code into the memory unit; and starting, stopping, and accounting for the computer system usage are automatically done by the system. A set of supervisory programs that permit such automatic operation is usually provided by the computer system manufacturer. This set, called the *operating system,* receives the information it needs through a set of command language statements from the user and manages the overall operation of the computer system. Figure I.3 is a simple rendering of the complete hardware-software environment of a general-purpose computer system.

I.2   Computer Evolution

Man has always been in search of mechanical aids for computation. The development of the abacus around 3000 B.C. introduced the positional notation of number systems. In seventeenth-century France, Pascal and Leibnitz developed mechanical calculators that were later developed into

Figure I.3 Hardware and software components

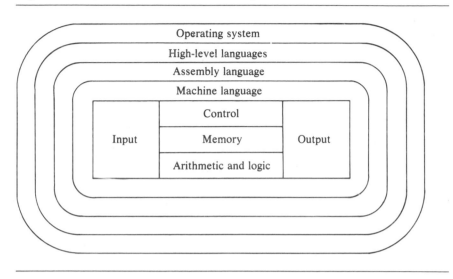

desk calculators. In 1801, Jacquard used punched cards to instruct his looms in weaving various patterns on cloth.

In 1822, Englishman Charles Babbage developed the difference engine, a mechanical device that carried out a sequence of computations specified by the settings of levers, gears, and cams. Data were entered manually as the computations progressed. Around 1820, Babbage proposed the analytical engine, which would use a set of punched cards for program input, another set of cards for data input, and a third set of cards for output of results. The mechanical technology was not sufficiently advanced and the analytical engine was never built; nevertheless, the analytical engine as designed probably was the first computer in the modern sense of the word.

Several unit-record machines to process data on punched cards were developed in the United States in 1880 by Herman Hollerith for census applications. In 1944, Mark I, the first automated computer, was announced. It was an electromechanical device that used punched cards for input and output of data and paper tape for program storage. The desire for faster computations than those Mark I could provide resulted in the development of ENIAC, the first electronic computer built out of vacuum tubes and relays by a team led by Americans Eckert and Mauchly. ENIAC employed the *stored-program concept* in which a sequence of instructions is stored in the memory for use by the machine in processing data. ENIAC had a control board on which the programs were wired. A rewiring of the control board was necessary for each computation sequence.

John von Neumann, a member of the Eckert-Mauchly team, developed EDVAC, the first stored-program computer. At the same time, M. V. Wilkes developed EDSAC, the first operational stored-program machine, which also introduced the concept of primary and secondary memory hierarchy. Von Neumann is credited for developing the stored-program concept, beginning with his 1945 first draft of EDVAC. The structure of EDVAC established the organization of the stored-program computer (von Neumann machine), which contains:

1. An input device through which data and instructions can be entered.
2. A storage into which results can be entered and from which instructions and data can be fetched.
3. An arithmetic unit to process data.
4. A control unit to fetch, interpret, and execute the instructions from the storage.
5. An output device to deliver the results to the user.

All contemporary computers are von Neumann machines, although various alternative architectures are being investigated.

Commercial computer system development has followed development of hardware technology and is usually divided into three generations.

First generation (1954–59)—Vacuum tube technology.
Second generation (1957–64)—Transistor technology.
Third generation (mid-1960s)—Integrated circuit technology.

We will not elaborate on the architectural details of the various machines developed during the three generations, except for the following brief evolution account.

First-generation machines such as the UNIVAC I and IBM 701, built out of vacuum tubes, were slow and bulky and accommodated a limited number of input/output devices. Magnetic tape was the predominant I/O medium. Data access time was measured in milliseconds.

Second-generation machines (IBM 1401, 7090; RCA 501; CDC 6600; Burroughs 5500; DEC PDP-1) used random-access core memories, transistor technology, multifunctional units, and multiple processing units. Data access time was measured in microseconds. Assembler and high-level languages were developed.

The integrated-circuit technology used in third-generation machines such as the IBM 360, UNIVAC 1108, ILLIAC-IV, and CDC STAR-100 contributed to nanosecond data access and processing times. Multiprogramming, array, and pipeline processing concepts came into being.

Computer systems were viewed as general-purpose data processors until the introduction in 1965 of DEC PDP-8, a *minicomputer*. Minicomputers were regarded as dedicated application machines with limited processing capability compared to that of large-scale machines. Since then, several new minicomputers have been introduced and this distinction between the mini and large-scale machines is becoming blurred due to advances in hardware and software technology.

The development of *microprocessors* in the early seventies allowed a significant contribution to the third class of computer systems: microcomputers. Microprocessors are essentially computers on an integrated-circuit (IC) chip that can be used as components to build a dedicated controller or processing system. Advances in IC technology leading to the current VLSI (very large scale integration) era have made microprocessors as powerful as minicomputers of the seventies.

Modern computer system architecture exploits the advances in hardware-software technology to the fullest extent. The current architectural trends are in development of systems of the following types:

1. Computer networks, in which several machines communicate with each other to share the processing load.
2. Distributed processing systems, in which the data base, processing, and control are distributed among various general-purpose resources (e.g., processors, memories, input/output devices) that work in a "cooperative autonomy."
3. Directly executable language oriented architectures that are tailored to execute programs written in particular languages as efficiently as possible.
4. Data flow architectures, non–von Neumann machines that activate an appropriate processor based on the attributes of data.

References

Burks, A. W., H. H. Goldstine, and J. von Neumann. "Preliminary Discussion of the Logical Design of an Electrical Computing Instrument." U.S. Army Ordnance Department Report, 1946.

Goldstine, H. H. *The Computer from Pascal to von Neumann*. Princeton, N.J.: Princeton University Press, 1972.

Siewiorek, D. P., C. G. Bell, and A. Newell. *Computer Structures: Principles and Examples*. New York, N.Y.: McGraw-Hill, 1982.

Stone, H. S., ed. *Introduction to Computer Architecture*. 2d ed. Chicago, Ill.: Science Research Associates, 1980.

Chapter 1

Combinational Logic

Each hardware component of a computer system is built of several logic circuits. A logic circuit is an interconnection of several primitive logic devices to perform a desired function. It has one or more inputs and one or more outputs. This chapter introduces some logic devices that are used in building one type of logic circuit called a *combinational circuit*. Each output of a combinational circuit is a function of all the inputs to the circuit. Further, the outputs at any time are each a function of inputs at that particular time and so the circuit does not have a memory. A circuit with a memory is called a *sequential circuit*. The output of a sequential circuit at any time is a function of not only the inputs at that time but also the *state* of the circuit at that time. The state of the circuit is dependent on what has happened to the circuit prior to that time and hence the state is also a function of the previous inputs and states. This chapter is an introduction to the analysis and design of combinational circuits. Details of sequential circuit analysis and design are given in Chapter 2.

1.1 Basic Operations and Terminology

Example 1.1 Consider the addition of two bits:

$$0 + 0 = 0$$

$$0 + 1 = 1$$

$$1 + 0 = 1$$

$$1 + 1 = 10 \text{ (i.e., a sum of 0 and a carry of 1)}$$

The addition of two single-bit numbers produces a SUM bit and a CARRY bit. The above operations can be arranged into the following table to separate the two resulting bits SUM and CARRY:

		A + B	
A	B	SUM	CARRY
0	0	0	0
0	1	1	0
1	0	1	0
1	1	0	1

A and B are the two operands. Each can take a value of either 0 or 1. The first two columns show the four combinations of values possible for the two operands A and B and the last two columns represent the sum of the two operands represented as a SUM and a CARRY bit.

Note that the CARRY is 1 only when A is 1 *and* B is 1, while the SUM bit is 1 when one of the following two conditions is satisfied: A is 0 AND B is 1; A is 1 AND B is 0. That is, SUM is 1 if (A is 0 AND B is 1) OR (A is 1 AND B is 0). Let us say $\bar{A}$ (pronounced ''A bar'') represents the opposite condition of A; that is, A is 0 if $\bar{A}$ is 1 and vice versa, and similarly, $\bar{B}$ represents the opposite condition of B. Then we can say SUM is 1 if ($\bar{A}$ is 1 AND B is 1) OR (A is 1 AND $\bar{B}$ is 1). Therefore,

$$\text{SUM} = (\bar{A} \cdot B) + (A \cdot \bar{B})$$
$$\text{CARRY} = A \cdot B$$

$$(1\text{--}1)$$

where

"+" represents the OR operation (not arithmetic addition),
"·" represents the AND operation, and
"–" represents the NOT operation (complement operation).

The definitions of AND, OR, and NOT operations are shown in Figure 1.1. The right side of equations (1–1) are Boolean *expressions*. A and B are Boolean *variables*. An expression is formed by combining variables with operations. The *value* (truth or falsity, 0 or 1) of SUM depends on the values of A and B. That is, SUM is a *function* of A and B and so is CARRY.

Example 1.2 Consider the following statement: Subtract if and only if an add instruction is given and the signs are different or a subtract instruction is given and the signs are alike.

Figure 1.1 Basic operations: AND, OR, and NOT

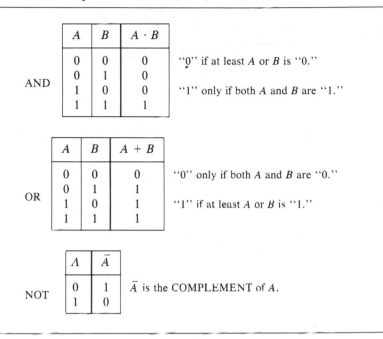

A	B	$A \cdot B$
0	0	0
0	1	0
1	0	0
1	1	1

AND

"0" if at least A or B is "0."

"1" only if both A and B are "1."

A	B	$A + B$
0	0	0
0	1	1
1	0	1
1	1	1

OR

"0" only if both A and B are "0."

"1" if at least A or B is "1."

A	$\bar{A}$
0	1
1	0

NOT

$\bar{A}$ is the COMPLEMENT of A.

Let

  S represent the "subtract" action,
  A represent "add instruction given" condition,
  B represent "signs are different" condition, and
  C represent "subtract instruction given" condition.

Then, the above statement can be expressed as

$$S = (A \cdot B) + (C \cdot \bar{B}) \qquad (1-2)$$

Usually, the "·" and "( )" are removed from expressions when there is no ambiguity. Thus, the above function can be written as

$$S = AB + C\bar{B} \qquad (1-3)$$

1.1.1 Evaluation of Expressions

Knowing the value of each of the component variables of an expression, we can find the value of the expression itself. The hierarchy of operations is important in the evaluation of expressions. We always perform NOT operations first, followed by AND and lastly OR, in the absence of parentheses. If there are parentheses, the expressions within the parentheses are evaluated first, observing the above hierarchy of operations, and then the remaining expression is evaluated. That is,

> Perform
>
>   NOT operations first,
>   AND operations next,
>   OR operations last,
>
> while evaluating an expression.

The following examples illustrate expression evaluation. The sequential order in which the operations are performed is shown by the numbers below each operation.

Example 1.3   Evaluate $A\bar{B} + B\bar{C}D$.

$$A \cdot \bar{B} + B \cdot \bar{C} \cdot D \qquad \text{Insert ``·''}$$

$$\phantom{A \cdot \bar{B}} 1 \qquad\qquad 2 \rule{1cm}{0.4pt}\text{Scan 1 for NOT operations.}$$

$$ 3 \qquad\qquad 4 \quad 5 \rule{0.6cm}{0.4pt}\text{Scan 2 for AND operations.}$$

$$ 6 \rule{2cm}{0.4pt}\text{Scan 3 for OR operations.}$$

Example 1.4   Evaluate $A(B + \bar{C}D) + A\bar{B} + \bar{C}\bar{D}$.

$$A(B + \bar{C} \cdot D) + A \cdot \bar{B} + \bar{C} \cdot \bar{D} \qquad\qquad\qquad \text{Insert ``·''}$$

1	NOT	⎫
2	AND	⎬ Within
3	OR	⎭ parentheses
4 5 6	NOT	
7 8 9	AND	
10 11	OR	

Example 1.5   Evaluate the function $Z = A\bar{B}C + (\bar{A}B)(B + \bar{C})$, given $A = 0$, $B = 1$, $C = 1$.

$$Z = (A \cdot \bar{B} \cdot C) + (\bar{A} \cdot B) \cdot (B + \bar{C}) \qquad \text{Insert ``·''}$$

$$= (0 \cdot \bar{1} \cdot 1) + (\bar{0} \cdot 1) \cdot (1 + \bar{1}) \qquad \text{Substitute values.}$$

$$= (0 \cdot 0 \cdot 1) + (1 \cdot 1) \cdot (1 + 0) \qquad \text{Evaluate NOT.}$$

$$= (0) + (1) \cdot (1) \qquad \text{Evaluate parenthetical expressions.}$$

$$= 0 + 1 \qquad \text{AND operation.}$$

$$= 1 \qquad \text{OR operation (value of } Z \text{ is 1).}$$

1.1.2 Truth Tables

Figure 1.1 shows truth tables for the three primitive operations AND, OR, and NOT. A truth table indicates the value of a function for all possible combinations of the values of the variables of which it is a function. There will be one column in the truth table corresponding to each variable and one column for the value of the function. Since each variable can take either of the two values (0 or 1), the number of combinations of values multiplies as the number of component variables increases. For instance, if there are two variables, there will be $2 \times 2 = 4$ combinations of values and hence four rows in a truth table. In general, there will be 2^N rows in a truth table for a function with N component variables. If the expression on the right-hand side of a function is complex, the truth table can be developed in several steps. The following example illustrates development of a truth table.

Example 1.6   Draw a truth table for $Z = A\bar{B} + \bar{A}C + \bar{A}\bar{B}C$.

There are three component variables, A, B, and C. Hence there will be 2^3 or 8 combinations of values of A, B, and C. The 8 combinations are shown on the left-hand side of the truth table in Figure 1.2. These combinations are generated by changing the value of C from 0 to 1 and from 1 to 0 as we move down from row to row, while changing the value of B once every two (i.e., 2^1) rows and changing the value for A once every four (i.e., 2^2) rows. These combinations are thus in a numerically increasing order in the binary number system, starting with $(000)_2$ or $(0)_{10}$ to $(111)_2$ or $(7)_{10}$, where the subscripts denote the base of the number system.

In general, if there are N component variables, there will be 2^N combinations of values ranging in their numerical value from 0 to $2^N - 1$.

To evaluate Z in the example function, knowing the values for A, B, and C at each row of the truth table in Figure 1.2, values for $\bar{A}$ and $\bar{B}$ are

Figure 1.2 Truth table for $Z = A\bar{B} + \bar{A}C + \bar{A}\bar{B}C$

A	B	C	$\bar{A}$	$\bar{B}$	$A\bar{B}$	$\bar{A}C$	$\bar{A}\bar{B}C$	Z
0	0	0	1	1	0	0	0	0
0	0	1	1	1	0	1	1	1
0	1	0	1	0	0	0	0	0
0	1	1	1	0	0	1	0	1
1	0	0	0	1	1	0	0	1
1	0	1	0	1	1	0	0	1
1	1	0	0	0	0	0	0	0
1	1	1	0	0	0	0	0	0

first generated; values for $(A\bar{B})$, $(\bar{A}C)$ and $(\bar{A}\bar{B}C)$ are then generated by ANDing the values in appropriate columns at each row; and finally the value of Z is found by ORing the values in the last three columns at each row. Note that evaluating $\bar{A}\bar{B}C$ corresponds to ANDing $\bar{A}$ and $\bar{B}$ values followed by ANDing the value of C. Similarly, if more than two values are to be ORed, they are ORed two at a time. The columns corresponding to $\bar{A}$, $\bar{B}$, $(A\bar{B})$, $(\bar{A}C)$, and $(\bar{A}\bar{B}C)$ are not usually shown in the final truth table.

1.1.3 Functions and Their Representation

There are two *constants* in the logic alphabet: 0 and 1 (true or false). A *variable* such as A, B, X, or Y can take the value of either 1 or 0 at any time. There are three basic operations: AND, OR, and NOT. When several variables are ANDed together, we get a *product* term (conjunction).

Example 1.7 $A\bar{B}C$, $A\bar{B}X\bar{Y}\bar{Z}$.

When several variables are ORed together we get a *sum* term (disjunction).

Example 1.8 $(A + B + \bar{C})$, $(X + \bar{Y})$, $(P + \bar{Q} + \bar{R})$.

Each occurrence of a variable either in *true* form or in *complemented* (inversed, NOT) form is a *literal*. For example, the product term XYZ has three literals; the sum term $(\bar{A} + \bar{B} + C + \bar{D})$ has four literals.

A product term (sum term) X is *included* in another product term (sum term) Y if Y has each literal that is in X.

Example 1.9 $X\bar{Y}$ is included in $X\bar{Y}$. $X\bar{Y}Z$ is included in $X\bar{Y}ZW$. $(\bar{X} + Y)$ is included in $(\bar{X} + Y + \bar{W})$. $X\bar{Y}$ is not included in XY. (Why?)

If the value of the variable Q is dependent on the value of several variables (say A, B, C)—that is, Q is a function of A, B, C—then Q can be expressed as a sum of several product terms in A, B, C.

Example 1.10 $Q = A\bar{B} + \bar{A}C + \bar{B}C$ is in sum of products (SOP) form.

If none of the product terms is included in the other product terms we get a *normal sum of products form*.

Example 1.11 $Q = AB + AC$, $Q = X + Y$, and $P = A\bar{B}C + \bar{A}CD$ $A\bar{C}\bar{D}$ are in normal SOP form.

Similarly, we can define a *normal product of sums form*.

Example 1.12 $P = (X + \bar{Y}) \cdot (\bar{X} + \bar{Y} + \bar{Z})$ and $Q = (A + \bar{B}) \cdot (\bar{A} + B + \bar{C}) \cdot (A + B + C)$ are in normal product of sums (POS) form.

A truth table can be used to derive the function in SOP or POS forms, as detailed below.

Example 1.13 Consider the following truth table for Q, a function of A, B, and C:

ABC	Q
0 0 0	0
0 0 1	1
0 1 0	0
0 1 1	1
1 0 0	1
1 0 1	1
1 1 0	0
1 1 1	0

From the truth table it can be seen that Q is 1 when $A = 0$ and $B = 0$ and $C = 1$. That is, Q is 1 when $\bar{A} = 1$ and $\bar{B} = 1$ and $C = 1$, which means Q is 1 when $(\bar{A} \cdot \bar{B} \cdot C)$ is 1. Similarly, corresponding to the other three ones in the Q column of the table, Q is 1 when $(\bar{A}BC)$ is 1 or $(A\bar{B}\bar{C})$ is 1 or $(A\bar{B}C)$ is 1. This argument leads to the following representation for Q:

$$Q = \bar{A}\bar{B}C + \bar{A}BC + A\bar{B}\bar{C} + A\bar{B}C$$

which is the normal SOP form.

In general, to derive an SOP form from the truth table, we can use the following procedure:

1. Generate a product term corresponding to each row where the value of the function is 1.
2. In each product term, consider the individual variables uncomplemented if the value of the variable in that row is 1 and complemented if the value of the variable in that row is 0.

The POS form for the function can be derived from the truth table by a similar procedure:

1. Generate a sum term corresponding to each row where the value of the function is 0.
2. In each sum term, consider the individual variables complemented if the value of the variable in that row is 1 and uncomplemented if the value of the variable in that row is 0.

$Q = (A + B + C) \cdot (A + \bar{B} + C) \cdot (\bar{A} + \bar{B} + C) \cdot (\bar{A} + \bar{B} + \bar{C})$ is the POS form for Q, in Example 1.13.

Example 1.14   Derivation of SOP and POS forms of representation for another three-variable function, P, is shown here:

	ABC	P	
0	0 0 0	1	$\leftarrow \bar{A}\bar{B}\bar{C}$
1	0 0 1	0	$\leftarrow (A + B + \bar{C})$
2	0 1 0	0	$\leftarrow (A + \bar{B} + C)$
3	0 1 1	0	$\leftarrow (A + \bar{B} + \bar{C})$
4	1 0 0	1	$\leftarrow A\bar{B}\bar{C}$
5	1 0 1	1	$\leftarrow A\bar{B}C$
6	1 1 0	0	$\leftarrow (\bar{A} + \bar{B} + C)$
7	1 1 1	0	$\leftarrow (\bar{A} + \bar{B} + \bar{C})$

SOP form: $P = \bar{A}\bar{B}\bar{C} + A\bar{B}\bar{C} + A\bar{B}C$

POS form: $P = (A + B + \bar{C}) \cdot (A + \bar{B} + C) \cdot (A + \bar{B} + \bar{C})$
$\cdot (\bar{A} + \bar{B} + C) \cdot (\bar{A} + \bar{B} + \bar{C})$

1.1.4   Canonical Forms

The SOP and POS forms of the functions derived from a truth table by the above procedures are *canonical forms*. In a canonical SOP form each component variable appears in either complemented or uncomplemented form in each product term.

Example 1.15 If Q is a function of A, B, and C, then $Q = \bar{A}\bar{B}C + A\bar{B}\bar{C} + \bar{A}B\bar{C}$ is a canonical SOP form, while $Q = \bar{A}B + AB\bar{C} + A\bar{C}$ is not because in the first and last product terms, all three variables are not present. A canonical POS form is similarly defined.

A canonical product term is also called a *minterm*, while a canonical sum term is called a *maxterm*. Hence, functions can be represented either in *sum of minterm* or in *product of maxterm* formats.

Example 1.16 From the truth table of Example 1.14:

$$P(A,B,C) = \bar{A}\bar{B}\bar{C} + A\bar{B}\bar{C} + A\bar{B}C$$

$$0\ 0\ 0 \quad 1\ 0\ 0 \quad 1\ 0\ 1 \qquad \leftarrow \text{Input combinations (0 for a complemented variable; 1 for an uncomplemented variable)}$$

$$0 \qquad\quad 4 \qquad\quad 5 \qquad \leftarrow \text{Decimal values}$$

$$= \Sigma m(0,\ 4,\ 5) \qquad\qquad \leftarrow \text{Minterm list form}$$

The minterm list form is a compact representation for the canonical SOP form.

$$P(A,B,C)=(A+B+\bar{C})\cdot(A+\bar{B}+C)\cdot(A+\bar{B}+\bar{C})\cdot(\bar{A}+\bar{B}+C)\cdot(\bar{A}+\bar{B}+\bar{C})$$

$$0\ 0\ 1 \qquad 0\ 1\ 0 \qquad 0\ 1\ 1 \qquad 1\ 1\ 0 \qquad 1\ 1\ 1$$

Input combinations (1 for a complemented variable and 0 for an uncomplemented variable)

$$1 \qquad\quad 2 \qquad\quad 3 \qquad\quad 6 \qquad\quad 7 \leftarrow$$

Decimal values

$$= \Pi_M(1,\ 2,\ 3,\ 6,\ 7) \qquad\qquad \leftarrow$$

Maxterm list form

The maxterm list form is a compact representation for the canonical POS form. Knowing one form, the other can be derived as shown by the following example.

Example 1.17   Given $Q(A,B,C,D) = \Sigma m(0,1,7,8,10,11,12,15)$.

Q is a four-variable function. Hence, there will be 2^4 or 16 combinations of input values whose decimal values range from 0 to 15. There are eight minterms. Hence, there should be $16 - 8 = 8$ maxterms; that is,

$$Q(A,B,C,D) = \Pi_M(2,3,4,5,6,9,13,14).$$

Also, note that the complement of Q is represented as

$$\bar{Q}(A,B,C,D) = \Sigma m(2,3,4,5,6,9,13,14)$$

$$= \Pi_M(0,1,7,8,10,11,12,15).$$

Note that for an n variable function,

$$\text{(Number of minterms)} + \text{(number of maxterms)} = 2^n. \qquad (1-4)$$

1.2   Boolean Algebra (Switching Algebra)

In 1854, George Boole introduced a symbolic notation to deal with symbolic statements that take a binary value of either *true* or *false*. This symbolic notation was adopted by Claude Shannon to analyze logic functions and has since come to be known as Boolean algebra or switching algebra. The definitions, theorems, and postulates of this algebra are described below.

Definition   A Boolean algebra is a closed algebraic system containing a set K of two or more elements and two binary operators "+" (OR) and "·" (AND); that is, for every X and Y in set K, $X \cdot Y$ belongs to K and $X + Y$ belongs to K. In addition, the following postulates must be satisfied.

Postulates

P1 Existence of 1 and 0	(a) $X + 0 = X$
	(b) $X \cdot 1 = X$
P2 Commutativity	(a) $X + Y = Y + X$
	(b) $X \cdot Y = Y \cdot X$
P3 Associativity	(a) $X + (Y + Z) = (X + Y) + Z$
	(b) $X \cdot (Y \cdot Z) = (X \cdot Y) \cdot Z$
P4 Distributivity	(a) $X + (Y \cdot Z) = (X + Y) \cdot (X + Z)$
	(b) $X \cdot (Y + Z) = X \cdot Y + X \cdot Z$

P5 Complement   (a) $X + \bar{X} = 1$ ($\bar{X}$ is the complement of X)

(b) $X \cdot \bar{X} = 0$

Definition Two expressions are said to be *equivalent* if one can be replaced by the other.

Definition The "dual" of an expression is obtained by replacing each "+" in the expression by "·", each "·" by "+", each 1 by 0, and each 0 by 1.

The *principle of duality* states that if an equation is valid in a Boolean algebra, its dual is also valid.

Example 1.18 Given $X + YZ = (X + Y) \cdot (X + Z)$, its dual is $X \cdot (Y + Z) = (X \cdot Y) + (X \cdot Z)$.

Note that part (b) of each of the postulates is the dual of the corresponding part (a).

Theorems The following theorems are useful in manipulating Boolean functions. They are traditionally used for converting Boolean functions from one form to another, deriving canonical forms, and minimizing (reducing the complexity of) Boolean functions. These theorems can be proven by drawing truth tables for both sides to see if the left-hand side has the same values as the right-hand side, for each possible combination of component variable values.

T1 Idempotency   (a) $X + X = X$

(b) $X \cdot X = X$

T2 Properties of 1 and 0   (a) $X + 1 = 1$

(b) $X \cdot 0 = 0$

T3 Absorption   (a) $X + XY = X$

(b) $X \cdot (X + Y) = X$

T4 Absorption   (a) $X + \bar{X}Y = X + Y$

(b) $X \cdot (\bar{X} + Y) = X \cdot Y$

T5 DeMorgan's law   (a) $\overline{(X + Y)} = \bar{X} \cdot \bar{Y}$

(b) $\overline{(X \cdot Y)} = \bar{X} + \bar{Y}$

T6 Consensus   (a) $XY + \bar{X}Z + YZ = XY + \bar{X}Z$

(b) $(X + Y) \cdot (\bar{X} + Z) \cdot (Y + Z) = (X + Y) \cdot (\bar{X} + Z)$

We can summarize some important properties thus:

$$X + 0 = X \qquad X + 1 = 1$$
$$X \cdot 0 = 0 \qquad X \cdot 1 = X$$
$$\bar{0} = 1, \bar{1} = 0, \bar{\bar{X}} = X$$

Algebraic proofs for the above theorems can be found in any of the references listed at the end of this chapter. Appendix B deals with the applications of Boolean algebra for minimization of logic functions. These minimization techniques are useful in reducing the complexity of logic circuits. We will not emphasize minimization in this book.

1.3   Primitive Hardware Blocks

A logic circuit is the physical implementation of a Boolean function. The primitive Boolean operations AND, OR, and NOT are implemented by electronic components known as *gates*. The Boolean constants 0 and 1 are implemented as two unique voltage levels or current levels. A gate receives these logic values on its inputs and produces a logic value that is a function of its inputs on its output. Each gate has one or more inputs and an output. The operation of a gate can be described by a truth table. The truth tables and standard symbols used to represent the three primitive gates are shown in Figure 1.3.

The NOT gate will always have one input and one output. Only two inputs are shown for the other gates in Figure 1.3 for convenience. The maximum number of inputs allowed on the gate is limited by the electronic technology used to build the gate. The number of inputs on the gate is termed its *fan-in*. We will assume that there is no restriction on the fan-in. A four-input AND gate is shown below.

$$F(A,B,C,D) = A \cdot \bar{B} \cdot C \cdot D$$

Figure 1.3 shows three other popular gates. The utility of these gates will be discussed later in this chapter.

Figure 1.3 Gates and truth tables

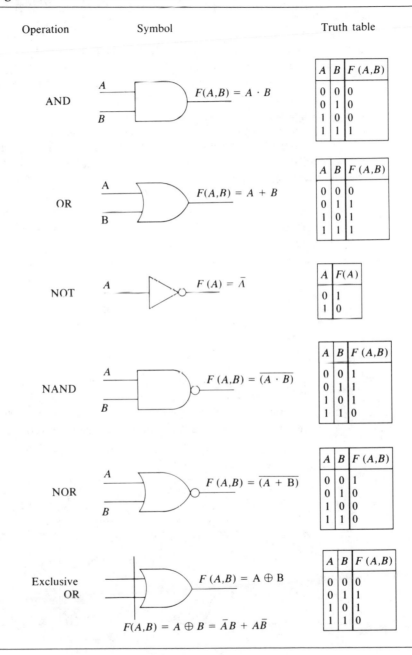

Operation	Symbol	Truth table

AND $F(A,B) = A \cdot B$

A	B	F(A,B)
0	0	0
0	1	0
1	0	0
1	1	1

OR $F(A,B) = A + B$

A	B	F(A,B)
0	0	0
0	1	1
1	0	1
1	1	1

NOT $F(A) = \bar{A}$

A	F(A)
0	1
1	0

NAND $F(A,B) = \overline{(A \cdot B)}$

A	B	F(A,B)
0	0	1
0	1	1
1	0	1
1	1	0

NOR $F(A,B) = \overline{(A + B)}$

A	B	F(A,B)
0	0	1
0	1	0
1	0	0
1	1	0

Exclusive OR $F(A,B) = A \oplus B$

$$F(A,B) = A \oplus B = \bar{A}B + A\bar{B}$$

A	B	F(A,B)
0	0	0
0	1	1
1	0	1
1	1	0

1.4 Functional Analysis of Combinational Circuits

A combinational circuit with n input variables and m outputs is shown in Figure 1.4. Since there are n inputs, there are 2^n combinations of input values. For each of these input combinations there is a unique combination of output values. Analysis of a combinational circuit is the process of determining the relations of its outputs to its inputs. These relations can be expressed as either Boolean functions or as truth tables. A truth table for the circuit in Figure 1.4 will have 2^n rows and $(n + m)$ columns. An m number of Boolean functions will be required to describe the circuit. We will demonstrate the analysis of combinational circuits through the following example.

Example 1.19   A circuit is shown in Figure 1.5. There are three input variables to the circuit: X, Y, and Z. Note that it is the number of input *variables* that count, not the number of input lines to the circuit. There are two outputs, P and Q.

We can trace through the signals in the circuit from its inputs to its outputs to derive P and Q as functions of X, Y, and Z. This is shown in Figure 1.5. The functions are

$$P(X,Y,Z) = X\bar{Y} + \bar{Z},$$

$$Q(X,Y,Z) = (X\bar{Y} + \bar{Z}) + X\bar{Z}.$$

The operation of the circuit can be described by a truth table. The truth table can be drawn from the above Boolean functions for P and Q or by

Figure 1.4 Combinational circuit

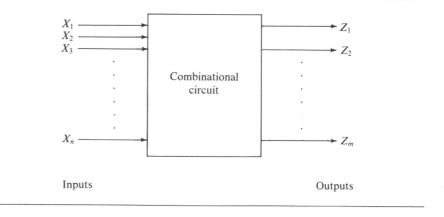

Inputs   Outputs

Figure 1.5 Circuit with three input variables

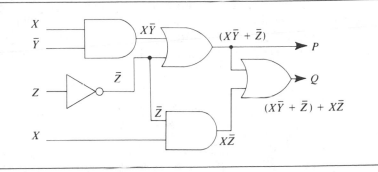

tracing through the circuit, as shown in Figure 1.6. There are three input variables, so first we draw a truth table with the eight combinations of input values [see Figure 1.6(b)]. Then we impose each combination of values on the input lines and note the values for the outputs. For example, Figure 1.6(a) shows the condition corresponding to $X = 0$, $Y = 0$, and $Z = 0$. Tracing through the circuit we note that $P = 1$ and $Q = 1$. We repeat the process for the other seven input combinations to determine the complete truth table as shown in Figure 1.6(b).

This procedure is called functional analysis of the logic circuit because we have derived only the logic function implemented by the circuit. Other detailed electronic analyses that include timing and loading problems are usually performed. We will briefly describe timing problems later in this

Figure 1.6 (a) Circuit with 000 input condition. (b) Truth table

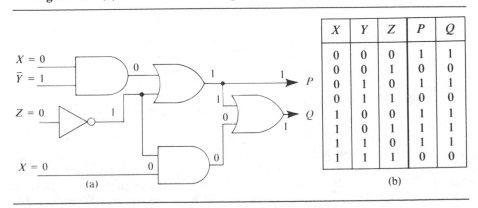

X	Y	Z	P	Q
0	0	0	1	1
0	0	1	0	0
0	1	0	1	1
0	1	1	0	0
1	0	0	1	1
1	0	1	1	1
1	1	0	1	1
1	1	1	0	0

(a)   (b)

chapter. The output of each gate can only be connected to a specified number of inputs (of other gates); that is, there is a limit on the number of other inputs a gate can *drive*. This limit is called the *fanout*. The *load* on the gate must be within the fanout limit for proper operation. For our discussion we will assume that all gates have sufficient fanout.

1.5 Synthesis of Combinational Circuits

Logic circuits can be synthesized (i.e., designed) starting with a truth table description of the problem. After the word statement of the process for which a logic circuit is to be built is given, the circuit designer must formulate the problem in the form of a truth table. This step requires identification of the input variables and the outputs corresponding to each combination of input values. Each output can then be expressed as a Boolean function of input variables. Using these functions, a switching circuit can be built.

Example 1.20   Build a circuit to implement function P shown in the truth table.

X	Y	Z	P
0	0	0	0
0	0	1	0
0	1	0	1
0	1	1	1
1	0	0	0
1	0	1	1
1	1	0	0
1	1	1	1

Inputs   Output

1.5.1 AND-OR Circuits

Let us express P as a function of X, Y, and Z in SOP form.

$$P = \bar{X} \cdot Y \cdot \bar{Z} + \bar{X} \cdot Y \cdot Z + X \cdot \bar{Y} \cdot Z + X \cdot Y \cdot Z$$

$P(X,Y,Z)$ is the sum of four product terms, so we use an OR gate with four inputs to generate P [see Figure 1.7(a)]. Each of the inputs to this OR gate is a product of three variables. Hence we use four AND gates, each realizing a product term. The outputs of these AND gates are connected to the four inputs of the OR gate as shown in Figure 1.7(b).

Figure 1.7 AND-OR circuit

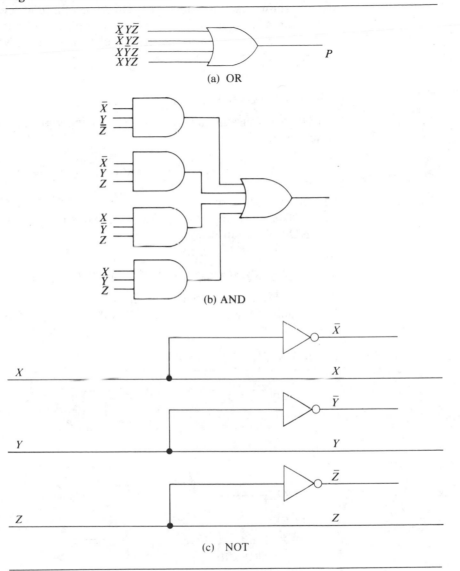

(a) OR

(b) AND

(c) NOT

A complemented variable can be generated using a NOT gate. Figure 1.7(c) shows the circuit needed to generate $\bar{X}$, $\bar{Y}$, and $\bar{Z}$. The final task in building the circuit is to connect these complemented and uncomplemented signals to appropriate inputs of AND gates. Often, the NOT gates are not specifically shown in the circuit. It is then assumed that the true and complemented values of variables are available. The logic circuit is usually shown as in Figure 1.7(b). This type of circuit, designed using the SOP form of Boolean function as the starting point, is called a two-level AND-OR circuit because the first level consists of AND gates and the second level consists of OR gates.

1.5.2 OR-AND Circuits

An OR-AND circuit can be designed starting with the POS form for the function:

$$P = (X + Y + Z) \cdot (X + Y + \bar{Z}) \cdot (\bar{X} + Y + Z) \cdot (\bar{X} + \bar{Y} + Z)$$

The design is carried out in three steps. The first two are shown in Figure 1.8(a). The third step of including NOT gates is identical to that required in AND-OR circuit design.

1.5.3 NAND-NAND and NOR-NOR Circuits

The NAND and NOR operations shown in Figure 1.3 are *universal* operations: each of the primitive operations AND, OR, and NOT can be real-

Figure 1.8 OR-AND circuit

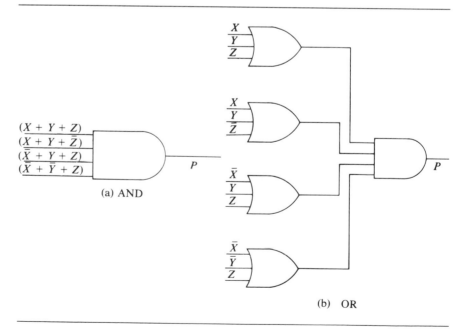

(a) AND

(b) OR

ized using only NAND operators or only NOR operators. Figure 1.9 shows the realization of the three operations using only NAND gates. The theorems used in arriving at the simplified form of expressions are also identified in the figure. The NOR gate can be used in a similar way to realize all three primitive operations.

The universal character of NAND and NOR gates permits building of logic circuits using only one type of gate (i.e., NAND only or NOR only).

Example 1.21 Figure 1.10 illustrates the transformation of an AND-OR circuit into a circuit consisting of only NAND gates. Each AND gate in the AND-OR circuit in (a) is replaced with two NAND gates. Each OR gate is replaced with an equivalent circuit comprising three NAND gates (see Figure 1.9). The circuit now has only NAND gates. There are some redundant gates in circuit (c). Gates 5 and 8 can be removed because these gates simply complement the input signal $(\overline{AB})$ twice and hence are not needed. Similarly, gates 7 and 9 can be removed. The circuit in (d) is

Figure 1.9 Realization of primitive operations using NAND

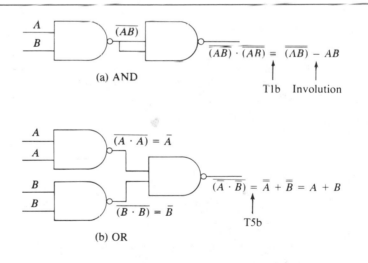

(a) AND

(b) OR

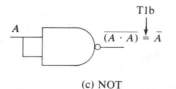

(c) NOT

Figure 1.10 NAND-NAND transformation

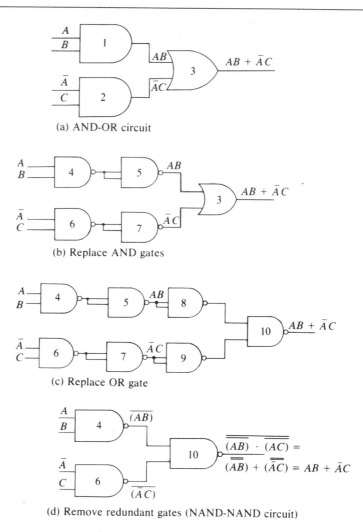

(a) AND-OR circuit

(b) Replace AND gates

(c) Replace OR gate

(d) Remove redundant gates (NAND-NAND circuit)

then a NAND-NAND circuit. The circuits in (a) and (d) are equivalent since both of them realize the same function ($AB + \bar{A}C$).

A NAND-NAND implementation can thus be derived from an AND-OR circuit by simply replacing each gate in the AND-OR circuit with a NAND gate having the same number of inputs as that of the gate it replaces. A NOR-NOR implementation likewise can be obtained by starting with an OR-AND implementation and replacing each gate with a NOR gate. Any input literal feeding the second level directly must be inverted.

These implementations are feasible because the gates are available commercially in the form of integrated circuits (ICs), in packages containing several gates of the same type. Using the same type of gates eliminates the need for different types of ICs. Since a whole IC containing several gates is required even though the circuit needs one gate of a type, using the same type of gates reduces the IC package count. Further, the NAND and NOR circuits are primitive circuit configurations in major IC technologies, and the AND and OR gates are realized by complementing the outputs of NAND and NOR, respectively. Thus, NAND and NOR gates are generally less complex to fabricate and more cost efficient than the corresponding AND and OR gates.

1.6 Some Popular Combinational Circuits

The design of four of the most commonly used combinational logic circuits is given in this section. These are available as IC components. Details of some available components are given in the next section. We will illustrate these designs in AND-OR circuit forms; the other three forms can be derived from the truth tables given here.

1.6.1 Adders

Addition is the most common arithmetic operation performed by processors. If a processor has hardware capable of adding two numbers, the other three primitive arithmetic operations can also be performed using the addition hardware. Subtraction is performed by adding the subtrahend expressed in either 2s or 1s complement form to the minuend; multiplication is repeated addition of multiplicand to itself by multiplier number of times; and division is the repeated subtraction of divisor from dividend.

Consider the addition of two 4-bit numbers A and B:

$$
\begin{array}{rccccc}
 & & c_2 & c_1 & c_0 & \\
A: & & a_3 & a_2 & a_1 & a_0 \\
+B: & & b_3 & b_2 & b_1 & b_0 \\
\hline
\text{SUM} & c_3 & s_3 & s_2 & s_1 & s_0
\end{array}
$$

Bits a_0 and b_0 are least significant bits (LSB); a_3 and b_3 are most significant bits (MSB). The addition is performed starting with the LSB position. Adding a_0 and b_0 will produce a SUM bit s_0 and a CARRY c_0. This CARRY c_0 is now used in the addition of the next significant bits a_1 and b_1, producing s_1 and c_1; this addition process is carried out through the MSB position.

A *half-adder* is a device that can add 2 bits producing a SUM bit and a CARRY bit as outputs. A *full adder* adds 3 bits, producing a SUM bit and a CARRY bit as its outputs. To add two *n*-bit numbers, we thus need one half-adder and $n - 1$ full adders. Figure 1.11 shows the half-adder and full adder arrangement to perform 4-bit addition. This is called a *ripple-carry adder* since the carry ripples through the stages of the adder starting at LSB to MSB. The time needed for this carry propagation is in proportion to the number of bits. Since the sum is of correct value only after the carry appears at MSB, the longer the carry propagation time, the slower the adder will be. There are several schemes to increase the speed of this adder. Some of them are discussed in Chapter 7.

Figure 1.12 shows the block diagram representations and truth tables for full adders and half-adders. From truth tables we can derive the SOP form functions for the outputs of the adders. They are:

Half-adder

$$S_0 = \bar{a}_0 b_0 + a_0 \bar{b}_0$$

$$C = a_0 b_0 \tag{1-5}$$

Figure 1.13 shows the circuit diagram.

Figure 1.11 A ripple-carry adder

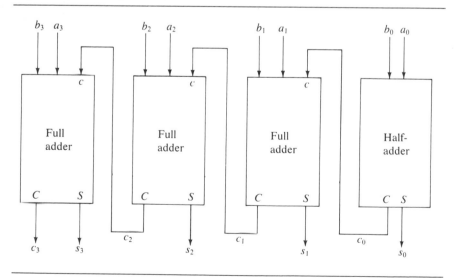

Note: INPUT: *c*, CARRY IN. OUTPUT: *C*, CARRY OUT; *S*, SUM.

Figure 1.12 Adders with truth tables

$s_0 \leftarrow \underline{\text{SUM}}$ Half- a_0
$C \leftarrow \underline{\text{CARRY}}$ adder b_0

$S_1 \leftarrow \underline{\text{SUM}}$ Full $\leftarrow C_{\text{in}}$
$C_{\text{out}} \leftarrow \underline{\text{CARRY}}$ adder $\leftarrow a_1$
 $\leftarrow b_1$

Truth Table

a_0	b_0	S_0	C
0	0	0	0
0	1	1	0
1	0	1	0
1	1	0	1

(a) Half-adder

Truth Table

C_{in}	a_1	b_1	S_1	C_{out}
0	0	0	0	0
0	0	1	1	0
0	1	0	1	0
0	1	1	0	1
1	0	0	1	0
1	0	1	0	1
1	1	0	0	1
1	1	1	1	1

(b) Full adder

Figure 1.13 Half-adder circuits

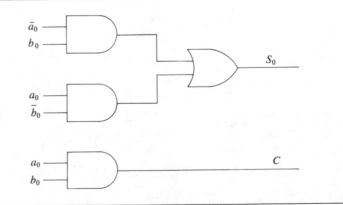

Full adder

$$S_1 = \bar{C}_{in}\bar{a}_1 b_1 + \bar{C}_{in}a_1\bar{b}_1 + C_{in}a_1 b_1 + C_{in}\bar{a}_1\bar{b}_1$$

$$C_{out} = \bar{C}_{in}a_1 b_1 + C_{in}\bar{a}_1 b_1 + C_{in}a_1\bar{b}_1 + C_{in}a_1 b_1$$

(1–6)

Figure 1.14 shows the circuit diagram.

Figure 1.14 Full adder circuits

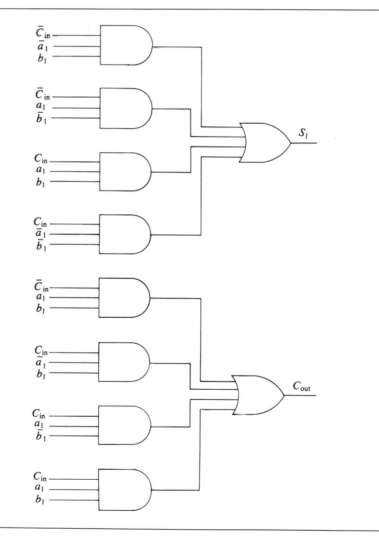

The equation for the C_{out} output of the full adder can be simplified using the theorems of Boolean algebra:

$$C_{out} = \bar{C}_{in}a_1b_1 + C_{in}\bar{a}_1b_1 + \underbrace{C_{in}a_1\bar{b}_1 + C_{in}a_1b_1}_{P4b}$$

$$= \bar{C}_{in}a_1b_1 + C_{in}\bar{a}_1b_1 + C_{in}a_1\underbrace{(\bar{b}_1 + b_1)}_{1} \qquad \text{P5a}$$

$$= \bar{C}_{in}a_1b_1 + \underbrace{C_{in}\bar{a}_1b_1 + C_{in}a_1}_{} \qquad \text{P1b}$$

$$= \bar{C}_{in}a_1b_1 + \underbrace{C_{in}(\bar{a}_1b_1 + a_1)}_{T4a} \qquad \text{P4b}$$

$$= \bar{C}_{in}a_1b_1 + C_{in}(b_1 + a_1)$$

$$= \underbrace{\bar{C}_{in}a_1b_1 + C_{in} \cdot b_1}_{} + C_{in} \cdot a_1 \qquad \text{P4b}$$

$$= \underbrace{(\bar{C}_{in}a_1 + C_{in})b_1}_{T4a} + C_{in}a_1 \qquad \text{P4b}$$

$$= (a_1 + C_{in})b_1 + C_{in}a_1 \qquad \text{P4b}$$

$$= a_1b_1 + C_{in}b_1 + C_{in}a_1$$

This equation has only 6 literals compared to the 12 literals of the original equation. This simplified equation can be realized with three 2-input AND gates and one 3-input OR gate. Such simplifications are usually performed while building a circuit using gates. Appendix B gives two more simplification procedures that are more mechanical to perform than the algebraic procedure shown above.

1.6.2 Decoders

A *code word* is a string of a certain number of bits. Appendix A lists the most common codes. The hexadecimal system, for example, uses a 4-bit code word for each digit 0, 1, 2, 3, . . . , D, E, F. An n-bit binary string can take 2^n combinations of values. An n-to-2^n decoder is a circuit that converts the n-bit input data into 2^n outputs (at the maximum). At any time only one output line corresponding to the combination on the input lines will be 1; all the other outputs will be 0. The outputs are usually numbered from 0 to $(2^n - 1)$. If, for example, the combination on the input of a 4-to-2^4 decoder is 1001, only output 9 will be 1; all other outputs will be 0.

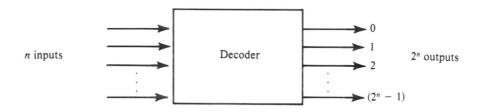

It is not usually necessary to draw a truth table for a decoder. There would be a single 1 in each output column of the truth table and the product (or SUM) term corresponding to that 1 could be easily derived. Figure 1.15 shows the circuit diagram of a 3-to-8 decoder. The 3 inputs are designated A, B, and C, with C as the LSB. The outputs are numbered 0 through 7.

Figure 1.15 A 3-to-8 decoder circuit

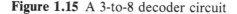

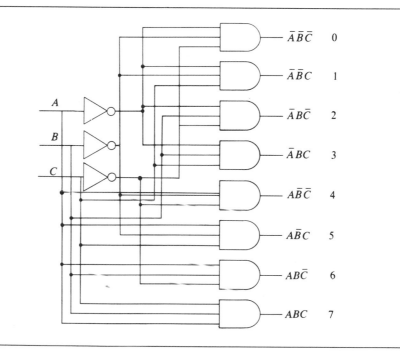

1.6.3 Code Converters

A code converter translates an input code word into an output bit pattern corresponding to a new code word. A decoder is a code converter that changes an n-bit code word into a 2^n-bit code word. We will illustrate the design of a circuit that converts the Binary Coded Decimal (BCD) into Excess-3 code. The truth table is shown in Figure 1.16. Both BCD and Excess-3 are 4-bit codes. BCD code extends from 0 to 9 and there are 16 combinations of 4 bits, so the last 6 combinations are not used in BCD. They will never occur as inputs to the circuit. Hence, we DON'T CARE what happens to the outputs, for these input values. These DON'T CARE conditions are shown as "d" on the truth table. They can be used to advantage in simplifying functions because they can be either a 0 or a 1 for our convenience. From Figure 1.16:

$$W = \bar{A}B\bar{C}D + \bar{A}BC\bar{D} + \bar{A}BCD + A\bar{B}\bar{C}\bar{D} + A\bar{B}\bar{C}D$$

$$X = \bar{A}\bar{B}\bar{C}D + \bar{A}\bar{B}C\bar{D} + \bar{A}\bar{B}CD + \bar{A}B\bar{C}\bar{D} + A\bar{B}\bar{C}D$$

$$Y = \bar{A}\bar{B}\bar{C}\bar{D} + \bar{A}\bar{B}CD + \bar{A}B\bar{C}\bar{D} + \bar{A}BCD + A\bar{B}\bar{C}\bar{D}$$

$$Z = \bar{A}\bar{B}\bar{C}\bar{D} + \bar{A}\bar{B}C\bar{D} + \bar{A}B\bar{C}\bar{D} + \bar{A}BC\bar{D} + A\bar{B}\bar{C}\bar{D}$$

Figure 1.16 Truth table for BCD to Excess-3 decoder

Decimal	A	B	C	D	W	X	Y	Z
		BCD Inputs				Excess-3 Output		
0	0	0	0	0	0	0	1	1
1	0	0	0	1	0	1	0	0
2	0	0	1	0	0	1	0	1
3	0	0	1	1	0	1	1	0
4	0	1	0	0	0	1	1	1
5	0	1	0	1	1	0	0	0
6	0	1	1	0	1	0	0	1
7	0	1	1	1	1	0	1	0
8	1	0	0	0	1	0	1	1
9	1	0	0	1	1	1	0	0
Not used	1	0	1	0	d	d	d	d
	1	0	1	1	d	d	d	d
	1	1	0	0	d	d	d	d
	1	1	0	1	d	d	d	d
	1	1	1	0	d	d	d	d
	1	1	1	1	d	d	d	d

In multiple-output designs such as this, it is possible that two or more output functions contain the same product term. For example, $\overline{A}\overline{B}\overline{C}\overline{D}$ appears in both Y and Z. It is not necessary to implement this product term twice. The output of the gate realizing this product term can be fanned out to be used in the realization of both Y and Z. Further simplification of these functions is possible when the DON'T CARE conditions are taken into account. Appendix B shows such a minimization for the BCD to Excess-3 code converter.

1.6.4 Encoders

An encoder generates an n-bit code word as a function of the combination of values on its input. At the maximum, there can be 2^n inputs.

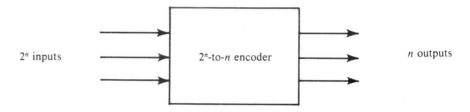

The design of an encoder is executed by first drawing a truth table that shows the n-bit output needed for each of the 2^n combinations of inputs. The circuit diagrams are then derived for each output bit.

Example 1.22 A partial truth table for a 4-to-2 line encoder is shown in Figure 1.17(a). Although there are 16 combinations of 4 inputs, only 4

Figure 1.17 A 4-to-2 encoder

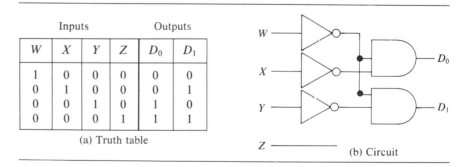

	Inputs			Outputs	
W	X	Y	Z	D_0	D_1
1	0	0	0	0	0
0	1	0	0	0	1
0	0	1	0	1	0
0	0	0	1	1	1

(a) Truth table

(b) Circuit

are used because the 2-bit output supports only 4 combinations. The output combinations identify which of the four input lines is at 1 at a particular time. The output functions as can be seen from this truth table are

$$D_0 = \bar{W}\bar{X}, \text{ and}$$
$$D_1 = \bar{W}\bar{Y}. \tag{1-7}$$

These functions may be simplified by observing that it is sufficient to have $W = 0$ and $X = 0$ for D_0 to be 1, no matter what the values of Y and Z are. Similarly, $W = 0$ and $Y = 0$ are sufficient for D_1 to be 1. Such observations, although not always straightforward, help in simplifying functions, thus reducing the amount of hardware needed. Alternatively, the truth table in Figure 1.17(a) can be completed by including the remaining 12 input combinations and entering don't cares for the outputs corresponding to those inputs. D_0 and D_1 can then be derived from the truth table and simplified. Figure 1.17(b) shows the circuit diagram for the 4-to-2 encoder.

1.6.5 Multiplexers

A multiplexer is a switch that connects one of its several inputs to the output. A set of n control inputs is needed to select one of the 2^n inputs that is to be connected to the output. A multiplexer with 4 inputs and two control signals is shown here:

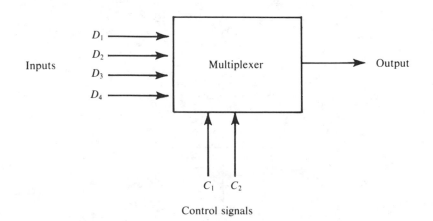

The operation of this multiplexer can be described by the following table:

C_1	C_2	Output
0	0	D_1
0	1	D_2
1	0	D_3
1	1	D_4

Although there are 6 inputs, a complete truth table with 2^6 rows is not required for designing the circuit, since the output simply assumes the value of one of the 4 inputs depending on the control signals C_1 and C_2. That is,

$$\text{Output} = D_1 \cdot \bar{C}_1\bar{C}_2 + D_2 \cdot \bar{C}_1C_2 + D_3 \cdot C_1\bar{C}_2 + D_4 \cdot C_1C_2. \quad (1\text{--}8)$$

The circuit for realizing the above multiplexer is shown in Figure 1.18.

Each of the inputs D_1, D_2, D_3, and D_4 and the output in this multiplexer circuit are single lines. If the application requires that the data lines to be

Figure 1.18 A 4-to-1 multiplexer

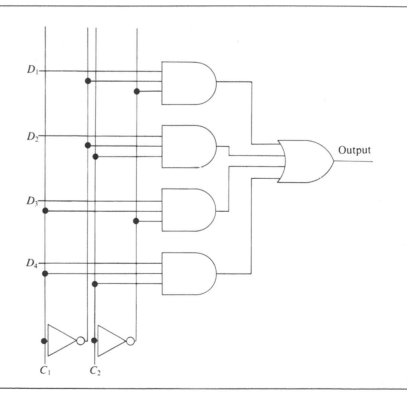

multiplexed have more than one bit each, the above circuit has to be duplicated once for each bit of data.

1.6.6 Demultiplexers

A demultiplexer has one input and several outputs. It switches (connects) the input to one of its outputs based on the combination of values on a set of control (select) inputs. If there are n control signals, there can be a maximum of 2^n outputs. A demultiplexer with 2^n outputs and n control signals is shown here:

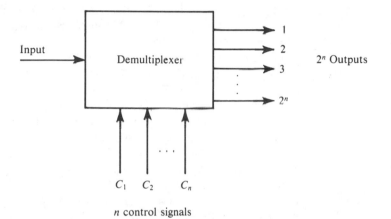

A typical application for a multiplexer is to connect one of the several input devices (as selected by a device number) to the input of a computer system. A demultiplexer can be used to switch the output of the computer on to one of the several output devices.

1.7 Integrated Circuits

The logic circuits we have designed in this chapter are shown in gate-level detail. These circuits are constructed in practice using integrated circuits (ICs). An IC is a small silicon semiconductor crystal or "chip" mounted in a metallic or plastic package. Several pins are welded to the chip to provide the external connections. The electronic components, such as transistors, diodes, resistors, and capacitors, are fabricated on the chip and interconnected to provide logic capabilities.

An IC consisting of several logic gates on a single package is a small-scale integrated circuit (SSI). A medium-scale integrated circuit (MSI) consists of the logic to perform an entire function such as adders and multiplexer and has a complexity equivalent to 10–100 gates. An IC with a complexity of more than 100 gates is a large-scale integrated circuit (LSI). There are very large scale integrated circuits (VLSI) now available that comprise thousands of gates.

1.7.1 Technologies

Two broad categories of integrated circuit technology are (1) bipolar and (2) metal-oxide-semiconductor (MOS). Bipolar technologies are based on transistors built out of (*p-n-p*) or (*n-p-n*) junctions of semiconductors; MOS technologies are based on transistors built out of metal-oxide semiconductors. Several logic families of ICs are available within each technology. The popular bipolar logic families are transistor-transistor logic (TTL) and emitter-coupled logic (ECL). P-channel MOS (PMOS), N-channel MOS (NMOS), and complementary MOS (CMOS) are the popular MOS logic families. Table 1.1 lists some characteristics of these logic families.

The supply voltage is the external voltage required to power the IC. The logic 0 and 1 values correspond to two distinct voltage ranges. For example, in TTL the logic 0 corresponds to 0 volts and the logic 1 corresponds to +5 volts. These are typical values. The acceptable ranges for these voltages are shown in Table 1.1. In the *positive logic* system, the high-level voltage (H) corresponds to 1 and the low-level voltage (L) corresponds to 0. In the *negative logic* system, the designations are opposite. We will follow the positive logic notation in this book.

Each gate introduces a delay into the signal propagation. That is, the change in the output of a gate with respect to the changes on its inputs is not simultaneous. Typical propagation delays are shown in Table 1.1. Because these delays accumulate as the signal passes through several gates, the circuit with the least number of levels will be the fastest. Hence, two-level circuits such as AND-OR and NAND-NAND circuits discussed in this chapter are preferred over multilevel designs for faster operations. Fanout for typical devices in each technology are also shown

Table 1.1 Characteristics of the popular logic families

Characteristic	TTL	ECL	CMOS
Supply voltage (volts)	5	−5.2	3 to 10
High-level voltage (H; volts)	2.4 to 5	−0.95 to −0.7	3 to 10
Low-level voltage (L; volts)	0 to 0.4	−1.9 to −1.6	0 to 0.5
Propagation delay (nanoseconds)	5 to 10	1 to 2	25
Fanout	10 to 20	25	50
Power dissipation (milliwatts)	2 to 10	25	0.1

in the table. Power dissipation per gate provides a measure of the overall power requirements for the circuit.

TTL is the most popular logic family. The ICs in this family have a numerical designation of either 7400 or 5400 series. 7400 series is for the industrial environments where the temperature variations are less severe. 5400 series is for military applications. Different numerical designations are used by different manufacturers. The equivalents are readily identified in a cross-reference table in the IC manufacturers' catalogs.

1.7.2 Some Popular Integrated Circuits

Figure 1.19 shows the mechanical details of an IC. The ICs are produced in two types of packages: (1) dual-in-line (DIP) ceramic or plastic and

Figure 1.19 Mechanical characteristics of ICs (Courtesy of Texas Instruments Incorporated)

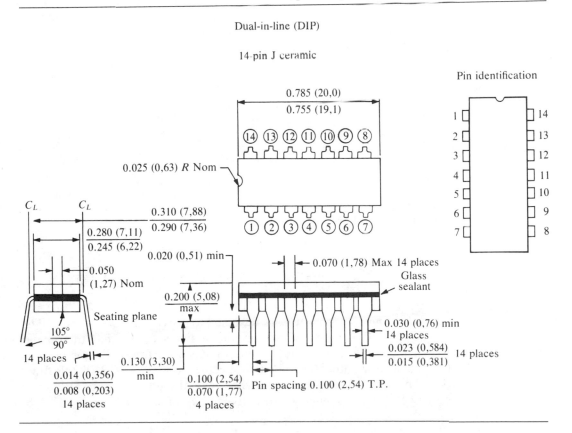

(2) flat-pack ceramic. The pins are numbered in the standard and easily identifiable format shown in the figure. The logical function realized by an IC and its other electrical characteristics such as propagation delay, fan-out, and the function of each pin are listed in IC manufacturers' catalogs.

Figure 1.20 shows logic diagrams for several 54/7400 series TTL circuits. The numbers on the logic diagrams correspond to the pin numbers on the IC. V_{cc} is the supply voltage (5V) and GND is the system ground (OV).

We will briefly discuss some of the important characteristics to be observed in designing logic circuits with these ICs. Manufacturers' catalogs are the best source for further details.

Inverted Signals.   The output and inputs of some ICs follow an inverse convention. For example, the BCD to decimal decoder (7442) provides a 0 on the selected output and a 1 on all the other outputs (which is opposite of the convention we used earlier in designing decoders and code converters). Signals that take a value of 0 when they are *active* are called low-active signals. These are indicated by a "bubble" on the logic diagrams. Signals that take a value of 1 when they are active are high-active signals. For example, in the following diagram of an IC, input *A* and output *E* are low-active, and inputs *B, C,* and *D* are high-active.

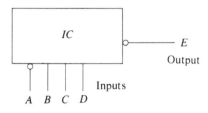

A bubble in the logic diagram normally denotes an inversion. Some examples are shown here:

Special Outputs.   Some ICs arc designed to provide special outputs. The ICs designated as buffers (7440) provide a higher fanout than the regular ICs in the 7400 series. The outputs of ICs with free collector outputs (open collector outputs) can be tied together to form a WIRED-OR function. This type of output is useful when several signals are to be ORed and only one of these signals will be active at any time (as in forming a BUS,

Figure 1.20 Logic diagrams and function tables of ICs (Courtesy of Texas Instruments Incorporated)

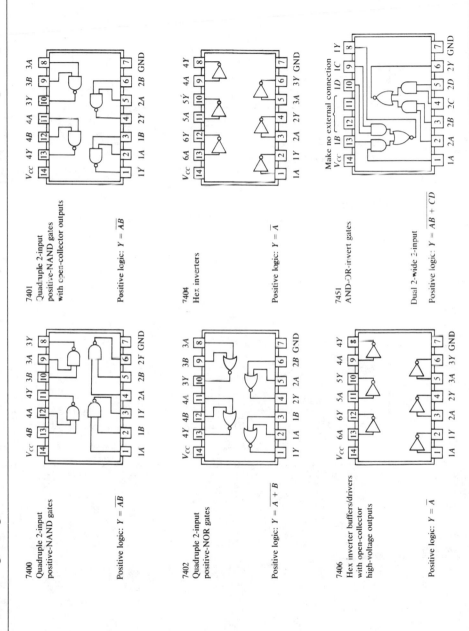

7400
Quadruple 2-input
positive-NAND gates

Positive logic: $Y = \overline{AB}$

7402
Quadruple 2-input
positive-NOR gates

Positive logic: $Y = \overline{A + B}$

7406
Hex inverter buffers/drivers
with open-collector
high-voltage outputs

Positive logic: $Y = \overline{A}$

7401
Quadruple 2-input
positive-NAND gates
with open-collector outputs

Positive logic: $Y = \overline{AB}$

7404
Hex inverters

Positive logic: $Y = \overline{A}$

7451
AND-OR-invert gates

Dual 2-wide 2-input

Positive logic: $Y = \overline{AB + CD}$

Figure 1.20 (Continued)

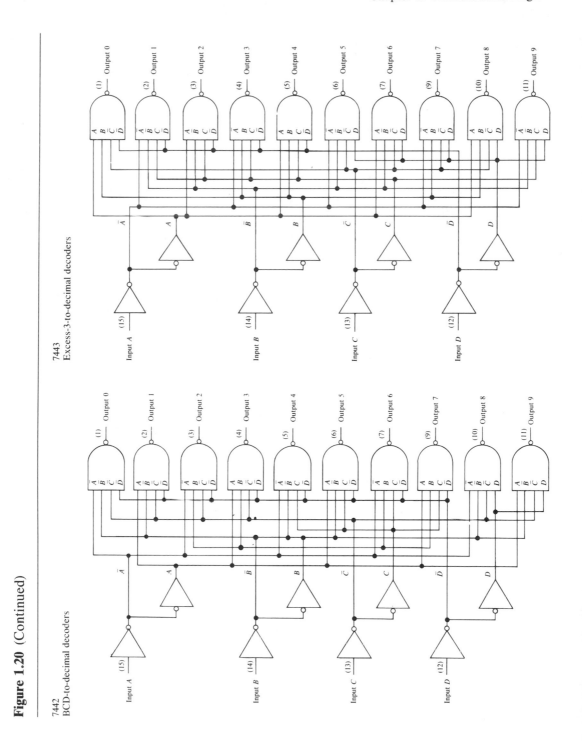

7442
BCD-to-decimal decoders

7443
Excess-3-to-decimal decoders

Functional block diagrams   '150

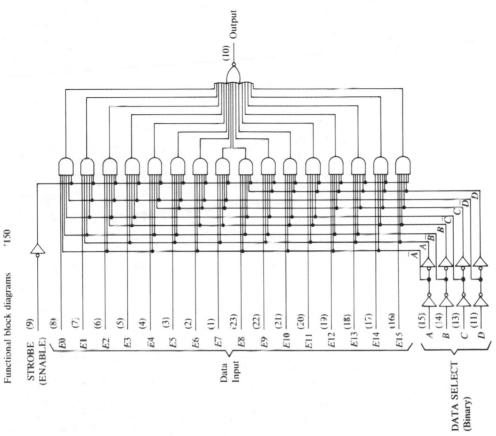

74150
Data Selector/Multiplexer

Logic   '150
Function table

Inputs					Output
SELECT				STROBE	
D	C	B	A	S	W
X	X	X	X	H	H
L	L	L	L	L	$\overline{E0}$
L	L	L	H	L	$\overline{E1}$
L	L	H	L	L	$\overline{E2}$
L	L	H	H	L	$\overline{E3}$
L	H	L	L	L	$\overline{E4}$
L	H	L	H	L	$\overline{E5}$
L	H	H	L	L	$\overline{E6}$
L	H	H	H	L	$\overline{E7}$
H	L	L	L	L	$\overline{E8}$
H	L	L	H	L	$\overline{E9}$
H	L	H	L	L	$\overline{E10}$
H	L	H	H	L	$\overline{E11}$
H	H	L	L	L	$\overline{E12}$
H	H	L	H	L	$\overline{E13}$
H	H	H	L	L	$\overline{E14}$
H	H	H	H	L	$\overline{E15}$

Figure 1.20 (Continued)

74154
4-line-to-16-line decoder/demultiplexer

Logic

Function Table

Inputs						Outputs															
G1	G2	D	C	B	A	0	1	2	3	4	5	6	7	8	9	10	11	12	13	14	15
L	L	L	L	L	L	L	H	H	H	H	H	H	H	H	H	H	H	H	H	H	H
L	L	L	L	L	H	H	L	H	H	H	H	H	H	H	H	H	H	H	H	H	H
L	L	L	L	H	L	H	H	L	H	H	H	H	H	H	H	H	H	H	H	H	H
L	L	L	L	H	H	H	H	H	L	H	H	H	H	H	H	H	H	H	H	H	H
L	L	L	H	L	L	H	H	H	H	L	H	H	H	H	H	H	H	H	H	H	H
L	L	L	H	L	H	H	H	H	H	H	L	H	H	H	H	H	H	H	H	H	H
L	L	L	H	H	L	H	H	H	H	H	H	L	H	H	H	H	H	H	H	H	H
L	L	L	H	H	H	H	H	H	H	H	H	H	L	H	H	H	H	H	H	H	H
L	L	H	L	L	L	H	H	H	H	H	H	H	H	L	H	H	H	H	H	H	H
L	L	H	L	L	H	H	H	H	H	H	H	H	H	H	L	H	H	H	H	H	H
L	L	H	L	H	L	H	H	H	H	H	H	H	H	H	H	L	H	H	H	H	H
L	L	H	L	H	H	H	H	H	H	H	H	H	H	H	H	H	L	H	H	H	H
L	L	H	H	L	L	H	H	H	H	H	H	H	H	H	H	H	H	L	H	H	H
L	L	H	H	L	H	H	H	H	H	H	H	H	H	H	H	H	H	H	L	H	H
L	L	H	H	H	L	H	H	H	H	H	H	H	H	H	H	H	H	H	H	L	H
L	L	H	H	H	H	H	H	H	H	H	H	H	H	H	H	H	H	H	H	H	L
L	H	X	X	X	X	H	H	H	H	H	H	H	H	H	H	H	H	H	H	H	H
H	L	X	X	X	X	H	H	H	H	H	H	H	H	H	H	H	H	H	H	H	H
H	H	X	X	X	X	H	H	H	H	H	H	H	H	H	H	H	H	H	H	H	H

H = high level. L = low level. X = irrelevant

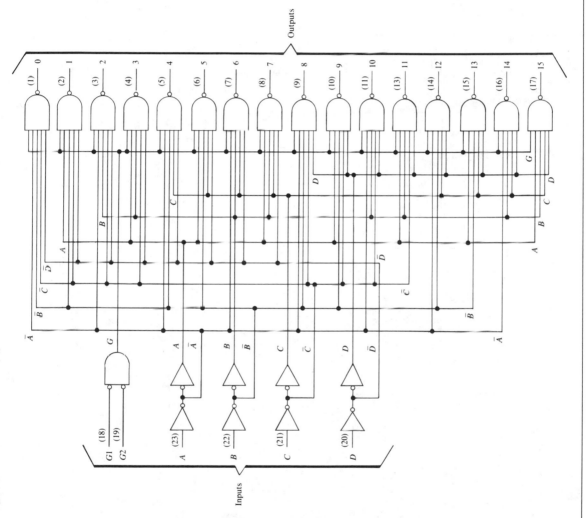

Functional block diagram and schematics of inputs and outputs

Figure 1.20 (Continued)

74155
Dual 2-line-to-4-line decoder/demultiplexer

Functional block diagram and logic

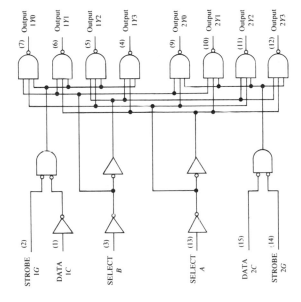

Function tables
2-line-to-4-line decoder
or 1-line-to-4-line demultiplexer

Inputs				Outputs			
SELECT		STROBE	DATA				
B	A	1G	1C	1Y0	1Y1	1Y2	1Y3
X	X	H	X	H	H	H	H
L	L	L	H	L	H	H	H
L	H	L	H	H	L	H	H
H	L	L	H	H	H	L	H
H	H	L	H	H	H	H	L
X	X	X	L	H	H	H	H

Inputs				Outputs			
SELECT		STROBE	DATA				
B	A	2G	2C	2Y0	2Y1	2Y2	2Y3
X	X	H	X	H	H	H	H
L	L	L	L	L	H	H	H
L	H	L	L	H	L	H	H
H	L	L	L	H	H	L	H
H	H	L	L	H	H	H	L
X	X	X	H	H	H	H	H

Function table
3-line-to-8-line decoder
or 1-line-to-8 line demultiplexer

Inputs				Outputs							
SELECT			STROBE or DATA	(0)	(1)	(2)	(3)	(4)	(5)	(6)	(7)
C†	B	A	G‡	2Y0	2Y1	2Y2	2Y3	1Y0	1Y1	1Y2	1Y3
X	X	X	H	H	H	H	H	H	H	H	H
L	L	L	L	L	H	H	H	H	H	H	H
L	L	H	L	H	L	H	H	H	H	H	H
L	H	L	L	H	H	L	H	H	H	H	H
L	H	H	L	H	H	H	L	H	H	H	H
H	L	L	L	H	H	H	H	L	H	H	H
H	L	H	L	H	H	H	H	H	L	H	H
H	H	L	L	H	H	H	H	H	H	L	H
H	H	H	L	H	H	H	H	H	H	H	L

† C = inputs 1C and 2C connected together
‡ G = inputs 1G and 2G connected together
H = high level. L = low level. X = irrelevant

discussed in Chapter 2). ICs with a TRISTATE output also provide the WIRED-OR capability. In addition to the 0 and 1 states, such ICs also stay in a high-impedance state. They have an ENABLE input to bring them into the normal operating states of 1 or 0. When not enabled, it is as though these gates were not connected to the circuit. ICs designated as *drivers* provide a driving capability usually for a special purpose. Some ICs have a STROBE (or ENABLE) input (74151), requiring the STROBE input to be active for these ICs to function. Some ICs provide both the true and complemented outputs (74151).

1.7.3 Designing with ICs

NAND-NAND or NOR-NOR implementations are extensively used in designing with ICs. NAND and NOR functions are basic to IC fabrication, and using a single type of gate in the implementation is preferable because several identical gates are available on one chip. Logic designers usually choose an available IC (decoder, adder, etc.) to implement functions rather than implement at the gate level as discussed earlier in this chapter.

Several nonconventional design approaches can be taken in designing with ICs. For example, since decoders are available as MSI components, the outputs of a decoder corresponding to the input combination where a circuit provides an output of 1 can be ORed to realize a function. An implementation of a full adder using a 3-to-8 decoder (whose outputs are assumed to be high-active) is shown here:

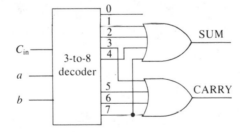

See Problem 1.21 for another example.

1.8   Loading and Timing

Two main problems to be resolved in designing with ICs are loading and timing. Loading problems occur in the event that the output of one gate cannot drive the subsequent gate when the fanout limit is exceeded. This can be compensated by providing a *buffer* at the output of the loaded gate, either a separate inverting or a noninverting buffer, or by replacing the gate with one that has a higher drive capability.

    Timing problems in general are not critical in a simple combinational circuit. However, a timing analysis is usually necessary in any complex circuit. Timing diagrams are useful in such analysis. Figure 1.21 shows

Figure 1.21 Timing characteristics and models of an IC

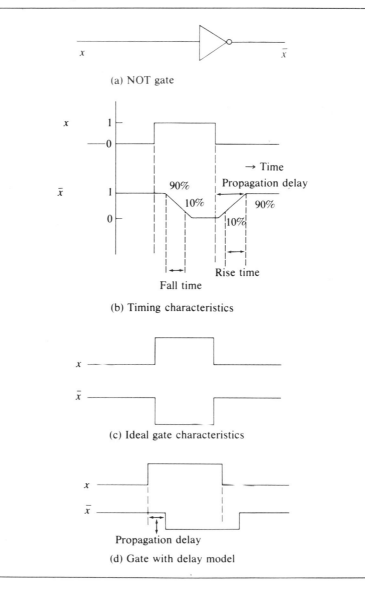

(a) NOT gate

(b) Timing characteristics

(c) Ideal gate characteristics

(d) Gate with delay model

the timing characteristics of a NOT gate. The X-axis indicates time. Logic values 1 and 0 are shown (as magnitudes of a voltage) on the Y-axis. Figure 1.22 shows the timing diagram for a simple combinational circuit. At t_0, all 3 inputs A, B, and C are at 0. Hence, Z_1, Z_2, and Z are all 0. At t_1, B changes to 1. Assuming gates with no delays (ideal gates), Z_1 changes to 1 at t_1 and hence Z also changes to 1. At t_2, C changes to 1 resulting in no changes in Z_1, Z_2, or Z. At t_3, A changes to 1, pulling $\bar{A}$ to 0; Z_1 to 0 and

Figure 1.22 Timing analysis of combinational circuit

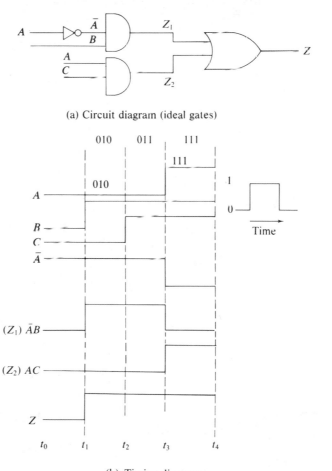

(a) Circuit diagram (ideal gates)

(b) Timing diagram

Z_2 to 1; Z remains at 1. This timing diagram can be expanded to indicate all the other combinations of inputs. It will then be a graphical way of representing the truth table.

We can also analyze the effects of gate delays using a timing diagram. Figure 1.23 is such an analysis for the above circuit, where the gate delays are shown as T_1, T_2, T_3, and T_4. Assume that the circuit starts at t_0 with all the inputs at 0. At t_1, B changes to 1. This change results in a change in Z_1

Figure 1.23 Timing analysis showing gate delays

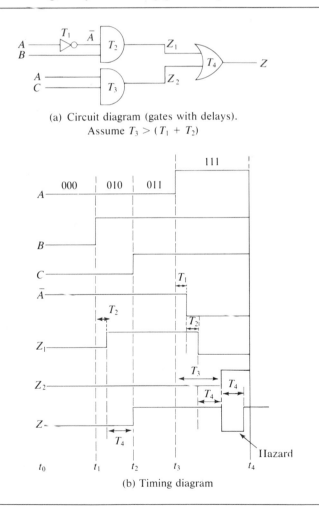

(a) Circuit diagram (gates with delays).
Assume $T_3 > (T_1 + T_2)$

(b) Timing diagram

at $(t_1 + T_2)$, rather than at t_1. This change in Z_1 causes Z to change T_4 later (i.e., at $t_1 + T_2 + T_4$). Changing of C to 1 at t_2 does not change any other signal value. When A is raised to 1 at t_3, $\bar{A}$ falls to 0 at $(t_3 + T_1)$, Z_1 falls to 0 at $(t_3 + T_1 + T_2)$, and Z_2 raises to 1 at $(t_3 + T_3)$. If $T_3 > (T_1 + T_2)$, there is a time period in which both Z_1 and Z_2 are 0, contributing a "glitch" at Z. Z rises back to 1, T_4 after Z_2 rises to 1. This momentary transition of Z to 0 might cause some problems in a complex circuit. Such hazards are the results of unequal delays in the signal paths of a circuit. They can be prevented by adding additional circuitry. This analysis indicates the utility of a timing diagram. Detailed discussion of hazards is beyond the scope of this book.

1.9 Summary

This chapter provided an introduction to the analysis and design of combinational logic circuits. Logic minimization procedures are discussed in Appendix B. Several intuitive methods to minimize logic circuits as used in some sections of this chapter, rather than the formal methods, will be used in the rest of the book. Readers familiar with formal methods can substitute those, to derive the minimum logic. Although the discussion on IC technology is brief, details on designing with ICs given here are sufficient to understand the information in an IC vendor's catalog and start building simple circuits. A complete understanding of the timing and loading problems helps, but is not mandatory, to understand the rest of the material in the book.

References

Friedman, A. D., and P. R. Menon. *Theory and Design of Switching Circuits*. Woodland Hills, Calif.: Computer Sciences Press, 1975.

Mano, M. M. *Digital Logic and Computer Design*. Englewood Cliffs, N.J.: Prentice-Hall, 1979.

MECL Integrated Circuits Data Book. Phoenix, Ariz.: Motorola Semiconductor Products, 1981.

Nagle, H. T., B. D. Carroll, and J. D. Irwin. *An Introduction to Computer Logic*. Englewood Cliffs, N.J.: Prentice-Hall, 1975.

Roth, C. H. *Fundamentals of Logic Design*. St. Paul, Minn.: West Publishing Co., 1979.

The TTL Data Book for Design Engineers. Dallas, Tex.: Texas Instruments, 1982.

Problems

1.1   If $A = 0$, $B = 1$, $C = 0$, and $D = 1$, find the value of F in each of the following:

    a. $F = A\bar{B} + C$

    b. $F = A\bar{B} + \bar{C}D + CD$

    c. $F = \bar{A}B(A + \bar{B} + \bar{C} \cdot D) + \bar{B}D$

    d. $F = (A + \bar{B})(\bar{C} + A)(A + B \cdot C)$

    e. $F = ((A + \bar{B})C + \bar{D})A\bar{B} + C\bar{D}(\bar{D} + \bar{A}(B + \bar{C}D))$

1.2   Draw a truth table for each of the following:

    a. $Q = X\bar{Y} + \bar{X}\bar{Z} + XYZ$

    b. $Q = (\bar{X} + Y)(\bar{X} + \bar{Z})(X + Z)$

    c. $Q = A\bar{B}(\bar{C} + D) + AB\bar{C} + \bar{C}D$

    d. $Q = \bar{A}BC + A\bar{B}(\bar{D}) + \bar{A} + \bar{B} + C\bar{D}$

    e. $Q = (X + Y + \bar{Z})(\bar{Y} + Z)$

1.3   State if the following identities are TRUE or FALSE.

    a. $X\bar{Y} + \bar{X}Z + \bar{Y}Z = \bar{X}Y + \bar{X}Z$

    b. $(\bar{B} + C)(\bar{B} + D) = \bar{B} + CD$

    c. $\bar{A}BC + AB\bar{C} + \bar{A}BD = B\bar{D} + AB\bar{C}$

    d. $\bar{X}Z + \bar{X}Y + XZ = \bar{X}Y\bar{Z} + \bar{X}YZ + \bar{X}Z$

    e. $(P + \bar{Q} + R)(P + \bar{Q} + \bar{R}) = \bar{Q} + P\bar{R} + R\bar{P}$

1.4   State if the following statements are TRUE or FALSE.

    a. $(X + \bar{Y})$ is a conjunction.

    b. $X\bar{Y}Z$ is a product term.

    c. $A\bar{B}\bar{C}$ is a disjunction.

    d. $(A + B + \bar{C})$ is a sum term.

    e. $A\bar{B}$ is not included in $ABCD$.

    f. $(A + \bar{B})$ is included in $(A + B + C)$.

    g. $A + B + \bar{C}$ is included in $AB\bar{C}$.

1.5   State if the following functions are in (1) normal POS form, (2) normal SOP form, (3) canonical POS form, or (4) canonical SOP form.

    a. $F(X,Y,Z) = X\bar{Y} + Y\bar{Z} + \bar{Z}\bar{Y}$

    b. $F(A,B,C,D) = (A + \bar{B} + \bar{C})(\bar{A} + C + D)(\bar{A} + \bar{C})$

    c. $F(P,Q,R) = P\bar{Q} + Q\bar{R}(P + \bar{Q}) + (\bar{R} + \bar{Q})$

    d. $F(A,B,C) = (A + B + \bar{C})(\bar{A} + \bar{B} + \bar{C})(\bar{A} + B + \bar{C})$

    e. $F(A,B,C,D) = AB\bar{C}D + AB\bar{C}D + \bar{A}\bar{B}CD$

    f. $F(A,B,C) = (A + \bar{B} + C)(A + \bar{B})(A + B + \bar{C})$

    g. $F(X,Y,Z) = X\bar{Y}Z + \bar{X}\bar{Y}Z + X\bar{Y} + XYZ$

    h. $F(A,B,C,D) = A\bar{B} + C\bar{D} + \bar{C}\bar{D}$

1.6   Express each of the following functions in (1) canonical POS form and (2) canonical SOP form. (Hint: Draw the truth table for each function.)

    a. $F(A,B,C) = (A + \bar{B})\bar{C} + \bar{A}C$

    b. $F(X,Y,Z) = (X + \bar{Y})(\bar{X} + Z) + Z\bar{Y}$

    c. $F(A,B,C,D) = A\bar{B}C + \bar{A}B\bar{C}D + \bar{A}BC\bar{D} + \bar{B}\bar{D}$

    d. $F(W,X,Y,Z) = W\bar{X} + \bar{Z}(\bar{Y} + \bar{W}) + \bar{W}\bar{Z}\bar{Y}$

1.7   Express F in minterm list form in each of the following:
    a. $F(A,B,C) = (A + \bar{B})\bar{C} + \bar{A}C$
    b. $F(X,Y,Z) = (X + \bar{Y})(\bar{X} + Z)(Z + \bar{Y})$
    c. $F(P,Q,R) = \Pi_M(0,1,5)$
    d. $F(A,B,C,D) = \Pi_M(1,2,3,7,9,10,15)$
    e. $F(W,X,Y,Z) = W\bar{Z} + (\bar{W} + \bar{X})Y\bar{Z} + \bar{W}\bar{Z}\bar{X}$

1.8   Express F in maxterm list form in each of the following:
    a. $F(A,B,C) = (A + \bar{B}) + \bar{C} + \bar{A}C$
    b. $\bar{F}(X,Y,Z) = (X + \bar{Y})(\bar{X} + Z) + Z\bar{Y}$
    c. $F(P,Q,R,S) = (P + \bar{Q})\bar{R} + \bar{P}\bar{S}\bar{R} + P\bar{Q}(\bar{S} + \bar{R} + \bar{Q})$
    d. $F(A,B,C,D) = \Sigma m(0,1,5,7,11,14,15)$
    c. $F(P,Q,R) = \Sigma m(2,3,5,7)$

1.9   Note that if two functions are equal, they will have the same minterms and the same maxterms. Use this fact to solve Problem 1.3.

1.10 Use only NOR gates to realize AND, OR, and NOT functions.

1.11 a. Design a combinational circuit with 3 inputs that produces an output that is 2s complement of the input. Refer to Appendix A for details on 2s complement system. Treat all input bits as magnitude bits, assuming there is no sign bit.
    b. Extend the design in (a) to include a sign bit. That is, the output should be the 2s complement of the input only if the sign bit is 1; otherwise, it is same as the input.

1.12 Design a comparator circuit with two 2-bit numbers A and B as inputs and three outputs indicating $A = B$, $A > B$, and $A < B$ conditions.

1.13 Design a BCD to 7-segment decoder: input is the 4 bit BCD code. There are 7 outputs, each of which drives one segment of a 7-segment display shown below, to form the numerical character corresponding to the input code.

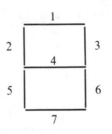

1.14 Build a full adder using two half-adders and other necessary gates.

1.15 Two 2-bit numbers are to be multiplied. Design a circuit with these numbers as input and the product as the output.

1.16 Two 2-bit numbers are to be added. Draw a truth table and design an AND-OR circuit. Compare the complexity of this circuit with the one built using a full adder and a half-adder. Which of these two circuits is faster?

1.17 Design a half-subtractor that has 2 inputs and 2 outputs: difference and borrow.

1.18 A full subtractor has 3 inputs: the 2 bits to be subtracted and a borrow-in. It produces a difference output and a borrow-out output. Design a NAND-NAND circuit.

1.19 Given

$$F_1(A,B,C) = \Sigma m(0,1,3) \quad + \quad d(2,7)$$

$$\qquad\qquad\qquad\qquad \uparrow \qquad\qquad\qquad \uparrow$$

$$\qquad\qquad\qquad\qquad \text{Minterms} \qquad \text{Don't cares}$$

$$\qquad\qquad\qquad\qquad \downarrow \qquad\qquad\qquad \downarrow$$

$$F_2(A,B,C) = \Sigma m(1,3,5,7) \quad + \quad d(6),$$

find
a. $\bar{F}_1$ in minterm list form.
b. $\bar{F}_1$ in maxterm list form.
c. $\bar{F}_1 \cdot F_2$.
d. $\bar{F}_1 + F_2$.

1.20 Note from the following table that the positive-logic OR gate performs as an AND gate in negative logic.

A	B	Z
L	L	L
L	H	H
H	L	H
H	H	H

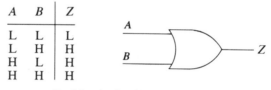

Positive logic: $H = 1, L = 0$
Negative logic: $H = 0, L = 1$

Find the equivalents of OR, NAND, NOR, and EXOR gates in negative logic.

1.21 Derive the exclusive-OR function using a 2-to-1 multiplexer.

Chapter 2

Sequential Circuits

The digital circuits described in Chapter 1 did not possess memory. In most digital systems, memory elements are added to the combinational logic circuits, thus making them *sequential circuits*. The output of a sequential circuit at any time is a function of its inputs at that time and the *state* of the circuit at that time. The state of the circuit is defined by the contents of the individual memory elements.

Figure 2.1 is a block diagram of a sequential circuit with m inputs, n outputs, and p internal memory elements. The output of p memory elements combined constitutes the state of the circuit at any time t. The combinational logic decides the output of the circuit and provides *next-state* information as a function of inputs and the state at time t. The next-state information at time t is stored in memory elements and constitutes the state at time $(t + \Delta t)$ where Δt is a time increment. The state of the circuit at time t is usually called the *present state*. We will denote the next time $(t + \Delta t)$ as $(t + 1)$ in this chapter.

There are two types of sequential circuits: *synchronous* and *asynchronous*. In a synchronous circuit, the behavior of the circuit can be defined by the knowledge of the signal values at discrete instants of time. In an asynchronous circuit, the circuit behavior depends on the order in which the input signals change and these changes can occur at any time.

The discrete time steps in the synchronous circuit are decided by a controlling signal, or *clock*. A clock is a signal that makes 0-to-1 and 1-to-0 transitions at regular intervals of time. Figure 2.2 shows a clock signal along with various terms used in describing a clock. This chapter deals with the analysis and design of clocked sequential circuits, the circuits in which the state transitions are controlled by clock pulses. Although the

Figure 2.1 Block diagram of a sequential circuit

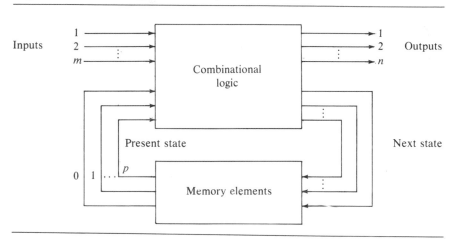

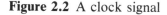

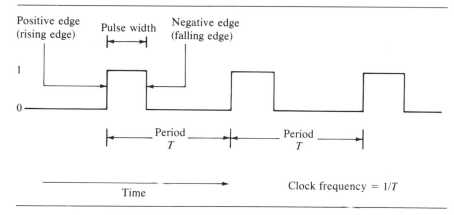

Figure 2.2 A clock signal

clock signal in Figure 2.2 is shown with regular period T, it is not required that the interval between two clock pulses be equal. The analysis and design procedures detailed in this chapter are thus valid as long as there is a clock pulse to bring in the state transition. Note that Δt must be less than or equal to T for proper operation of the circuit.

Synchronous sequential circuits use *flip-flops* as memory elements. A flip-flop is an electronic memory device that can store either a 0 or a 1 and stay in that logic state as long as changes in input do not bring in a state change. Normally, there will be two outputs from a flip-flop, one corresponding to the normal state (Q) and the other to the complementary state ($\bar{Q}$). We will discuss four popular types of flip-flops in the next section.

Asynchronous circuits normally use delay elements as memory. A delay element introduces a specified amount of delay into signal propagation. Sometimes the propagation delay of logic gates in the circuit is sufficient to produce the needed delay. This property allows an asynchronous circuit to be treated as a combinational circuit with feedback. Asynchronous circuits are difficult to analyze and design, although if properly designed, they are generally faster than synchronous circuits.

2.1 Flip-Flops

The four types of flip-flops most commonly used are the set-reset (SR) flip-flop, the delay (D) flip-flop, the modified SR (JK) flip-flop, and the trigger (T) flip-flop. The essential characteristics of each of these are discussed in this section.

2.1.1 SR Flip-Flop

Figure 2.3(a) shows a cross-coupled NOR circuit and (b) a partial truth table for its operations at any time t. When $S = 1$ and $R = 0$ are applied at t, $\bar{Q}$ assumes 0 and Q assumes 1 at time $t + 1$. If S is changed to 0 as shown in the second row of the table, then Q and $\bar{Q}$ values will not change. If R is changed to 1, then the output values change to $Q = 0$ and $\bar{Q} = 1$. Again, an $S = 0$, $R = 0$ input condition does not change the output values. When an $S = 1$, $R = 1$ is applied, both outputs assume 0 values, which is not desired because Q and $\bar{Q}$ must always be complements.

The outputs do not change instantaneously after a change in the input and hence the time slot Δt is assumed to be long enough for the outputs to stabilize. This cross-coupled NOR-circuit is the *set-reset flip-flop* (SR flip-flop). The input combination $S = 1$, $R = 0$ "sets" the flip-flop circuit (i.e., $Q = 1$); $S = 0$, $R = 1$ "resets" the flip-flop circuit (i.e., $Q = 0$); $S = 0$, $R = 0$ is a "no change" condition; and $S = 1$, $R = 1$ is not allowed because the $\bar{Q}$ output must always be the complement of Q. S input is called the SET input, and R is the RESET input.

Figure 2.3(c) shows the *state table* for this flip-flop circuit. The present state $Q(t)$ (the state at time t) is either a 0 or a 1. The two inputs $S(t)$ and $R(t)$ can assume four combinations of values: 00, 01, 10, and 11. For each input combination and the present-state value, the next-state value $Q(t + 1)$ is shown in the state table. This SR flip-flop formed by cross-coupling two NOR gates is essentially an asynchronous circuit: the outputs change as and when the inputs change. A clock input can be added to this asynchronous circuit to derive a "clocked" SR flip-flop [Figure 2.3(d)]. Here,

Figure 2.3 Basic SR flip-flop circuit

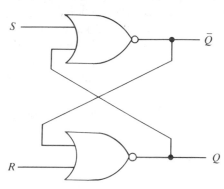

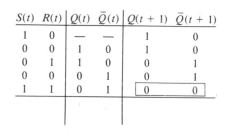

$S(t)$	$R(t)$	$Q(t)$	$\bar{Q}(t)$	$Q(t+1)$	$\bar{Q}(t+1)$
1	0	—	—	1	0
0	0	1	0	1	0
0	1	1	0	0	1
0	0	0	1	0	1
1	1	0	1	0	0

(a) Logic diagram

(b) Partial truth table

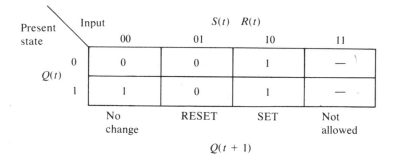

Present state \ Input	$S(t)$ $R(t)$			
$Q(t)$	00	01	10	11
0	0	0	1	—
1	1	0	1	—
	No change	RESET	SET	Not allowed

$Q(t+1)$

(c) State table

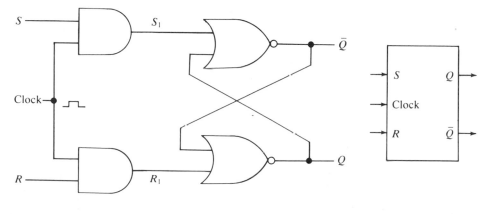

(d) Clocked SR flip-flop

(e) Graphic symbol

as long as the clock stays at 0, the outputs of the two AND gates (S_1 and R_1) are 0, so the Q and $\bar{Q}$ outputs do not change. The S and R values are impressed on the cross-coupled gates only during the clock pulse. Hence, the clock controls all state transitions. Figure 2.3(e) shows the graphic symbol of the clocked SR flip-flop. Figure 2.4 shows an SR flip-flop with both clocked (SET-RESET) and asynchronous (PRESET-CLEAR) inputs. A clock is not needed to activate the asynchronous inputs.

A flip-flop circuit requires a certain amount of time after the change in input conditions to attain the new state. The pulse width of the clock must be large enough to allow this transition. Input values should not change during the transition; a change in input would drive the flip-flop to a new state, thus overriding the response from the first set of input conditions. If all input changes are to be recognized, the pulse width must be short enough and the clock frequency must be increased. The clock frequency and pulse width thus must be adjusted to accommodate the flip-flop circuit transition time and the rate of input change.

Figure 2.4 Clocked SR flip-flop with PRESET-CLEAR

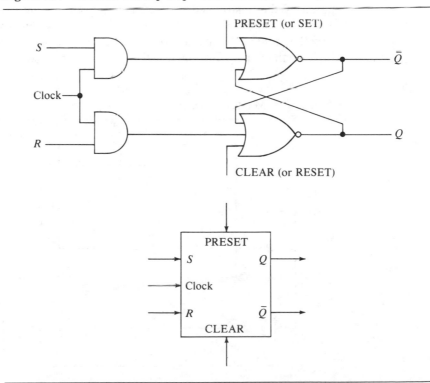

"Edge-triggered" flip-flops are normally used to avoid unnecessary state transitions due to changes in inputs. These flip-flops will have additional circuitry that recognizes the inputs at either the positive edge or the negative edge of the clock rather than during the complete clock pulse. Hence, changes in input values, after the triggering edge has passed, do not bring any state transition. In practice, these flip-flops require that the inputs be stable for a period of time known as *setup time* just before the triggering edge occurs.

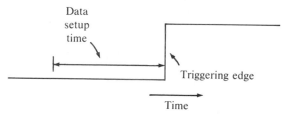

Another common method of inhibiting undesirable state changes due to changes in inputs is by using a "master-slave" flip-flop configuration as shown in Figure 2.5. Here, two flip-flops are used. The "master" is triggered by the positive edge of the clock and the state change is seen at Y and $\bar{Y}$ terminals. The "slave" is triggered by the negative edge transferring the state of the master to the slave. In this arrangement, the S and R inputs can change after the positive edge of the clock, since these changes

Figure 2.5 Master-slave flip-flop

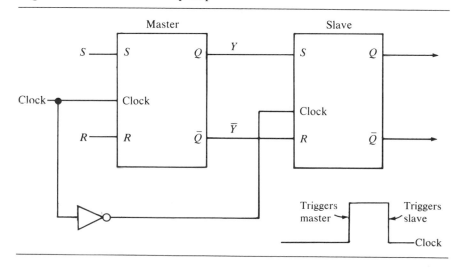

are not recognized until the next positive edge and hence the operation of the flip-flop is not affected. Such flip-flops are especially useful when the input to the flip-flop is a function of its own output.

We will now discuss the other three types of flip-flops that are commonly used. The preset-clear and master-slave configurations discussed above apply to each of these flip-flops also. In the remaining portions of this chapter, if a reference to a signal does not show a time associated with it, it is assumed to be the current time t.

2.1.2 D Flip-Flop

Figure 2.6 shows a D (delay) flip-flop and its state table. The D flip-flop assumes the state of the D input; if $D = 1$, $Q(t + 1) - 1$; if $D = 0$, $Q(t + 1) = 0$. Note that the function of this flip-flop is to introduce a unit delay (Δt) in the signal input at D, hence the name "delay" flip-flop.

2.1.3 JK Flip-Flop

A JK flip-flop is a modified SR flip-flop in that the $J = 1$ and $K = 1$ input combination is allowed to occur. When this input combination occurs, the flip-flop complements its state. J input corresponds to SET and K corresponds to RESET of an SR flip-flop. Figure 2.7 shows a JK flip-flop and its state table.

2.1.4 T Flip-Flop

Figure 2.8 shows a T (trigger) flip-flop. A T flip-flop complements itself when $T = 1$ and remains in the same state as it was when $T = 0$.

Figure 2.6 D flip-flop

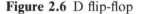

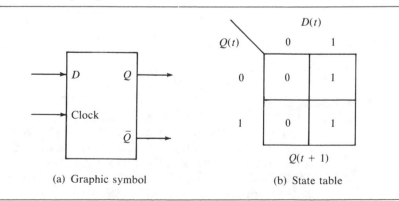

(a) Graphic symbol   (b) State table

Figure 2.7 JK flip-flop

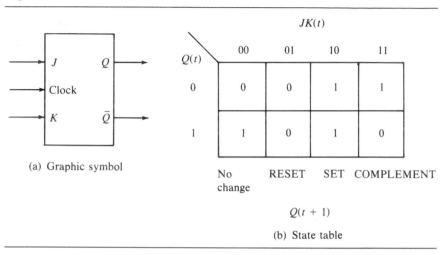

(a) Graphic symbol

(b) State table

Figure 2.8 T flip-flop

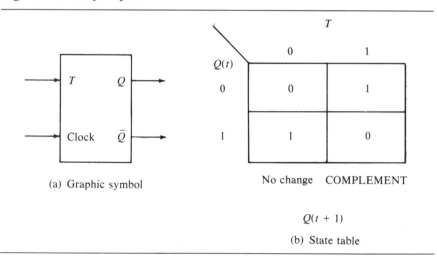

(a) Graphic symbol

(b) State table

Figure 2.9 summarizes the characteristics of the four types of flip-flops. Here, the state table for each flip-flop is rearranged to show that $Q(t + 1)$ is a function of $Q(t)$ and flip-flop inputs. These *characteristic* tables are useful in the analysis of sequential circuits since they provide the next-state information as a function of present state and inputs.

Figure 2.9 Characteristic tables for flip-flops

$Q(t)$	SR	$Q(t + 1)$	$Q(t)$	D	$Q(t + 1)$	$Q(t)$	JK	$Q(t + 1)$
0	00	0	0	0	0	0	00	0
0	01	0	0	1	1	0	01	0
0	10	1	1	0	0	0	10	1
0	11	—	1	1	1	0	11	1
1	00	1				1	00	1
1	01	0		(b) D flip-flop		1	01	0
1	10	1				1	10	1
1	11	—				1	11	0

(a) SR flip-flop

$Q(t)$	T	$Q(t + 1)$
0	0	0
0	1	1
1	0	1
1	1	0

(d) T flip-flop

(c) JK flip-flop

The *excitation table* (input table) for each flip-flop shown in Figure 2.10 is useful in the design of sequential circuits since it provides the excitation information for the flip-flop to bring in a state change from $Q(t)$ to $Q(t + 1)$. Some inputs are not defined in these tables. For example, an SR flip-flop makes a transition from 0 to 0 as long as $S = 0$ and R is 0 or 1. This excitation requirement is shown in Figure 2.10 as "$0d$." Similarly, for the SR flip-flop to make a transition from 1 to 1, the excitation required is "$d0$" ($SR = 10$ or 00). These "don't care" input conditions can be utilized in reducing the input circuitry of the flip-flop.

Figure 2.10 Excitation tables for flip-flops

$Q(t)$	$Q(t + 1)$	SR	D	JK	T
0	0	$0d$	0	$0d$	0
0	1	10	1	$1d$	1
1	0	01	0	$d1$	1
1	1	$d0$	1	$d0$	0

d = "don't care" (0 or 1)

2.2 Analysis of Sequential Circuits ˙

The analysis of a sequential circuit is the process of determining the functional relation that exists between its outputs, its inputs, and its internal states. The combined outputs of all the flip-flops in the circuit determine the state of the circuit. If there are n flip-flops, the circuit can be in one of 2^n states. Knowing the present state of the circuit and the input to it at any time t, we should be able to derive its next state (state at $t + 1$) and its output at t. A sequential circuit can be fully described by a state table similar to the ones shown for flip-flops in Figures 2.6 through 2.8. For a sequential circuit with n flip-flops, there will be 2^n rows in the state table. If there are m input lines, there will be 2^m columns. At the intersection of a row and a column, the next-state and output information is represented. A *state diagram* is a graphic representation of a state table. The analysis of a sequential circuit is, then, the process of generating the state table and/or state diagram starting from a circuit diagram. This procedure is detailed in the example that follows.

Example 2.1 A sequential circuit is shown in Figure 2.11(a). There are two clocked flip-flops, one input line X, and one output line Z. The Q outputs of the flip-flops (Y_1, Y_2) constitute the present state of the circuit at any time t. The signal values of J and K determine the next state $Y_1(t + 1)$ of the JK flip-flop. The value of D determines the next state $Y_2(t + 1)$ of the D flip-flop. Both flip-flops make the state transition at the same time because they are connected to the same clock.

In practice, only one type of flip-flop is actually used in a given circuit. We have used several different types of flip-flops in examples of sequential circuits in this chapter for the purposes of illustration.
By analyzing the combinational portion of the circuit it is seen that

$$J = XY_2 \text{ and } K = X + \bar{Y}_2$$

and
$$(2\text{--}1)$$

$$D = \bar{Y}_1 Y_2 + \bar{X}\bar{Y}_2.$$

These equations are called flip-flop *input equations* (excitation equations). They express each input of flip-flops in the circuit as a function of the present state of the circuit and circuit inputs at time t. Similarly, an analysis of the circuit yields the following equation for the circuit output Z:

$$Z = XY_1Y_2. \qquad (2\text{--}2)$$

This is called the circuit *output equation*.

Figure 2.11 Sequential circuit with two flip-flops

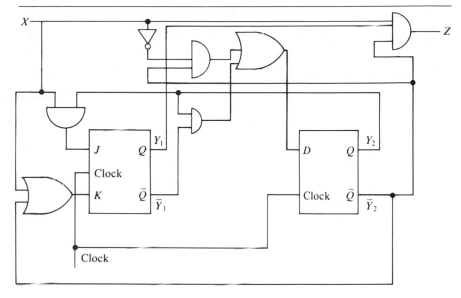

(a) Circuit diagrams

$$J = XY_2 \qquad\qquad D = \bar{Y}_1 Y_2 + \bar{X} Y_2$$
$$K = X + \bar{Y}_2 \qquad\quad Z = XY_1 \bar{Y}_2$$

(b) Excitation and output equations

$Y_1 Y_2$	X 0	1
0 0	0	0
0 1	0	1
1 0	0	0
1 1	0	1
	J	

$Y_1 Y_2$	X 0	1
0 0	1	1
0 1	0	1
1 0	1	1
1 1	0	1
	K	

$Y_1 Y_2$	X 0	1
0 0	01	01
0 1	00	11
1 0	01	01
1 1	00	11
	↑ JK	

State of
flip-flop 1

$Y_1 Y_2$	X 0	1
0 0	0	0
0 1	0	1
1 0	0	0
1 1	1	0
	$Y_1(t + 1)$	

(c) JK flip-flop transitions

$Y_1 Y_2$	X 0	1
0 0	1	0
0 1	1	1
1 0	1	0
1 1	0	0
	↑ D	

State of
flip-flop 2

$Y_1 Y_2$	X 0	1
0 0	1	0
0 1	1	1
1 0	1	0
1 1	0	0
	$Y_2(t + 1)$	

(d) D flip-flop transitions

(continued)

Figure 2.11 (Continued)

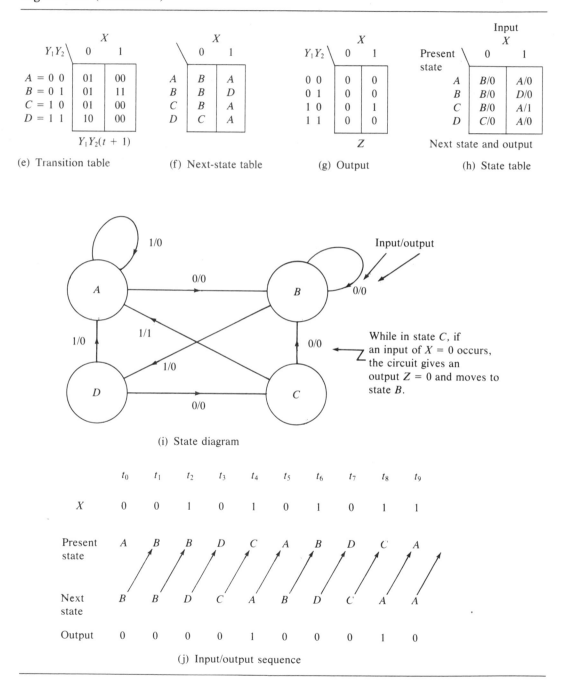

Y_1Y_2 \ X	0	1
A = 0 0	01	00
B = 0 1	01	11
C = 1 0	01	00
D = 1 1	10	00

$Y_1Y_2(t+1)$

(e) Transition table

X	0	1
A	B	A
B	B	D
C	B	A
D	C	A

(f) Next-state table

Y_1Y_2 \ X	0	1
0 0	0	0
0 1	0	0
1 0	0	1
1 1	0	0

Z

(g) Output

Present state \ Input X	0	1
A	B/0	A/0
B	B/0	D/0
C	B/0	A/1
D	C/0	A/0

Next state and output

(h) State table

(i) State diagram

While in state C, if an input of $X = 0$ occurs, the circuit gives an output $Z = 0$ and moves to state B.

	t_0	t_1	t_2	t_3	t_4	t_5	t_6	t_7	t_8	t_9
X	0	0	1	0	1	0	1	0	1	1
Present state	A	B	B	D	C	A	B	D	C	A
Next state	B	B	D	C	A	B	D	C	A	A
Output	0	0	0	0	1	0	0	0	1	0

(j) Input/output sequence

Since there are two flip-flops, there will be $2^2 = 4$ states for the circuit. Since X can be either 0 or 1, there will be two columns in the state table. Further, the rows are identified with present-state vectors $Y_1Y_2 = 00, 01,$ 10, and 11 and columns are identified as $X = 0$ and $X = 1$.

In general, the inputs to flip-flops and the circuit output are functions of the circuit inputs and the present state of the circuit. For example, since Y_1 is missing in the equation for J in equation (2–1), it can be expressed as

$$J = XY_2(Y_1 + \bar{Y}_1)$$
$$= XY_1Y_2 + X\bar{Y}_1Y_2. \tag{2–3}$$

From equation (2–3) a truth table for J can be drawn. Similarly, the equation for K can be expanded to include all the variables (X_1, Y_1, and Y_2) and a truth table can be drawn. Figure 2.11(c) shows the values of J and K derived from the excitation equations (2–1) in a tabular form. These tables are simply the truth tables for J and K, rearranged to show the present-state information along the rows and input information along the column. The third table in (c) merges the tables for J and K column by column for ease of observing J and K values together. Knowing J and K values and the present state of the JK flip-flop Y_1, the next state $Y_1(t + 1)$ can be derived by referring to the characteristic table (see Figure 2.9) of the JK flip-flop.

In Figure 2.11(c), consider the J and K values shown boxed in the first row of the JK table. Here, J is 0 and K is 1. Hence, the JK flip-flop will reset, resulting in $Y_1(t + 1) = 0$, as shown in the top left corner entry of the $Y_1(t + 1)$ table. Similarly, in the boxed entry in the second row of the JK table, J is 1 and K is 1 and hence the JK flip-flop changes its state. Since Y_1 is 0 corresponding to this entry, $Y_1(t + 1)$ will be 1. This process is repeated six times, resulting in the complete $Y_1(t + 1)$ table.

Figure 2.11(d) shows a similar analysis of D flip-flop transitions resulting in a $Y_2(t + 1)$ table. These tables are the *next-state tables* for individual flip-flops. We merge the individual next-state tables column by column to form the combined *transition table* for the circuit as shown in Figure 2.11(e). This table lists the next-state transitions of the complete circuit. Instead of denoting the states by state vectors 00, 01, 10, and 11, a letter designation can be given for each vector as shown, resulting in the next-state table, Figure 2.11(f).

From equation (2–2) a truth table for Z can be drawn. A rearranged truth table for the circuit output Z is shown in Figure 2.11(g). It is merged with the next-state table in (f) to derive the state table for the circuit shown in (h). The state table fully represents the behavior of the sequential circuit.

The state diagram is shown in Figure 2.11(i). In the state diagram, each circle corresponds to a state; arcs between the states represent the transitions between the states in the direction of the arrow. The input/output values during the transition are shown on the arcs.

An input sequence to the circuit and the corresponding output sequence are shown in Figure 2.11(j). The circuit is assumed to be in the *starting state* A at time t_0. With input $X = 0$ at t_0, the circuit moves to B with an output of 0 as shown by the state table. B is thus the state at t_1. The rest of the output sequence is similarly derived by referring to either the state table or the state diagram. Note that the output sequence indicates that the output is 1 only when the circuit input is the sequence 0101. Thus, this is a 0101 sequence detector.

This heuristic analysis can be formalized into the following step-by-step procedure for the analysis of synchronous sequential circuits:

1. Analyze the combinational part of the circuit to derive excitation equations for each flip-flop and the circuit output equations.
2. Note the number of flip-flops (p) and determine the number of states (2^p). Express each flip-flop input equation as a function of circuit inputs and the present state and derive the transition table for each flip-flop using the characteristic table for the flip-flop.
3. Derive the next-state table for each flip-flop and merge them into one, thus forming the transition table for the entire circuit.
4. Assign names to state vectors in the transition table to derive the next-state table.
5. Draw a truth table for each output of the circuit from output equations and rearrange these tables in state table form. If there are more outputs than one, then merge the output tables column by column to form the circuit output table.
6. Merge the next-state and output tables into one to form the state table for the entire circuit.
7. Draw the state diagram.

The state table and state diagram for a sequential circuit permit a functional analysis whereby the behavior of the circuit can be determined if the starting or initial state of the circuit and the input sequence is known. A timing analysis can also be performed by drawing timing diagrams based on the information in the state table or state diagram.

2.3   Design of Sequential Circuits

The first step in the design of a sequential circuit is to derive a state diagram or a state table from the problem statement. This step is often the most difficult one because no definite rules to derive a state diagram can be established. The designs provided in this section illustrate the complete design process. It is not always necessary to follow the classical design procedure outlined here, because some problems lend themselves to easier design methods. The design of the shift register is one example. The classical design procedure for sequential circuits comprises the following steps:

1. Derive the state diagram (or state table) for the circuit from the problem statement.
2. Derive the number of flip-flops (p) needed for the design from the number of states in the state diagram, by the formula

$$2^{p-1} < n \le 2^p$$

   where n = number of states.
3. Decide on the types of flip-flops to be used. (This often simply depends on the type of flip-flops available for the particular design.)
4. Assign a unique p bit pattern (state vector) to each state.
5. Derive the state transition table and the output table.
6. Separate the state transition table into p tables, one for each flip-flop.
7. Derive an input table for each flip-flop input, using the excitation tables (see Figure 2.10).
8. Derive an input equation for each flip-flop input and the circuit output equations.
9. Draw the circuit diagram.

The design procedure is illustrated in the three examples that follow.

Example 2.2   *1011 sequence detector*. Design a sequential circuit that detects an input sequence of 1011. The sequences may overlap. A 1011 sequence detector gives an output of 1 when the input completes a sequence of 1011. With overlap allowed, the last 1 in the 1011 can be the first bit of the next 1011 sequence and hence a further input of 011 is enough to produce an output of 1. The input sequence 1011011, for example, consists of two overlapping sequences.

Figure 2.12(a) shows the state diagram. The sequence begins with a 1. Assuming a starting state A, the circuit stays in A as long as the input is 0, giving an output of 0 waiting for a 1 to occur. The first 1 input takes it to a new state B. As long as the inputs continue to be 1, it will stay in B waiting for a 0 to occur to continue the sequence and hence to move to a new state C. While in C, if a 0 is received, then the sequence of inputs is 100, and the current sequence can not lead to 1011. The circuit returns to state A. If a 1 is received while in C, however, then the circuit moves to a new state D,

Figure 2.12 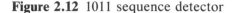 1011 sequence detector

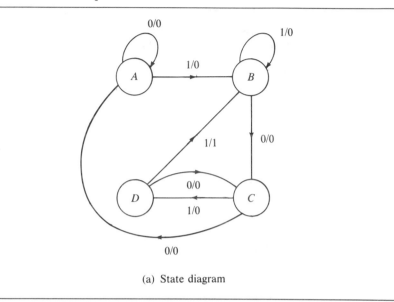

(a) State diagram

continuing the sequence. While in D, a 1 input completes the 1011 sequence. The circuit gives a 1 output and goes to B, in preparation for a 011 for a new sequence. If 0 input is received while at D (a possibility of the overlap), then the circuit returns to C so that it can detect the 11 subsequence required to complete the sequence.

Drawing a state diagram is solely a trial-and-error process. In general, we start with an initial state. At each state, we move either to a new state or to one of the already-reached states, depending on the input values. The state diagram is complete when all the input combinations are tested and accounted for at each state. Note that the number of states in the diagram can not be determined beforehand and a choice of several diagrams is normally possible for a given problem statement. The amount of hardware needed to synthesize the circuit increases with the number of states. Hence, it is desirable to reduce the number of states, if possible. The reader is referred to the books listed at the end of this chapter for procedures to reduce to a minimum the number of states in a state diagram.

The state table for the example is shown in Figure 2.12(b). Since there are four states, we need two flip-flops. The four 2-bit patterns are arbitrarily assigned to the states and the transition table (c) and output table (d) are drawn. From the output table it is seen that

$$Z = XY_1Y_2. \qquad\qquad (2-4)$$

Figure 2.12 (Continued)

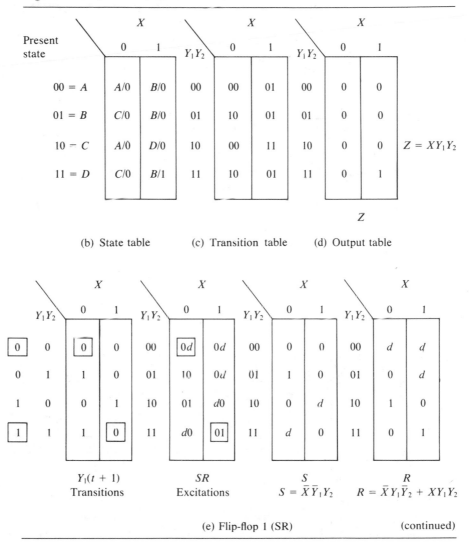

(b) State table (c) Transition table (d) Output table

(e) Flip-flop 1 (SR) (continued)

We will use an SR flip-flop and a T flip-flop. (Remember that it is common practice to use only one kind of flip-flop in a given circuit; different types are used here for illustration purposes only.) The transitions of flip-flop 1 (SR) extracted from Figure 2.12(c) are shown in the first table $Y_1(t + 1)$ of (e). From these transitions and using the excitation tables for the SR flip-flop (see Figure 2.10), the S and R excitations are derived.

Figure 2.12 (Continued)

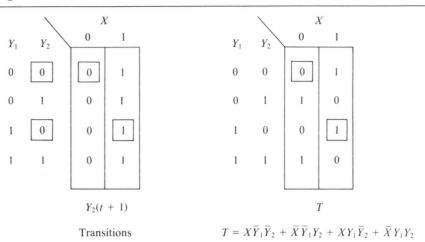

Transitions

$$T = X\bar{Y}_1\bar{Y}_2 + \bar{X}\bar{Y}_1Y_2 + XY_1\bar{Y}_2 + \bar{X}Y_1Y_2$$

(f) Flip-flop 2 (T)

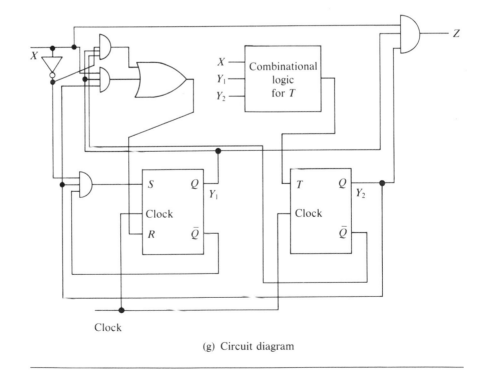

(g) Circuit diagram

(For example, the 0-to-0 transition of the flip-flop requires $S = 0$ and $R = $ d; and a 1-to-0 transition requires $S = 0$ and $R = 1$). The S and R excitations (which are functions of X, Y_1, and Y_2) are separated into individual tables and the excitation equations are derived. These equations are shown in Figure 2.12(e). The input equation for the second flip-flop (T) is similarly derived and is shown in Figure 2.12(f); the circuit diagram is shown in (g).

Note that no attempt was made in this design to reduce the circuitry. The number of states must be reduced, if possible. Appropriate assignment of state vectors to states also results in minimization of the circuitry. (State-assignment procedures to perform such logic minimization are not included in this book but can be found in reference works such as Kohavi, Nagle, and Dietmeyer cited at the end of this chapter.) The equations for S, R, T, and Z can usually be minimized by the methods detailed in Appendix B.

Example 2.3 *Modulo-4 up/down counter.* The modulo-4 counter will have four states: 0, 1, 2, and 3. It will count either up or down depending on the value of a control signal. This control signal is the input to the circuit. The state of the circuit (i.e., the count) itself is the output. The state diagram is shown here:

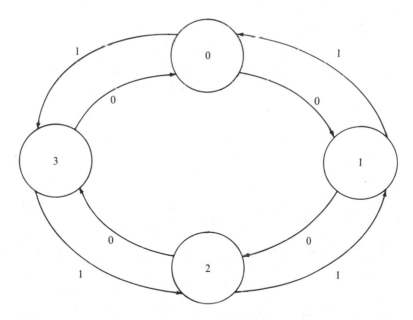

Derivation of a state diagram for this counter is straightforward, since the number of states and the transitions are completely defined by the problem statement. Note that only input values are shown on the arcs — the output of the circuit is the state of the circuit itself. We will need two flip-flops and the assignment of 2-bit vectors for states is also defined to be 00, 01, 10, and 11 to correspond to 0, 1, 2, and 3, respectively. The state table and transition table are shown below: the control signal is X; $X = 0$ indicates "count up"; $X = 1$ indicates "count down."

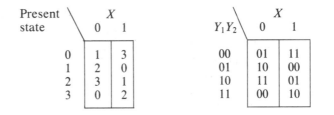

Present state	X 0	1
0	1	3
1	2	0
2	3	1
3	0	2

Y_1Y_2	X 0	1
00	01	11
01	10	00
10	11	01
11	00	10

We will use a JK flip-flop and a D flip-flop. The input equations are derived below:

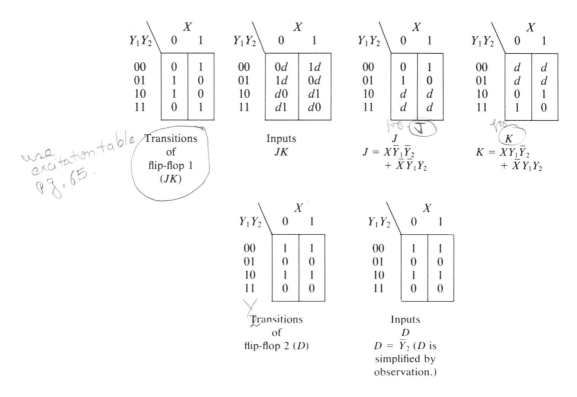

Y_1Y_2	X 0	1
00	0	1
01	1	0
10	1	0
11	0	1

Transitions of flip-flop 1 (JK)

Y_1Y_2	X 0	1
00	0d	1d
01	1d	0d
10	d0	d1
11	d1	d0

Inputs JK

Y_1Y_2	X 0	1
00	0	1
01	1	0
10	d	d
11	d	d

J
$J = X\bar{Y}_1\bar{Y}_2 + \bar{X}\,\bar{Y}_1Y_2$

Y_1Y_2	X 0	1
00	d	d
01	d	d
10	0	1
11	1	0

K
$K = XY_1\bar{Y}_2 + \bar{X}Y_1Y_2$

use excitation table pg. 65.

Y_1Y_2	X 0	1
00	1	1
01	0	0
10	1	1
11	0	0

Transitions of flip-flop 2 (D)

Y_1Y_2	X 0	1
00	1	1
01	0	0
10	1	1
11	0	0

Inputs D
$D = \bar{Y}_2$ (D is simplified by observation.)

Figure 2.13 shows the circuit.

Figure 2.13 Circuit for modulo-4 counter

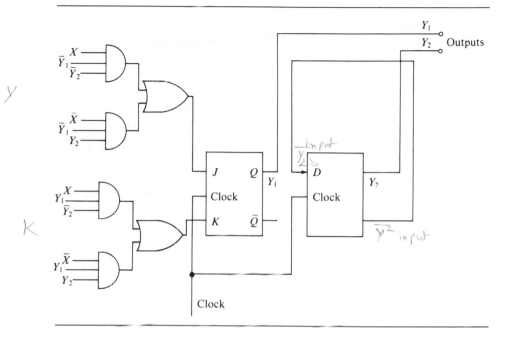

Example 2.4 *Three-stage counter.* Figure 2.14(a) shows the circuit diagram for a three-stage counter. Recall that the T flip-flop complements its state when the T input is 1. If input X is held at 1, the flip-flop on the least significant end (flip-flop 3) complements at each clock pulse; flip-flop 2 complements only when Q_3 is 1 and flip-flop 1 complements only when Q_2 is 1. If all three flip-flops are initially reset, the counter will be in $Q_1 Q_2 Q_3 = 000$ state. The first clock pulse will take it to 001 state; the next pulse will take it to 010 and on to 111 during the next pulse. The counter returns to 000 state during the fourth pulse. One other four-state sequence is possible, if the counter starts in state 100 as shown in Figure 2.14(b). Thus, this is also a modulo-4 counter.

2.4　Registers

A register is a storage device capable of holding binary data; it is a collection of flip-flops. An n-bit register is built of n flip-flops. Figure 2.15 shows a 4-bit register built out of four D flip-flops. There are four input lines, IN_1, IN_2, IN_3, and IN_4, each connected to the D input of the correspond-

Figure 2.14 A three-stage counter

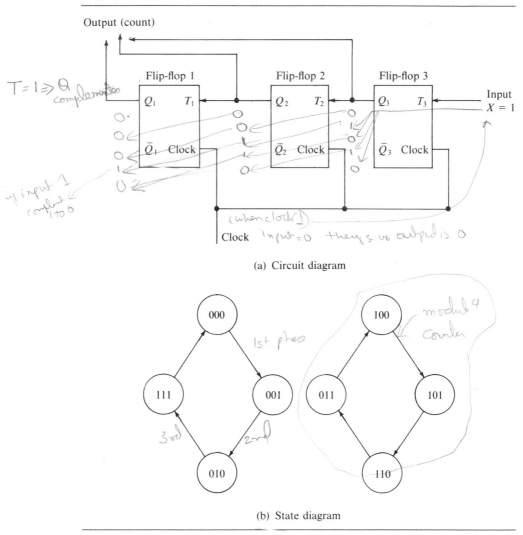

(a) Circuit diagram

(b) State diagram

ing flip-flop. When a clock pulse occurs, the data from input lines IN_1 through IN_4 enter the register. The clock thus *loads* the register. The loading is in *parallel*, since all 4 bits enter the register simultaneously. Q outputs of flip-flops are connected to output lines OUT_1 through OUT_4 and hence all 4 bits of data (i.e., contents of the register) are available simultaneously (i.e., in parallel) on the output lines. Hence, this is a parallel-input (parallel-load), parallel-output register.

Figure 2.15 A 4-bit register

loading in ||

parallel input.

Parallel output.

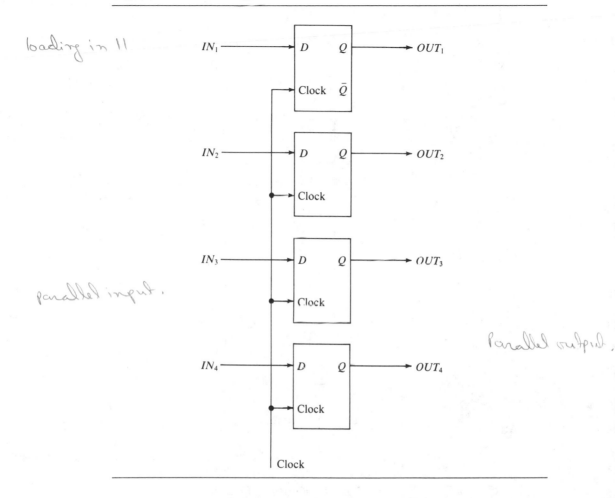

At each clock pulse, a 4-bit data input enters the register from input lines IN_1 through IN_4 and remains in the register until the next clock pulse. The clock controls the loading of the register as shown in Figure 2.16. LOAD must be 1 for data to enter the register. The CLEAR signal shown in Figure 2.16 loads zeros into the register (i.e., *clears* the register). Clearing a register is a common operation and is normally done through the asynchronous clear input (RESET) provided on flip-flops. Thus, when asynchronous inputs are used, a clearing operation can be done independent of the clock. The CLEAR signal shown in Figure 2.17 clears the register asynchronously. In this scheme, the CLEAR input

Figure 2.16 A 4-bit register with CLEAR and LOAD

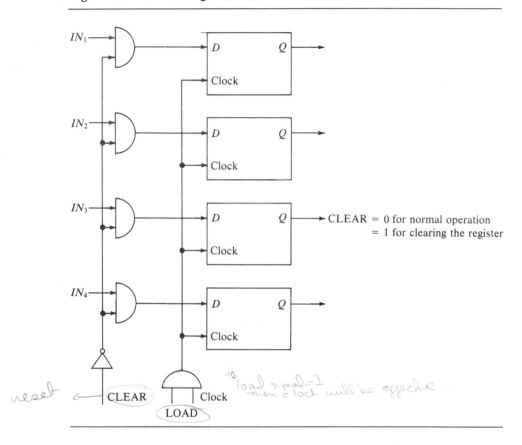

CLEAR = 0 for normal operation
= 1 for clearing the register

handwritten annotations:
D = 0
Q = 0
copy

reset

"load normal = 1
then clock will be effective

must be set to 1 for clearing the register and should be brought to 0 to deactivate RESET and allow resumption of normal operation. Figure 2.18 shows a 4-bit register built out of JK flip-flops.

A common operation on the data in a register is to *shift* it either right or left. A left shift of the register multiplies the register contents by 2 and a right shift divides them by 2. Figure 2.19 shows the diagram of a 4-bit *shift register* built out of four D flip-flops. The Q output of each flip-flop is connected to the D input of the flip-flop to its right. At each clock pulse, content of d_1 moves to d_2, content of d_2 moves to d_3, and that of d_3 moves into d_4, simultaneously. The *output* is the content of d_4 at any time. If *input* is set to 1, a 1 is entered into the d_1 bit of the register at each shift pulse. Similarly, a 0 can be loaded by setting *input* to 0. Any 4-bit pattern can be loaded into the register by setting the *input* to the corresponding bit value at each shift pulse. The bits are input from least significant (right-most) to the most significant (left-most). An n-bit shift register can be

Figure 2.17 A 4-bit register with asynchronous CLEAR

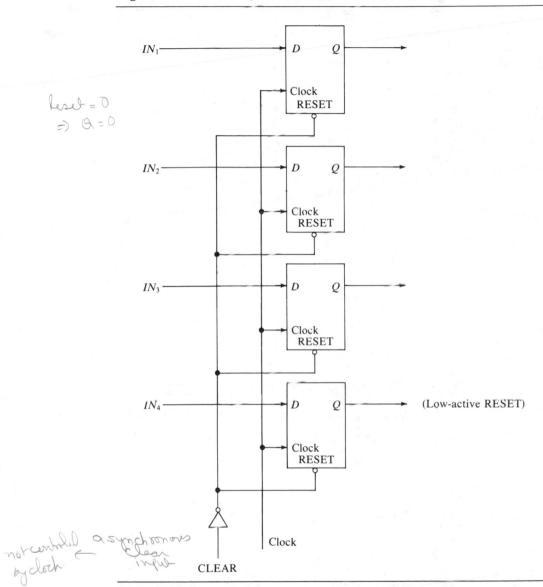

*Reset = 0
⇒ Q = 0*

(Low-active RESET)

*not controlled
by clock* ← *asynchronous
Clear
input*

CLEAR

Clock

loaded serially in n clock pulses and the contents of the register can be monitored (or output) using the *output* line in n clock pulses. After n shifts, the contents of the register will be either all 0s or all 1s depending on whether the *input* is set at 0 or 1, respectively. If the *output* is connected to the *input*, the contents of the register "circulate" since the bit output by d_4 enters the register at the *input*.

Figure 2.18 A 4-bit register using JK flip-flops

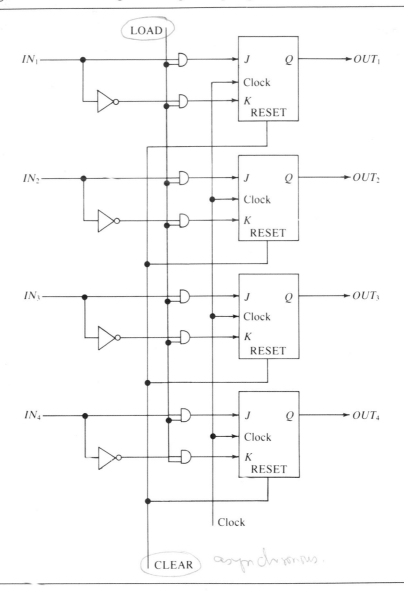

Figure 2.20 shows a shift register with serial-input, serial-output, parallel-output, circulate (left or right), and shift (left or right) capabilities. Each *D* input can receive data from the flip-flop to the right or left of it, depending on whether the DIRECTION signal is 0 or 1, respectively. Since *right* and *left* signals are complements, the register can shift only in

Figure 2.19 A 4-bit shift register

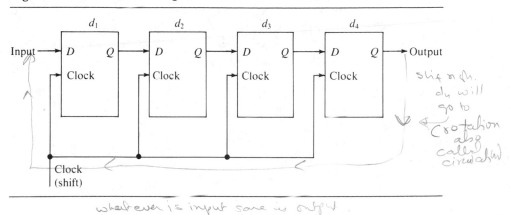

Figure 2.20 A 4-bit universal shift register

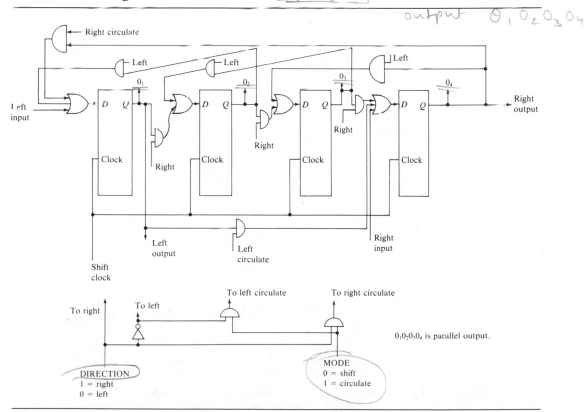

one direction at any time. The register performs shift or circulate based on the value of the MODE signal. When in shift mode, the data on left input enter the register if DIRECTION is 1 and the data on right input enter the register if DIRECTION is 0. The content of the register can be output in parallel through $0_1 0_2 0_3 0_4$ or in a serial mode through 0_4.

A 3-bit shift register using SR flip-flops with right-shift and parallel or serial input capabilities is shown in Figure 2.21. The following examples illustrate the utility of shift registers in sequential circuit design.

Figure 2.21 A 3-bit shift register

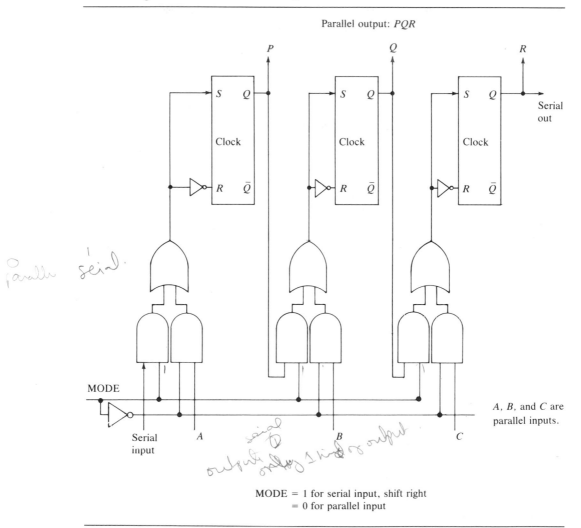

MODE = 1 for serial input, shift right
      = 0 for parallel input

Example 2.5 *Serial adder*. The adder circuit designed in Section 1.7 uses $(n - 1)$ full adders and one half-adder to generate the SUM of two n-bit numbers. The addition is done in parallel, although the CARRY has to propagate from the least significant bit (LSB) position to the most significant bit (MSB) position. This CARRY propagation delay determines the speed of the adder. If a slower speed of addition can be tolerated by the system, a *serial adder* can be utilized. The serial adder uses one full adder and two shift registers. The bits to be added are brought to full adder inputs and the SUM output of the full adder is shifted into one of the operand registers while the CARRY output is stored in a flip-flop and is used in the addition of next most significant bits. The n-bit addition is thus performed in n cycles (i.e., n clock pulse times) through the full adder.

Figure 2.22 shows the serial adder for 6-bit operands stored in shift registers A and B. The addition follows the stage-by-stage addition process (as done on paper) from LSB to MSB. The CARRY flip-flop is reset at the beginning of addition since the carry into the LSB position is 0. The full adder adds the LSBs of A and B with C_{in} and generates SUM and C_{out}. During the first shift pulse, C_{out} enters the CARRY flip-flop, SUM enters the MSB of A, and A and B registers are shifted right, simultaneously. Now the circuit is ready for the addition of the next stage. Six pulses are needed to complete the addition at the end of which the least significant n

Figure 2.22 Serial adder

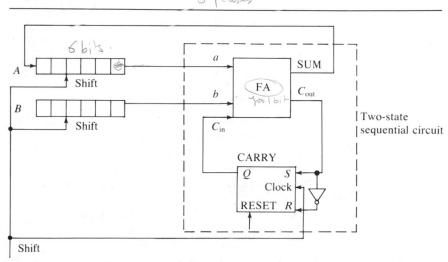

bits of the SUM of A and B will be in A and the $(n + 1)$th bit will be in the CARRY flip-flop. Operands A and B are lost at the end of the addition process.

If the LSB output of B is connected to its MSB input, then B will become a circulating shift register. The contents of B are unaltered due to addition, since the bit pattern in B after the sixth shift pulse will be the same as that before addition began. If the value of A is also required to be preserved, A should be converted into a circulating shift register and the SUM output of the full adder must be fed into a third shift register.

The circuit enclosed by dotted lines in Figure 2.22 is a sequential circuit with one flip-flop and hence two states, two input lines (a and b) and one output line (SUM). C_{in} is the present-state vector and C_{out} is the next-state vector.

Example 2.6 *Serial 2s complementer.* A serial 2s complementer follows the COPY-COMPLEMENT algorithm for 2s complementing the contents of a register (see Appendix A). The algorithm examines the bits of the register starting from the LSB. The zero bits from the LSB until and including the first nonzero bit are retained as they are (that is, "copied") and the remaining bits until and including MSB are "complemented," to convert a number into its 2s complement. An example is given below.

```
1 0 1 1 0 1 0  ¦  1 0 0 0       An 11-bit number
↑_____   ¦  ←_____
               ¦
COMPLEMENT     ¦  COPY
               ¦
0 1 0 0 1 0 1  ¦  1 0 0 0       Its 2s complement
```

There are two distinct operations in this algorithm: COPY and COMPLEMENT. Further, the transition from a copying mode to complementing mode is brought about by the first nonzero bit. The serial complementer circuit must be a sequential circuit because the mode of operation at any time depends on whether the nonzero bit has occurred or not. There will be two states and hence one flip-flop in the circuit; one input line on which bits of the number to be complemented are entering starting with LSB; and one output line that is either the copy or the complement of the input. The circuit starts in the COPY state and changes to COMPLE-MENT state when the first nonzero bit enters through the input line. At the beginning of each 2s complement operation, the circuit must be set to the COPY state.

Figure 2.23 shows the design of this circuit. From the state diagram in (a), the state table in (b) is derived, followed by the output equation in (c) and the input equations for the SR flip-flop in (e). The circuit is shown in (f). The circuit is set to the COPY state by resetting the flip-flop before each complementation.

Figure 2.23 Serial 2s complementer

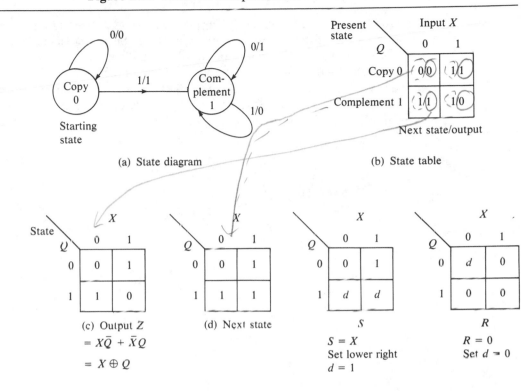

(a) State diagram

(b) State table

(c) Output Z
$= X\bar{Q} + \bar{X}Q$
$= X \oplus Q$

(d) Next state

S
$S = X$
Set lower right
$d = 1$

R
$R = 0$
Set $d = 0$

(e) Input equations

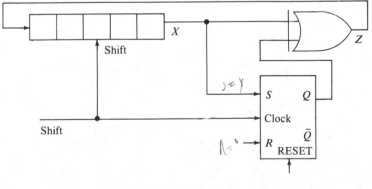

(f) Circuit diagram

2.5   Register Transfer Logic

Manipulation of data in most digital systems involves the movement of data between registers. This data movement can be accomplished either in *serial* or in *parallel*. Transfer of an *n*-bit data from one register to the other (each of *n* bits) takes *n* shift pulses if done in serial mode, while it is done in one pulse time in parallel mode. A data path that can transfer 1 bit between the registers is sufficient for serial mode operation. This path is repeatedly used for transferring all *n* bits one at a time. For a parallel

Figure 2.24 Register transfers

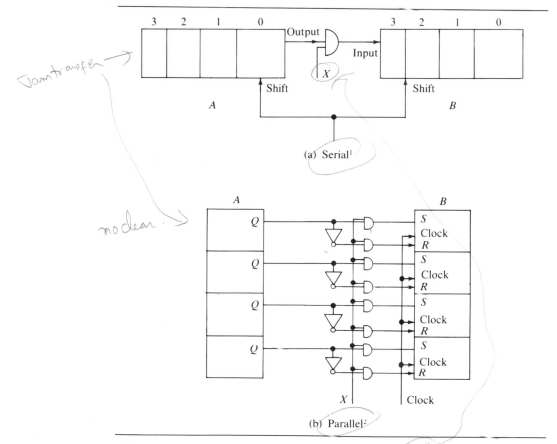

(a) Serial[1]

(b) Parallel[2]

[1] *A* and *B* are 4-bit shift registers; *X* for transfer control; and $X = 1$ for transfer contents of *A* into *B*.

[2] *A* and *B* are 4-bit registers. *X* must be 1 at clock pulse for transfer to occur.

transfer scheme, *n* such data paths are needed. Thus, a serial transfer scheme is less expensive in terms of hardware and slower than the parallel scheme. Figure 2.24 shows serial and parallel data transfer schemes.

The transfer circuit shown in Figure 2.24 is usually referred to as a *jam transfer* circuit. The other method of transfer shown in Figure 2.25 is the *clear-and-copy* transfer. This circuit shows a 1-bit transfer path from the source register to the destination register. Clear-and-copy transfer requires two clock pulses and is slower than the jam transfer, which requires one clock pulse time.

All data processing done in the processing unit of a computer is accomplished by one or more register transfer operations. It is often required that data in one register be transferred into several other registers or a register receive its inputs from one or more other registers. Figure 2.26 shows two schemes for transferring the contents of either register *A* or register *B* into register *C*. When the *control* signal "*A* to *C*" is on, contents of *A* are moved into *C*. When "*B* to *C*" signal is on, contents of *B* are moved into *C*. Only one control signal can be active at any time. This can be accomplished by using the true and complement of the same control signal to select one of the two transfer paths. Figure 2.26(b) shows the use of a 4-line 2-to-1 multiplexer to accomplish the register transfer required in (a). In this figure, the number shown next to "/" indicates the number of bits (lines). This is a common convention used to represent multiple bits of any signal in a circuit diagram.

Figure 2.25 CLEAR and COPY transfer scheme

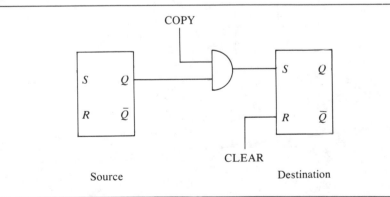

Note: The destination register is first cleared and the source is then copied. Two clock pulses are thus required for each transfer operation.

Figure 2.26 Transfer from multiple-source registers

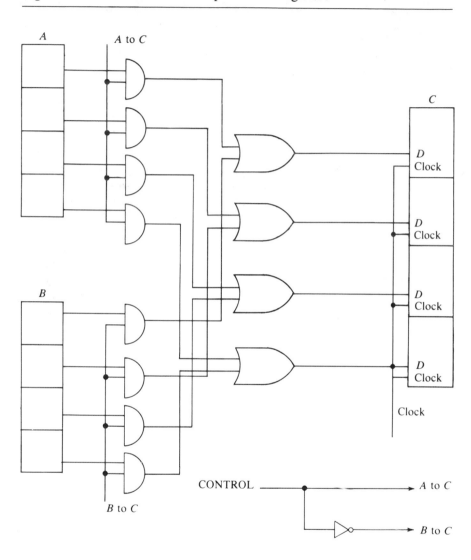

(a) Transfer by control signals

Figure 2.26 (Continued)

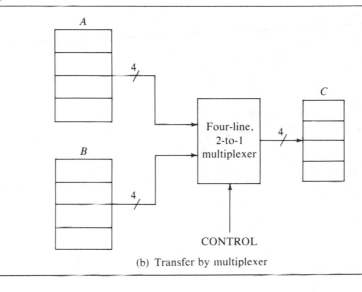

(b) Transfer by multiplexer

2.6 Register Transfer Schemes

When it is required to transfer data between several registers to complete a processing sequence in a digital computer, one of two transfer schemes is generally used: (1) point-to-point and (2) bus. In a point-to-point scheme there will be one transfer path between each of the two registers involved in the data transfer. In a bus scheme, one common path is time shared for all register transfers.

2.6.1 Point-to-Point Transfer

The hardware required for a *point-to-point* transfer between three 3-bit registers *A*, *B*, and *C* is shown in Figure 2.27. Only a few of the paths are shown. "*A* to *C*" and "*B* to *C*" are control signals used to bring the data transfer. This scheme allows more than one transfer to be made at the same time (in parallel) because independent data paths are available. For example, the control signals "*A* to *C*" and "*C* to *B*" can both be enabled at the same time. The disadvantage of the scheme is that the amount of hardware required for the transfer increases rapidly as additional registers are included and each new register is connected to other registers through newer data paths. This growth makes the scheme too expensive; hence, a point-to-point scheme is used only when fast, parallel operation is desired.

Figure 2.27 Point-to-point transfer

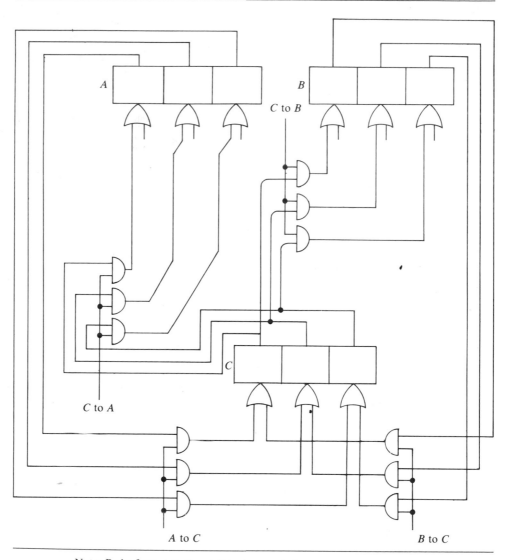

Note: Paths from *A* to *B* and *B* to *A* are not shown.

2.6.2 Bus Transfer

Figure 2.28(a) shows a *bus* scheme for the transfer of data between three 3-bit registers. A bus is a common data path (highway) that each register either feeds data into (i.e., contents of the register ON the bus) or takes data from (i.e., register OFF the bus). At any time, only one register can be putting data on the bus. This requires that bits in the same position in each register be ORed and connected to the corresponding bit (line) of the bus. Figure 2.28(b) shows typical timing for the transfer from A to C. Control signals "A to BUS" and "BUS to C" have to be 1 simultaneously for the transfer to take place. Several registers can receive data from the bus simultaneously, but only one register can put data on the bus at any time. Thus the bus transfer scheme is slower than the point-to-point scheme, but the hardware requirements are considerably less. Further, additional registers can be added to the bus structure just by adding two paths, one each from bus to register and register to bus. For these reasons, bus transfer is the most commonly used data transfer scheme.

In practice, a large number of registers are connected to a bus. This requires the use of OR gates with many inputs to form the bus interconnection. Two special types of outputs available on certain gates permit an easier realization of the OR function: gates with "open-collector" output or "tristate" output. Figure 2.29(a) shows 1 bit of a bus built using the *open-collector gates*. The outputs of these special gates can be tied together to provide the OR function. One other commonly used device, a *tristate gate*, is shown in Figure 2.29(b). When the gate is enabled (enable = 1), the output is a function of the input; if disabled (enable = 0), the output is nonexistent electrically. The scheme shown in Figure 2.29(c) realizes the OR function using tristate inverters. Note that now the bus signals are inverted. These signals are to be reinverted in paths from bus to each register (by using NAND gates in place of AND gates).

2.7 Register Transfer Languages

Since register transfer is the basic operation in a digital computer, several register transfer notations have evolved over the past decade. These notations, complete enough to describe any digital computer at the register transfer level, have come to be known as *register transfer languages*. Since they are used to describe the hardware structure and behavior of digital systems, they are more generally known as *hardware description languages* (HDL). One such language, Computer Design Language (CDL), is described in Appendix C. For our purposes, a relatively simple HDL is sufficient and will be used to describe register transfers throughout the book.

Figure 2.28 Bus transfer

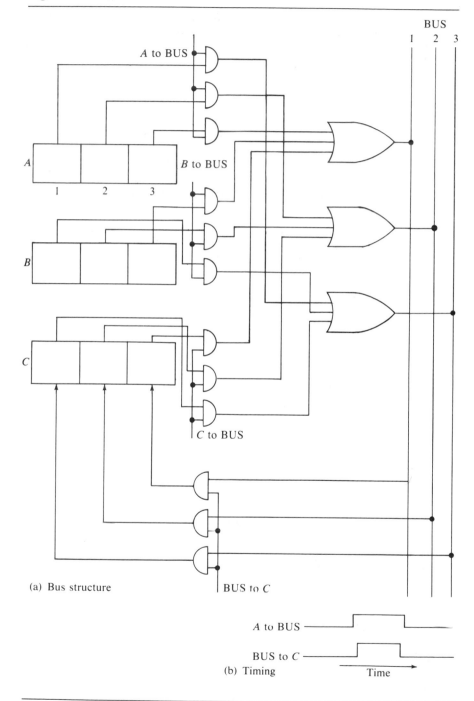

(a) Bus structure

(b) Timing

Note: BUS to A and BUS to B are not shown.

Figure 2.29 Special devices for BUS interface

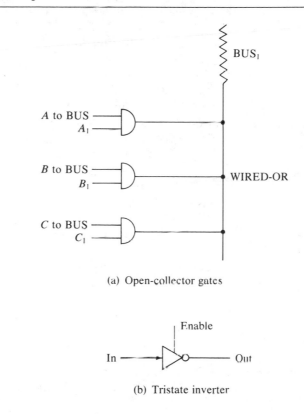

(a) Open-collector gates

(b) Tristate inverter

Enable = 1
output exists.
Enable = 0
output non-exist.

(c) OR using tristates

Table 2.1 and Table 2.2 show the basic operators and constructs of our HDL. The general format of a register transfer is

$$\text{Destination} \leftarrow \text{Source.}$$

where "Source" is a register or an expression consisting of registers and operators, and "Destination" is a register or a concatenation (linked series) of registers. The number of bits in source and destination must be equal. A period (".") terminates a register transfer statement.

A transfer controlled by a control signal has the format

$$\text{Control: transfer.}$$

Multiple transfers controlled by a control signal are indicated by

$$\text{Control: transfer}_1, \text{transfer}_2, \ldots, \text{transfer}_n.$$

The transfers are simultaneous.

The general format of a conditional register transfer is

$$\text{IF condition THEN transfer}_1$$

$$\text{ELSE transfer}_2.$$

where "condition" is a Boolean expression, "transfer$_1$" occurs if condition is TRUE (or 1), and "transfer$_2$" occurs if condition is FALSE (or 0).

Table 2.1 HDL operators

Operator	Description	Examples
Left arrow ←	Transfer operator	$Y \leftarrow X$. Contents of register X are transferred to register Y.
Plus +	Addition	$Z \leftarrow X + Y$.
Minus −	Subtraction	$Z \leftarrow X - Y$.
¢	Concatenation	$C \leftarrow A \, ¢ \, B$.
Overbar $^{-}$	Complement	$D \leftarrow \bar{A}$.
$\wedge$	Logical AND	$C \leftarrow A \wedge B$.
$\vee$	Logical OR	$C \leftarrow A \vee B$.
SHL	Shift left 1 bit; zero filled on right	$A \leftarrow SHL\,(A)$.
SHR	Shift right 1 bit; copy most significant bit on left	$A \leftarrow SHR\,(A)$.

Table 2.2 HDL constructs

Construct	Description	Examples	
Capital-letter strings	Denote registers	ACC, A, MBR	Single bit.
Subscripts	Denote a bit or a range of bits of a register	A_0, A_{15}	Bits are numbered left to right, bits 5 through 15.
		A_{5-15}	
		A_{5-0}	Bits are numbered right to left, bits 0 through 5.
Parentheses ( )	Denote a portion of a register (subregister)	IR (ADR)	ADR portion of the register IR; this is a symbolic notation to address a range of bits.
Colon:	Serves as control function delimiter	ADD:	Terminates the control signal definition.
Comma,	Separates register transfers; implies that transfers are simultaneous	$Y \leftarrow X$, $Q \leftarrow P$.	
Period.	Terminates register transfer statement	$Y \leftarrow X$.	

The ELSE clause is optional. Thus,

$$\text{IF condition THEN transfer.}$$

is valid.

A control signal can be associated with a conditional register transfer:

$$\text{Control:} \quad \text{IF condition THEN transfer}_1$$

$$\text{ELSE transfer}_2.$$

Example 2.7 illustrates the features of the HDL.

Example 2.7

$B \leftarrow A.$	A and B must have the same number of bits.
$C \leftarrow A + \bar{B} + 1.$	2s complement of B added to A, transferred to C.
$B \leftarrow A, A \leftarrow B.$	A and B exchange. (A and B must be formed using master-slave flip-flops, to accomplish this exchange.)

$T1: \quad B \leftarrow A.$

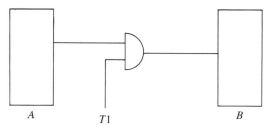

$A \leftarrow C \, \mathfrak{c} \, D.$ The total number of bits in C and D must be equal to that in A.

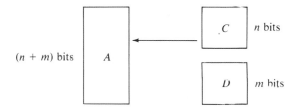

$C \, \mathfrak{c} \, D \leftarrow A.$	Reverse operation of the above.
$T1: \quad \text{IF } C \text{ THEN } B \leftarrow A$	Equivalent to $T1 \wedge C: B \leftarrow A$ and
$\text{ELSE } B \leftarrow D.$	$T1 \wedge \bar{C}: B \leftarrow D.$

Table 2.3 CDL equivalents to HDL statements (Example 2.7)

HDL	CDL
$B \leftarrow A.$	$B = A$
$C \leftarrow A + \bar{B} + 1.$	$A = A + B' + 1$
$B \leftarrow A, A \leftarrow B.$	$B = A, A = B$
$T1: \quad B \leftarrow A.$	$/T1/ \; B = A$
$A \leftarrow C \, \raisebox{0.2ex}{\textcent} \, D.$	$A = C - D$
$C \, \raisebox{0.2ex}{\textcent} \, D \leftarrow A.$	$C - D = A$
$T1: \quad$ IF C THEN $B \leftarrow A$	$/T1/$ IF (C) THEN $(B = A)$
ELSE $B \leftarrow D.$	ELSE $(B = D)$

The transfers in Figure 2.26 can be described by the statement

$$\text{IF control THEN } C \leftarrow A$$

$$\text{ELSE } C \leftarrow B.$$

Table 2.3 shows the CDL equivalents of HDL constructs in the above example. CDL is a popular HDL and several versions of software packages that can simulate a CDL description are available. Appendix C summarizes the capabilities of one such package.

2.8 Designing Sequential Circuits with ICs

Figure 2.30 shows some small- and medium-scale integrated circuits from the transistor-transistor logic (TTL) family. The reader is referred to IC manufacturer catalogs for further details on these ICs. A sequential circuit can be designed by following the classical design procedure described in this chapter. As a final step in the design, the circuit components (flip-flops, registers, etc.) are selected by referring to manufacturer catalogs.

It is often possible to design sequential circuits without following the classical design procedure. The serial adder design (see Example 2.5) is one example. Where the number of states in practical circuits becomes so large that the classical design procedure becomes impractical, the circuit functions are usually partitioned and each partition is separately designed. Ad hoc methods of design based on familiarity with available ICs may be used in designing a partition or the complete circuit. Example 2.8 on page 104 illustrates the design process using ICs.

Figure 2.30 Some SSI/MSI circuits (courtesy of Texas Instruments Incorporated)

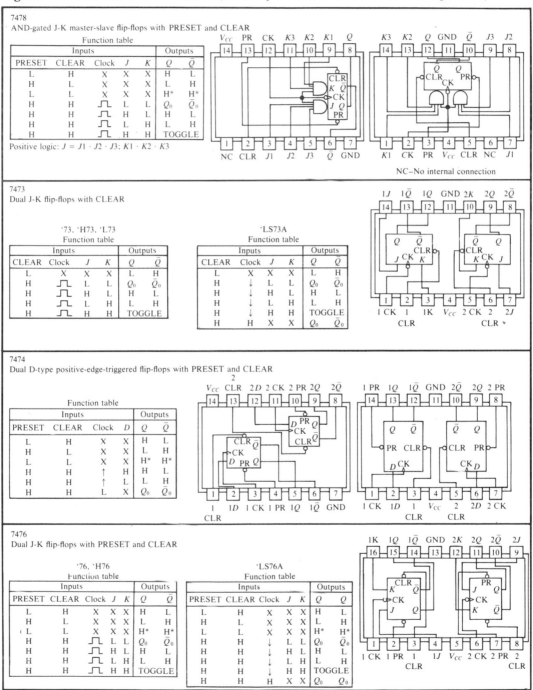

7478
AND-gated J-K master-slave flip-flops with PRESET and CLEAR

Function table

Inputs					Outputs	
PRESET	CLEAR	Clock	J	K	Q	$\bar{Q}$
L	H	X	X	X	H	L
H	L	X	X	X	L	H
L	L	X	X	X	H*	H*
H	H	⎍	L	L	Q_0	$\bar{Q}_0$
H	H	⎍	H	L	H	L
H	H	⎍	L	H	L	H
H	H	⎍	H	H	TOGGLE	

Positive logic: $J = J1 \cdot J2 \cdot J3$; $K1 \cdot K2 \cdot K3$

NC–No internal connection

7473
Dual J-K flip-flops with CLEAR

'73, 'H73, 'L73
Function table

Inputs				Outputs	
CLEAR	Clock	J	K	Q	$\bar{Q}$
L	X	X	X	L	H
H	⎍	L	L	Q_0	$\bar{Q}_0$
H	⎍	H	L	H	L
H	⎍	L	H	L	H
H	⎍	H	H	TOGGLE	

'LS73A
Function table

Inputs				Outputs	
CLEAR	Clock	J	K	Q	$\bar{Q}$
L	X	X	X	L	H
H	↓	L	L	Q_0	$\bar{Q}_0$
H	↓	H	L	H	L
H	↓	L	H	L	H
H	↓	H	H	TOGGLE	
H	H	X	X	Q_0	$\bar{Q}_0$

7474
Dual D-type positive-edge-triggered flip-flops with PRESET and CLEAR

Function table

Inputs				Outputs	
PRESET	CLEAR	Clock	D	Q	$\bar{Q}$
L	H	X	X	H	L
H	L	X	X	L	H
L	L	X	X	H*	H*
H	H	↑	H	H	L
H	H	↑	L	L	H
H	H	L	X	Q_0	$\bar{Q}_0$

7476
Dual J-K flip-flops with PRESET and CLEAR

'76, 'H76
Function table

Inputs					Outputs	
PRESET	CLEAR	Clock	J	K	Q	$\bar{Q}$
L	H	X	X	X	H	L
H	L	X	X	X	L	H
L	L	X	X	X	H*	H*
H	H	⎍	L	L	Q_0	$\bar{Q}_0$
H	H	⎍	H	L	H	L
H	H	⎍	L	H	L	H
H	H	⎍	H	H	TOGGLE	

'LS76A
Function table

Inputs					Outputs	
PRESET	CLEAR	Clock	J	K	Q	$\bar{Q}$
L	H	X	X	X	H	L
H	L	X	X	X	L	H
L	L	X	X	X	H*	H*
H	H	↓	L	L	Q_0	$\bar{Q}_0$
H	H	↓	H	L	H	L
H	H	↓	L	H	L	H
H	H	↓	H	H	TOGGLE	
H	H	H	X	X	Q_0	$\bar{Q}_0$

Figure 2.30 (Continued)

7490 Decade counter

'90A, 'L90, 'LS90
BCD COUNT sequence
(See Note A)

COUNT	Output			
	Q_D	Q_C	Q_B	Q_A
0	L	L	L	L
1	L	L	L	H
2	L	L	H	L
3	L	L	H	H
4	L	H	L	L
5	L	H	L	H
6	L	H	H	L
7	L	H	H	H
8	H	L	L	L
9	H	L	L	H

'90A, 'L90, 'LS90
RESET/COUNT function table

RESET inputs				Output			
$R_{0(1)}$	$R_{0(2)}$	$R_{9(1)}$	$R_{9(2)}$	Q_D	Q_C	Q_B	Q_A
H	H	L	X	L	L	L	L
H	H	X	L	L	L	L	L
X	X	H	H	H	L	L	H
X	L	X	L	COUNT			
L	X	L	X	COUNT			
L	X	X	L	COUNT			
X	L	L	X	COUNT			

Notes: A. Output Q_A is connected to input B for *BCD* count.
     B. Output Q_D is connected to input A for bi-quinary count.
     C. Output Q_A is connected to input B.
     D. H = high level, L = low level, X = irrelevant

Functional block diagram

'90A, 'L90, 'LS90

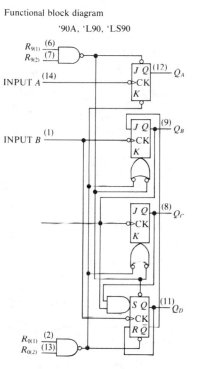

(continued)

Figure 2.30 (Continued)

SN7494
4-bit shift registers

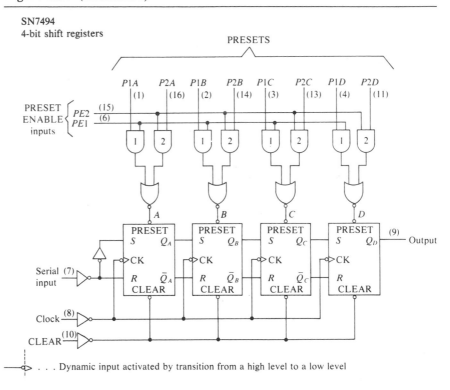

 . . . Dynamic input activated by transition from a high level to a low level

7495
4-bit parallel-access shift register

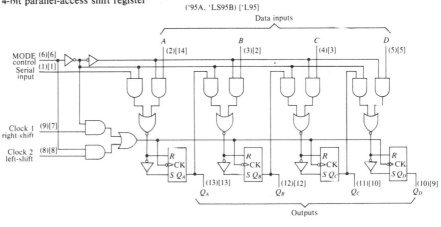

Figure 2.30 (Continued)

SN74160
Synchronous decade counters

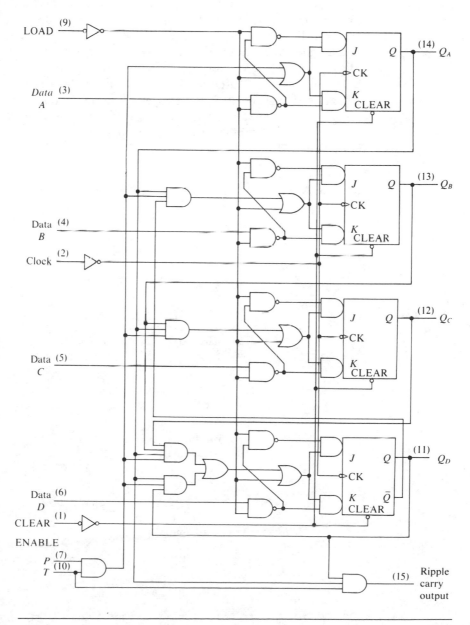

Example 2.8 *Parallel-to-serial data converter*. The object of our design is a parallel-to-serial data converter that accepts 4-bit data in parallel and produces as its output a serial-bit stream of the data input into it. The input consists of the sign bit (a_0) and three magnitude bits ($a_1a_2a_3$). The serial device expects to receive the sign bit a_0 first, followed by the three magnitude bits in the order $a_3a_2a_1$ as shown in Figure 2.31(a).

Note that the output bit pattern can be obtained by circulating the input data right three times and then shifting right one bit at a time. To perform this, a 4-bit shift register that can be loaded in parallel and can be right-shifted is required. TTL 7495 is one such circuit. From the 7495 circuit diagram, it can be deduced that the "mode" input must be 1 for the parallel load operation and has to be 0 for serial input and right shift modes. The D output must be connected to the "serial" input line, for circulating the data.

Figure 2.31 A parallel-to-serial data converter

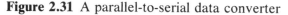

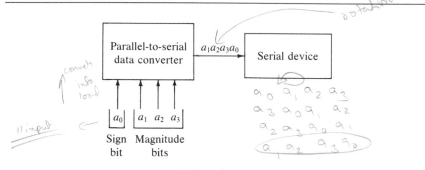

(a) Requirements

Count	Event	Action	Mode
0	Load the register (Parallel)	Parallel in	1
1	↑	Shift circular	0
2	Circulate	"	0
3	↓	"	0
4	↑	Shift right	0
5	Serial	"	0
6	Output	"	0
7	↓	"	0
8	Idle	Idle	d
9	Idle	Idle	d

(b) Operation details

Figure 2.31 (Continued)

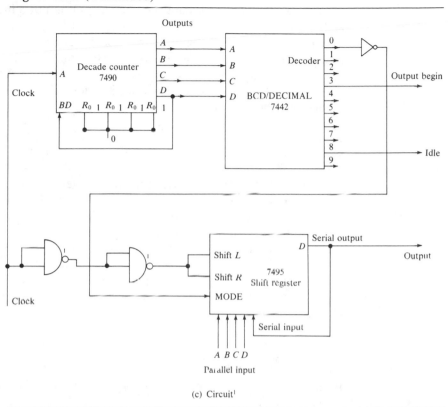

(c) Circuit[1]

[1] These gates compensate for delays introduced by the counter and decoder.

Figure 2.31(b) shows the details of the circuit operation. The complete operation needs eight steps, designated 0 through 7. Two more idle steps 8 and 9 are shown, since a decade counter (7490) is available that can count from 0 through 9. The circuit is shown in Figure 2.31(c). The 4-bit output of the decade counter 7490 is decoded using a BCD-to-decimal decoder (7443). Since the outputs of 7443 are low-active, output "0" will have a value of 0 during the 0 time step and a value of 1 during other times. Hence, it can be used as MODE control signal for 7495. "Shift-L" and "shift-R" of 7495 must be tied together so that the circuit receives "clock" in both modes. Two NAND gates are shown in the path from external clock input to shift inputs of 7495. These gates compensate for the delay introduced by 7490 and 7443 in generating the mode input signal for 7495. Since the same external clock is used for triggering both 7490 and 7495, this delay compensation is needed. Output 3 of 7442 is used to alert the serial device for data acceptance and output 8 indicates the idle state.

This example illustrates a simple design using ICs. In practice, the timing problems will be more severe. The triggering of flip-flops, data setup times, clock skews (i.e., arrival of clock on parallel lines at slightly different times due to differences in path delays), and other timing elements must be considered in detail.

2.9   Summary

The analysis and design of synchronous sequential circuits described in this chapter are given as an overview of the subject. The reader is referred to the logic design texts listed at the end of this chapter for further details on these topics and also on asynchronous circuit analysis and design. IC manufacturer catalogs are an important source of information for logic designers, although the detailed electrical characteristics given in these catalogs are not required for the purposes of this book. Register transfer logic concepts described in this chapter will be used extensively in Chapter 5 in the logical design of a simple computer.

References

Blakeslee, T. R. *Digital Design With Standard MSI and LSI*. New York, N.Y.: John Wiley, 1975.

Chu, Y. *Computer Organization and Microprogramming*. Englewood Cliffs, N.J.: Prentice-Hall, 1972.

Computer, Special issues on Hardware Description Languages, Vol. 7, No. 12 (December 1974); Vol. 10, No. 16 (June 1977).

Dietmeyer, D. *Logical Design of Digital Systems*. Boston, Mass.: Allyn and Bacon, 1971.

Foster, C. C. *Computer Architecture*. New York, N.Y.: Van Nostrand Reinhold, 1976.

Greenfield, J. D. *Practical Digital Design Using ICs*. 2d ed. New York, N.Y.: John Wiley, 1983.

Kline, R. M. *Digital Computer Design*. Englewood Cliffs, N.J.: Prentice-Hall, 1977.

Kohavi, Z. *Switching and Finite Automata Theory*. New York, N.Y.: McGraw-Hill, 1970.

Lewin, M. H. *Logic Design and Computer Organization*. Reading, Mass: Addison-Wesley, 1983.

Nagle, H. T., J. D. Irwin, and B. D. Carroll. *An Introduction to Computer Logic*. Englewood Cliffs, N.J.: Prentice-Hall, 1975.

TTL Data Book for Design Engineers. Dallas, Tex.: Texas Instruments, 1976.

Problems

2.1 You are given a JK flip-flop. Design the circuitry around it to convert it into a (a) T flip-flop, (b) D flip-flop, and (c) SR flip-flop. Hint: A flip-flop is a sequential circuit. Start the design with the state table of the required flip-flop. Use a JK flip-flop in the design.

2.2 A *set-dominate flip-flop* is similar to an SR flip-flop, except that an input of $S = R = 1$ will result in setting the flip-flop. Draw the state table and excitation table for the flip-flop.

2.3 There are two 4-bit registers A and B, built out of SR flip-flops. There is a control signal C. The following operations are needed:

If $C = 0$, send contents of A to B.

If $C = 1$, send 1s complement of contents of A into B.

Draw the circuit to perform these functions
   a. in parallel mode.
   b. in serial mode.

2.4 There are three 2-bit registers A, B, and C. Design the logic to perform:

$$\text{AND: } C \leftarrow A \wedge B.$$

$$\text{OR: } C \leftarrow A \vee B.$$

AND and OR are control signals. Each bit in the register is a D flip-flop.

2.5 A 2 bit counter C controls the register transfers shown below:

$C = 0: B \leftarrow A.$ $C = 2: B \leftarrow A + B.$
$C = 1: B \leftarrow \bar{A}.$ $C = 3: B \leftarrow 0.$

A and B are 2-bit registers. Draw the circuit. Use 4-to-1 multiplexers in your design. Show the details of register B.

2.6 Draw a bus structure to perform the operations in Problem 2.5.

2.7 Connect four 5-bit registers A, B, C, and D using a bus structure capable of performing the following:

$C0: B \leftarrow A.$ $C4: A \leftarrow C + D.$
$C1: C \leftarrow A \vee B.$ $C5: B \leftarrow \bar{C} \wedge \bar{D}.$
$C2: D \leftarrow A \wedge B.$ $C6: D \leftarrow A + C.$
$C3: A \leftarrow A + \bar{B}.$ $C7: B \leftarrow A + \bar{C}.$

$C0$ through $C7$ are control signals. Use a 3-bit counter and a decoder to generate those signals. Assume tristate outputs for each register.

2.8 Assume regular outputs for each register in Problem 2.7. How many OR gates are needed to implement the bus structure?

2.9 Design a 11011 detector. The sequences may overlap. Use JK flip-flops.

2.10 Design the circuit in Problem 2.3a for a 2s complement transfer.

2.11 Design the circuit for a soft drink machine. Each bottle costs thirty cents. The machine accepts nickels, dimes, and quarters. Assume a coin sorter that accepts coins and provides three signals, one each for the three types of coins. Assume that the signals on these three lines are separated far enough so that the other circuits can make a state transition between pulses received on any two of these lines. Correct change must be released. The sequential circuit must generate signals to release correct change (one signal for each type of coin) and the soft drink bottle. Use JK flip-flops in your design.

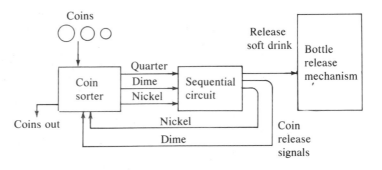

(The coin sorter produces a pulse on its appropriate output line for each coin it receives. It releases an appropriate coin when it receives a coin release signal.)

2.12 To add two positive numbers A and B, A can be incremented by 1, B times. Design the circuit to perform the addition of two 4-bit numbers A and B. A and B registers could each be an up/down counter. You have to stop incrementing A when B reaches 0. Assume B is positive.

2.13 Repeat Problem 2.8 for B, a negative number, represented in 2s complement system.

2.14 For the circuit shown here,

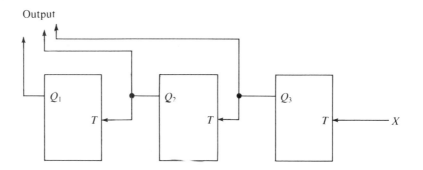

assume that the T flip-flops are triggered by the 1-to-0 edge (negative edge) transition on the T input. Note that the flip-flops are not clocked. Assume the transitions of X are as shown at the top of page 109 and complete the timing diagram for Q_1, Q_2, and Q_3. (Hint: This is a *ripple counter*.)

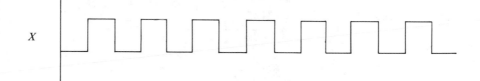

2.15   For the following circuit, derive the state table. Use the assignments $Y_1 Y_2$:
$00 = A$, $01 = B$, $10 = C$, and $11 = D$.

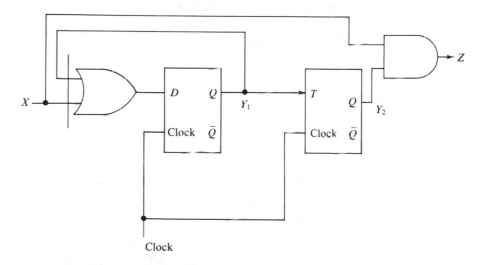

2.16   For the following circuit,
   a. Complete the timing diagram starting with $Y_1 Y_2 = 00$ (at time $= 0$).
   b. Derive excitation tables.
   c. Derive the state table, using $Y_1 Y_2$: $00 = A$, $01 = B$, $11 = C$, and $10 = D$.
   Assume that the flip-flops are triggered by the raising edge of the clock.

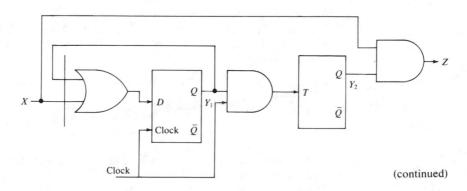

(continued)

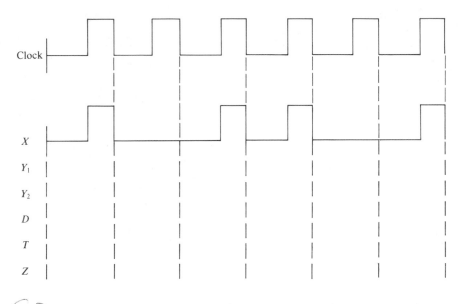

2.17 The circuit shown below gave an output sequence of $Z = 11011111$ for an input sequence $X = 1101010$. What was the starting state?

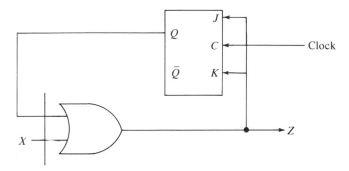

2.18 It is required to transmit data on a serial line. The data are in an 8-bit register. The receiver expects the 8-bit data followed by a parity bit. Odd parity is used; i.e., if the number of 1s in the data is even, the parity bit will be 1, otherwise 0.

Design the data converter/formatter circuit. Use existing ICs from a catalog, if possible.

Chapter 3

Memory and Storage

We have demonstrated the use of flip-flops in storing binary information. Several flip-flops put together form a register. A register is used either to store data temporarily or to manipulate data stored in it using the logic circuitry around it. The *memory* subsystem of a digital computer is functionally a set of such registers where data and programs are stored. The instructions from the programs stored in memory are retrieved by the control unit of the machine (digital computer system) and are decoded to perform the appropriate operation on the data stored either in memory or in a set of registers in the processing unit.

For optimum operation of the machine, it is required that programs and data be accessible by control and processing units as quickly as possible. The *main memory* (primary memory) allows such a fast access. This fast-access requirement adds a considerable amount of hardware to the main memory and thus makes it expensive. To reduce memory cost, data and programs not immediately needed by the machine are normally stored in a less expensive *secondary memory* subsystem. They are brought into the main memory as the processing unit needs them. The larger the memory, the more information it can store and hence the faster the processing, since most of the information required is immediately available. But because main-memory hardware is expensive, a speed-cost tradeoff is needed to decide on the amounts of main and secondary storage needed. This chapter provides models of operation for the most commonly used types of memories, followed by a brief description of memory devices and organization.

3.1   Types of Memory

Depending on the mechanism used to store and retrieve data, a memory system can be classified as one of the following four types:

1. Random-access memory (RAM):
   a. Read-write memory (RWM).
   b. Read-only memory (ROM).
2. Content-addressable memory (CAM) or associative memory (AM).
3. Sequential-access memory (SAM).
4. Direct-access memory (DAM).

The models of operation for these memories are described next.

3.1.1   Random-Access Memory

In a random-access memory (RAM), any addressable location in the memory can be accessed in a random manner. That is, the process of reading from and writing into a location in a RAM is the same and requires an equal amount of time no matter where the location is physically in the memory. The two types of RAM available are (1) read-write and (2) read-only memories.

Read-Write Memory.   The most common type of main memory is the read-write memory (RWM), the model of which is shown in Figure 3.1. In a RWM, each memory register or memory location has an "address" associated with it. Data is input into (written into) and output from (read from) a memory location by accessing the location using its "address." The memory address register (MAR) of Figure 3.1 stores such an address. With n bits in the MAR, 2^n locations can be addressed and they are numbered from 0 through $2^n - 1$. Transfer of data in and out of memory is usually in terms of a set of bits known as a *memory word*. A memory buffer register (MBR) is used to store data to be written into or read from a memory word.

To read the memory, the address of the memory word to be read from is provided in MAR and the READ signal is set to 1. A copy of the content of the addressed memory word is then brought by the memory logic into MBR. The content of the memory word is thus not altered by a READ operation. To write a word into the memory, the data to be written are placed in MBR by external logic, the address of the location into which the data is to be written is placed in MAR, and the WRITE signal is set to 1. The memory logic then transfers MBR content into the addressed memory location. The content of the memory word is thus altered during a WRITE operation.

Figure 3.1 Read-write memory

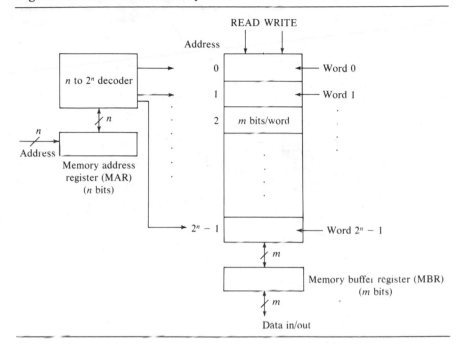

A memory word is defined as the most often accessed unit of data. Word sizes of 8, 16, 32, 36, and 64 bits are typically used in memory organizations of commercially available machines. In addition to addressing a memory word, it is possible to address a portion of it (half-word, quarter-word, etc.) or a multiple of it (double word, quad word, etc.) depending on the memory organization. In a "byte-addressable" memory, for example, an address is associated with each byte (usually 8 bits per byte) in the memory and a memory word consists of one or more bytes.

The acronym RAM is routinely used in computer literature to refer to read-write memory (RWM). We will follow this popular practice and use RWM only when the context requires us to be specific.

Read-Only Memory. Read-only memory (ROM) is also a random-access memory, except that data can only be read from it. Data are usually written into a ROM either by the memory manufacturer or by the user in an off-line mode; i.e., by special devices that can write (burn) the data pattern into the ROM. A model of ROM is shown in Figure 3.2. A ROM is also used as main memory and contains data and programs that are not usually altered in real time during the system operation. The memory

Figure 3.2 Read-only memory

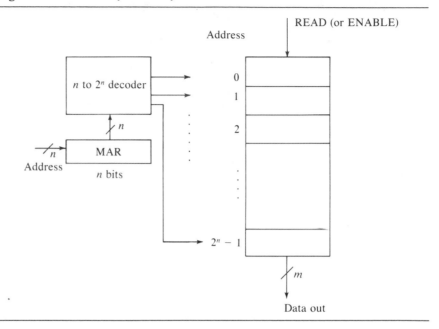

buffer register is not shown in Figure 3.2. In general, we assume that the data on output lines are available as long as the memory enable signal is on and it is latched into an external buffer register. A buffer is provided as part of the memory system, in some technologies.

3.1.2 Content-Addressable Memory or Associative Memory

In this type of memory, the concept of addresses is not usually present; rather, the memory logic searches for the locations containing a specified data pattern and hence the descriptor "content-addressable" or "associative." A model of an *associative memory* (AM) is shown in Figure 3.3. The data pattern to be searched for is first placed in the *data register*. The *mask register* designates the portion of the data register that is of interest. The memory logic compares each memory word with data and mask registers. As a result, the bits of the *results register* corresponding to words of the memory that have the required data pattern are set to 1. The *word-select register* acts as a word mask: if a bit in this register is set, the corresponding memory word is included in the search; if the bit is reset, the memory word is excluded from the search.

Associative memories are useful when an identical operation needs to be performed on several pieces of data simultaneously or when a search for a particular data pattern in parallel is required. For example, if each memory word is a record in a personnel file, the records corresponding to the set of female employees 25 years old can be searched for by setting the data and mask register bits appropriately. If sufficient logic is provided, all records responding to the search can also be updated simultaneously. In practice, *content-addressable memories* (CAM) are built out of RAM components and as such have addressing capability. In fact, the multiple match resolver returns the address of the responding word or words in response to a search. The major application of CAM is for storage of data on which fast search and update operations are performed.

3.1.3 Sequential-Access Memory

Figure 3.4 shows the model of a sequential-access storage system. In this type of storage, data are written in the sequence in which they appear.

Figure 3.3 Associative memory

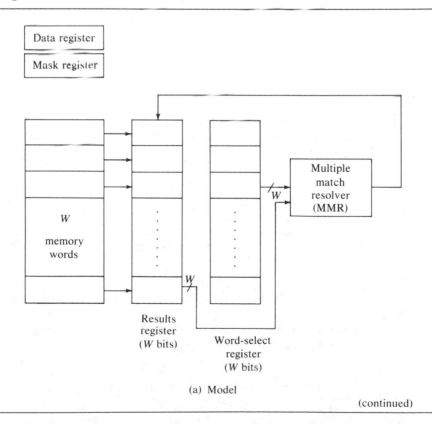

(a) Model

(continued)

Figure 3.3 (Continued)

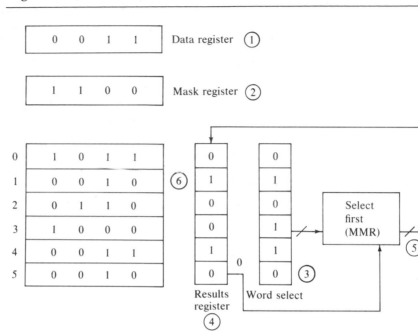

(b) Operation

The circled numbers indicate the sequence of operation.

1. The "data" word being searched for is 0011.

2. Most significant 2 bits of "mask" are 1s. Hence, only the corresponding 2 bits of "data" are compared with those of memory words 0 through 5.

3. "Word select" register bit setting indicates that only words 1, 3, and 4 are to be involved in the search process.

4. "Results" register indicates that words 1 and 4 have the needed data.

5. The "select first (MMR)" circuit resets the "results" register bit, corresponding to word 4.

6. Word 1 is the final respondent.

The information provided in Figure 3.3(b) can be used for updating word 1 contents.

Note that comparison of data register with memory words is done in parallel. The addresses shown (0 through 5) are for reference only.

While reading the data, each unit of data on the storage medium is examined in sequence until the desired data are found. SAMs are secondary storage devices and the most common sequential storage devices are magnetic tape, paper tape, and punched cards.

3.1.4 Direct-Access Memory

Figure 3.5 shows the model of a direct-access memory device (a magnetic disk) in which the data are accessed in two steps: (1) the transducers

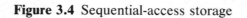

Figure 3.4 Sequential-access storage

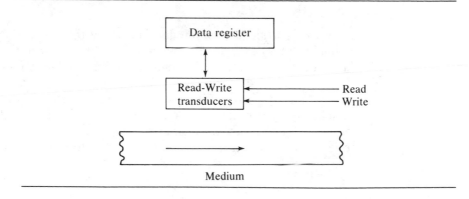

Medium

Figure 3.5 Direct-access storage

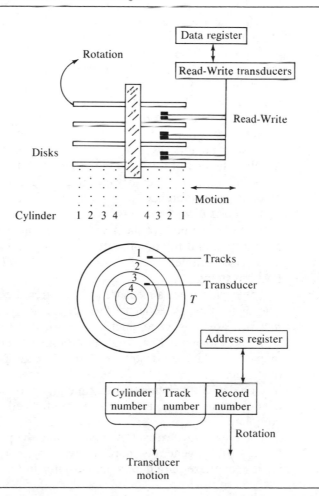

move to a particular position determined by the addressing mechanism (cylinder, track) and, once in this position, (2) the transducers access the data on the selected track sequentially until the data are found. This type of memory is used for secondary storage. It is also called "semirandom access" memory since the movement of read-write transducers to a selected cylinder is random and only the accessing of data within a track is sequential. These devices can also be used as sequential devices. Magnetic disks and drums are the most common direct-access devices.

3.2   Memory System Parameters

The most important characteristics of any memory system are its capacity, data access time, the data transfer rate, and the frequency at which memory can be accessed or the cycle time and cost.

The *capacity* of the storage system is the maximum number of units (bits, bytes, or words) of data it can store. The capacity of a RAM, for example, is the product of the number of memory words and the word size. A 2K × 4 memory can store 2K (K $= 1024 = 2^{10}$) words each containing 4 bits or a total of 2 × 1024 × 4 bits.

The *access time* is the time taken by the memory module to access the data, after an address is provided to the module. The data appear in the MBR at the end of this time in the event of a RAM. The access time in a non-random-access memory is a function of the location of the data on the medium with reference to the position of read-write transducers.

The *data transfer rate* is the number of bits per second at which the data can be read out of the memory. It is the product of the reciprocal of access time and the number of bits in the unit of data (data word) being read. This parameter is of more significance in non-RAM systems than in RAM systems.

The *cycle time* is a measure of how often the memory can be accessed. The cycle time is equal to the access time in nondestructive readout memories (e.g., semiconductor memories) in which the data can be read without destroying them. In some storage systems (such as magnetic core memories), data are destroyed during a read operation (destructive readout). A rewrite operation is necessary to restore the data. The cycle time in such devices is defined as the time taken to read and restore data, since a new read operation can not be performed until after the rewrite is complete.

The *cost* is the product of capacity and the price of memory device per bit. RAMs are generally more costly than other memory devices. Typical values for these parameters appear later in this chapter.

3.3   Memory Devices and Organizations

The basic property a memory device must possess is that of two well-defined states that can be used for the storage of binary information. In addition, the ability to switch from one state to another (i.e., reading and writing a 0 or 1) is required and the switching time needs to be minimal to make the memory system fast. Further, the cost per bit of storage should be as low as possible.

The address-decoding mechanism and its implementation distinguishes random-access memory from non-random-access memory. Since a RAM needs to be fast, the address decoding is done all electronically, thus involving no physical movement of the storage media. In a non-RAM, either the storage media or the read-write mechanism (transducers) is usually moved until the appropriate address (or data bit) is found. This sharing of the addressing mechanism makes non-RAM cheaper than RAM, while the mechanical movement makes it slower than RAM in terms of data access times. In addition to the memory device characteristics, decoding of the external address and read-write circuitry affect speed and cost of the storage system.

Semiconductor and magnetic memory technologies have been the most popular device technologies. In each technology, memory devices can be organized into various configurations with a range of cost and speed characteristics. Memory device technologies and organizations used in de signing the four types of memories are described in this section.

3.3.1   Random-Access Memory Systems

Semiconductor technology became the most popular random-access memory technology of the eighties. Advances in integrated circuit technology brought memory costs down while making it possible to have an enormous storage capability on an IC chip. Magnetic-core memories, although now superseded, were widely used in computer systems built during the seventies and eighties. We will describe RAM system organizations using these technologies in this section.

The major components of a random-access memory are the address decoding circuit, read-write circuit, and the set of memory devices organized into several words. The memory device that can store a bit and has appropriate hardware to support decoding and read-write operations is a *memory cell*.

Semiconductor RAMs.   A flip-flop is the basic storage device for a semiconductor RAM. Figure 3.6(a) shows a memory cell built out of a JK flip-

Figure 3.6 A semiconductor memory cell

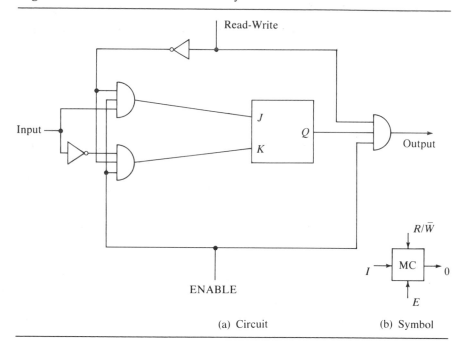

(a) Circuit   (b) Symbol

flop. The flip-flop is not clocked. When the ENABLE signal is 1, either the INPUT signal enters the flip-flop or the contents of the flip-flop are seen on the OUTPUT based on the value of the READ-WRITE signal. If ENABLE is 0, the cell outputs 0 and also makes $J = K = 0$, thereby not changing the contents of the flip-flop. The READ-WRITE signal is 1 for reading (OUTPUT $\leftarrow Q$) and 0 for writing ($Q \leftarrow$ INPUT). A symbol for this memory cell (MC) is also shown in Figure 3.6(b).

A four-word RAM with 3 bits per word built out of such MCs is shown in Figure 3.7. The 2-bit address in the MAR is decoded by a 2-to-4 decoder to select one of the four memory words. The memory ENABLE line has to be 1 for the memory to be active. If not, none of the words is selected (all outputs of the decoder are 0). When it is 1 and the $R/\overline{W}$ line is 1, the outputs of memory cells enabled by the selected word line will be input into the set of OR gates whose outputs are connected to the OUTPUT lines. OUTPUT lines receive signals from MCs that are in the enabled word only, since all other MC outputs in each bit position are 0. If the memory is enabled and the $R/\overline{W}$ line is 0, only the selected word will receive the INPUT information.

Figure 3.7 A four-word, 3-bit semiconductor memory

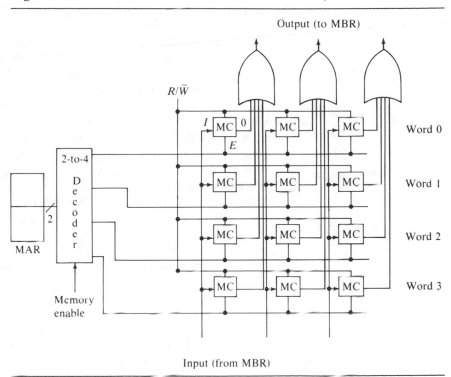

If the number of words is large, as in any practical semiconductor RAM, the OR gates shown in Figure 3.7 become impractical. To eliminate these gates, the MCs are fabricated with either open-collector or tristate outputs. If open-collector outputs are provided, outputs of MCs in each bit position are tied together to form a WIRED-OR, thus eliminating an OR gate. The pull-up resistors required and the current dissipation by the gates, however, limit the number of the outputs of gates that can be WIRE-ORed. Memory cells with tristate outputs can be used in such limiting cases. Outputs of MCs in each bit position are then tied together to form an output line.

In a commercial memory IC, there might be more than one "memory enable" signal to provide a chip selection feature when several such ICs are used to form larger memories. Outputs of such ICs are usually fabricated as either WIRED-OR or tristate.

Contents of a semiconductor RAM are lost when the power is removed. This property is called "volatility." A backup power source is thus required to retain the memory content. Alternatively, memory contents can be copied over to a secondary storage just before the power is removed and restored after the power is turned on.

Semiconductor RAMs with cells resembling the MC shown in Figure 3.6 are known as *static* RAMs, since the content of each MC remains 1 or 0 as long as the power is on. In *dynamic* RAMs, each MC is fabricated as a capacitor rather than as a flip-flop. The 1 and 0 states correspond to two charge levels. Because the charge on a capacitor dissipates over time, dynamic RAMs must be "refreshed" with data periodically. Due to the refresh cycle, dynamic RAMs are slower than static RAMs. But since fabricating a capacitor is much less complex than fabricating a flip-flop, a large number of bits can be fabricated on a dynamic memory chip. Dynamic RAMs are thus slower but less expensive than static RAMs.

Figure 3.8 shows the organization and characteristics of one commercially available memory, Intel 2114. This is a 1K word, 4 bits per word (1K $\times$ 4) static memory. There are 10 address lines (A_0–A_9). The active-low chip select ($\overline{CS}$) must be 0 to enable this chip. When 0, write enable ($\overline{WE}$) puts the IC into write mode; otherwise the memory will be in read mode (if $\overline{CS}$ = 0). There are four input/output pins. Internally, the memory cells are fabricated in a 64 $\times$ 64 array. This array is divided into sixteen 4-bit groups (columns), one of which is selected by address lines A_0, A_1, A_2, and A_9. One of the 64 rows (in the selected column) is selected by the address lines A_3–A_8. Intersection of the selected row and column corresponds to one 4-bit word. The $\overline{WE}$ and $\overline{CS}$ together control the 4-bit data input/output. Table 3.1 shows typical characteristics of some semiconductor RAMs.

Magnetic-Core RAMs.   The basic storage cell in magnetic-core memories is a donut-shaped core made of magnetic material. Two magnetic flux patterns can be stored on the core. A current passing through a magnetizing wire wound around the core induces a flux to magnetize the core. The direction of magnetic flux induced on the core depends on the direction of the current. The flux follows the square hysteresis loop shown in Figure 3.9. As the magnitude of the current is increased, the flux reaches a saturating level ($+\phi$ for 1, $-\phi$ for 0) and stays at that level even if the current is removed. To reverse the flux pattern, the direction of the current must be reversed. If the core is not saturated, it returns to the previous state once the current is removed. Thus, a current magnitude of less than I does not bring any state change on the core.

To sense the direction of flux stored on the core, a sense wire wound on the core is used. A voltage is induced in the sense winding whenever there is a change in flux on the core. As shown in Figure 3.9, if a 0 is stored on the core, and the current I is passed through the magnetizing

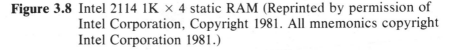

Figure 3.8 Intel 2114 1K × 4 static RAM (Reprinted by permission of Intel Corporation, Copyright 1981. All mnemonics copyright Intel Corporation 1981.)

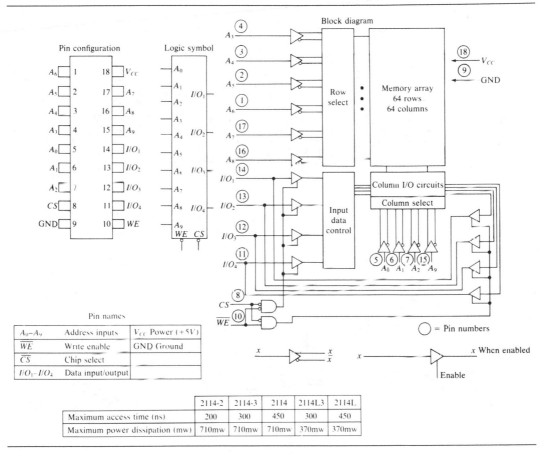

		2114-2	2114-3	2114	2114L3	2114L
Maximum access time (ns)		200	300	450	300	450
Maximum power dissipation (mw)		710mw	710mw	710mw	370mw	370mw

wire, the flux pattern changes from negative to positive, thus inducing a voltage V at the sense wire terminals. If the original flux on the core was positive (corresponding to a 1), no voltage would be seen at the sense wire terminals when the current is I. Thus, the voltage on sense wire can be used to detect the binary data stored on the core. Note that this method of reading the contents of the core is "destructive," because the flux on the core is changed (for example, from negative to positive when the current is I) while reading. Hence, core memories are called *destructive readout* (DRO) memories. To retain the information on the cell, it must be restored (or rewritten) after each read operation and cannot be accessed

Table 3.1 Semiconductor memory characteristics

Type	Manufacturer	Part number	Technology	Access time (nanoseconds)	Power dissipation (watts)	Capacity (bits)
Static RAM	Intel	2125H	NMOS (HMOS II)	20–35	0.53	1K × 1
Static RAM	Intel	2114A	HMOS	120–250	1.0	1K × 4
Dynamic RAM	Intel	2164	NMOS	150–200	1.0	64K × 1
PROM	Texas Instruments	SN 74S478	Schotky	45 (access) 40 (enable)	0.630	8K × 1
Ultraviolet EPROM	Intel	2716	NMOS	350–650	0.525	2K × 8
EPROM	Texas Instruments	TMS 2516	N–channel Silicon gate	350–450	0.285	16K × 1
Electrical EPROM	Intel	2817	HMOS-E	250–450	—	2K × 8
CAM	Semionics	REM S-100	NMOS	200 (access) 200 (cycle)	—	4K × 8

Figure 3.9 Magnetic core

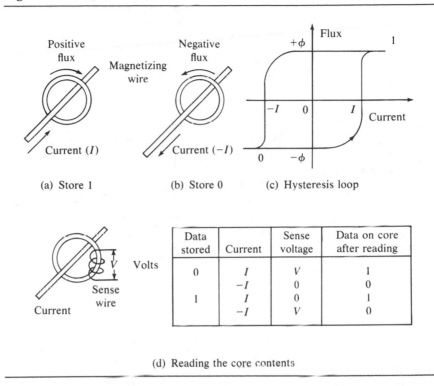

(a) Store 1   (b) Store 0   (c) Hysteresis loop

Data stored	Current	Sense voltage	Data on core after reading
0	I	V	1
	$-I$	0	0
1	I	0	1
	$-I$	V	0

(d) Reading the core contents

again until the rewrite is complete. The cycle time of the memory is thus the time required to read and rewrite the information.

Figure 3.10 shows a four-word core memory with 3 bits per word. The MAR contents are decoded to select one of the four memory words.

This organization of the core memory is referred to as the *two-dimensional* (2-D) organization. A general 2-D core memory with W bits and B bits per word is shown in Figure 3.11. It requires W word lines, $n = \log_2 W$ bits in the MAR, W word drivers, B bit drivers, and B sense amplifiers. As the number of words increases, the memory array gets thinner (longer), requiring that the bit lines be longer and contributing larger delays through the bit lines (and higher loss compensation). This limits the number of words. Hence, 2-D organization is useful for smaller memory sizes where the memory array is nearly square. Since only two wires are needed at each core, the cores can be smaller in size and can switch faster, thus making the memory fast. But the number of components (at least W gates) required for decoding makes this organization expensive for larger values of W.

Figure 3.10 A four-word, 3-bits-per-word core memory

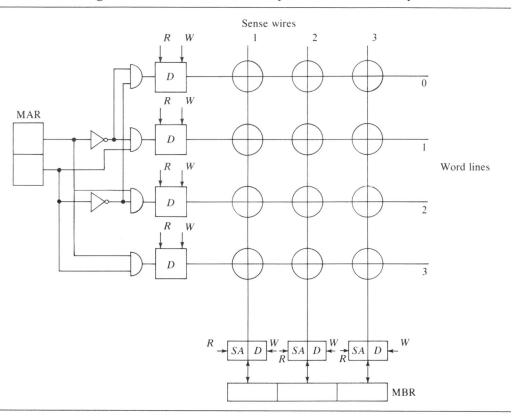

Note: *SA*: sense amplifier; *D*: driver; *R*: read; *W*: write.

The 2½-D and 3-D organizations of cores are also used in building core memories. These organizations attempt to make the memory array as nearly a square as possible. Analysis of cost and speed characteristics of such organizations can be found in reference works listed at the end of this chapter.

The main advantage of the core memory is its *nonvolatile* property; that is, the information is not lost when the power is removed. This characteristic has made the core a popular main-memory device. Typical characteristics of the core memory are: core diameter around 18 mils (1 mil = 1/1,000 inch); switching time, 140 nanoseconds; access time, 350 nanoseconds; cycle time, 500 nanoseconds; word current, 400 milliamps; and sense signal, 50 millivolts.

In addition to magnetic cores, other magnetic devices have been used to construct RAMs; thin-film and plated-wire memories are two popular

Figure 3.11 Two-dimensional core memory (W, B bit words)

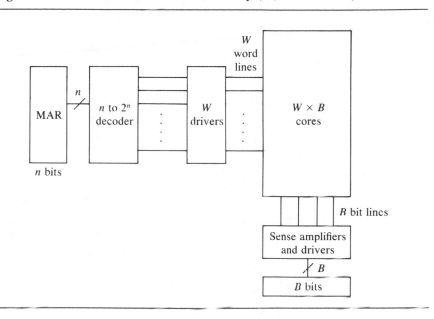

ones. Operating principles of these memory devices are similar to that of magnetic cores, although thin-film memory is composed of dots of magnetic material on a glass surface while plated-wire memories are composed of a thin layer of magnetic material on wires. Both of these memories are nondestructive readout memories and hence are faster than core memories.

3.3.2 Read-Only Memory

A read-only memory (ROM) is a random-access memory with data permanently stored in it. When the n-bit address is input to the ROM, the data stored at the addressed location are output on its output lines. ROM is basically a combinational logic device. Figure 3.12 shows a four-word ROM with 3 bits per word. The links at junctions of word lines and bit lines are either open or closed depending on whether a 0 or a 1 is stored at the junction, respectively. When a word is selected by the address decoder, each output line (i.e., bit line) with a closed link at its junction with the selected word line will output a 1 while the other output lines output a 0. In Figure 3.12, contents of locations 0 through 3 are 101, 010, 111, and 001, respectively.

Figure 3.12 A four-word, 3-bit-per-word ROM

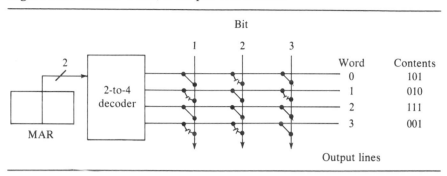

Two types of ROMs are commercially available, *mask-programmed* ROMs and *user-programmed* ROMs. Mask-programmed ROMs are used when a large number of ROM units containing a particular program and/or data is required. The IC manufacturer can be asked to "burn" the program and data into the ROM unit. The program is given by the user on a compatible medium such as paper tape or punched cards. The IC manufacturer prepares a mask and uses it to fabricate the program and data into the ROM as the last step in the fabrication. The ROM is thus custom fabricated to suit the particular application. Since custom manufacturing of an IC is expensive, mask-programmed ROMs are not cost effective unless the application requires a large number of units, thus spreading the cost among the units. Further, since the contents of these ROMs are unalterable, any change requires new fabrication.

A user-programmable ROM (programmable ROM or PROM) is fabricated with either all 1s or all 0s stored in it. A special device called a *PROM programmer* is used by the user to "burn" the required program, by sending the proper current through each link. Contents of this type of ROM can not be altered after initial programming. Erasable PROMs (EPROM) are available. An ultraviolet light is used to restore the content of an EPROM to its initial value of either all 0s or all 1s. It can then be reprogrammed using a PROM programmer. Electrically alterable ROMs (EAROMs) are another kind of ROM that uses a specially designed electrical signal to alter its contents. Table 3.1 lists the characteristics of some commercially available ROM chips.

ROMs are used for storing programs and data that are not expected to change during program execution (i.e., in real time). They are also used in implementing complex Boolean functions, code converters, and the like. An example of ROM-based implementation follows.

Example 3.1 Implement a binary coded decimal (BCD)-to-Excess-3 decoder using a ROM.

Figure 3.13 shows the BCD-to-Excess-3 conversion. Since there are ten input (BCD) combinations, a ROM with sixteen words ($2^3 < 10 < 2^4$) must be used. The first ten words of the ROM will contain the ten Excess-3 code words. Each word is 4 bits long. The BCD input appears on the four address input lines of the ROM. The content of the addressed word is output on the output lines. This output is the required Excess-3 code.

Programmable Logic Arrays (PLA). In a ROM with n address lines, there will be 2^n words. In some applications, it is not necessary to have the complete 2^n word space. PLAs are used instead of ROMs in such applications. We will illustrate the utility of PLAs with the following example.

Example 3.2 Consider the implementation of a four-variable Boolean function:

$$F(A, B, C, D) = A\bar{B}C + \bar{C}\bar{D}.$$

A ROM can be used to implement this function. The four address lines correspond to variables A, B, C, and D. The sixteen 1-bit words of the ROM will each contain the value of F, corresponding to each input combination. When a particular combination of inputs is provided to the ROM (as an address), the corresponding F value is output by the ROM.

Figure 3.14 shows a PLA implementation of the above function. A PLA consists of an AND array and an OR array. These semiconductor arrays are fabricated to provide AND and OR functions at the intersections of the horizontal and vertical lines (in practice, they are NAND-

Figure 3.13 ROM-based implementation of code converter

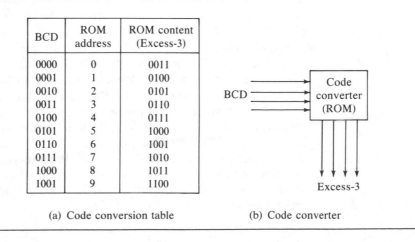

BCD	ROM address	ROM content (Excess-3)
0000	0	0011
0001	1	0100
0010	2	0101
0011	3	0110
0100	4	0111
0101	5	1000
0110	6	1001
0111	7	1010
1000	8	1011
1001	9	1100

(a) Code conversion table   (b) Code converter

Figure 3.14 PLA implementation of $A\bar{B}C + \bar{C}\bar{D}$

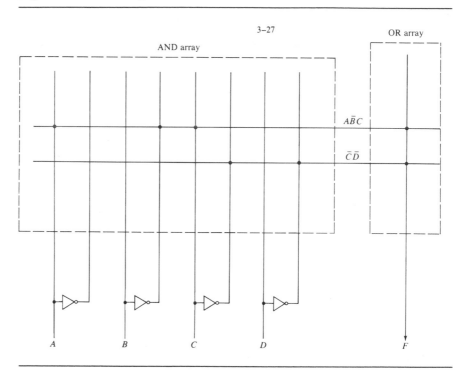

NAND or NOR-NOR arrays). A vertical line corresponds to either an input variable or its complement. Each horizontal line in the AND array implements a product term. Appropriate junctions of the AND array are connected to form product terms. This can be done during IC fabrication. Each vertical line in the OR array forms the OR of the connected product terms. There will thus be a vertical line in OR array corresponding to each output. In Figure 3.14, two horizontal lines are used to implement the two product terms in F. These lines are ORed to form F.

Just as in the case of ROM, the user provides a PLA program to the IC manufacturer, who programs the PLA during fabrication. Thus, PLAs can be used as ROMs. To implement an n variable function, a ROM with 2^n words is needed. Since all the 2^n product terms do not occur in practical functions, a PLA can be more cost effective because the PLA uses one horizontal line in the AND array for each product term in the function. For example, the four-variable function of Example 3.2 requires only two horizontal lines in the PLA implementation. It would have required a 16×1 ROM.

Standard PLA patterns of various configurations are available from IC manufacturers. These configurations differ with respect to the number of AND and OR lines, the number of inputs, and the number of outputs. Programming of standard PLA modules is done during the last step of fabrication, saving design and fabrication time and costs.

PLAs are basically combinational logic devices that can be programmed to implement logic functions. Sequential circuits can be implemented by including flip-flops external to a PLA. Figure 3.15 shows the implementation of a two-input, four-state, one-output sequential circuit using a PLA.

3.3.3 Associative Memory Cells

A typical associative memory cell (AMC) built from a JK flip-flop is shown in Figure 3.16. The *response* is 1 when either (1) the data bit D and the memory bit Q match while *mask* bit M is 1 or (2) the mask bit is 0 (corresponding to a "do not compare"). A truth table and a block diagram

Figure 3.15 A two-input, four-state, one-output sequential circuit

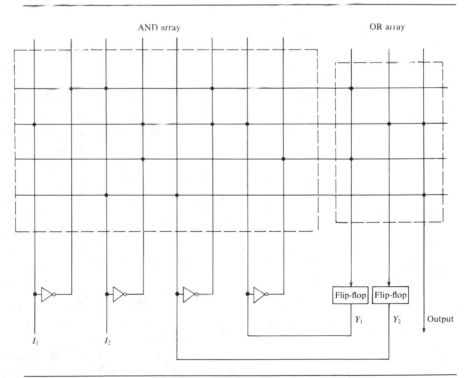

Figure 3.16 A simplified associative memory cell

Data (D)	Mask (M)	Q	Response
0	0	0	1
0	0	1	1
0	1	0	1
0	1	1	0
1	0	0	1
1	0	1	1
1	1	0	0
1	1	1	1

$$\text{Response} = \bar{M} + \bar{D}\bar{Q} + DQ.$$

for the simplified cell are also shown in the figure. In addition to the response circuitry, an AMC will have read, write, and enable circuits similar to the RWM cell shown in Figure 3.6.

A four-word, 3-bits-per-word associative memory built out of the above cells is shown in Figure 3.17. Data and mask registers are each 3 bits long. For simplicity we will assume that all memory words are selected for comparison. Hence, we will not need a word-select register. Response outputs of all cells in a word are ANDed together to form the word response signal. Thus, a word is a *respondent* if response output of each cell in the word is a 1. The multiple-match-resolver circuit shown selects the first respondent. The first respondent drives to zero the response outputs of other words following it.

The input (or write) and output (or read) circuitry is also needed. It is similar to that of the RWM system shown in Figure 3.7 and hence is not shown in Figure 3.17.

Small associative memories are available as IC chips. Their capacity is of the order of eight words, 8 bits per word. Larger associative memory systems are designed using RAM chips. As such, these memories can be used in both RAM and CAM modes. Because of increased logic complexity of an associative memory cell, however, the cost of a CAM system is much greater than that of an RAM of equal capacity.

3.3.4 Sequential-Access Memory Devices

Magnetic tape is the most common sequential-access memory device. A magnetic tape is a mylar tape coated with magnetic material (similar to that used in home music systems) on which data is recorded as magnetic patterns. The tape moves past a read-write head to read or write data.

Figure 3.17 A 3-bit, 4-word associative memory

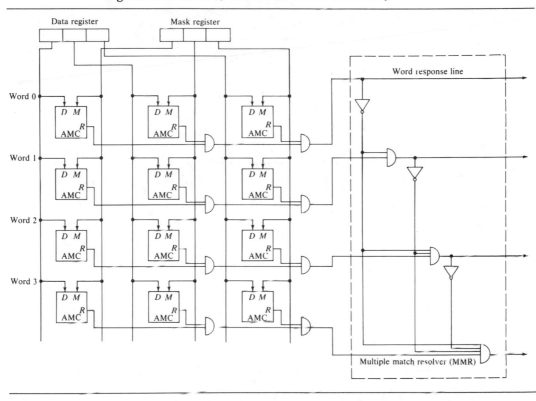

Figure 3.18 shows the two popular tape formats: the reel-to-reel tape used for storing large volumes of data (usually with large-scale and minicomputer systems) and the cassette tape used for small data volumes (usually with microcomputer systems). Data are recorded on tracks. A track on a magnetic tape runs along the length of the tape and occupies a width just sufficient to store a bit. On a seven-track tape for example, the width of the tape is divided into seven tracks and each character of data is represented with 7 bits (one bit on each track). One or more of these bits is usually a parity bit, which facilitates error detection and correction.

Several characters grouped together form a *record*. The records are separated by an inter-record gap (about ¾ inch) and an end-of-record mark (which is a special character). A set of records forms a *file*. The files are separated by an end-of-file mark and a gap (about 3 inches). On cassette tapes, the data are recorded in a serial mode on one track as shown in Figure 3.18(b). Table 3.2 summarizes magnetic tape characteristics.

Figure 3.18 Magnetic tape formats

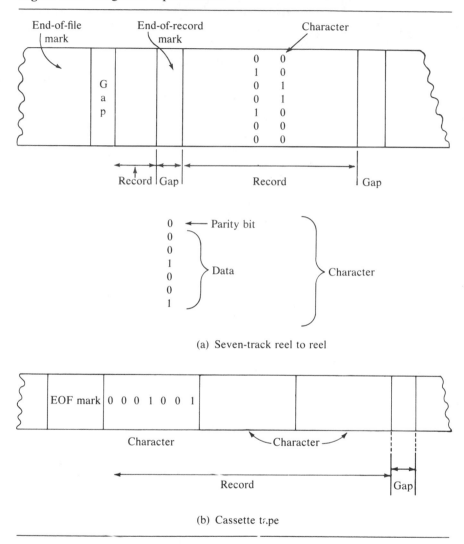

(a) Seven-track reel to reel

(b) Cassette tape

The recording or *writing* on magnetic devices is the process of creating magnetic flux patterns on the device: the sensing of the flux pattern when the medium moves past the read-write head constitutes the *reading* of the data. In reel-to-reel tapes, the data are recorded along the tracks digitally. In a cassette tape, each bit is converted into an audio frequency and is recorded. Digital cassette recording techniques are also becoming popular. Note that the information on a magnetic tape is nonvolatile.

Table 3.2 Mass memory system parameters

Magnetic disk (hard)
Density	1100–6000 bits/inch
	100–200 tracks/inch
Rotation	1200–3600 revolutions/minute
Data rates	0.5–10 million bits/second
Access time	200–500 milliseconds

Magnetic tapes (reel-to-reel)
Speed	18.75–200 inches/second
Data rate	15–1250K bytes/second
Density	800–6250 bits/inch
Inter-record gap	0.3–0.75 inch

Magnetic bubble memories
Access time	4–7 milliseconds
Shift rate	100K bits/second (transfer rate)
Density	10^6 bits/inch^2

Floppy disks
Access time	300 milliseconds
Data rate	250K bits/second
Storage capacity	2–5 million bits

Paper tape is also a sequential-access device. Since data are recorded with a pattern of holes along tracks of paper tape, the tape is not reusable.

Magnetic and paper tapes permit recording of vast amounts of data at a very low cost. But the access time, being a function of the position of the data on the tape with respect to the read-write head position along the length of the tape, can be very long. Sequential-access devices thus form low-cost secondary memory devices.

3.3.5 Direct-Access Storage Devices

The most popular direct- or semirandom-access storage devices are *magnetic drums* and *magnetic disks*. Accessing data in these devices usually requires two steps: random or direct movement of read-write heads to the vicinity of data, followed by a sequential access. These mass-memory devices are used as secondary storage devices in a computer system for storing data and programs. Figure 3.19 shows a magnetic drum. This is a rotating cylinder with a thin coating of magnetic material. There are several read-write heads, for recording and reading the magnetic patterns on the drum surface. Each head records or reads data on one track. A track consists of several cells, each of which can store a bit. A timing track serves as the reference to identify the position of the drum. To access the data on the drum, heads are first positioned to the proper track or tracks.

Figure 3.19 A magnetic drum

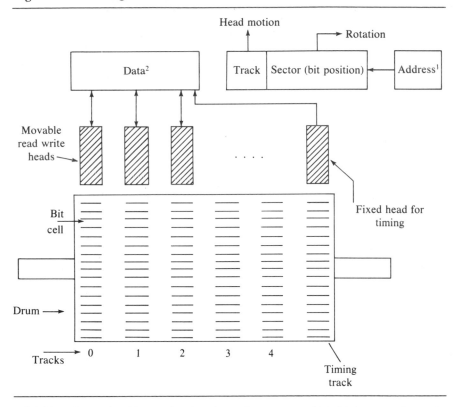

[1] Address is translated into (a) head motion to the proper track(s); (b) drum rotation to the proper sector or bit position along the track.
[2] Data read-write is through the read-write heads.

The data on these tracks are then accessed sequentially. Hence, the access time depends on the track positioning time plus the sequential data access time (within the track).

Magnetic Disk. A magnetic disk (see Figure 3.5) is a flat circular surface coated with a magnetic material, much like a phonograph record. Several such disks are mounted on a rotating spindle. Each surface will have a read-write head. Each surface is divided into several concentric circles (tracks). By first positioning read-write heads to the proper track, the data on the track can be accessed sequentially. A track is normally divided into several sectors, each of which correspond to a data word. The address of a data word on the disk thus corresponds to a track number and a sector number.

Floppy Disks.   Floppy disks have emerged as the most popular low-cost secondary memory devices, especially for microcomputer systems. The data storage and access format on these devices is similar to that on hard disks. The disk surface is flexible (unlike hard disks) and hence the term "floppy." Floppy disks are enclosed in a paper envelope with a window to permit read and write operations. Floppy disks are now available in 5¼-inch and 8-inch diameters. They can store 250,000 to 500,000 bytes of data and the data storage density is continually being increased. Their data transfer rate is slower than that of hard-disk devices.

Semiconductor Direct-Access Devices.   In the direct-access devices just discussed, the storage medium moves past the read-write mechanism for data access while the data remain static. In semiconductor direct-access memories such as *charge-coupled devices* (CCD) and *magnetic bubble memories* (MBM), data are moved past the read-write mechanism while the storage medium is static. This organization eliminates mechanical movements of the medium and also provides for memory access at electronic speeds.

A track on a magnetic disk or drum is equivalent in function to a circulating shift register. Consider the circulating shift register shown in Figure 3.20(a), in which data can be input or output at bit position 0. To read from or write into a bit position, it is necessary that the particular bit occupy position 0. Hence the data access time is a function of the distance of the selected bit from bit position 0. Figure 3.18(b) shows a five-word, 3-bits-per-word memory built out of three 5-bit shift registers. The *shift counter* counts modulo 5 and indicates the number (or *address*) of the bit occupying position 0 at any time. All three registers circulate simultaneously and when the address matches the shift counter, a read or write operation is performed in parallel at bit position 0 into or from MBR, respectively. The average access time is thus a function of the number of bits in each shift register. When the number of bits per data word is less than the number of shift registers in the memory system, proper subset of registers is first selected and bits in the same position in these selected registers are then accessed. Thus, the procedure is in two steps, as with disks and drums, but faster, because all operations are electronic. Next, we will discuss one semiconductor technology useful in building direct-access storage devices.

Magnetic Bubble Memories.   Magnetic bubble memory technology has advanced considerably since the concept was introduced by Bell Telephone Laboratories in 1967. The operation of this memory system is based on small cylindrical magnetic domains referred to as magnetic bubbles. These bubbles can be produced in single crystal-thin films of syn-

Figure 3.20 A five-word shift register memory with 3 bits per word

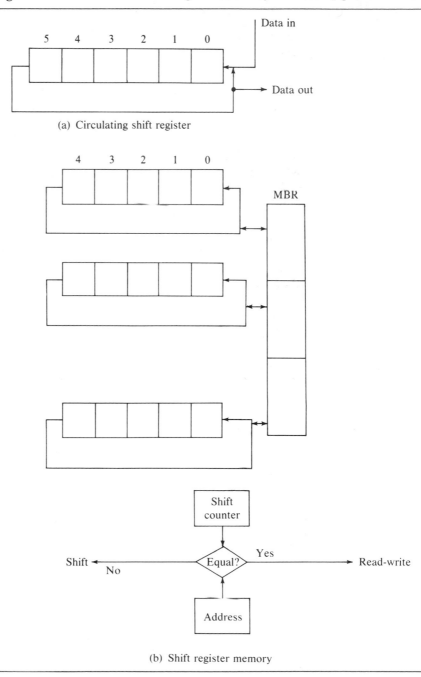

(a) Circulating shift register

(b) Shift register memory

thetic ferrites or garnets when an external magnetic field is applied perpendicular to the surface of the film. The bubbles can be moved laterally through the film by the use of a varying magnetic field. The movement can be restricted to certain paths or tracks. These characteristics of magnetic bubbles make them suitable for devising semiconductor shift-register memories where each track is equivalent to a shift register in its operation. The presence or absence of a bubble at a particular bit position in the track is used to define the logic state at that position. Because the diameter of a bubble is of the order of $1/10$ micrometer, a very large number of data bits can be stored in a single bubble memory chip.

Magnetic film is depicted in Figure 3.21(a). In the absence of an external magnetic field, the average number of upward magnetic domains is equal to that of the downward magnetic domains, minimizing the magnetic energy within the film. These magnetic domains form random serpentine patterns of equal area. The magnetic fields of the serpentine domains line up primarily along a single axis called the "easy" axis, which is normal to the plane of the film. When an external magnet field is applied to the film, its energy tends to expand domains polarized in the direction of the field and to shrink those polarized in the direction opposite to the field until they become small cylinders embedded in a background of opposite magnetization. When viewed on end, these cylinders have the appearance of small circles or bubbles with diameters of from 2 to 30 micrometers. By increasing the field strength, the bubble can be made to collapse or be annihilated. This magnetic field (bias field) can be produced by a permanent magnet, with no power expenditure.

Four basic mechanisms are required in order to use magnetic bubbles for memory: (1) generation of bubbles, (2) control of their direction of movement to form tracks, (3) detection of the presence or absence of a bubble at a bubble position on the track, and (4) transfer of a bubble from one track to the other.

Bubbles are generated by locally altering the bias field with a magnetic field produced by a pulse of current through a microscopic one-turn metallized loop. This loop is located on a secondary layer immediately above the magnetic film on the surface of the chip. By sending a current of appropriate amplitude and polarity through the one-turn loop, a localized vertical magnetic field opposite to that of the permanent magnet is produced. This localized field generates a bubble.

Once a bubble has been created, a method of forming tracks on which bubbles can move is required. This is accomplished by the deposition of patterns of a soft magnetic material on the chip surface above the magnetic film. When magnetized sequentially by a magnetic field rotating in the same plane, these propagation patterns set up magnetic polarities that attract the bubble domains and establish motion. Figure 3.21(b) shows

Figure 3.21 Magnetic bubble memories

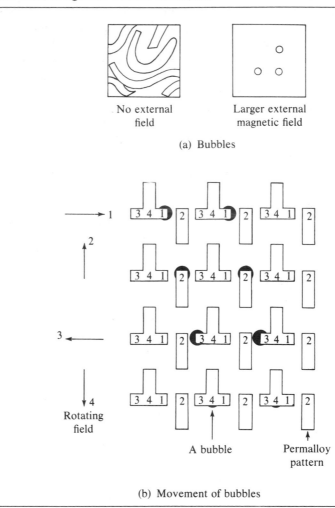

(a) Bubbles

(b) Movement of bubbles

various polarities at different positions of the rotating magnetic field. In practice, the rotating in-plane magnetic field is implemented by applying a two-phase alternating current through two coils placed around the chip.

The phenomenon in which a magnetic material varies its electrical resistance when subjected to the influence of a magnetic field is called the *magnetoresistive effect*. Detection of magnetic bubbles exploits this property. Since electrical resistance varies to a large degree as the size of the bubble increases, the bubble to be detected is extended. For this purpose, a pattern referred to as a *stretcher* is used. Each time the bubble shifts in the advance direction by 1 bit, it is also extended in the direction perpendicular to that of the advance. The magnetic bubble, stretched to an appropriate degree, is passed beneath a *detector* pattern, which detects the presence of the bubble through the magnetoresistivity.

A bubble *annihilator* clears the bubbles and is commonly combined with a *replicator*. Replication of bubbles allows a nondestructive read operation by duplicating bubbles. One copy is read and destroyed while the other copy is retained in the memory.

One possible implementation for the magnetic bubble memory resembles a long serial shift register as shown in Figure 3.22. Bubbles shift under the influence of the rotating magnetic field, following the path determined by the placement of the patterns of soft magnetic material. For each bubble in the loop, the replicator creates another bubble that in turn is detected by the detector. The annihilator destroys the bubbles while the *generator* creates new bubbles and feeds them into the loop. This organization offers the simplest design and interface control but also has the slowest access time because the data bit (bubble) must circulate through the entire loop before it can be read and retrieved. Another problem with this single-loop design is that a single fault in the shift-register structure results in a defective memory chip. This results in a low processing yield and hence high cost to the end user.

A better organization is the *major/minor loop configuration,* where the

Figure 3.22 Single-loop organization of magnetic bubble memories

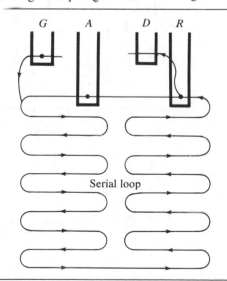

Note: *G:* generator; *A:* annihilator; *D:* detector; *R:* replicator.

long single-shift register is reorganized into several registers. The major/minor loop organization has a shorter access time and is suitable for a large storage capacity. Figure 3.23 shows such an organization consisting of a major loop to read and write data and several minor loops for data storage.

During the write operation, data are first transferred into the major loop. The major loop is essentially a unidirectional circular-shift register from which data can be transferred in parallel to minor loops. A block of data is thus entered into the major loop and shifted until the first data bit is aligned with the most remote minor loop. At that time, each parallel transfer element receives a current pulse that produces a localized magnetic field. This causes a parallel transfer of all the bubbles in the major loop to the top bit position of the corresponding minor loop. Once data are written into minor loops, new data may be written after first removing the old data by performing a destructive read. In this operation, bubbles are first transferred from the minor loop and annihilated and the new data are transferred into the minor loops.

During a read operation, loops are rotated until the data to be accessed are adjacent to the major loop. At this time, a parallel transfer is made to

Figure 3.23 Major/minor loop organizations for MBMs

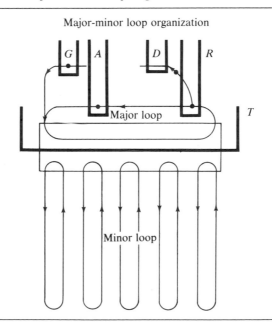

Major-minor loop organization

Note: *G:* generator; *A:* annihilator; *D:* detector; *R:* replicator; *T:* transfer gate.

the major loop. The block of data is shifted to the replicator, where it is duplicated. The duplicated data are sent to the detector. The original data remain in the major loop and are transferred back into minor loops.

Magnetic bubble memories (MBMs) offer several advantages: non-volatility, fabrication ease and higher yields relative to other semiconductor memory devices, and faster access time and higher reliability than disks. Table 3.3 shows some MBM system characteristics.

Charge-Coupled Devices. Charge-coupled devices (CCDs) can also be used for electronic direct-access storage. MOS processing is used in fabricating shift registers made of CCDs, where a CCD cell consists of MOS capacitors capable of storing a charge. The stored charge can then be moved by application of proper voltage levels, thus forming CCD shift-register memories. CCDs permit faster access time than MBMs and are comparable to them in cost.

3.4 RAM Design Using ICs

Memory system designers normally use commercially available RAM chips as components in implementing larger memories. Major steps in such memory designs are

1. Calculating the number of RAM chips needed to implement the RAM of required capacity.
2. Designing the decoding circuitry to uniquely address each memory word formed out of RAM chips.

A memory system design is given in Example 3.3.

Table 3.3 Magnetic bubble memory characteristics

Manufacturer	Model	Capacity	Organization	Package	Cost
Fujitsu	FBM 0102	64K bits	Major/minor	18 pin	$ 100
Fujitsu	FBM 0301	256K bits	Major/minor block-replicate	16 pin	$ 500
Intel	7110	1M bit	Major/minor block-replicate	Leadless	$2000
Rockwell	RBM 256	256K bits	Major/minor block-replicate	18 pin	$ 500
Texas Instruments	TIB 0303	254K bits	Major/minor block-replicate	18 pin	$ 500

Example 3.3   Design a 4K × 8 memory, using Intel 2114 RAM chips.

1. Number of chips needed $= \dfrac{total\ memory\ capacity}{chip\ capacity} = \dfrac{4K \times 8}{1K \times 4} = 8.$

2. Memory system MAR will have 12 bits, since $4K = 4 \times 1024 = 2^{12}$; the MBR will have 8 bits.
3. Since 2114s are organized with 4 bits per word, two chips are used in forming a memory word of 8 bits. Thus, the eight 2114s are arranged in four rows with two chips per row.
4. 2114 has 10 address lines. The least significant 10 bits of memory system MAR are connected to the ten address lines of each 2114. A 2-to-4 decoder is used to decode the most significant 2 bits of MAR to select one of the four rows of 2114 chips through $\overline{CS}$ signal on each 2114 chip.
5. Input/output lines of chips in each row are connected to MBR. Note that these I/O lines are configured as tristate. $\overline{WE}$ lines of all 2114 chips are tied together to form the system $\overline{WE}$.

The memory system is shown in Figure 3.24.

3.5 Memory Hierarchy

The *primary memory* of a computer system is always built out of RAM devices, thereby allowing the processing unit to access data and instructions in the memory as quickly as possible. It is necessary that the program or data be in the primary memory when the processing unit needs them. This would call for a large primary memory when programs and data blocks are large, thereby increasing the memory cost. In practice, it is not really necessary to store the complete program or data in the primary memory as long as the portion of the program or data needed by the processing unit is in the primary memory.

A *secondary memory* built out of direct or serial access devices is then used to store programs and data not immediately needed by the processing unit. Since random-access devices are more expensive than secondary memory devices, a cost-effective memory system results when the primary memory capacity is minimized. But this organization introduces an overhead requirement into the memory operation, since mechanisms to bring the required portion of the programs and data into primary memory

Figure 3.24 A 4K × 8 memory

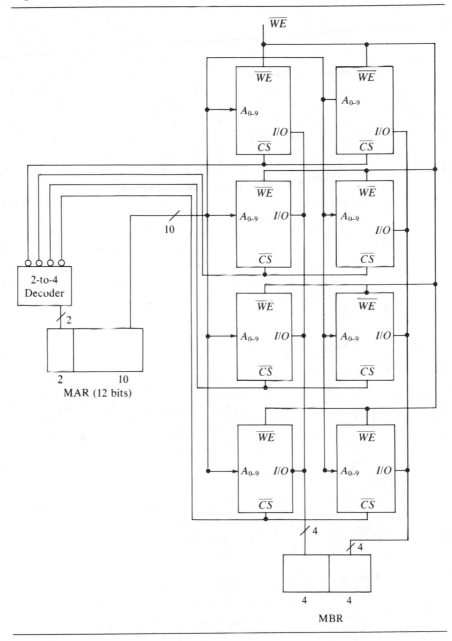

Note: Power and GND not shown.

as needed will have to be devised. These mechanisms form what is called a *virtual memory* scheme.

In a virtual memory scheme, the user assumes that the total memory capacity (primary plus secondary) is available for programming. The operating system manages the moving in and out of portions (segments or pages) of program and data into and out of the primary memory.

Even with current technologies, the primary memory hardware is slow compared to the processing unit hardware. To reduce this speed gap, a small but faster memory is usually introduced between the main memory and the processing unit. This memory block is called *cache memory* and is usually 10 to 100 times faster than the primary memory. A virtual memory mechanism similar to that between primary and secondary memories is then needed to manage operations from main memory to cache. The set of instructions and data that are immediately needed by the processing unit are brought from the primary memory into cache and retained there. A parallel fetch operation is possible in that while the cache unit is being filled from the main memory, the processing unit can fetch from the cache, thus narrowing the memory-to-processor speed gap.

Note that the registers in the processing unit are temporary storage devices. They are the fastest components of the computer system memory.

Figure 3.25 Memory hierarchy

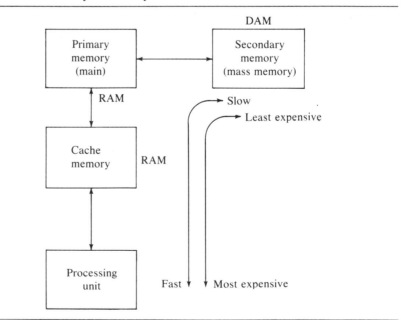

Thus, in a general purpose computer system there is a memory hierarchy in which the highest speed memory is closest to the processing unit and is most expensive. The least expensive and slowest memory devices are farthest from the processing unit. Figure 3.25 shows the memory hierarchy. Chapter 6 gives further details on memory hierarchy and virtual memory schemes.

3.6 Summary

Four types of memories were introduced in this chapter. The main memory of large computer systems was predominantly magnetic core memory. Semiconductor RWMs have replaced core memory since advances in semiconductor technology have brought memory cost down drastically. Memory hierarchies and efficient memory management schemes to utilize secondary storage can now be seen even on smaller computer systems. Magnetic bubble memory systems have already been used and continue to replace hard and floppy-disk memories. Optical memories using holographic techniques are at the experimental stage and promise faster, dense memories. The speed-versus-cost tradeoff is the basic parameter in designing memory systems. Figure 3.26 shows relative costs of memory devices.

Figure 3.26 Memory cost comparison

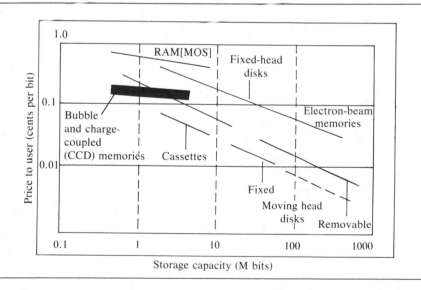

References

Beausoleil, W. F., D. T. Brown, and B. E. Phelps. "Magnetic Bubble Memory Organization," *IBM Journal of Research and Development,* Vol. 16, 1972, pp. 587–591.

Bipolar Microcomputers Components Data Book. Dallas, Tex.: Texas Instruments, 1980.

Bobeck, A. H., and E. Della Torre. *Magnetic Bubbles.* New York, N.Y.: American Elsevier, 1975.

Computer. Long Beach, Calif.: IEEE Computer Society. Published monthly.

Computer Design. Littleton, Mass.: Computer Design Publishing Corp. Published monthly.

Elphick, M. "Magnetic Bubbles Muscle into Memory Territory," *High Technology,* February 1980.

Foster, C. C. *Computer Architecture.* New York, N.Y.: Van Nostrand Reinhold, 1976.

Mano, M. M. *Digital Logic and Computer Design.* Englewood Cliffs, N.J.: Prentice-Hall, 1979.

Riley, W. B. *Electronic Computer Memory Technology.* New York, N.Y.: McGraw-Hill, 1971.

Snigier, P. "Magnetic Bubble Memories," *Digital Design,* December 1979.

Stone, H. S. *Introduction to Computer Architecture.* Chicago, Ill.: Science Research Associates, 1975.

The TTL Data Book for Design Engineers. Dallas, Tex.: Texas Instruments, 1976.

Problems

3.1   Complete the following table:

Memory-system capacity	Number of bits in MAR	Number of bits in MBR	Number of chips needed if chip capacity is		
			1K × 4	2K × 1	1K × 8
64K × 4					
64K × 8					
32K × 4					
32K × 16					
32K × 32					
10K × 8					
10K × 10					

3.2 What is the storage capacity and maximum data transfer rate of
   a. a magnetic tape, 800 bits per inch, 2400 feet long, 10 inches per second?
   b. a magnetic drum with 50 tracks including a timing track, 4K bits per track, rotates at 3600 RPM? What is the maximum access time assuming a track-to-track move time of 1 millisecond?

3.3 Implement the following functions using a PLA:

$$F_1(A,B,C) = \bar{A}BC + A\bar{B} + AB\bar{C}$$
$$F_2(A,B,C) = \bar{A}\bar{B} + \bar{A}BC + \bar{C}$$

Is it advantageous to reduce the Boolean functions before implementing them using PLAs?

3.4 Implement the sequential circuit of problem 2.15 using PLA.

3.5 Design a 16K $\times$ 8 memory using the following ICs:
   a. 1024 $\times$ 1   b. 2K $\times$ 4   c. 1K $\times$ 8
   Each IC has onchip decoding, tristate outputs, and an "enable" pin.

3.6 The computations in a particular computer system with an associative memory require that the contents of any field in the associative memory word be incremented by 1.
   a. Design a circuit to perform this increment operation on a selected field in all memory words that respond to a search.
   b. Extend the circuit in (a) to accommodate addition of a constant value greater than 1 to the selected field of all respondents, simultaneously.

3.7 Design the decoding, read-write circuitry for a core memory with W words and B bits per word. The memory is organized as T segments each containing W/T, B bit words as shown:

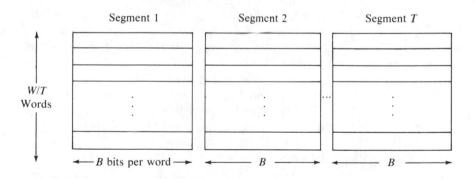

This is called a 2½-D organization.

3.8 Design the decoding, read-write circuit for a core memory with 64 words and 8 bits per word. The memory is organized into eight planes with each plane containing the corresponding bit from each word. The bits in each plane are organized into an 8 $\times$ 8 array. The decoding circuitry consists of eight row-lines and eight column-lines on each plane selecting a bit from the plane where the X and Y currents add up to I. Corresponding bits from each plane form a word. There is a sense winding for each plane, through each core in the plane. (This is called a 3-D organization).

3.9   You are given a 16K $\times$ 32 RAM unit. Convert it into a 64K $\times$ 8 RAM. Treat the 16K $\times$ 32 RAM as one unit you can not alter. You can only include logic external to the RAM unit.

3.10   A 256-word memory has its words numbered from 0 to 255. Define the address bits for each of the following. Each address bit should be specified as 0, 1, or d ("don't care").
       a. Word 48.
       b. Lower half of the memory (words 0 through 127).
       c. Upper half of the memory (words 128 through 255).
       d. Even memory words (0, 2, 4, etc.).
       e. Any of the eight words 48 through 55.

3.11   A processor has a memory-addressing range of 64K with 8 bits per word. It is required that the lower and upper 4K of the memory be ROM and the rest of the memory be RAM. Use 1K $\times$ 8 ROM and 4K $\times$ 4 RAM chips and design the memory system. Design a circuit to generate an error signal if an attempt is made to write into a ROM area.

3.12   An 8K memory is divided into 32 equal size blocks (or pages) of 256 words each. The address bits are then grouped into two fields: the page number and the number of the memory word within a page. Draw the memory, MAR, and MBR configurations.

3.13   Four of the 32 pages of the memory of problem 3.12 must be accessible at any time. Four auxiliary 5-bit registers, each containing a page address, are used for this purpose. The processor outputs a 10-bit address; the most significant 2 bits select one of the auxiliary registers and the least significant 8 bits select a word within a page, the page number obtained from the selected auxiliary register. Design the circuit to convert the 10-bit address output by the processor into the 13-bit address required.

3.14   Draw a schematic for a magnetic bubble memory system with sixteen minor loops and one major loop, assuming the data transfer in and out of the system is serial (1 bit at a time).

3.15   Repeat the design in problem 3.14 assuming that the data transfer is parallel
       a. 8 bits at a time.
       b. 4 bits at a time.

Chapter 4

Computer Organization and Programming

Chapters 1, 2, and 3 provided the hardware design and analysis information needed to understand the organization and design of a computer. The purpose of this chapter is to introduce the terminology and basic functions of a simple but complete computer, mainly from a programmer's (user's) point of view. We will call the simple hypothetical computer ASC (*A Simple Computer*). Although ASC appears very primitive in comparison with any commercially available machine, its organization reflects the basic structure of the most complex modern computer. The instruction set is limited but complete enough to write powerful programs. Assembly language programming and understanding of assembly process are a must for a system designer. We defer the discussion of organization of commercially available computers to Chapters 6 and 7. The detailed hardware design of ASC is provided in Chapter 5.

4.1 A Simple Computer

We will assume that ASC is a 16-bit machine and hence the unit of data manipulated by and transferred between various registers of the machine is 16 bits long. It is a binary, stored-program computer and uses 2s complement representation for negative numbers. Since one can address 64K memory words with a 16-bit address, we will assume a memory with 64K, 16-bit words. A 16-bit-long memory address register (MAR) is thus required. The memory buffer register (MBR) is also 16 bits long. MAR stores the address of a memory location to be accessed and MBR receives the data from the memory word during a memory read operation and retains the data to be written into a memory word during a memory write operation. These two registers are not normally accessible by the programmer.

In a stored-program machine, programs are stored in the memory. During the execution of the program, each instruction from the stored program is first *fetched* from the memory into the control unit and then the operations called for by the instruction are performed (i.e., the instruction is *executed*). Two special registers are used for performing fetch-execute operations: *A program counter* (PC) and an *instruction register* (IR). The PC contains the address of the instruction to be fetched from the memory and is usually incremented by the control unit to point to the next instruction address at the end of an instruction fetch. The instruction is fetched into IR. The circuitry connected to IR decodes the instruction and generates appropriate control signals to perform the operations called for by the instruction. PC and IR are both 16 bits long in ASC.

There is a 16-bit *accumulator register* (ACC) used in all arithmetic and logic operations. As the name implies, it accumulates the result of arithmetic and logic operations.

There are three *index registers* (INDEX 1, 2, and 3) used in manipulation of addresses. We will discuss the function of these registers later in this chapter.

A *console* is needed to permit operator interaction with the machine. ASC console permits the operator to examine and change the contents of memory locations and initialize the program counter. Power ON/OFF and START/STOP controls are also on the console. The console has a set of sixteen switches through which a 16-bit data can be entered into ASC memory. There are sixteen lights (monitors) that can display 16-bit data from either a memory location or a specified register. To execute a program, the operator first loads the programs and data into the memory, then sets the PC contents to the address of the first instruction in the program and STARTs the machine. During execution of the program, additional data input (or output) is done through an input (or output) device. We will assume that there is one input device from which a 16-bit data word can be "read" into the ACC and one output device that outputs the 16-bit data in the ACC onto the output medium. Note that the data in the ACC are not altered due to the output, but an input operation replaces the original ACC contents with the new data. Figure 4.1 shows the hardware components of ASC.

4.1.1 Data Format

ASC memory is an array of up to 64K, 16-bit words. Each of these 16-bit words will be either an instruction or 16-bit data. The exact interpretation depends on the context in which the machine accesses a particular mem-

Figure 4.1 ASC hardware components

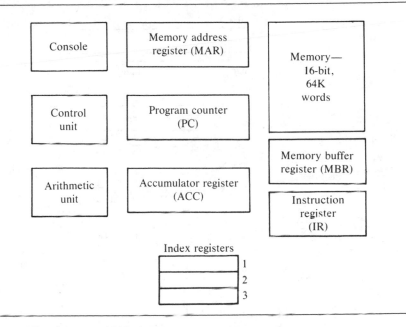

Note: All registers are 16 bits long.

ory word. The programmer should be aware (at least at the assembly and machine-language programming levels) of the data and program segments in the memory and should make certain that a data word is not accessed during a phase in which the processor is accessing an instruction and vice versa.

Figure 4.2 shows the data format of ASC for both positive and negative numbers. Only fixed-point (integer) arithmetic is allowed on ASC. Note also the four-digit hexadecimal notation to represent a 16-bit data word. This notation is used to denote a 16-bit quantity irrespective of whether it is data or an instruction.

4.1.2 Instruction Format

Each instruction in an ASC program occupies a 16-bit word. An instruction word has four fields as shown below:

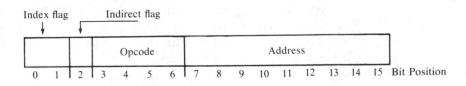

Figure 4.2 ASC data format

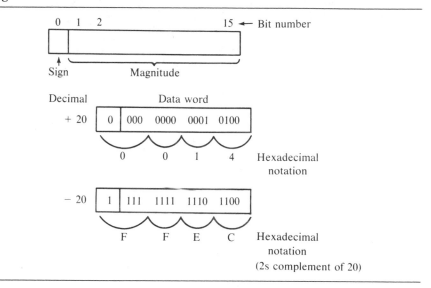

Bits 0 and 1 of the instruction word select one of the three index registers when indexed addressing is called for or if the instruction manipulates an index register:

Bit 0	Bit 1	
0	0	No indexing
0	1	Index register 1
1	0	Index register 2
1	1	Index register 3

Bit 2 of the instruction word is the *indirect* flag. If indirect addressing is used, bit 2 is 1; otherwise, it is 0.

Bits 3 through 6 of the instruction word are used for the operation code (opcode). An *opcode* is a unique bit pattern that encodes a primitive operation that the computer can perform. Thus, ASC can have $2^4 = 16$ unique instructions.

Bits 7 through 15 of the instruction word are allowed for memory address. Thus, $2^9 = 512$ memory locations can be addressed directly. Indexed and indirect addressing modes can be used to extend this address range to 64K. Thus, ASC has direct addressing, indirect addressing, index addressing, and indexed-indirect addressing (or indirect-indexed addressing) modes. We will describe these addressing modes after the description of the instruction set that follows.

Table 4.1 ASC instruction set

Mnemonic	Opcode (Hexadecimal)	Description
LDA	0	$ACC \leftarrow M[MEM]$
STA	1	$M[MEM] \leftarrow ACC$
ADD	2	$ACC \leftarrow ACC + M[MEM]$
TCA	3	$ACC \leftarrow \overline{ACC} + 1$ (2s complement)
HLT	4	Halt
BRU	5	Branch unconditional
BIP	6	Branch if $ACC > 0$
BIN	7	Branch if $ACC < 0$
RWD	8	Read a word into ACC
WWD	9	Write a word from ACC
SHL	A	Shift left ACC once
SHR	B	Shift right ACC once
LDX	C	$INDEX \leftarrow M[MEM]$
STX	D	$M[MEM] \leftarrow INDEX$
TIX	E	Test index increment $INDEX \leftarrow INDEX + 1$ Branch if $INDEX = 0$
TDX	F	Test index decrement $INDEX \leftarrow INDEX - 1$ Branch if $INDEX \neq 0$

Note: *MEM* refers to a memory word; i.e., the symbolic address of a memory word. *M[MEM]* refers to the contents of the memory word *MEM* when used as a source and to the memory word when used as a destination.

4.1.3 Instruction Set

Table 4.1 lists the complete instruction set of ASC. Each hexadecimal (H) opcode (as defined by 4 bits in the instruction format) is also identified by a symbolic name. This symbolic name is called the *mnemonic*.

We add one more construct to our HDL (hardware description language) described in Chapter 2. The memory is designated as *M*. A memory read operation is shown as

$$MBR \leftarrow M[MAR].$$

and a memory write operation is shown as

$$M[MAR] \leftarrow MBR.$$

The operand within the [ ] can be

1. A register; the content of the register is a *memory address*.

2. A symbolic address; the *symbolic address* will eventually be associated with an *absolute address*.
3. An absolute address.

Thus,

$$ACC \leftarrow M[27].$$

$$M[28] \leftarrow ACC.$$

$$IR \leftarrow M[X1]. \text{ and}$$

$$M[X1] \leftarrow ACC. \qquad (X1 \text{ is a symbolic address.})$$

are all valid data transfers. Further,

$$ACC \leftarrow X1.$$

implies that the absolute address value corresponding to X1 is transferred to ACC. Thus,

$$X1 \leftarrow ACC.$$

is not valid.

The ASC instruction set consists of the following three classes of instructions:

1. Zero address (TCA, HLT, SHL, and SHR).
2. One address (LDA, STA, ADD, BRU, BIP, BIN, LDX, STX, TIX, and TDX).
3. Input/output (RWD, WWD).

A description of instructions and their representation follows. In this description, hexadecimal numbers are distinguished from decimal numbers with a preceding "H."

Zero-Address Instructions. In this class of instructions, the opcode represents the complete instruction. The operand (if needed) is implied to be in the ACC. The address field and the index and indirect flags are not used. A description of each instruction follows:

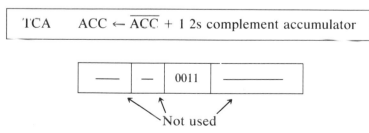

TCA complements each bit of the ACC to produce the 1s complement and then a 1 is added to produce the 2s complement. The 2s complement of the ACC is stored back into the ACC.

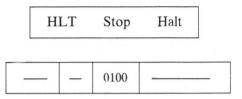

| HLT | Stop | Halt |

| —— | — | 0100 | ————— |

The HLT instruction indicates the logical end of a program and hence stops the machine from fetching the next instruction (if any).

| SHL | $ACC_{0-14} \leftarrow ACC_{1-15}$ | Shift left |
| | $ACC_{15} \leftarrow 0$ | |

| —— | — | 1010 | ————— |

The SHL instruction shifts the contents of the ACC 1 bit to the left and fills a 0 into the least significant bit of the ACC.

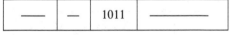

| SHR | $ACC_{1-15} \leftarrow ACC_{0-14}$ | Shift right |
| | $ACC_0 \leftarrow ACC_0$ | |

| —— | — | 1011 | ————— |

The SHR instruction shifts the contents of the ACC 1 bit to the right and the most significant bit of the ACC remains unchanged. The contents of the least significant bit position are lost.

One-Address Instructions. These instructions use all 16 bits of an instruction word. In the following, MEM is a *symbolic address* of an arbitrary memory location. An *absolute address* is the physical address of a memory location, expressed as a numeric quantity. A symbolic address is mapped to an absolute address when an assembly language program is translated into machine language. The description assumes a direct addressing mode in which MEM is the *effective address* (the address of the operand). The 9-bit address is usually modified by the indirect and index operations to generate the effective address of a memory operand for each of these instructions. A description of one-address instruction follows:

LDA	MEM	ACC ← M[MEM].	Load accumulator

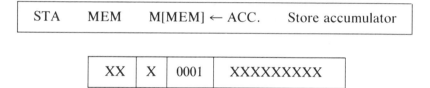

~Used~

LDA loads the ACC with the contents of the memory location (MEM) specified. Contents of MEM are not changed, but the contents of the ACC before the execution of this instruction are replaced by the contents of MEM.

STA	MEM	M[MEM] ← ACC.	Store accumulator

XX	X	0001	XXXXXXXXX

STA stores the contents of the ACC at the specified memory location. ACC contents are not altered.

ADD	MEM	ACC ← ACC + M[MEM].	Add

XX	X	0010	XXXXXXXXX

ADD adds the contents of the memory location specified to the contents of the ACC. Memory contents are not altered.

BRU	MEM	PC ← MEM.	Branch unconditional

XX	X	0101	XXXXXXXXX

BRU transfers the program control to the address MEM. That is, the next instruction to be executed is at MEM.

BIP	MEM	IF ACC > 0 THEN PC ← MEM.	Branch if ACC is positive

XX	X	0110	XXXXXXXXX

The BIP instruction tests the ACC; if it is >0, then the program execution resumes at the address (MEM) specified; if not, execution continues with the next instruction in sequence. Since the program counter (PC) must contain the address of the instruction to be executed next, the branching operation corresponds to transferring the address into PC.

BIN	MEM	IF ACC < 0 THEN PC ← MEM.	Branch if accumulator negative

XX	X	0111	XXXXXXXXX

The BIN instruction tests the most significant bit (sign bit) of the ACC; if it is 1, program execution resumes at the address specified; if not, the execution continues with the next instruction in sequence.

LDX	MEM, INDEX	INDEX ← M[MEM].	Load index register

XX	X	1100	XXXXXXXXX

The LDX loads the index register (specified by INDEX) with the contents of memory location specified. In the assembly language instruction format, INDEX will be 1, 2, or 3.

| STX   MEM, INDEX | M[MEM] ← INDEX. | Store index register |

| XX | X | 1101 | XXXXXXXXX |

The STX stores a copy of the contents of the index register specified by the index flag into the memory location specified by the address. The index register contents remain unchanged.

| TIX   MEM, INDEX | INDEX ← INDEX + 1.
IF INDEX = 0 THEN PC ← MEM. | Test index
increment |

| XX | X | 1110 | XXXXXXXXX |

TIX increments the index register content by 1. Next, it tests the index register content; if it is 0, the program execution resumes at the address specified; otherwise, execution continues with the next sequential instruction.

| TDX   MEM, INDEX | INDEX ← INDEX − 1.
IF INDEX ≠ 0 THEN PC ←MEM. | Test index
decrement |

| XX | X | 1111 | XXXXXXXXX |

TDX decrements the index register content by 1. Next it tests the index register content; if it is not equal to 0, the program execution resumes at the address specified; otherwise, execution continues with the next sequential instruction.

Input/Output Instructions. Since ASC has one input and one output device, the address, index, and indirect fields in the instruction word are not used. Thus, these are also zero-address instructions.

RWD	ACC ← Input data. Read a word

—	—	1001	—————

RWD instruction reads a 16-bit word from the input device into the ACC. The contents of the ACC before RWD are thus lost.

WWD	Output ← ACC. Write a word

—	—	1001	—————

WWD instruction writes a 16-bit word from the ACC onto the output device. ACC contents remain unaltered.

4.1.4 Addressing Modes

ASC instruction format allows several addressing modes. They are illustrated below with reference to LDA ("load accumulator") instruction. Here, X is assumed to be the symbolic address of the memory location AH (i.e., location 10 in decimal). For each mode, the assembly language format of the instruction is shown first, followed by the instruction format encoded in binary. The effective address calculation and the effect of the instruction are also illustrated. The effective address is the address of the memory word where the operand is located.

Direct addressing

Instruction format: LDA X

00	0	0000	000001010

Effective address: X or AH
Effect: ACC ← $M[X]$.

The effect of this instruction is illustrated below. We will use hexadecimal notation to represent all data and addresses in the following diagrams.

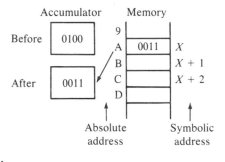

Indexed addressing

Instruction format: LDA   X,2

10	0	0000	000001010

Effective address: X + index register 2
Effect: ACC ← M[X + index register 2].

The number in the operand field after the comma denotes the index register used. Assuming that index register 2 contains 3, the following diagram illustrates the effect of this instruction. The numbers in circles show the sequence of operations. Contents of index register 2 are added to X to derive the effective address X + 3. Contents of location X + 3 are then loaded into the accumulator.

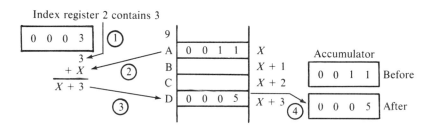

Note that the *address field* of the instruction refers to X and the contents of the index register specify an offset from X. Contents of an index register can be varied by using LDX, TIX, and TDX instructions, thereby accessing various memory locations as offsets of X. Indexing in this way allows us to access consecutive memory locations dynamically, by changing the contents of the index register. Further, since index registers are 16 bits wide, the effective address can be 16 bits long, thereby extending the memory addressing range to 64K from the range of 512 locations possible with 9 address bits.

Note that LDX, STX, TDX and TIX are index register manipulation instructions. The *index field* for these instructions refers to the index register being manipulated. The address field is thus not modified by the index field.

Indirect addressing

Instruction format: LDA* X

00	1	0000	00000 1010

Effective address: $M[X]$
Effect: $MAR \leftarrow M[X]$.
                            $ACC \leftarrow M[MAR]$.
                            i.e., $ACC \leftarrow M[M[X]]$.

The asterisk next to the mnemonic denotes the indirect addressing mode. In this mode, the address field points to a location where the address of the operand can be found.

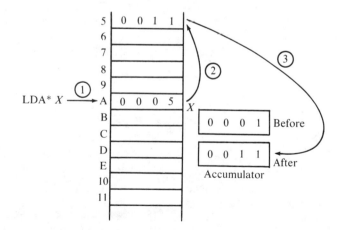

Since a memory word is 16 bits long, the indirect addressing mode can also be used to extend the addressing range to 64K. Further, by simply changing the contents of location A in the above illustration, we can refer to various memory addresses using the same instruction. This feature is useful, for example, in creating a multiple jump instruction in which contents of A are dynamically changed to refer to the appropriate address to be jumped to.

If both indirect and index flags are used, there are two possible modes of effective address computation, depending on whether indirecting or indexing is performed first. They are illustrated below.

Indexed-indirect addressing (preindexed-indirect)

Instruction format: LDA* $X,2$

10	1	0000 0	0000 1010

Effective address: $M[X + \text{index register 2}]$
Effect: $ACC \leftarrow M[M[X + \text{index register 2}]]$.

Indexing ① is done first, followed by indirection ② to compute the effective address whose contents are loaded ③ into the accumulator as shown:

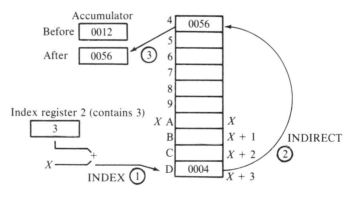

Indirect-indexed addressing (postindexed-indirect)

Instruction format: LDA* $X,2$

10	1	0000	000001010

Effective address: $M[X] + \text{index register 2}$
Effect: $ACC \leftarrow M[M[X] + \text{index register 2}]$.

Indirection ① is performed first, followed by indexing ② to compute the effective address whose contents are loaded ③ into the accumulator.

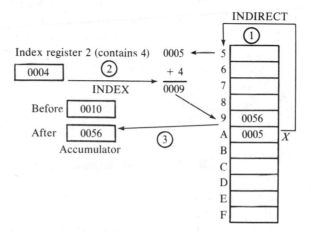

Note that the instruction formats in the above two modes are identical. ASC can not distinguish between these two modes. The indirect flag must be expanded to 2 bits, if both of these modes are to be allowed. Instead, we assume that ASC always performs preindexed-indirect and postindexing is not supported.

The above addressing modes are applicable to all single-address instructions. The only exceptions are the index-reference instructions (LDX, STX, TIX, and TDX) in which indexing is not permitted.

These are the most popular addressing modes. Various other modes are used in machines commercially available. Addressing modes and address range extension mechanisms of some practical machines are discussed further in Chapter 6.

4.1.5 Machine Language Programming

It is possible to write a program for ASC using absolute addresses (actual physical memory addresses) and opcodes only, since the instruction set and instruction and data formats are now known. Such programs are called *machine language programs*. They need not be further translated for the hardware to interpret them since they are already in binary form. Programming at this level is tedious, however. A program in machine language to add two numbers and store the sum in a third location is

$$0000\ 0000\ 0000\ 0100$$

$$0000\ 0100\ 0000\ 0101$$

$$0000\ 0010\ 0000\ 0111$$

Can you decode these instructions and determine what the program is doing?

Modern-day computers are seldom programmed at this level. All programs must be at this level, however, before execution of the program can begin. Translators (assemblers and compilers) are used in converting programs written in assembly and high-level languages into this machine language. We will discuss a hypothetical assembler for ASC assembly language in the next section.

4.2   ASC Assembler

An assembler that translates ASC assembly language programs into machine language programs is available. We will provide details of the language as accepted by this assembler and outline the assembly process in this section.

An assembly language program consists of a sequence of statements (instructions) coded in mnemonics and symbolic addresses. Each statement consists of four fields: label, operation (mnemonic), operand, and comments, as shown in Figure 4.3. The *label* is a symbolic name denoting the memory location where the instruction itself is located. It is not necessary to provide a label for each statement. Only those statements that are referenced from elsewhere in the program need labels. When provided, the label is a set of alphabetic and numeric characters the first of which must be an alphabetic character. The *mnemonic* field contains the instruc-

Figure 4.3 Assembly language statement format

Label[1]	Mnemonic	Operand	Comments[1]
Consists of alphabetic and numeric characters. First character must be alphabetic. An "*" as first character denotes that complete statement is a comment.	Comprises three-character standard symbolic opcodes. An "*" as fourth character signifies indirect addressing.	Consists of absolute and symbolic addresses. Indexes register designations following a ",".	Starts with a ".". Assembler ignores it.

[1] Optional field.

Note: A space (partition) is required between label and mnemonic fields and between mnemonic and operand fields.

tion mnemonic. An "*" following the instruction mnemonic denotes indirect addressing. The *operand* field consists of symbolic addresses, absolute addresses, and index register designations. Typical operands are:

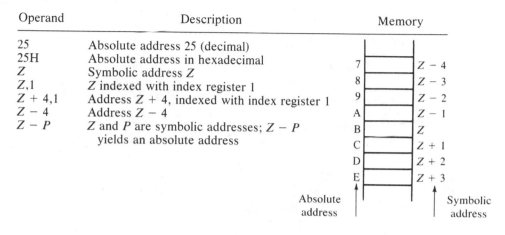

Operand	Description	Memory
25	Absolute address 25 (decimal)	
25H	Absolute address in hexadecimal	
Z	Symbolic address Z	
Z,1	Z indexed with index register 1	
Z + 4,1	Address Z + 4, indexed with index register 1	
Z − 4	Address Z − 4	
Z − P	Z and P are symbolic addresses; Z − P yields an absolute address	

The *comments* field starts with a ".". This optional field consists only of comments by the programmer. It does not affect the instruction in any way and is ignored by the assembler. An "*" as the first character in the label field designates that the complete statement is a comment.

Each instruction in an assembly language program can be classified as either an *executable instruction* or an *assembler directive* (or a pseudo-instruction). Each of the sixteen instructions in ASC instruction set is an executable instruction. The assembler generates a machine language instruction corresponding to each such instruction in the program. A *pseudo-instruction* is a directive to the assembler. This instruction is used to control the assembly process, to reserve memory locations, and to establish constants required by the program. The pseudo-instructions when assembled do not generate machine language instructions and as such are not executable. Care must be taken by the assembly language programmer to partition the program such that an assembler directive is not in the execution sequence. A description of ASC pseudo-instructions follows:

ORG Address	Origin

If used, ORG must be the first statement in the program. If ORG is not used, the assembler assumes a default starting address of 0. The operand field of ORG shows the address of the first instruction of the program. Its function is to provide the assembler a starting memory address at which the program is assumed to be located.

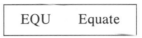

| END | Address | Physical end |

END indicates the physical end of the program and is the last statement in a program. The operand field of the END normally contains the label of the first executable statement in the program.

| EQU | Equate |

EQU provides a means of giving multiple symbolic names to memory locations as shown by the following example:

Example 4.1

A	EQU	B	A is another name for B.
A	EQU	B + 5	A is the name of location B + 5.
A	EQU	10	A is the name of the absolute address 10.

| BSS | Block storage starting |

BSS is used to reserve blocks of storage locations for intermediate or final results.

Example 4.2

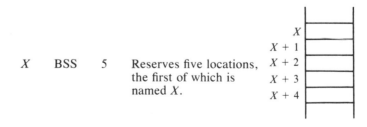

| X | BSS | 5 | Reserves five locations, the first of which is named X. |

The operand field always designates the number of locations to be reserved. Contents of these reserved locations are not defined.

| BSC | Block storage of constants |

BSC provides a means of storing constants in memory locations in addition to reserving those locations. The operand field consists of one or more operands (separated by a ","). Each operand requires one memory word.

Example 4.3

Z   BSC   5   Reserves one location named Z containing a 5.
P   BSC   5, -6, 7   Reserves three locations: P containing 5, $P + 1$ containing -6, and $P + 2$ containing 7.

Literal Addressing Mode.   It is convenient for the programmer to be able to define constants (data) as a part of the instruction. This feature also makes an assembly language program more readable. Literal addressing mode enables this. A literal is a constant preceded by an "=". For example,

$$LDA = 2$$

implies loading a constant 2 (decimal) into the accumulator, and

$$ADD = 10H$$

implies adding a $10H$ to the accumulator. ASC assembler recognizes such literals, reserves an available memory location for the constant in the address field, and substitutes the address of the memory location into the instruction.

Figure 4.4 provides a complete assembly language program as an example. This program performs an integer division.

Example 4.4   *Division.* Division can be treated as the repeated subtraction of the divisor from the dividend until a zero or negative result is obtained. The quotient is equal to the maximum number of times the subtraction can be performed without yielding a negative result. Figure 4.4 shows the division routine.

The division program (Figure 4.4) is generated by the ASC assembler. The first column contains the memory addresses, the second column the object code in hexadecimal notation, and the third column simply the statement numbers. The generation of the object code is the subject of the next subsection.

Figure 4.4 ASC division program

```
LOC    OBJECT CODE   STMT   SOURCE STATEMENT
0000                 1      *            SOURCE PROGRAM
0000                 2      *                            . DIVISION ALGORITHM FOR ASC (A/B)
0000                 3      *                            . A AND B ARE INTEGERS
0000                 4      *
0000                 5                   ORG   0
0000    1000         6      BEGIN        RWD            . READ A
0001    0222         7                   STA   A
0002    0C05         8                   BIP   R2
0003    0E05         9                   BIN   R2
0004    0A1F        10                   BRU   OUT      . IF A=0, QUOTIENT=0
0005    1000        11      R2           RWD            . READ B
0006    0223        12                   STA   B
0007    0C0C        13                   BIP   INIT
0008    0E0C        14                   BIN   INIT
0009    0027        15                   LDA   ERR      . IF B=0 ,PRINT NEGATIVE NUMBER
000A    0600        16                   TCA              (ERROR)
000B    0A20        17                   BRU   OUT1
000C                18      *
000C    0025        19      INIT         LDA   ZERO     . INITIALIZE QUOTIENT TO 0
000D    0224        20                   STA   COUNT
000E    0023        21                   LDA   B
000F    0600        22                   TCA
0010    0223        23                   STA   B        . STORE NEGATIVE B IN B
0011    0023        24      LOOP         LDA   B
0012    0422        25                   ADD   A        . A-(I*B), I=NUMBER OF LOOPS
0013    0222        26                   STA   A
0014    0E19        27                   BIN   FINISH   . RESULT NEGATIVE, FINISHED
0015                28      *                           . DO NOT INCREMENT COUNTER
0015    0C1B        29                   BIP   FINISH+2
0016    0024        30                   LDA   COUNT    . REMAINDER IS ZERO
0017    0426        31                   ADD   ONE
0018    0A20        32                   BRU   OUT1
0019    0024        33      FINISH       LDA   COUNT    . LOAD FINAL COUNT
001A    0A20        34                   BRU   OUT1
001B    0024        35                   LDA   COUNT    . INCREMENT QUOTIENT
001C    0426        36                   ADD   ONE      . RESULT IS 0 OR POSITIVE
001D    0224        37                   STA   COUNT
001E    0A11        38                   BRU   LOOP
001F    0025        39      OUT          LDA   ZERO
0020    1200        40      OUT1         WWD            . WRITE RESULT
0021    0800        41                   HLT
0022                42      A            BSS   1
0023                43      B            BSS   1
0024                44      COUNT        BSS   1
0025    0000        45      ZERO         BSC   0
0026    0001        46      ONE          BSC   1
0027    0001        47      ERR          BSC   1
0028                48                   END   BEGIN
```

4.2.1 Assembly Process

The major functions of the assembler program are (1) to generate an address for each symbolic name in the program and (2) to generate the binary equivalent of each assembly instruction. The assembly process is usually carried out in two scans over the source program. Each of these scans is called a *pass* and the assembler is called a *two-pass assembler*. The first pass is used for allocating a memory location for each symbolic name used in the program; during the second pass, references to these symbolic names are resolved. If the restriction is made that each symbol must be defined before it can be referenced, one pass will suffice.

Details of the ASC two-pass assembler are given in Figure 4.5 and Figure 4.6. The assembler uses a counter known as *location counter* (LC) to keep track of the memory locations used. If the first instruction in the program is ORG, the operand field of ORG defines the initial value of LC;

Figure 4.5 Assembler pass 1

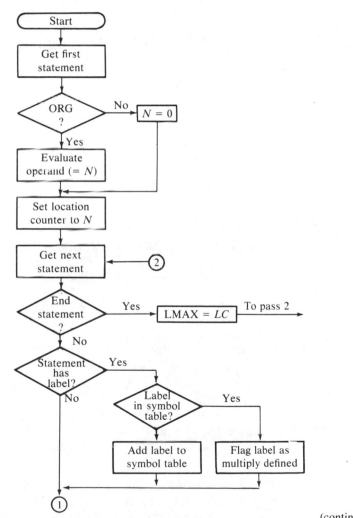

(continued)

Figure 4.5 (Continued)

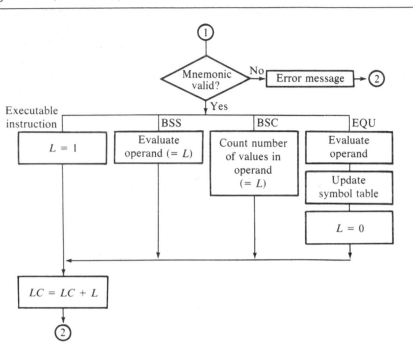

otherwise, LC is set to 0. LC is incremented appropriately during the assembly process. Content of LC at any time is the address of the next available memory location.

The assembler performs the following tasks during the first pass:

1. Enters labels into a symbol table along with the LC value as the address of the label.
2. Validates mnemonics.
3. Interprets pseudo-instructions completely.
4. Manages the location counter.

The major activities during the second pass are

1. Evaluation of the operand field.
2. Insertion of opcode, address, and address modifiers into the instruction format.
3. Resolution of literal addressing.

The assembler uses an opcode table to extract opcode information. The opcode table is a table storing each mnemonic, the corresponding opcode, and any other attribute of the instruction useful for the assembly process.

Figure 4.6 Assembler pass 2

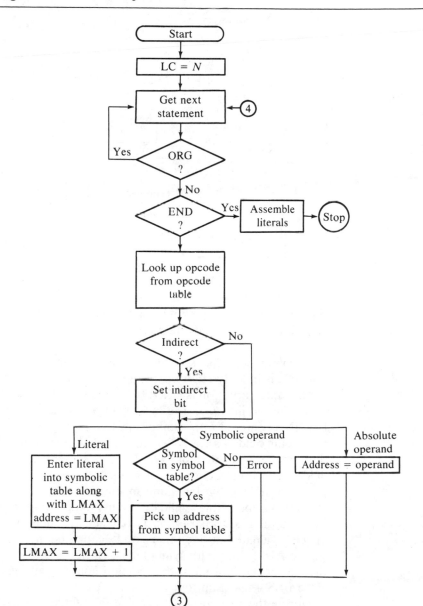

(continued)

Figure 4.6 (Continued)

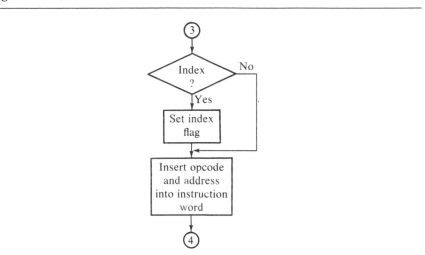

The symbol table created by the assembler consists of two entries for each symbolic name: the symbol itself and the address in which the symbol will be located. We will illustrate the assembly process in Example 4.5.

Example 4.5   Consider the program shown in Figure 4.7(a). The symbol table is initially empty. Location counter starts at the default value of 0. The first instruction is ORG. Its operand field is evaluated and the value (0) is entered into LC. The label field of the next instruction is BEGIN. BEGIN is entered into symbol table and assigned the address of 0. The mnemonic field has LDX, which is a valid mnemonic. Since this instruction takes up one memory word, LC is incremented by 1. The operand field of LDX instruction is not evaluated during the first pass. This process of scanning the label and mnemonic fields, entering labels (if any) into the symbol table, validating mnemonic, and incrementing LC continues until END instruction is reached. Pseudo-instructions are completely evaluated during this pass. Location counter values are shown in Figure 4.7(a) along with symbol table entries at the end of pass 1 in (b). By the end of the first pass, the location counter will have advanced to E, since BSS 4 takes up four locations (A through D).

During the second pass, machine instructions are generated using the source program and the symbol table. The operand fields are evaluated during this pass and instruction format fields are appropriately filled for each instruction. Starting with $LC = 0$, the label field of instruction at 0 is ignored and the opcode (1100) is substituted for the mnemonic LDX. Since this is a one-address instruction, the operand field is evaluated.

Figure 4.7 Assembly process

LC		Instruction	
		ORG	0
0	BEGIN	LDX	C,1
1		LDX	= 0,2
2	LOOP	LDA	D,2
3		ADD	SUM
4		STA	SUM
5		TIX	TEMP,2
6	TEMP	LDX	LOOP,1
7		HLT	
8	SUM	BSC	0
9	C	BSC	4
A	D	BSS	4
		END	BEGIN

(a) Program

Symbol	Address (H)
BEGIN	0
LOOP	2
TEMP	6
SUM	8
C	9
D	A

LMAX = EH

(b) Symbol table after pass 1

LC	Index	Indirect	Opcode	Address	Object code (H)
0	01	0	1100	0 0000 1001	5809
1	10	0	1100	0 0000 1110	980E
2	10	0	0000	0 0000 1010	800A
3	00	0	0010	0 0000 1000	0408
4	00	0	0001	0 0000 1000	0208
5	10	0	1110	0 0000 0110	9C06
6	01	0	1111	0 0000 0010	5E02
7	—	—	0100	— — —	0800[1]
8	00	0	0000	0 0000 0000	0000
9	00	0	0000	0 0000 0100	0004
A					dddd
B			4 Locations		dddd
C					dddd
D					dddd
E	00	0	0000	0 0000 0000	0000

A, B, C, D: } Undefined

(c) Object code

[1] Assume 0 for undefined bits.

Symbol	Address (H)
BEGIN	0
LOOP	2
TEMP	6
SUM	8
C	9
D	A
= 0	E

LMAX = EH

(d) Symbol table after pass 2

There is no "*" next to the mnemonic and hence the indirect flag is set to 0. The absolute address of X is obtained from the symbol table and entered into the address field of the instruction and the index flag is set to 01. This process continues for each instruction until END is reached. The object code is shown in Figure 4.7(c) in binary and hexadecimal formats.

The symbol table shown in (d) has one more entry corresponding to the literal = 0. Note that the instruction LDX = 0,2 has been assembled as LDX EH, 2, with the location EH containing a 0. Contents of the words reserved in response to BSS are not defined and unused bits of HLT instruction words are assumed to be 0s.

4.3 Program Loading

The object code must be loaded into the machine memory before it can be executed. ASC console can be used to load programs and data into the memory. Loading through the console is tedious and time consuming, however, especially when programs are large. In such cases, a small program that reads the object code statements from the input device and stores them in appropriate memory locations is first written, assembled, and loaded (using the console) into machine memory. This loader program is then used to load the object code or data into the memory. Table 4.2 shows a loader program for ASC. Additional details on loading programs are provided in Section 4.6 of this chapter.

4.4 Program Execution

Once the object code is loaded into the memory, it can be executed by initializing the program counter to the starting address and activating the START switch on the console. Instructions are then fetched from the

Table 4.2 A loader for ASC

Label	Mnemonic	Operand	Comment
	ORG	200H	
START	RWD		.Read starting address
	STA	SAVE	
	LDX	SAVE,2	.Starting address in index register 2
	RWD		.Input number of statements N
	TCA		.$-N$
	STA	SAVE	.SAVE contains $-N$
	LDX	SAVE,1	.Load $(-N)$ into index register 1
LOOP	RWD		.Input an object code statement
	STA	0,2	.Store the object code statement
LL	TIX	LL,2	.Increment index register 2
	TDX	LOOP,1	.Decrement N by 1 and loop
	HLT		
SAVE	BSS	1	
	END	START	

memory and executed in sequence until an HLT instruction is reached or an error condition occurs. The execution of an instruction consists of two phases:

1. Instruction fetch.
2. Instruction execute.

Each of these two phases is referred to as a "cycle," since memory read-write cycles are used during fetch and execute operations.

4.4.1 Instruction Fetch Cycle

During instruction fetch, the instruction word is transferred from the memory into the *instruction register* (*IR*). To accomplish this, the contents of the program counter are first transferred into MAR, a memory read operation is performed to transfer the instruction into MBR, and the instruction is then transferred to IR. While memory is being read, the control unit uses its internal logic to add 1 to the contents of the program counter so that the program counter points to the memory word following the one from which the current instruction is fetched. This sequence of operations constitutes the fetch cycle and is the same for all instructions.

4.4.2 Instruction Execution Cycle

Once the instruction is in the instruction register (IR), the opcode is decoded and a sequence of operations is brought about to retrieve the operands (if needed) from the memory and to perform the processing called for by the opcode. This is the execution cycle and is unique for each instruction in the instruction set. For example, for LDA instruction the effective address is first calculated, then the contents of the memory word at the effective address are read and transferred into ACC. At the end of an execute cycle, the machine returns to a fetch mode. The fetch and execute cycles together form an *instruction cycle*.

ASC uses one more cycle to compute the effective address if an indirect addressing is used, since such computation involves reading an address from the memory. This cycle is termed *defer cycle*. Thus, an ASC instruction cycle consists of three machine cycles at the maximum, two machine cycles if no indirect addressing is used, and one machine cycle for instructions that do not involve a memory address, and the operations called for by the instruction can typically be accommodated completely in the fetch cycle. Further details on instruction cycles are provided in Chapter 5.

Figure 4.8 gives a sample program along with the object code and shows contents of ASC registers during the execution of the program (i.e., trace of the program).

Figure 4.8 Execution process of sample program

PC	Label	Mnemonic[1]	Operand
0		ORG	16
0010	*BEG*	LDA*	*X*
0011	*L*1	STA	*X* − 1
0012		LDX	*X*,3
0013		TIX	*L*1,3
0014		HLT	
0015	*X*	BSC	5
0016	*Z*	BSS	7
	P	EQU	*Z* − 1
001D		END	*BEG*

(a) Source

```
00 1 0000 0 0001 0101   (2015H)
00 0 0001 0 0001 0100   (0214H)
11 0 1100 1 0001 0101   (D815H)
11 0 1110 0 0001 0001   (DC11H)
00 0 0100 0 0000 0000   (0800H)
00 0 0000 0 0000 0101   (0005H)
RESERVE 7 MEM LOCATION
```

(b) Object code

Symbol	Location[2]
BEG	0010
*L*1	0011
X	0015
Z	0016
P	0015

(c) Symbol table

Cycle	Operations	Comments
INITIALIZE	$PC \leftarrow 0010H.$	
FETCH	$MAR \leftarrow 0010H.$	
	Read memory.	
	$MBR \leftarrow$ *Instruction LDA* X.*	
	$IR \leftarrow MBR.$	Instruction in IR
	$PC \leftarrow 0011H.$	(end of Fetch)
	$MAR \leftarrow X.$	needs a defer cycle
DEFER	Read memory.	
	$MBR \leftarrow M[X].$	
	$MAR \leftarrow MBR.$	Effective address in MAR
EXECUTE	Read memory.	
	$MBR \leftarrow M[M[X]].$	
	$ACC \leftarrow MBR.$	Execution complete

(d) Execution trace

[1] An asterisk as fourth character indicates indirect addressing.
[2] Assume location 5 contains an HLT instruction.

Figure 4.8 (Continued)

Cycle	Operations	Comments
FETCH	$MAR \leftarrow PC$. $MBR \leftarrow$ Instruction STA $X\text{-}1$. $IR \leftarrow MBR$. $PC \leftarrow 0012H$.	Fetch next instruction Instruction in IR
EXECUTE	$MAR \leftarrow X\text{-}1$. $MBR \leftarrow ACC$. Write memory.	 Execution complete
FETCH	$MAR \leftarrow PC$. Read memory. $MBR \leftarrow$ Instruction LDX $X,3$. $IR \leftarrow MBR$. $PC \leftarrow 0013H$.	 Instruction in IR
EXECUTE	$MAR \leftarrow X$. Read memory. $MBR \leftarrow M[X]$. Index register 3 $\leftarrow MBR$.	 Execution complete
FETCH	$MAR \leftarrow PC$. Read memory. $MBR \leftarrow$ Instruction IIX $L1,3$. $IR \leftarrow MBR$. $PC \leftarrow 0014H$.	 Instruction in IR
EXECUTE	Index register 3 $\leftarrow$ Index register 3 + 1. Since (index register 3) $\neq$ 0: No operation.	 Execution complete
FETCH	$MAR \leftarrow PC$. Read memory. $MBR \leftarrow$ Instruction HLT. $IR \leftarrow MBR$. $PC \leftarrow 0015H$.	 Instruction in IR
EXECUTE	Machine halts.	Execution complete

(d) Execution trace (continued)

4.5 Relocation of Programs

The ORG pseudo-instruction provides a starting address for the program during assembly. Prior to execution, the program may not be loaded into the memory starting at this address because

1. The memory locations may not be free if another program has been loaded there.

2. A program and its subprograms could be assembled separately, loaded into different memory locations (relocated), and linked together.

A relocation of the program is needed under the above conditions. The relocation of the program results in the addition of a relocation factor to each symbolic address. The relocation factor is the number of locations the program has been moved during loading from the starting address assumed during its assembly. The absolute addresses and some addresses such as the difference of two symbolic addresses remain unchanged even after relocation. Figure 4.9 shows the object code of Figure 4.7 relocated to location 20H. The relocation factor (RF) is $20H - 0H = 20H$.

In addition to providing the object code, the assembler also provides the relocation information. This relocation information is useful when the object code is loaded into the memory just before execution. Basically, the assembler provides a flag bit for each instruction to specify whether its address is *relocatable* (RF is to be added) or *absolute* (no relocation required). Typical address expressions that need the addition of RF when programs are relocated are:

$$X$$
$$X - 1$$
$$X + 3$$
$$X + 3, 2 \quad (X \text{ is a symbolic address.})$$

Figure 4.9 Relocated program

Location	Object code
20	5829
21	982F
22	802A
23	0428
24	0228
25	9C26
26	5E22
27	0800
28	0000
29	0004
2A	*dddd*
2B	*dddd*
2C	*dddd*
2D	*dddd*
2E	0000

Note: The starting address is 20H; the relocation factor is 20H.

The following address expressions evaluate to absolute addresses and hence remain unaltered during relocation:

$$25$$
$$25H$$
$$25H, 1$$
$$X - Y \qquad \text{Why?} \quad (X \text{ and } Y \text{ are symbolic addresses.})$$

4.6 Program Linking

In a very simple computer system, once the source programs are translated, the object code would be directly loaded into the memory for execution and program relocation may or may not be needed depending upon the flexibility of the system. In such simple systems, the loading function is a part of the assembler or compiler.

In practice, a program uses several subprograms. Some of these subprograms (e.g., user-written subprograms) may be translated along with the main program and some may be already in the object code format from previous translations (e.g., a system or user library routine). In general, it is desirable to have the capability to translate each subprogram individually. To accommodate such a flexible program development environment, mechanisms to translate and load individual subprograms (or parts of the same program) and link them together just before the execution are needed.

Figure 4.10 shows an example of linking three subroutines to a main program. When a subprogram is CALLed, the execution is transferred to the beginning of the subprogram (equivalent to a jump). When a RETURN instruction in the subprogram is executed, the execution control is returned to the main program. To facilitate this return, the processor saves the PC value (return address) during the CALL. We will assume for our purposes that CALL and RETURN are new instructions added to the ASC instruction set. Assume that each program (main program and subprogram) is assembled separately. Note from Figure 4.10(a) the inclusion of EXTERNAL statements to identify names of subprograms that are assembled separately (this information may be implied by CALL, if the assembler is designed to treat references to names that are not defined within a program as EXTERNAL calls). Each call to an external routine is changed by the assembler to a CALL* to a location at the beginning of the routine as shown in Figure 4.10(b). One such location is reserved for each CALL. For example, CALL SUB1 is changed to CALL* 100. Note that during this assembly, the memory availability or loading location

Figure 4.10 Linking subroutines to main program

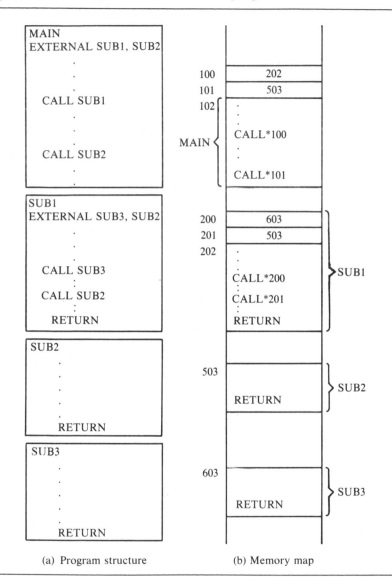

(a) Program structure   (b) Memory map

address information is not needed. We could have assumed that the main program starts at 0 as well. Then, CALL SUB1 would change to CALL*0, with 0 and 1 being the reserved locations for external calls. Once all routines are assembled and relocated to available slots in the memory, a *linker* program fills in the *pointer* information into each reserved location at the beginning of each program. (Example: 202 and 503 are entered into locations 100 and 101 by the linker.) The memory map shown in Figure 4.10(b) is the completely linked program, ready to be executed.

Note that the loader, linker, assembler, and compilers are also programs and must be translated, linked, and loaded before we can use them to process other source programs. The loader program shown in Table 4.2 can be used to load other programs. This program is usually called *initial program loader* (IPL). Loading of the complete loader by IPL is usually called *bootstrap loading*. IPL is a required routine and is either stored in a read-only memory (ROM) or loaded into machine memory through console switches.

Assembler is usually a large assembly language program. It has to be assembled first, to execute it on other source programs. This translation is either done manually or in a bootstrap mode, just as for the loader.

4.7 Compilers

Assembler, linker, and loader constitute the minimum software needed to support hardware components in their efficient operation. Several high-level languages including FORTRAN, COBOL, Pascal, PL/1, and BASIC are now used in programming digital computers. It is preferable to program in a high-level language because of the improved readability and portability as well as decreased machine dependence of such programs over assembly language programs. High-level language programming necessitates one compiler for each programming language used.

A user of such a general computer system would like to have his or her programs run with as little manual "housekeeping" as possible. The operating system programs help in the housekeeping aspects of the computer system. A set of control statements are provided to the user. This control language is used to direct the operating system to call the proper compiler for the language used, direct the object code to the proper device, call the linker and loader and supply appropriate memory availability information to system programs, and direct results of execution to the appropriate output devices. In addition to these functions, the operating system monitors status of devices, processor, and the memory loads; keeps the accounting information on users and their programs; and manages the distribution of shared facilities such as peripherals, processors, and memory for efficient throughput of the system.

4.8 Summary

This chapter is a programmer's introduction to ASC organization. Various components of ASC were assumed to be existent and no justification was given as to why a component was needed. Chapter 5 answers some questions and provides the detailed design of ASC. Descriptions of loaders, linkers, and translators provided here is brief although complete. Selected reference works listed at the end of this chapter deal with these topics in more detail.

References

Calingaert, P. *Assemblers, Compilers, and Program Translation*. Rockville, Md.: Computer Science Press, 1979.

Deitel, H. M. *An Introduction to Operating Systems*. Reading, Mass.: Addison-Wesley, 1984.

Donovan, J. J. *Systems Programming*. New York, N.Y.: McGraw-Hill, 1972.

Gear, C. W. *Computer Organization and Programming*. New York, N.Y.: McGraw-Hill, 1974.

Sloan, M. E. *Computer Hardware and Organization*. 2d ed. Chicago, Ill.: Science Research Associates, 1983.

Stone, H. S. *Introduction to Computer Architecture*. Chicago, Ill.: Science Research Associates, 1980.

Problems

4.1 Write ASC assembly language programs for the following. Start programs at location 0H, using ORG 0 Statement.

   a. Subtract an integer stored at memory location A from that at B and store the result at C.

   b. Read several cards, each containing an integer, and store the sum of positive integers only at location POS in memory. A "0" on the card should terminate the reading process.

   c. Location 50H contains an address pointing to the first entry in a table of integers. The table is also in the memory and the first entry is the number of entries in the table, excluding itself. Store the maximum and minimum valued integers at memory locations MAX and MIN, respectively.

   d. SORT the entries in a table of n entries in increasing order of *magnitude*.

   e. Multiply integers stored at memory locations A and B and store the result in C. Assume the product is small enough and can be represented in 16 bits. Note that multiplication is the repeated addition of multiplicand to itself multiplier times.

       f. Compute the absolute value of each of the 50 integers located at the memory block starting at *A* and store them at the block starting at *B*.

4.2   a. Assemble each program in Problem 4.1 and list the object code in binary and hexadecimal forms.

       b. Relocate each program to location 90H.

4.3   Extend the current ASC instruction set to include subroutine CALL and RETURN. List the sequence of register transfers needed to accomplish CALL and RETURN. Assume that only one subroutine is called at a time; i.e., a subroutine can not call another subroutine.

4.4   Usually several parameters are passed into the subroutine and returned to the main program after execution of the subroutine is completed. Discuss various implementations possible to pass two parameters into a subroutine in ASC.

4.5   What restrictions are to be imposed on the assembly language if a single-pass assembler is needed?

4.6   Numbers larger than $(2^{15} - 1)$ are required for certain applications. Two ASC words can be used to store each such number. What changes to the ASC instruction set are needed to enable addition of numbers that are each stored in two consecutive memory words?

4.7   SHR instruction must be enhanced to allow multiple shifts. The address field can be used to represent the shift count; for example,

$$\text{SHR} \quad 5$$

implies a shift right 5 bits. Discuss the assembler modifications needed to accommodate multiple-shift SHR. The hardware is capable of performing only one shift at a time.

4.8   Calculate the effective address for each of the following instructions. (Remember: an "*" as the fourth symbol denotes indirect addressing.)

$$
\begin{array}{lll}
\text{STA} & Z & \\
\text{STA} & Z,3 & \\
\text{STA*} & Z & \\
\text{STA*} & Z,3 & \text{(Pre-index)} \\
\text{STA*} & Z,3 & \text{(Post-index)}
\end{array}
$$

Assume index register 3 contains 5; *Z* is memory location 10H and is the first location of a memory block containing 25, 7, 4, 86, 46, and 77.

4.9   Assume that the two-address instruction

$$\text{MOVE} \quad \text{MEM1, MEM2}$$

that moves the contents of memory location MEM1 to memory location MEM2 is available in ASC. Compare the data transfers needed to accomplish this instruction to those required for performing the MOVE using LDA and STA instructions.

Chapter 5

Design of a Simple Computer

The organization of a simple computer (ASC) provided in Chapter 4 is the programmer's view of the machine. We will illustrate the complete hardware design of ASC in this chapter. Assume that the design follows the sequence of eight steps listed here.

1. Selection of an instruction set.
2. Word size selection.
3. Selection of instruction and data formats.
4. Register set and memory design.
5. Data and instruction flowpath design.
6. Arithmetic and logic unit design.
7. Input/output mechanism design.
8. Generation of control signals and design of control unit.

In practice, design of a digital computer is an iterative process. A decision made early in the design process may have to be altered to suit some parameter at a later step. For example, instruction and data formats may have to be changed to accommodate a better data or instruction flowpath design.

Some architectural issues of concern at each of the above steps are identified in this chapter. Chapters 6 and 7 discuss these issues further with reference to architectures of commercially available machines. In general, a computer architect selects an architecture for the machine based on cost and performance tradeoffs and a computer designer implements the architecture using the hardware and software components available. The complete process of the development of a computer system thus can also be viewed as consisting of two phases, design and implementation. Once the architect derives an architecture (design phase), each subsystem in the architecture can be implemented in several ways depending on the available technology and requirements. We will not distinguish between these two phases in this chapter. We restrict this chapter to the design of hardware components of ASC and use memory elements, registers, flip-flops, and logic gates as components in the design.

5.1 Instruction Set

The first step in designing a computer is the selection of a satisfactory set of instructions. This selection is influenced by the projected application of the computer. For a business-applications-oriented machine, operations on data represented in decimal (BCD) form are a requirement. Some scientific applications require operations on arrays of floating-point numbers as primitive operations. If the computer is to be a general-purpose machine, the set of instructions must be capable of performing the basic arithmetic and logic operations efficiently. In any case, the requirements for the instruction set will center around the following basic functions to be performed by the machine:

1. Data movement: Memory location to memory location, register to register, register to memory, and memory to register.
2. Arithmetic: Add, subtract, multiply, and divide.
3. Logic: Shift, circulate, AND, OR, and NOT.
4. Control: Conditional and unconditional branch, subroutine jump and return, and halt.
5. Other: E.g., no operation, stack processing.

A computer with a large instruction set provides optimum programming flexibility. The design of such a machine becomes complex, however, as its control unit and data paths are designed to accommodate the complete instruction set. When a large instruction set is available, efficient use of the instruction set is also complex and typically a subset of instructions is used more often than the others in an application. A smaller instruction set, on the other hand, makes the design of the computer less complex, but requires elaborate programming steps to compensate for the reduced set of instructions. Thus, the performance measure of an instruction set is not just the number of instructions in the set but the complete set of operations that the instruction set provides.

The speed of program execution depends on how fast each instruction is executed by the machine. Instructions that involve memory reference take longer to execute than those that involve only register reference because a register-to-register transfer is typically faster than a memory read or write operation. Thus, the majority of operations in a fast machine are usually register-to-register operations, necessitating a large number of registers.

The ASC instruction set was selected to provide the basic arithmetic capabilities of add and subtract (via TCA), multiply (via SHL), and divide (via SHR). Housekeeping instructions such as branch, input/output, and load and store were added to complete the set. The number of instructions was limited to 16 to keep the design details manageable.

5.2   Word Size

A word is the most often transferred or manipulated unit of data in the machine. The number of bits in a word is usually determined by the standard components available. Word sizes of a multiple of a byte (8, 16, or 32 bits per word) are common although machines of 36- and 60-bit words are available. The word size influences the selection of all register and memory word sizes. The data paths in a parallel machine are usually of the same size as its registers. If the machine is intended for a special application, data sizes in the application environment will also influence the word size of the machine. Selection of word size thus is one major factor in determining the complexity of the hardware. In general, the machine word must be large enough to accommodate the most often processed unit of data in the machine in order to maintain the throughput and small enough to minimize the hardware needed.

With recent advances in IC technology, it is now possible to implement larger word size machines on a single chip. Microprocessors with 16-bit word sizes are available and new 32-bit-word microprocessors have been designed. A 16-bit word size was chosen for ASC to make it representative of contemporary machines.

5.3   Instruction Format

Major components of instruction are the *operation code* (opcode) and the *address*. The number of bits in the opcode is determined by the number of instructions in the instruction set. With n bits in the opcode, 2^n instructions are possible. All the 2^n combinations may not be used if future expansion of the instruction set is envisioned. Note that the address field of an instruction is not used in a zero-address instruction. This field may be used for the expansion of the instruction set without increasing the number of bits in the opcode.

The *assignment* of opcodes to instructions (operations) can be arbitrary. In practice, an opcode is composed of subfields where each subfield represents a class of operations. For example, five of the eight combinations of a 3-bit subfield can be assigned to reflect the five basic classes of operations listed in section 5.1. The remaining bits in the opcode further identify the operations in each class of operations. This type of opcode assignment reduces the complexity of the decoding hardware.

The size of the address field is determined by the address range required. Address modifier fields are determined by the addressing modes allowed in the instruction set.

A 4-bit opcode is needed to represent the 16 instructions in the ASC instruction set. The instruction set was divided into two classes: instructions that required an indexed addressing mode, which were assigned opcodes ranging from 0000 through 0111 (HLT is an exception); and instructions not requiring an indexed address computation, which were assigned opcodes 1000 through 1111. Thus, the most significant bit (MSB) of the opcode indicates the class to which the instruction belongs. Two bits were used to address the three index registers and 1 bit was used for indirect addressing. Thus, 7 bits in all are needed for opcode and address modifiers. Nine bits remain for the address field. This gives a direct addressing range of $2^9 = 512$ words — the words 0 to 511 of the memory. Any memory location beyond this range must be addressed using either the indexed or indirect mode. If both modes are used, preindexing is assumed for the design.

The instruction format design assumes that each instruction is of the same size. Alternatively, since only 4 bits are needed to represent four zero-address instructions, it would have been possible to represent four zero-address instructions per memory word; also, a one-address instruction could have been made two words long, thus obtaining 25 bits for direct addressing. Instructions of variable length are used in actual machines. To retain simplicity of design, a uniform instruction length (of one word) was used for ASC.

5.4 Memory and Registers

Once the memory word size is selected, the memory buffer register (MBR) size is determined (16 bits for ASC). The size of the memory address register (MAR) is equal to the maximum number of bits in the address. In ASC, MAR is 16 bits long, since indirect and indexed addressing modes generate 16-bit addresses. The maximum memory size for ASC is thus 2^{16} or 64K (K = 1024 = 2^{10}) words and the addresses range from 0 to ($2^{16} - 1$). We will use four hexadecimal digits to represent an address. The address range thus is 0000H to FFFFH.

The program counter (PC) was chosen to be 16 bits long to allow the flexibility of the program's being located anywhere in the 64K address range. Three index registers were assumed. The number of index registers varies from one to several in actual machines. Since the content of an index register is always added to that of the address field of an instruction, it is sufficient to have 15 bits in the index register to generate a 16-bit address (note that the sum of two n-bit numbers in general is $n + 1$ bits long). To retain the simplicity (uniformity) of the design, ASC index registers were assumed to be 16 bits long. A 16-bit instruction register (IR) is also required. The instruction set implies an accumulator (ACC) that must also be 16 bits long since the most often processed unit of data is 16 bits long.

Registers of ASC are specialized in their function. A current trend in computer design is to include several general-purpose registers that can be used as accumulators, index registers, stack pointers, and so on, as required. Although such register organization increases the complexity of the design, it provides high programming flexibility.

5.5   Data and Instruction Flow

A detailed analysis of the flow of instructions and data during instruction *fetch* and *execution* cycles for each instruction is required to determine the data flowpaths needed between registers and memory. Such an analysis for ASC follows.

5.5.1   Fetch Phase

Assuming that the PC is loaded with the address of the first instruction in the program, the following set of register transfers and manipulations is needed during the fetch phase of each instruction:

$MAR \leftarrow PC$.	
READ memory.	Instruction is transferred to MBR; i.e., $MBR \leftarrow M[MAR]$.
$PC \leftarrow PC + 1$.	Increment PC by 1.
$IR \leftarrow MBR$.	Transfer instruction to IR.

5.5.2   Address Calculations

For one-address instructions the following address computation capabilities are needed:

Direct:	$MAR \leftarrow IR_{7-15}$.	$MAR \leftarrow IR(ADRS)$
Indexed:	$MAR \leftarrow IR_{7-15} + \text{INDEX}$.	(INDEX refers to the index register selected by the index flag.)
Indirect:	$MAR \leftarrow IR_{7-15}$. READ Memory. $MAR \leftarrow MBR$.	Get the new address. Address to MAR.
Preindexed-indirect:	$MAR \leftarrow IR_{7-15} + \text{INDEX}$. READ Memory. $MAR \leftarrow MBR$.	 Get the new address.

In the above, *effective address* is assumed to be in MAR at the end of address calculation, just before the execution of the instruction begins. Using the concatenation operator "¢," the transfer $MAR \leftarrow IR_{7-15}$ should be further refined as

$$MAR \leftarrow 0000000 \ ¢ \ IR_{7-15},$$

meaning that the most significant 7 bits of MAR receive 0s. The concatenation of 0s to the address field of IR as above is assumed whenever the contents of the IR address field are transferred to a 16-bit destination or the IR address field is added to an index register. The memory operations are designated as

READ memory $MBR \leftarrow M[MAR]$.   and

WRITE memory $M[MAR] \leftarrow MBR$.

Assuming that all arithmetic is performed by one arithmetic unit, the instruction and address flowpaths required for fetch cycle and address computation in ASC are as shown in Figure 5.1. (For a list of mnemonic codes, see Table 4.1, page 155.)

5.5.3 Instruction Execution

The detailed data flow during the execution of each instruction is determined by the analysis shown in Table 5.1.

5.6 Bus Structure

The data and address transfers shown in Figure 5.1(b) can be brought about either by a point-to-point interconnection of registers or by a bus structure connecting all the registers in ASC. Bus structures are com-

Figure 5.1 Register transfer paths of a simple computer (ASC)

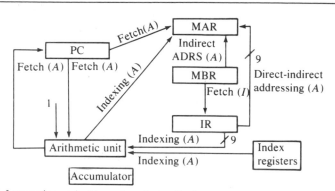

(a) Instruction and address flow during fetch cycle and address computation

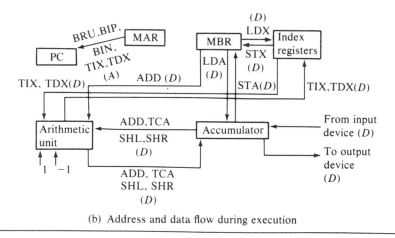

(b) Address and data flow during execution

Note: *A* indicates address, *I* indicates instruction, and *D* indicates data.
All paths are 16 bits wide unless indicated otherwise.
Input 1 into the arithmetic unit is a constant input required to increment PC.
Constant inputs are required for incrementing and decrementing PC and index registers.
Refer to Table 4.1, ASC instruction set.

monly used because a point-to-point interconnection becomes complex as the number of registers to be connected increases.

The most common bus structures are *single bus* and *multibus*. In a single-bus structure, all data and address flow is through one bus. A multibus structure typically consists of several buses, each dedicated to certain transfers; for example, one bus could be a data bus and the other could be an address bus. Multibus structures provide the advantage of tailoring each bus to the set of transfers it is dedicated to, while single-bus structures have the advantage of uniformity of design. Other characteris-

Table 5.1 Analysis of data flow during execution

Mnemonic	Operations	Comments
LDA	READ memory.	Data into MBR. (The effective address of the operand is in MAR.)
	$ACC \leftarrow MBR$.	
STA	$MBR \leftarrow ACC$. WRITE memory.	
ADD	READ memory. $ACC \leftarrow ACC + MBR$.	Data into MBR.
TCA	$ACC \leftarrow \overline{ACC}$.	Two-step computation of the 2s complement.
	$ACC \leftarrow ACC + 1$.	
HLT	STOP.	
BRU	$PC \leftarrow MAR$.	Address goes to PC.
BIP	IF $ACC_0 = 0$ and $ACC_{1-15} \neq 0$ THEN $\quad PC \leftarrow MAR$.	
BIN	IF $ACC_0 \neq 0$ THEN $PC \leftarrow MAR$.	
RWD	$ACC \leftarrow$ Input.	Input device data buffer contents to ACC.
WWD	Output $\leftarrow ACC$.	ACC to output device.
SHL	$ACC \leftarrow ACC_{1-15} \, \xi \, 0$.	Zero fill.
SHR	$ACC_{1-15} \leftarrow ACC_{0-14}$.	ACC_0 not altered.
LDX	READ memory. INDEX $\leftarrow MBR$.	
STX	$MBR \leftarrow$ INDEX. WRITE memory.	
TIX	INDEX $\leftarrow$ INDEX $+ 1$. IF INDEX $= 0$ THEN $PC \leftarrow MAR$.	
TDX	INDEX $\leftarrow$ INDEX $- 1$. IF INDEX $\neq 0$ THEN $PC \leftarrow MAR$.	

Note: The data paths required for the operations given in Table 5.1 are shown in Figure 5.1. All paths are 16 bits wide unless indicated otherwise. Also note that indexing is not allowed in index-register reference instructions LDX, STX, TIX, and TDX.

tics to be considered in evaluating bus structures are the amount of hardware required and the data transfer rates possible.

Figure 5.2 shows a bus structure for ASC. The bus structure is realized by recognizing that two operands are required for arithmetic operations using the arithmetic unit of ASC. Each operand will be on a bus (BUS1 and BUS2) feeding the arithmetic unit. The output of the arithmetic unit will be on another bus (BUS3). For transfers that do not involve any arithmetic operation, two direct paths are assumed through the arithmetic unit. These paths either transfer BUS1 to BUS3 or transfer BUS2 to BUS3. The bus that is not involved in these direct transfers contains all 0s

Figure 5.2 ASC bus structure

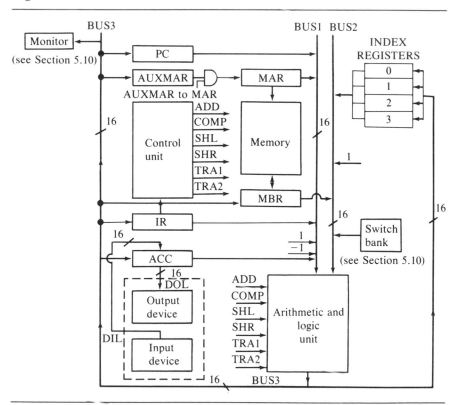

Note: AUXMAR is used to prevent MAR being changed during a memory restore operation (see Section 5.9).

Each bit of PC and ACC is a master-slave flip-flop.

Index register 0 always contains a 0 (see Section 5.9).

1 and −1 represent constant registers connected to the respective bus; they are 16-bit constants represented in 2s complement form.

during these transfers. The contents of each bus during other typical operations are listed below:

Operation	BUS1	BUS2	BUS3
Increment *PC*	*PC*	1 (constant)	*PC* + 1
Indexing	$0000000 \; ¢ \; IR_{7-15}$	INDEX	Indexed address
ADD	*ACC*	*MBR*	*ACC* + *MBR*

To perform the increment PC operation shown above, *PC* and 1 must be gated *onto* BUS1 and BUS2, respectively, an ADD command must be sent to ALU, and the output of the ALU on BUS3 must be gated *into PC*. The control signals required to perform this operation must all be generated simultaneously and should last long enough to complete the operation, as shown in Figure 5.3. When PC is on BUS1, all other signals connected to BUS1 must be 0, since a bus is formed by ORing all the signals that are connected to it and only one of those signals must be active at any time.

Input and output transfers are performed on two separate 16-bit paths: data input lines (DIL) and data output lines (DOL) connected to and from the accumulator. This input/output scheme was selected for simplicity. Alternatively, DIL and DOL could have been connected to one of the three buses.

Figure 5.3 Control signals required to increment the program counter (PC)

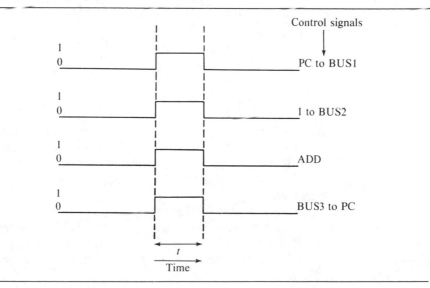

A single bus structure is possible for ASC. In this structure, either one of the operands of the two operand operations or the result must be stored in a buffer register before it can be transmitted to the destination register. Thus, there will be some additional transfers in the single-bus structure and some operations will take longer to complete, thereby making the structure slower than the multibus structure.

Transfer of data, instructions, and addresses on the bus structure is controlled by a set of control signals generated by the control unit of the machine. Detailed design of the control unit is illustrated in Section 5.8.

5.7   Arithmetic and Logic Unit

The arithmetic and logic unit (ALU) of ASC is the hardware which performs all arithmetic and logical operations. The instruction set implies that the ALU of ASC must perform addition of two numbers, compute the 2s complement of a number, and shift the contents of the accumulator either right or left by one bit. Additionally, the ASC ALU must directly transfer either of its inputs to its output to support data transfer operations such as $IR \leftarrow MBR$ and $MAR \leftarrow IR$.

We will assume that the control unit of the machine provides the appropriate control signals to enable the ALU to perform one of these operations. Since BUS1 and BUS2 are the inputs and BUS3 is the output of ALU, the following operations must be performed by the ALU:

$$
\begin{aligned}
&\text{ADD:} && \text{BUS3} \leftarrow \underline{\text{BUS1}} + \text{BUS2.} \\
&\text{COMP:} && \text{BUS3} \leftarrow \overline{\text{BUS1}}. \\
&\text{SHR:} && \text{BUS3} \leftarrow \text{BUS1}_0 \text{ c } \text{BUS1}_{0-14}. \\
&\text{SHL:} && \text{BUS3} \leftarrow \text{BUS1}_{1-15} \text{ c } 0. \\
&\text{TRA1:} && \text{BUS3} \leftarrow \text{BUS1.} \\
&\text{TRA2:} && \text{BUS3} \leftarrow \text{BUS2.}
\end{aligned}
$$

ADD, COMP, SHR, SHL, TRA1, and TRA2 are the control signals generated by the control unit, and bit positions of the buses are numbered 0 through 15, left to right. Each of the control signals activates a particular operation in ALU. Only one of these control signals may be active at any time. Figure 5.4 shows a typical bit of ALU and its connections to the bits of BUS1, BUS2, and BUS3. A functional description follows of the ALU corresponding to the above control signals.

ADD: The addition circuitry consists of fifteen full adders and one half-adder for the least significant bit (bit 15). The sum output of each adder is gated through an AND gate with the ADD control signal. The carry output of each adder is input to the carry-in of the adder for the next most

Figure 5.4 Logic diagram of ASC ALU

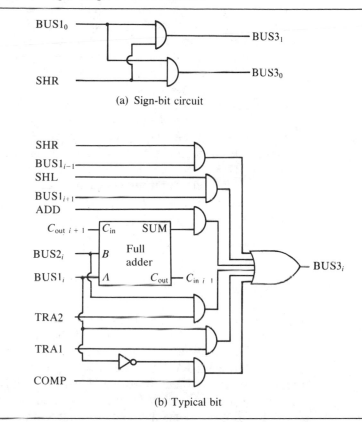

(a) Sign-bit circuit

(b) Typical bit

Note: During SHL, all lines connected to $BUS3_{15}$ are 0, and hence the LSB is automatically zero filled; no special circuitry is needed.

significant bit. The half-adder for bit 15 has no carry-in and the carry output for bit 0 is not used. Each adder has an input from both of the input buses and addition is performed on operands from the accumulator and the memory, with the result being stored in the accumulator.

COMP: The complement circuitry consists of sixteen NOT gates, one for each bit on BUS1. Thus, the circuitry produces the 1s complement of a number. The output of each NOT gate is gated through an AND gate with the COMP control signal. The operand for complement is the contents of the accumulator and the result is stored in the accumulator. TCA (2s complement accumulator) command is accomplished by taking the 1s complement of an operand first and then adding 1 to the result.

SHR: For shifting a bit pattern right, each bit of BUS1 is routed to the next least significant bit of BUS3. This transfer is gated by SHR control signal. The least significant bit of BUS1 ($BUS1_{15}$) is lost in the shifting process, while the most significant bit of BUS1 ($BUS1_0$) is routed to both the most significant bit ($BUS3_0$) and the next least significant bit ($BUS3_1$) of BUS3. Thus, the left-most bit of the output is "sign" filled.

SHL: For shifting a bit pattern left, each bit of BUS1 is routed to the next most significant bit of BUS3. SHL control signal is used to gate this transfer. The most significant bit on BUS1 ($BUS1_0$) is lost in the shifting process, while the least significant bit of BUS3 ($BUS3_{15}$) is zero filled.

TRA1: This operation transfers each bit from BUS1 to the corresponding bit on BUS3, each bit gated by TRA1 signal.

TRA2: This operation transfers each bit of BUS2 to the corresponding bit of BUS3, each bit gated by TRA2 control signal.

5.8   Input/Output

ASC is assumed to have one input device, *reader,* and one output device, *printer.* The input and output devices transfer a 16-bit data word into and from the accumulator. We will base our design on the simplest (and slowest) input/output (I/O) scheme, called the *programmed I/O.* Chapter 7 provides the details of other popular I/O schemes. In the programmed I/O scheme, during the RWD instruction, the processor (CPU) commands the reader to send a 16-bit data word and waits until it is ready in the reader's data buffer register (the reader indicates when the data is ready). Data are then moved into the accumulator through data input lines and the CPU proceeds to the next instruction. During the WWD, the CPU sends data on data output lines, commands the printer to accept data, and waits until the data are accepted by the printer. When the printer signals data acceptance, the CPU proceeds to the next instruction.

The CPU and the peripheral device have to communicate with each other (handshake) to perform the data transfer. A DATA flip-flop is used to facilitate the handshake. The RWD and WWD handshakes are described in detail:

RWD
1. CPU resets DATA flip-flop.
2. CPU sends a 1 on INPUT line indicating the READ DATA mode.
3. CPU waits for DATA flip-flop to be set by the reader.
4. Reader gathers data, gates it onto DIL, and sets the DATA flip-flop.
5. CPU gates DIL into the accumulator and resumes instruction execution.

WWD
1. CPU sets DATA flip-flop.
2. CPU sends a 1 on the OUTPUT line indicating the WRITE DATA mode and gates accumulator on DOL.
3. CPU waits for DATA flip-flop to be reset by the printer.
4. Printer, when ready, gates DOL into its buffer register and resets DATA flip-flop.
5. CPU resumes program execution.

In this I/O scheme, the CPU controls the complete I/O process and waits until the data are ready to be input or data are accepted by the printer. Since the I/O devices are much slower than CPU and the CPU idles waiting for I/O, this scheme is the slowest of the I/O schemes used in practice. But it is simple to design and generally has a low overhead (in terms of the design and implementation of CPU, peripheral handshake), especially when small amounts of data are to be transferred. Faster I/O schemes such as interrupt mode I/O, direct memory access, and channels are discussed in Chapter 7.

5.9 Control Unit

The control unit is the most complex block of computer hardware from a designer's point of view. Its function is to generate control signals needed by the other blocks of the machine in a predetermined sequence to bring about the sequence of actions called for by each instruction. The ASC instruction cycle in general consists of three phases: fetch, calculate effective address, and execute (see Section 5.5). Each of these phases further constitutes several microoperations, where each microoperation corresponds to a simple register transfer or a register transfer with an arithmetic or logic operation.

Inputs to the control unit are

1. The opcode, indirect bit, and index flag from IR.
2. Accumulator contents: $A_0 \neq 0$ indicates a negative accumulator; $A_{1-15} \neq 0$ indicates a nonzero accumulator. These conditions are used in BIP and BIN instructions.
3. Index register bits 0–15, to test for the zero or nonzero index register in TIX and TDX instructions.

In addition to these inputs, control signals generated by the control unit are functions of the contents of the following:

1. DATA flip-flop: Used to facilitate the handshake between the CPU and I/O devices.

2. RUN flip-flop: Set by the START switch on the console (see Section 5.9), indicates the RUN state of the machine. RUN flip-flop must be set for control signals to activate a microoperation. RUN flip-flop is reset by the HLT instruction.
3. STATE register: A 2-bit register used to distinguish between the three phases (states) of the instruction cycle. The control unit is thus viewed as a three-state sequential circuit.

Figure 5.5(a) shows a block diagram of the ASC control unit. A set of control signals needed to complement the contents of the accumulator are shown in (b). The accumulator is gated *onto* BUS1, COMP control signal of ALU is activated, and BUS3 is gated *into* the accumulator. The control signals required to bring about this transfer are

ACC to BUS1,

COMP, and

BUS3 to *ACC*.

Figure 5.5 Control unit

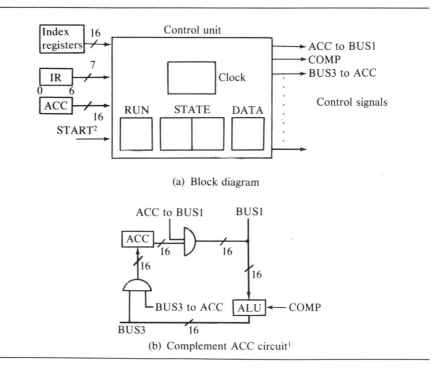

(a) Block diagram

(b) Complement ACC circuit[1]

Figure 5.5 (Continued)

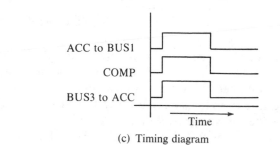

ACC to BUS1

COMP

BUS3 to ACC

Time

(c) Timing diagram

External inputs

OPCODE
ACC_{0-15}
IR_{0-15}
SWITCH BANK[2]
START SWITCH[2]
DATA FLIP-FLOP SET-RESET
MASTER CLEAR[2]

Internal inputs

RUN flip-flop
DATA flip-flop
STATE register
CLOCK (CP1, CP2, CP3, CP4)

State change signals

Fetch
Calculate effective address
Execute

Control signals (outputs of control unit)

To memory	To ALU	To I/O
READ	TRA1	INPUT
WRITE	TRA2	OUTPUT
	ADD	DIL to *ACC*
	COMP	*ACC* to DOL
	SHL	SET DATA flip-flop
	SHR	RESET DATA flip-flop

To the bus structure

ACC to BUS1[1]	INDEX to BUS2	BUS3 to *ACC*[1]
MAR to BUS1	*MBR* to BUS2	BUS3 to INDEX
IR_{7-15} to BUS1	1 to BUS2	BUS3 to *AUXMAR*
PC to BUS1	SWITCH BANK[2] to BUS2	BUS3 to *MBR*
2s COMP of 1 to BUS1		BUS3 to *PC*
AUXMAR to *MAR*		BUS3 to MONITOR[2]

(d) Signals

[1] *ACC* must be built out of master-slave flip-flops since its outputs are connected to its inputs through the ALU.
[2] Denotes a console facility.

Control signals must have a value of 1 to activate a microoperation. For example, the signal *ACC* to BUS1 activates the transfer

$$BUS1 \leftarrow ACC.$$

Similarly, when COMP is high, the ALU performs a complement microoperation. Figure 5.5(c) shows that all of the control signals must be maintained at 1 for a certain amount of time to allow for the signal propagation from the source through the ALU to the destination. This time unit is the *register transfer time,* determined by the delay time of the gates in the path of the signal, physical bus characteristics, and the setup time needed for the flip-flops forming the destination register. In practice, the design must allow for the slowest register transfer (along the longest path). This determines the speed with which the data can be transferred and hence the time required to complete an instruction cycle. Figure 5.5(d) lists the complete set of inputs, outputs, and internal signals of the ASC control unit.

5.9.1 Types of Control Units

Once the inputs and outputs of the control unit (CU) and their relationships are determined, one of the following schemes can be used to generate the control signals:

1. *Hardwired control unit* (*HCU*). The output signals (control signals) of the CU are generated by logic circuitry built of gates and flip-flops.
2. *Microprogrammed control unit* (*MCU*). The sequence of microoperations corresponding to each instruction are stored in a read-only memory called *control ROM* (CROM). The execution of this microinstruction sequence is controlled by a simpler hardwired control unit.

The MCU scheme is more flexible than the HCU scheme because in it the meaning of an instruction can be changed by changing the microinstruction sequence corresponding to that instruction, and the instruction set can be extended simply by including a new ROM containing the corresponding microoperation sequences. Hardware changes to the control unit thus are minimal in this implementation. In an HCU, any such change to the instruction set requires substantial changes to the hardwired logic. HCUs, however, are generally faster than MCUs and are used where the control unit must be fast. Most of the more recent machines have microprogrammed control units.

Among the machines that have an MCU, the degree to which the microprogram (the microinstruction sequence) can be changed by the user varies from machine to machine. Some do not allow the user to change the microprogram, some allow partial changes and additions, and some machines do not have an instruction set of their own and allow the user to microprogram the complete instruction set suitable for his application. This latter type of machine is called a *soft machine*. We will design an HCU for ASC in this section. An MCU design for ASC is provided in Section 5.11.

5.9.2 Hardwired Control Unit for ASC

A hardwired CU can either be synchronous or asynchronous. In a synchronous CU, each operation is controlled by a clock and the control-unit state can be easily determined knowing the state of the clock. In an asynchronous CU, completion of one operation triggers the next and hence no clock exists. Because of its nature, the design of an asynchronous CU is complex, but if it is designed properly it can be made faster than a synchronous CU. In a synchronous CU, the clock frequency must be such that the time between two clock pulses is sufficient to allow the completion of the slowest microoperation. This characteristic makes a synchronous CU relatively slow. We will design a synchronous CU for ASC.

5.9.3 Memory versus Processor Speed

The memory hardware, whether it is built using semiconductors or cores, is slower than the processor hardware, although this gap is narrowing with the advances in hardware technology. Some memory organizations to help reduce this speed gap are discussed in Chapter 6. When the memory is destructive readout type, the processor can not access memory until after the rewrite (restore) operation is complete. We will assume a core memory for ASC with a read time and restore time each equal to two times the register transfer time. The memory cycle time then equals four times the register transfer time.

5.9.4 Machine Cycles

In a synchronous CU, the time between two clock pulses is the register transfer time, as defined earlier. The interval between two clock pulses is usually called a *minor cycle*. A *major cycle* (or machine cycle) consists of several minor cycles. Both fixed- and variable-length major cycles have been used in practical machines. An instruction cycle typically consumes one or more major cycles.

To determine how long a machine cycle needs to be, we will examine the fetch, address calculation, and execute states in detail. The microoperations required during fetch state can be allocated to minor cycles:

Minor cycle	Microoperations	
T_1:	$MAR \leftarrow PC$, READ memory.	
T_2:	Wait.	Memory read time
T_3:	$IR \leftarrow MBR$, WRITE memory.	
T_4:	Wait.	Memory restore time

Once the READ memory signal is issued at T_1, the instruction to be fetched will be available at the end of T_2, because the memory read operation requires two minor cycles. Since ASC has a core memory, two more minor cycles (T_3 and T_4) are needed to restore the memory location just read. To ensure proper memory restoration, contents of MAR can not be altered during T_2 and those of MAR and MBR can not be altered during T_3 and T_4. The rest of the processor hardware (buses 1, 2, and 3) can be used during T_2 and T_4.

T_2 can be used to increment PC as required by a fetch cycle. Since T_4 is required, it can be used for transferring the address portion of IR into MAR for single-address instructions. But MAR can not be changed until the end of T_4. A new register (AUXMAR) is introduced between BUS3 and MAR that will hold the address from IR until the rewrite operation is complete. Contents of AUXMAR are transferred to MAR just before the next read operation. Without AUXMAR, it would have been necessary to include one more minor cycle T_5 to complete the fetch cycle.

Since the instruction is available in IR by the end of T_3 and the address portion of IR must be transferred to MAR during T_4, address indexing (if called for) can also be performed during T_4 without any additional time requirement. To accomplish this, a 2-to-4 decoder must be connected to IR_{0-1} to select one of the three index registers. A fourth index register (index 0) containing all zeros is included. Thus when the index flag contains (00), indexing is performed with index 0, which in effect is equivalent to no indexing. The revised microoperation sequence for fetch cycle then is

T_1: $AUXMAR \leftarrow PC$, $MAR \leftarrow AUXMAR$, READ.
T_2: $PC \leftarrow PC + 1$.
T_3: $IR \leftarrow MBR$, WRITE.
T_4: $AUXMAR \leftarrow IR_{7-15} + INDEX$.

Note that both transfers in T_1 can be accomplished in one minor cycle because the second transfer does not use the bus structure.

Indexing in T_4 is not needed for zero-address instructions. If the assembler inserts 0s into the unused fields of zero-address instructions, the indexing operation during T_4 will not affect the execution of those instructions in any way. Also note that indexing is not allowed in LDX, STX, TIX, and TDX instructions. Microoperations in T_4 thus need to be altered for these instructions. From the opcode assignment it is seen that indexing is not required for instructions with an opcode in the range of 1000 through 1111. Hence, microoperations in T_4 can use the MSB of opcode IR_3 to inhibit indexing for index reference instructions. Thus,

T_4: IF $IR_3 = 0$ THEN $AUXMAR \leftarrow IR_{7-15} + $ INDEX
ELSE $AUXMAR \leftarrow IR_{7-15}$.

The fetch machine cycle thus consists of four minor cycles and also accomplishes direct and indexed (if called for) address calculation. When indirect addressing is called for, address calculation requires a memory read (and restore) cycle that would consume four minor cycles. We will thus redefine the three phases of ASC instruction cycle as follows:

FETCH: Includes direct and indexed address calculation.
DEFER: Entered only when indirect addressing is called for.
EXECUTE: Unique to each instruction.

Since the address (indexed if needed) is in AUXMAR at the end of fetch state, the defer state can use the following time allocation:

T_1: $MAR \leftarrow AUXMAR$, READ.
T_2:   Wait.   Memory being read.
T_3: $AUXMAR \leftarrow MBR$, WRITE.
T_4:   Wait.   Memory being restored.

The effective address is in AUXMAR at the end of the defer state. Defer and fetch states thus each need a minimum of four minor cycles.

The execute state differs for each instruction. For LDA instruction, the microoperations required during the execute state are

T_1: $MAR \leftarrow AUXMAR$, READ.
T_2: Wait.
T_3: $ACC \leftarrow MBR$, WRITE.
T_4: Wait.

From this analysis it can be seen that four minor cycles for each machine cycle is a good choice. If the execution state of an instruction can not be completed in four minor cycles, additional machine cycles must be allocated for that instruction.

We will now analyze the microoperations needed by each ASC instruction and allocate them to whatever number of machine cycles they require. We will maintain the machine cycles of constant length of four minor cycles, for simplicity. For zero-address instructions where no address calculation is required, we will use the four minor cycles of the fetch state to perform execution phase microoperations, if possible.

ASC instruction cycle thus consists of one machine cycle for those zero-address instructions in which there is enough time left in the fetch machine cycle to complete the execution of the instruction; two machine cycles for some zero-address and single-address instructions with no indirect addressing; three cycles for single-address instructions with indirect addressing; and multiple machine cycles (depending on I/O wait time) for I/O instructions.

Table 5.2 lists the complete set of microoperations for LDA instruction and the control signals needed to activate those microoperations. Control signals are listed in this order: gating onto BUS1, gating onto BUS2, command to ALU, gating from BUS3, and command to memory. The set of control signals to activate a microoperation must be generated simultaneously by the control unit. Note that the microoperations (and control signals) that are simultaneous are separated by a comma (,). A period (.) indicates the end of such a set of operations (signals). The conditional microoperations (signals) are represented using the notation:

IF condition   THEN operation(s)   ELSE operation(s).

The ELSE clause is optional, if an alternate set of operations is not required when the "condition" is not true (or 1).

The transitions between fetch (F), defer (D), and execute (E) states are allowed only in minor cycle 4 (CP4) of each machine cycle, to retain the simplicity of design. If a complete machine cycle is not needed for a particular set of operations, these state transitions can occur earlier in the machine cycle. Then the state transition circuit will be more complex. The state transitions are represented by the operations $STATE \leftarrow E$, $STATE \leftarrow D$, and $STATE \leftarrow F$. These are equivalent to transferring the codes corresponding to each state into the STATE register. We will use the following coding:

Code	State
00	F
01	D
10	E
11	Not used

Table 5.2 Microoperations for LDA

Machine cycle	Minor cycle (clock pulse)	Microoperations	Control signals
FETCH	CP1	$AUXMAR \leftarrow PC$, $MAR \leftarrow AUXMAR$, READ MEMORY.	PC to BUS1, TRA1, BUS3 to $AUXMAR$, $AUXMAR$ to MAR, READ.
	CP2	$PC \leftarrow PC + 1$.	1 to BUS2, PC to BUS1, ADD, BUS3 to PC.
	CP3	$IR \leftarrow MBR$, RESTORE (WRITE) MEMORY.	MBR to BUS2, TRA2, BUS3 to IR, WRITE.

	CP4	IF $IR_3 = 0$ THEN
		 $AUXMAR \leftarrow IR_{7-15} +$
		 INDEX ELSE
		 $AUXMAR \leftarrow IR_{7-15}$,
		 IF $IR_2 = 1$ THEN
		 STATE $\leftarrow D$
		 ELSE STATE $\leftarrow E$.
			IF $IR_3 = 0$, THEN
			 $IR_{7\ 15}$ to BUS1,
			 INDEX to BUS2, ADD,
			 BUS3 to $AUXMAR$,
			 ELSE
			 IR_{7-15} to BUS1, TRA1,
			 BUS3 to $AUXMAR$,
			 IF $IR_2 = 1$, THEN
			 D to STATE
			 ELSE E to STATE.

DEFER	CP1	$MAR \leftarrow AUXMAR$, READ MEMORY.	$AUXMAR$ to MAR.
	CP2	WAIT.	—
	CP3	$AUXMAR \leftarrow MBR$, RESTORE MEMORY.	MBR to BUS2, TRA2, BUS3 to $AUXMAR$, WRITE.
	CP4	STATE $\leftarrow E$.	E to STATE.
EXECUTE	CP1	$MAR \leftarrow AUXMAR$, READ MEMORY.	$AUXMAR$ to MAR, READ.
	CP2	WAIT.	—
	CP3	$ACC \leftarrow MBR$, WRITE MEMORY.	MBR to BUS2, TRA2, BUS3 to ACC, WRITE.
	CP4	STATE $\leftarrow F$.	F to STATE.

Note that in CP2 of the fetch cycle, a constant register containing a 1 is needed to facilitate increment PC operation. Such a constant register is connected to BUS2 by the signal 1 to BUS2. In CP4 of the fetch cycle, indexing is controlled by IR_3 and indirect address computation is controlled by IR_2. The state transition is either to defer (D) or to execute (E), depending on whether IR_2 is 1 or 0, respectively.

The microoperation sequence shown in Table 5.2 is usually called the *microprogram* for the LDA instruction. It consists of three segments, one corresponding to each state; the execution of LDA by the machine corresponds to the execution of the microprogram by the control unit. Execution of each microoperation results in the generation of the corresponding control signals. The control-signal sequence of Table 5.2 is also a microprogram for LDA except that it is more detailed (low level).

Table 5.3 Microoperations for one-address instruction

Machine cycle	Minor cycle or clock cycle	STA
EXECUTE	CP1	$MAR \leftarrow AUXMAR$, READ.
	CP2	—
	CP3	$MBR \leftarrow ACC$, WRITE.
	CP4	$STATE \leftarrow F$.

Machine cycle	Minor cycle or clock pulse	TIX
EXECUTE	CP1	$MAR \leftarrow AUXMAR$, INDEX $\leftarrow$ INDEX $+ 1$.
	CP2	IF INDEX = 0 THEN $PC \leftarrow MAR$.
	CP3	—
	CP4	$STATE \leftarrow F$.

We will now analyze the remaining instructions to derive the complete set of control signals required for ASC.

5.9.5 One-Address Instructions

Fetch and defer states are identical to the ones shown in Table 5.1 for all one-address instructions. Table 5.3 lists the execute-phase microprograms for these instructions.

5.9.6 Zero-Address Instructions

The microoperations during the first three minor cycles of fetch cycle will be similar to that of LDA, for zero-address instructions also. Since there is no address computation, some of the execution-cycle operations can be

ADD	BRU	LDX	STX
$MAR \leftarrow AUXMAR$, READ.	$MAR \leftarrow AUXMAR$, $PC \leftarrow MAR$.	$MAR \leftarrow AUXMAR$, READ.	$MAR \leftarrow AUXMAR$, READ.
—	—	—	—
$ACC \leftarrow MBR +$ ACC, WRITE.	—	$INDEX \leftarrow MBR$, WRITE.	$MBR \leftarrow INDEX$, WRITE.
$STATE \leftarrow F$.	$STATE \leftarrow F$.	$STATE \leftarrow F$.	$STATE \leftarrow F$.

TDX	BIP	BIN
$MAR \leftarrow AUXMAR$, $INDEX \leftarrow INDEX - 1$.	$MAR \leftarrow AUXMAR$.	$MAR \leftarrow AUXMAR$.
IF INDEX $\neq$ 0 THEN $PC \leftarrow MAR$.	—	
$STATE \leftarrow F$.	IF $ACC_0 = 0$ AND $ACC_{1-15} \neq 0$ THEN $PC \leftarrow MAR$, $STATE \leftarrow F$.	IF $ACC_0 \neq 0$ THEN $PC \leftarrow MAR$, $STATE \leftarrow F$.

performed during the fourth minor cycle and no defer cycle is needed. Microprograms for all zero-address instructions are listed in Table 5.4. TCA is performed in two steps and hence needs the execution cycle. SHR, SHL, and HLT are completed in the fetch cycle itself.

5.9.7 Input/Output Instructions

During RWD and WWD, the processor waits until the end of the execute cycle to check to see if the incoming data is ready ($DATA = 1$) or if it has been accepted ($DATA = 0$). The transition to fetch state occurs only if these conditions are satisfied. If not, the processor waits (loops) in the execute state until the conditions are met. Hence, the number of cycles needed for these instructions depends on the speeds of reader and printer.

Table 5.5 lists the control signals as implied by the microprograms in Tables 5.3 and 5.4. Logic diagrams that implement an HCU can be derived from the control-signal information in Tables 5.2 and 5.5.

Figure 5.6 (page 216) shows the implementation of the four-phase clock to generate CP1, CP2, CP3, and CP4. A 4-bit shift register is used in the implementation. The master clock is an oscillator that starts emitting

Table 5.4 Microprograms for zero-address instructions

Cycle	Clock pulse	RWD
FETCH	CP1	
	CP2	Same microoperations as those for LDA.
	CP3	
	CP4	$DATA \leftarrow 0$, INPUT $\leftarrow 1$, $STATE \leftarrow E$.
EXECUTE	CP1	—
	CP2	—
	CP3	—
	CP4	IF $DATA = 1$ THEN $ACC \leftarrow DIL$, INPUT $\leftarrow 0$, $STATE \leftarrow F$.

clock pulses as soon as the power to the machine is turned on. When the START button on the console (discussed in the next section) is pushed, the RUN flip-flop and the MSB of the shift register are set to 1. The master clock pulse is used to circulate the 1 in the MSB of the shift register through the other bits on the right, to generate the four clock pulses. The sequence of these pulses continues as long as RUN flip-flop is set. The HLT instruction resets the RUN flip-flop, thus stopping the four-phase clock. A ''Master Clear'' button on the console clears all the flip-flops when the RUN is not on.

Figure 5.7 (page 217) shows the opcode and index flag decoding circuitry and Figure 5.8 (page 217) the index register selection circuitry. Figure 5.9 (page 218) shows the circuitry to test whether the accumulator is positive (nonzero) or negative. A similar circuit connected to BUS2 will detect whether the selected index register is zero or not, as required by TIX and TDX instructions.

A 2-to-4 decoder is used to generate F, D, and E signals corresponding to the fetch (00), defer (01), and execute (10) states. Figure 5.9 shows the state change circuitry and its derivation, assuming D (delay) flip-flops. The CP4 is used as the clock for the state register, which along with the transition circuits is shown in Figure 5.10 (pages 218–219).

WWD	TCA	SHR	SHL	HLT
$DATA \leftarrow 1$, $OUTPUT \leftarrow 1$, $STATE \leftarrow E$, $DOL \leftarrow ACC$.	$STATE \leftarrow E$.	$ACC \leftarrow SHR(ACC)$.	$ACC \leftarrow SHL$ (ACC).	$RUN \leftarrow 0$
—	$ACC \leftarrow \overline{ACC}$.			
—	$ACC \leftarrow ACC + 1$.	Execution cycle not needed.		
—	—			
IF $DATA = 0$ THEN $OUTPUT \leftarrow 0$, $STATE \leftarrow F$.	$STATE \leftarrow F$.			

Table 5.5 (a) Control signals for one-address instructions

Machine cycle	Minor cycle or clock pulse	STA	ADD
EXECUTE	CP1	*AUXMAR* to *MAR*, READ.	*AUXMAR* to *MAR*, READ.
	CP2	—	—
	CP3	*ACC* to BUS1, TRA1, BUS3 to *MBR*, WRITE.	*ACC* to BUS1, *MBR* to BUS2, ADD, BUS3 to *ACC*, WRITE.
	CP4	*F* to *STATE*.	*F* to *STATE*.

Machine cycle	Clock pulse	TIX	TDX
EXECUTE	CP1	*AUXMAR* to *MAR*, INDEX to BUS2, 1 to BUS1, ADD, BUS3 to INDEX.	*AUXMAR* to *MAR*, INDEX to BUS2, 2s COMP of 1 to BUS1, ADD, BUS3 to INDEX.
	CP2	IF INDEX = 0 THEN *MAR* to BUS1, TRA1, BUS3 to *PC*.	IF INDEX ≠ 0 THEN *MAR* to BUS1, TRA1, BUS3 to *PC*.
	CP3	—	—
	CP4	*F* to *STATE*.	*F* to *STATE*.

BRU	LDX	STX
AUXMAR to *MAR*, *MAR* to BUS1, TRA1, BUS3 to *PC*.	*AUXMAR* to *MAR*, READ.	*AUXMAR* to *MAR*, READ.
—	—	WRITE.
—	*MBR* to BUS2, TRA2, BUS3 to INDEX, WRITE.	INDEX to BUS2, TRA2, BUS3 to *MBR*, WRITE.
F to *STATE*.	*F* to *STATE*.	*F* to *STATE*.

BIP	BIN
AUXMAR to *MAR*.	*AUXMAR* to *MAR*.
—	—
—	—
IF $(ACC)_0 = 0$ AND $(ACC)_{1-15} \neq 0$ THEN *MAR* to BUS1, TRA1, BUS3 to *PC*, *F* to *STATE*.	IF $(ACC)_0 \neq 0$ THEN *MAR* to BUS1, TRA1, BUS3 to *PC*, *F* to *STATE*.

Table 5.5 (b) Control signals for zero-address instructions

Machine cycle	Clock pulse	RWD
FETCH	CP1	
	CP2	Same as those for LDA in Table 5.1
	CP3	
	CP4	0 to DATA, 1 to INPUT, *E* to *STATE*.
EXECUTE	CP1	—
	CP2	—
	CP3	—
	CP4	IF DATA = 1 THEN DIL to ACC, 0 to INPUT, *F* to *STATE*.

Figure 5.11 (pages 219–220) shows the logic needed to generate the control signals for the fetch cycle, Figure 5.12 (page 220) for the defer cycle, and Figure 5.13 (pages 221–223) for the execute cycle. The state transition signals of Figure 5.9 are not shown (again) in these figures. No logic minimization is attempted here.

5.10   Console

Figure 5.14 (page 224) shows the ASC console. The console (control panel) enables the operator to control the machine. It can be used for loading programs and data into memory, observing the contents of registers and memory locations, and starting and stopping the machine. There are sixteen lights (monitors) on the console that can display the contents of a selected register or memory location. There is a *switch bank* consist-

WWD	TCA	SHR	SHL	HLT
1 to DATA, 1 to OUTPUT, *E* to *STATE*, *ACC* to DOL.	*E* to *STATE*.	*ACC* to BUS1, SHR, BUS3 to *ACC*.	*ACC* to BUS1, SHL, BUS3 to *ACC*.	0 to RUN.
—	*ACC* to BUS1, COMP, BUS3 to *ACC*.			
—	*ACC* to BUS1, 1 to BUS2, ADD, BUS3 to *ACC*.	Execution cycle not needed.		
—	—			
IF DATA = 0 THEN 0 to INPUT, *E* to *STATE*.	*F* to *STATE*.			

ing of sixteen two-position switches that can be used for loading a 16-bit pattern into either PC or a selected memory location. There are two LOAD switches: LOAD PC and LOAD MEM. When LOAD PC is pushed, the bit pattern set on the switch bank is transferred to PC. When LOAD MEM is pushed, the contents of the switch bank are transferred to the memory location addressed by PC. There is a set of DISPLAY switches to enable the display of contents of ACC, PC, IR, index registers, or the memory location addressed by PC. The DISPLAY and LOAD switches are push-button switches and are mechanically ganged together so that only one of these switches is pushed (operative) at any time. The switch that was previously pushed pops out when a new switch is pushed. The MASTER CLEAR switch clears all ASC registers and starts the four-phase clock. The START/STOP switch sets or resets the RUN flip-flop. There is also a POWER ON/OFF switch on the console.

Figure 5.6 Four-phase clock using SR flip-flops

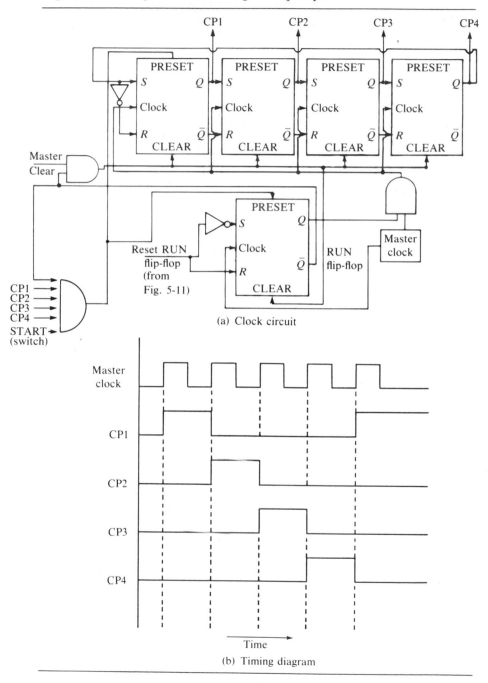

(a) Clock circuit

(b) Timing diagram

Figure 5.7 IR decoders

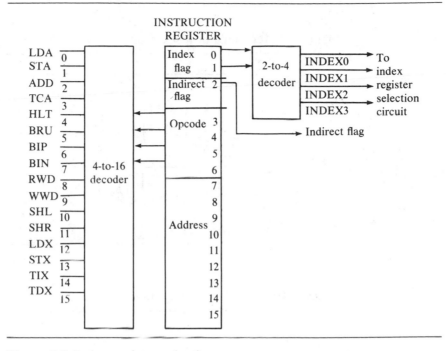

Figure 5.8 Index register selection

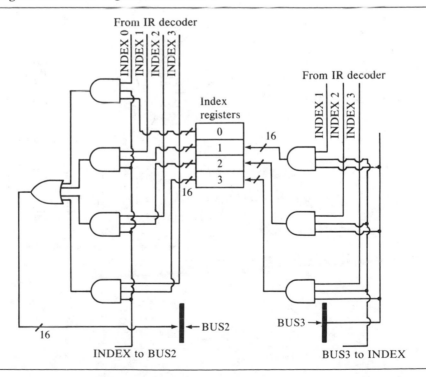

Figure 5.9 Accumulator test circuitry

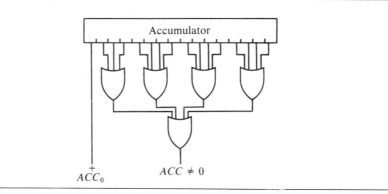

$\overset{+}{ACC_0}$ $ACC \neq 0$

Figure 5.10 State register and transition circuits

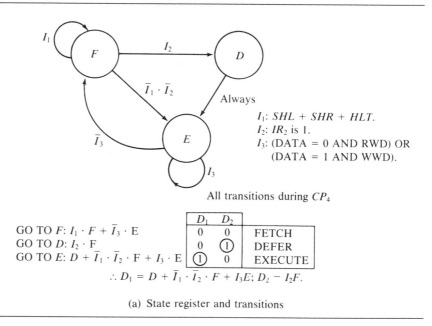

I_1: SHL + SHR + HLT.
I_2: IR_2 is 1.
I_3: (DATA = 0 AND RWD) OR (DATA = 1 AND WWD).

All transitions during CP_4

GO TO F: $I_1 \cdot F + \bar{I}_3 \cdot E$
GO TO D: $I_2 \cdot F$
GO TO E: $D + \bar{I}_1 \cdot \bar{I}_2 \cdot F + I_3 \cdot E$

D_1	D_2	
0	0	FETCH
0	①	DEFER
①	0	EXECUTE

$\therefore D_1 = D + \bar{I}_1 \cdot \bar{I}_2 \cdot F + I_3 E; \; D_2 - I_2 F.$

(a) State register and transitions

Figure 5.10 (Continued)

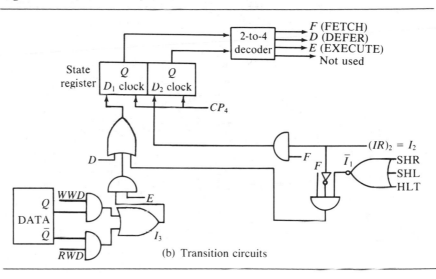

(b) Transition circuits

Figure 5.11 Fetch cycle

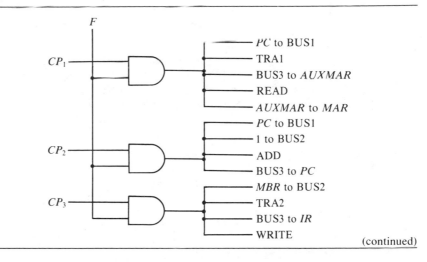

(continued)

Figure 5.11 (Continued)

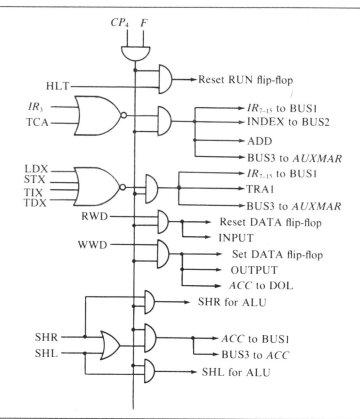

Note: State change signals are shown in Figure 5.9.

Figure 5.12 Defer cycle

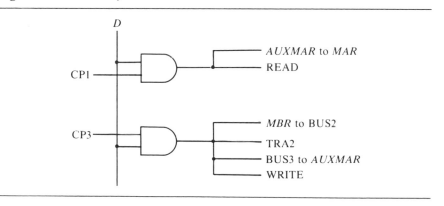

Figure 5.13 Execute cycle

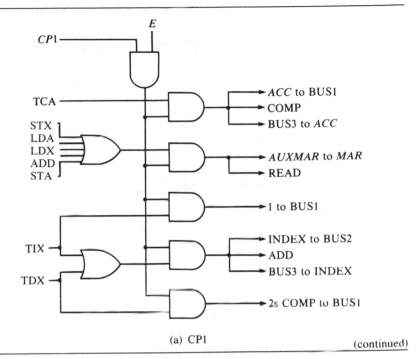

(a) CP1

(continued)

Figure 5.13 (Continued)

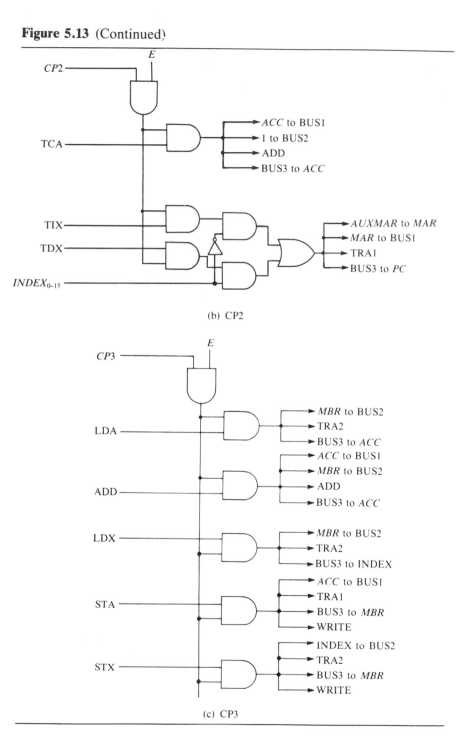

(b) CP2

(c) CP3

Figure 5.13 (Continued)

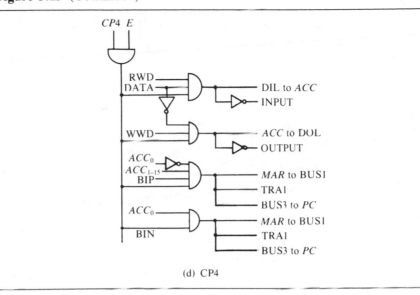

(d) CP4

Figure 5.14 ASC console

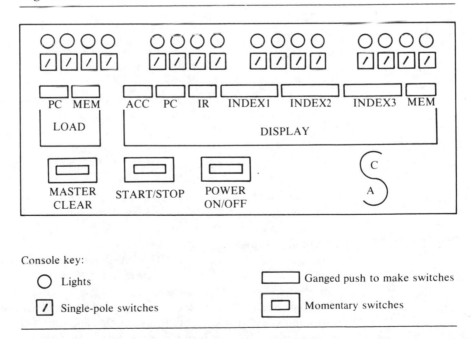

Console key:

◯ Lights   ▭ Ganged push to make switches

▱ Single-pole switches   ▭ Momentary switches

Each switch on the console invokes a sequence of microoperations. Typical operations possible using the console along with the sequences of microoperations invoked are listed here:

Loading PC

Set the switch bank to the required 16-bit pattern.

LOAD *PC*   *PC* ← Switch bank.

Loading memory

Load *PC* with the memory address.
Set switch bank to the data to be loaded into the memory location.

LOAD MEM   *MAR* ← *PC*, READ.
                                                WAIT
                                                MBR ← Switch bank
                                                        WRITE.
                                                PC ← *PC* + 1.

Display registers

Each of the register contents can be displayed on monitors (lights) by pushing the corresponding display switch.

MONITOR ← Selected register

Display memory

Set *PC* to the memory address.

DISPLAY MEM   *MAR* ← *PC*, READ.
                                                PC ← *PC* + 1.
                                                MONITOR ← *MBR*, WRITE.

While loading and displaying memory, the PC value is incremented by 1 at the end of a load or a display. This enables easier loading and monitoring of the consecutive memory locations. To execute a program, the program and data are first loaded into the memory, PC is set to the address of the first executable instruction, and the execution is started by pushing the START switch. Since the content of any register or memory location can be placed on BUS3, a 16-bit *monitor* register is connected to BUS3. The lights on the console display the contents of this register. The switch bank is connected to BUS2.

Figure 5.15 shows the control circuitry needed to display memory. The console is active only when the RUN flip-flop is RESET. When one of the LOAD or DISPLAY switches is depressed, the *console active* flip-flop is set for a time period equal to three clock pulses (all the console functions can be completed in three-clock-pulse time). The RUN flip-flop is also set during this period, thus enabling the clock. The clock circuitry is active long enough to give three pulses and deactivated by resetting the RUN

Figure 5.15 Console circuits for DISPLAY MEMORY.

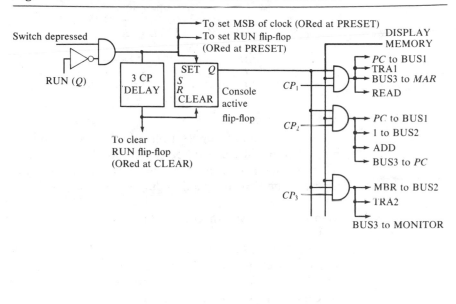

flip-flop. The START/STOP switch complements the RUN flip-flop each time it is depressed, thus starting or stopping the clock. Note that except for the START/STOP switch, the console is inactive when the machine is RUNning. Circuits to generate control signals corresponding to each LOAD and DISPLAY switch must be included to complete the console design. The console designed here is very simple compared to the consoles of machines available commercially. Some of the other features normally available include displays for error conditions (overflow, parity error, and the like) and single step (enabling execution of one instruction).

5.11 Hardware Design Language Description

The set of microoperations in Table 5.2 can be described using the hardware design language (HDL) as follows:

$F \wedge CP1$: $AUXMAR \leftarrow PC, MAR \leftarrow AUXMAR, READ$.
$F \wedge CP2$: $PC \leftarrow PC + 1$.
$F \wedge CP3$: $IR \leftarrow MBR$, WRITE.
$F \wedge CP4$: IF $IR_3 = 0$ THEN $AUXMAR \leftarrow IR_{7-15} + $ INDEX.
             IF $IR_2 = 1$ THEN $STATE \leftarrow D$ ELSE $STATE \leftarrow E$.

$D \wedge CP1$: $MAR \leftarrow AUXMAR$, READ.
$D \wedge CP2$:   No operation.
$D \wedge CP3$: $AUXMAR \leftarrow MBR$, WRITE.
$D \wedge CP4$: $STATE \leftarrow E$.

$LDA \wedge E \wedge CP1$: $MAR \leftarrow AUXMAR$, READ.
$LDA \wedge E \wedge CP2$:   No operation.
$LDA \wedge E \wedge CP3$: $ACC \leftarrow MBR$, WRITE.
$LDA \wedge E \wedge CP4$: $STATE \leftarrow F$.

Here F, D, and E represent the three states of the control unit. LDA is high when the instruction register contains an LDA instruction. Since the fetch and defer states are the same for all instructions, LDA is not used as a part of the control function during these states. The wait states during CP2 of defer and execute are shown as "No operation." These statements are not really needed in the description but are included for completeness.

The above description can be expanded to include the microoperation sequence for the remaining fifteen instructions. To make the description complete, each of the facilities (registers, memory, bus, and so on) in ASC must be declared. We will now provide an HDL structure suitable for facility declarations. Appendix C describes a popular HDL, the Computer Design Language, along with some examples. Details as to the utility of HDLs in simulation, description, and synthesis are also given in that appendix.

5.11.1 Declarations

Register declarations are of the form:

$$\text{REGISTER, Name}_{\text{Subscript}}.$$

where Name is a string of characters starting with an alphabetic character, and Subscript is of the form

$$n$$

implying n bits numbered 1 through n, left to right; $n > 0$; or

$$n_1 - n_2$$

implying a range of bits n_1 through n_2, left to right; $n_1 \geq 0$, $n_2 \geq 0$. Absence of a subscript implies a single-bit register.

Example 5.1

$$\text{REGISTER, } PC_{0-15}.$$

$$\text{REGISTER, } MAR_{0-15}.$$

$$\text{REGISTER, } MBR_{0-15}.$$

Facilities of the same type can be declared in the same statement, separated by a comma. Thus, the above declaration is equivalent to

$$\text{REGISTER, } PC_{0-15}, MAR_{0-15}, MBR_{0-15}.$$

Registers also can be declared with subregisters using the general form

$$\text{REGISTER, Name}_{\text{Subscript}} = \text{Name}_{\text{Subscript}} \, \xi \, \text{Name}_{\text{Subscript}} \, \xi \ldots$$

$$\text{REGISTER, } IR_{0-15} = \text{INDEX FLAG}_2 \, \xi \, \text{INDIRECT FLAG}$$
$$\xi \, \text{OPCODE}_4 \, \xi \, \text{ADDRESS}_9.$$

The other facilities that use the declaration statements of the above type are

BUS:	Declares buses.
SWITCH:	Declares a set of switches.
LIGHT:	Declares a set of monitors.

Example 5.2

$$\text{BUS, BUS1}_{0-15}, \text{BUS2}_{0-15}, \text{BUS3}_{0-15}.$$

$$\text{SWITCH, START.}$$

$$\text{LIGHT, MONITOR}_{1-16}.$$

A set of registers can also be declared by using a double subscript, as in Example 5.3.

Example 5.3 $\text{REGISTER, INDEX}_{0-3, \, 0-15}.$

Memory is declared using the format

$$\text{MEMORY, } M_{p,q}$$

where p is the number of words numbered 0 through p-1 and q is the number of bits per word and can take all the forms of the subscript above.

Example 5.4

MEMORY, $M_{1023, 16}$, or

MEMORY, $M_{1023, 1-16}$, declare a 1K × 16 memory.

A *decoder* can be declared by using the format

DECODER, (Inputs: outputs).

DECODER, (STATE: F, D, E).

Assuming that STATE has been declared as a 2-bit register, the decoder should have four outputs. Only the first three are used.

These examples describe various ASC facilities. We will leave the complete description of ASC for an exercise.

5.12 Microprogrammed Control Unit

A hardwired control unit requires extensive redesign of the hardware if the instruction set has to be expanded or if the function of an instruction has to be changed. In practice, a flexible control unit is desired to enable tailoring the instruction set to the application environment. A microprogrammed control unit (MCU) offers such a flexibility. In an MCU, microprograms corresponding to each instruction in the instruction set are stored in a ROM called control ROM (CROM). A microcontrol unit (μCU) executes the appropriate microprogram based on the instruction in IR. The execution of a microinstruction is equivalent to the generation of control signals to bring about that microoperation. The μCU is usually hardwired and is comparatively simple to design since its function is only to execute microprograms in the CROM.

Figure 5.16 shows a block diagram of an MCU. Microprograms corresponding to fetch, defer, and execute cycles of each instruction are stored in the CROM. The beginning address of the fetch sequence is loaded into μMAR when the power is turned on. Then the CROM transfers the first microinstruction of fetch into μMBR. The μCU decodes this microinstruction to generate control signals required to bring about that microoperation. The μMAR is normally incremented by 1 at each clock pulse to execute the next microinstruction in sequence. This sequential execution is altered at the end of the fetch microprogram, since the execution of the microprogram corresponding to the execute cycle of the instruction now residing in IR must be started. Hence the μMAR must be set to the CROM address where the appropriate execute microprogram

Figure 5.16 Microprogrammed control unit (MCU) model

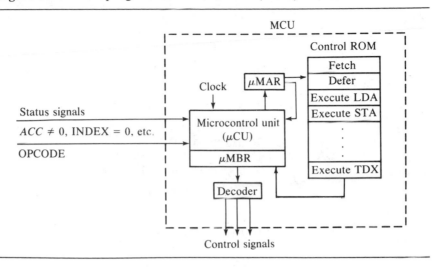

begins. The defer microprogram can be called from the execute microprogram if the indirect flag is on. At the end of execution of each execute
microprogram, control is transferred to the fetch sequence. The function
of the μCU is thus to set the μMAR to the proper value; i.e., the current
value incremented by 1 or a jump address depending on the opcode and
the status signals such as INDEX = 0 and $ACC \neq 0$.

For illustration purposes, a typical microinstruction might be $PC \leftarrow PC$
+ 1. When this microinstruction is brought into μMBR, the decoder
circuits generate the following control signals: PC to BUS1, 1 to BUS2,
ADD, BUS3 to PC, and the μMAR is incremented by 1. We will discuss
the design of an MCU for ASC next.

5.12.1 MCU for ASC

Table 5.5 shows the complete microprogram for the ASC instruction set.
A microinstruction corresponds to a set of operations that can be performed simultaneously (during one register transfer time). The microprogram resembles an assembly language program and includes jumps and
calls. Execute sequence for ASC instructions is arranged in the opcode
order following the fetch sequence. The defer sequence is called by each
single address instruction if $(IR)_2 = 1$. GO TO * OPCODE implies a jump
to the execution sequence corresponding to the opcode residing in IR at
that time. The last column in Table 5.5 shows that there are twelve types
of operations in the microprogram numbered 0 through 11. Type 0 is a

Table 5.5 ASC Microprogram

Address		Microinstruction	Type
0	FETCH	$MAR \leftarrow PC$, READ.	0
1		$PC \leftarrow PC + 1$.	0
2		$IR \leftarrow MBR$, WRITE.	0
3		$AUXMAR \leftarrow IR_{7-15}$.	0
4		IF $IR_3 \neq 0$ OR OPCODE = TCA THEN GO TO L.	1
5		$AUXMAR \leftarrow IR_{7-15} + $ INDEX.	0
6	L	GO TO * OPCODE.	2
8	LDA	IF $IR_2 = 1$ THEN CALL DEFER.	3
9		$MAR \leftarrow AUXMAR$, READ.	0
10		WAIT.	4
11		$ACC \leftarrow MBR$, WRITE.	0
12		GO TO FETCH.	5
16	STA	IF $IR_2 = 1$ THEN CALL DEFER.	3
17		$MAR \leftarrow AUXMAR$, READ.	0
18		WAIT.	4
19		$MBR \leftarrow ACC$, WRITE.	0
20		GO TO FETCH.	5
24	ADD	IF $IR_2 = 1$ THEN CALL DEFER.	3
25		$MAR \leftarrow AUXMAR$, READ.	0
26		WAIT.	4
27		$ACC \leftarrow MBR + ACC$, WRITE.	0
28		GO TO FETCH.	5
32	TCA	$ACC \leftarrow \overline{ACC}$	0
33		$ACC \leftarrow ACC + 1$.	0
34		GO TO FETCH.	5
40	HLT	INHIBIT CLOCK.	0
48	BRU	IF $IR_2 = 1$ THEN CALL DEFER.	3
49		$MAR \leftarrow AUXMAR$.	0
50		$PC \leftarrow MAR$.	0
51		GO TO FETCH.	5
56[1]	BIP	IF $ACC_0 \neq 0$ OR $ACC_{1-15} = 0$ THEN GO TO FETCH.	6
57	L1	IF $IR_2 = 1$ THEN CALL DEFER.	3
58		$MAR \leftarrow AUXMAR$.	0
59		$PC \leftarrow MAR$.	0
60		GO TO FETCH.	5
64	BIN	IF $ACC_0 \neq 0$ THEN GO TO FETCH.	7
65		GO TO $L1$.	5
72	RWD	$DATA \leftarrow 0$, INPUT $\leftarrow 1$.	0
73	L2	WAIT.	4
74		IF $DATA \neq 1$ THEN GO TO L2.	8
75		$ACC \leftarrow DIL$, INPUT $\leftarrow 0$.	0
76		GO TO FETCH.	5
80[2]	WWD	$DATA \leftarrow 0$, OUTPUT $\leftarrow 1$, DOL $\leftarrow ACC$.	0

Table 5.5 (Continued)

81	L3	WAIT.	4
82		IF $DATA \neq 1$ THEN GO TO L3.	8
83		OUTPUT $\leftarrow 0$.	0
84		GO TO FETCH.	5
88	SHL	$ACC \leftarrow$ SHL(ACC).	0
89		GO TO FETCH.	5
96	SHR	$ACC \leftarrow$ SHR(ACC).	0
97		GO TO FETCH.	5
104	LDX	IF $IR_2 = 1$ THEN CALL DEFER.	3
105		$MAR \leftarrow AUXMAR$, READ.	0
106		WAIT.	4
107		INDEX $\leftarrow MAR$, WRITE.	0
108		GO TO FETCH.	5
112	STX	IF $IR_2 = 1$ THEN CALL DEFER.	3
113		$MAR \leftarrow AUXMAR$, READ.	0
114		WAIT.	4
115		$MBR \leftarrow$ INDEX, WRITE.	0
116		GO TO FETCH.	5
120	TIX	INDEX $\leftarrow$ INDEX $+ 1$.	0
121		IF INDEX $\neq 0$ THEN GO TO FETCH.	9
122	L4	IF $IR_2 = 1$ THEN CALL DEFER.	3
123		$MAR \leftarrow AUXMAR$.	0
124		$PC \leftarrow MAR$.	0
125		GO TO FETCH.	5
128	TDX	INDEX $\leftarrow$ INDEX $- 1$.	0
129		IF INDEX $= 0$ THEN GO TO FETCH.	10
130		GO TO $L4$.	5
131	DEFER	MAR $\leftarrow AUXMAR$, READ.	0
132		WAIT.	4
133		$AUXMAR \leftarrow$ MBR, WRITE.	0
134		RETURN.	11

[1] Effective address is calculated during BIP and BIN only if needed.
[2] Data flip-flop operation is changed to make it identical to RWD operation.

microinstruction that generates control signals for the macromachine (ASC); other types are instructions to the μCU to load the appropriate address into μMAR for subsequent operation. Note that the CROM addresses assigned to the beginning of each microinstruction sequence (shown in column 1 of Table 5.5) differ by 8 between each sequence. This was done to simplify the computation of the jump address during GO TO * OPCODE. Since the jump address = (opcode + 1)*8, it can be easily calculated by the μCU by first adding 1 to the opcode and shifting it left three times. This method simplifies the multibranch implementation but could result in a larger CROM size than needed by the complete microprogram; the multiplication factor above should correspond to the longest microinstruction sequence and sequences shorter than this maximum length waste CROM space. If CROM size is a restriction, some other method should be used to implement the multijump.

To distinguish between the twelve types of microinstructions a 4-bit μopcode is needed. Additional bits are needed to represent various control signals (in type 0) and microprogram jump address (in other types). Since the highest microprogram address is 134, an 8-bit address field would be sufficient for representing the address field in other than type 0 microinstructions.

To encode type 0 microinstructions, an analysis of control signals to connect registers to BUS1 and BUS2 and ALU commands and signals to connect BUS3 to a register must be generated simultaneously. Four fields, therefore, are needed to encode these signals. We will call these fields ON BUS1, ON BUS2, ALU, and OFF BUS3. Control signals for memory operations (READ, WRITE, No operation) can be grouped into one field. Other miscellaneous control signals can be partitioned into one or more fields. Figure 5.17 shows such a partitioning and encoding for type 0 microinstructions. Note that total number of bits to represent a type 0 microinstruction thus is 24.

To retain the uniformity, we will use a CROM with 24 bits per word. Figure 5.18 shows the microinstruction formats. Figure 5.19 shows two typical microinstructions in the encoded format. The microprogram in Table 5.5 must be encoded using Figures 5.17 and 5.18 and loaded into the CROM.

The μCU executes the microprogram in CROM to generate control signals. Each microinstruction is first brought into μMBR and based on the μopcode, μCU performs the various functions shown in Table 5.6. Table 5.6 is the complete specification for designing the μCU. The design of this hardware block is left as an exercise.

The signals required for the console are also omitted in the above design. Control sequences for each of the console operations form a part of the microprogram and are invoked by the console operations as are other sequences.

Note that the microprogram of Table 5.5 is an HDL description of ASC. This description is *procedural*, since the program statements are executed in sequence and hence the position of a statement with respect to others matters. The HDL description shown in the previous section is *nonprocedural*, because a statement is activated only when the control function has a value of 1 and hence the sequence of statements does not imply a sequential order of execution.

Figure 5.17 Signal partitioning and encoding for microinstruction type 0

Code	ON BUS1	ON BUS2	ON BUS3	ALU
0 0 0	None	None	None	None
0 0 1	*ACC*	INDEX	*ACC*	TRA1
0 1 0	*MAR*	*MBR*	INDEX	TRA2
0 1 1	$(IR)_{ADRS}$	1	IR	ADD
1 0 0	*PC*	SWITCH BANK	*AUXMAR*	COMP
1 0 1	1		*MBR*	SHL
1 1 0	−1		*PC*	SHR
1 1 1			MONITOR	

(a) 3-bit fields

Code	FIELD1	FIELD2	FIELD3	MEMORY
0 0	None	None	None	None
0 1	*AUXMAR* to *MAR*	DIL to *ACC*	0 to INPUT	READ
1 0	1 to INPUT	*ACC* to DOL	0 to OUTPUT	WRITE
1 1	1 to OUTPUT	INHIBIT CLOCK	0 to DATA	Not used

(b) 2-bit fields

Figure 5.18 Microinstruction formats

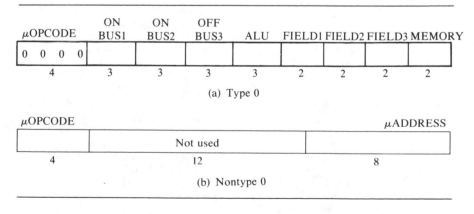

(a) Type 0

(b) Nontype 0

Figure 5.19 Typical encoded microinstructions

	ACC to		BUS3 to		AUXMAR to			
μOPCODE	BUS1	NONE	MBR	TRA1	MAR	NONE	NONE	WRITE
0000	001	000	101	001	01	00	00	10

$MAR \leftarrow AUXMAR$, $MBR \leftarrow ACC$, WRITE.

(a) Type 0

μOPCODE		ADDRESS	
0101	Not used	0000	0000

GO TO FETCH

(b) Type 5

In an MCU, the time required to execute an instruction is a function of the number of microinstructions in the corresponding sequence. The MCU returns to fetch the new instruction once the sequence is executed (the hardwired HCU waited until CP4 for a state change). The overall operation is, however, slower than that of an HCU since each microin-

Table 5.6 μCU requirements

μopcode	Type	Action required by μCU
0 0 0 0	0	Decode the remaining bits in μMBR and generate control signals; $\mu MAR \leftarrow \mu MAR + 1$.
0 0 0 1	1	IF $IR_3 = 0$ or OPCODE = TCA THEN $\mu MAR \leftarrow \mu ADDRESS$ ELSE $\mu MAR \leftarrow \mu MAR + 1$.
0 0 1 0	2	$\mu MAR \leftarrow (OPCODE + 1)*8$.
0 0 1 1	3	TEMP $\leftarrow \mu MAR$, $\mu MAR \leftarrow \mu ADDRESS$.
0 1 0 0	4	All-zero μMBR, No operation; (i.e., WAIT, No control signals).
0 1 0 1	5	$\mu MAR \leftarrow \mu ADDRESS$.
0 1 1 0	6	IF $ACC_0 \neq 0$ OR $ACC_{1-15} = 0$ THEN $\mu MAR \leftarrow \mu ADDRESS$ ELSE $\mu MAR \leftarrow \mu MAR + 1$.
0 1 1 1	7	IF $ACC \neq 0$ THEN $\mu MAR \leftarrow \mu ADDRESS$ ELSE $\mu MAR \leftarrow \mu MAR + 1$.
1 0 0 0	8	IF $DATA \neq 1$ THEN $\mu MAR \leftarrow \mu ADDRESS$ ELSE $\mu MAR \leftarrow \mu MAR + 1$.
1 0 0 1	9	IF INDEX $\neq 0$ THEN $\mu MAR \leftarrow \mu ADDRESS$ ELSE $\mu MAR \leftarrow \mu MAR + 1$.
1 0 1 0	10	IF INDEX $= 0$ THEN $\mu MAR \leftarrow \mu ADDRESS$ ELSE $\mu MAR \leftarrow \mu MAR + 1$.
1 0 1 1	11	$\mu MAR \leftarrow$ TEMP $+ 1$.

struction is to be retrieved from the CROM and the time required between two clock pulses is thus equal to

Slowest register transfer time + CROM access time.

The function of an instruction is easily altered by changing the microprogram. This requires a new CROM. Other than this, no hardware changes are needed. This attribute of an MCU is used in the "emulation" of computers where an available machine (host) is made to execute another (target) machine's instructions by changing the control store of the host.

In practice, CROM size is a design factor. The length of the microprogram must be minimized to reduce CROM size, thereby reducing the cost of MCU. This requires that each microinstruction contain as many microoperations as possible, thereby increasing the CROM word size, which in turn increases the cost of MCU. A compromise is thus needed. As in ASC-MCU, each microinstruction has to be encoded and the number of such encoded fields in an instruction has to be kept low to reduce the CROM width. A microoperation then will span more than one CROM word. Facilities are then needed to buffer the CROM words corresponding to a microoperation so that all required control signals are generated simultaneously. In a *horizontally microprogrammed* machine, a microoperation typically is represented in one CROM word; in a *vertically microprogrammed* machine, a microoperation spans more than one CROM word. Variations in microinstruction formats are discussed in Chapter 6.

We conclude this section with the following procedure for designing an MCU, once the bus structure of the machine is established:

1. Arrange the microinstruction sequences into one complete program (microprogram).
2. Determine the number of distinct operations needed and derive the number of bits needed for the micro opcode (μopcode).
3. Count the number of control signals to be generated. Each bit in the microinstruction can be used to represent a control signal (being ON or OFF). Then, the number of bits needed in the microinstruction might be too large. To reduce the CROM word size, partition the control signals into distinct groups (i.e., signals to BUS1, signals to BUS2, etc., or signals that never occur at the same time so that the same bit can be used for representing them). Assign fields in the microinstruction for each group and encode them.
4. Determine the size of μMAR from the number of microinstructions

and the encoding of control signals. Then determine the widths of CROM and μMBR from the width of the microinstruction.

5. Code the microprogram using the microinstruction format derived above and load it into the CROM.

6. Design the microcontrol unit, following the HCU design for ASC.

5.13 Summary

The detailed design of ASC provided here illustrates the sequence of steps in the design of a digital computer. In practice, the chronological order shown here can not be strictly followed. Several iterations between the steps are needed in the design cycle before a complete design is obtained. Some architectural issues were identified at each step. These points are further discussed with respect to commercially available architectures in Chapters 6, 7, and 8. The MCU as discussed here gives a brief introduction to microprogramming. The majority of modern-day computers have microprogrammed control units. Microprogramming is especially popular now because of the technological advances in memory fabrication and the cost effectiveness of semiconductor memory devices.

References

Ahmad, S. I., and K. T. Fung. *Introduction to Computer Design and Implementation.* Rockville, Md.: Computer Science Press, 1981.

Baer, J. L. *Computer Systems Architecture.* Rockville, Md.: Computer Science Press, 1980.

Chu, Y. *Computer Organization and Microprogramming.* Englewood Cliffs, N.J.: Prentice-Hall, 1972.

Foster, C. C. *Computer Architecture.* New York, N.Y.: Van Nostrand Reinhold, 1976.

Hill, F. J., and G. R. Peterson. *Digital Systems: Hardware, Organization and Design.* 2d ed. New York, N.Y.: John Wiley, 1978.

Mano, M. M. *Computer Systems Architecture.* Englewood Cliffs, N.J.: Prentice-Hall, 1976.

Problems

5.1   Rewrite the control sequence for conditional branch instructions of ASC so that the instruction cycle terminates in one major cycle if the condition is not satisfied. Discuss the effect of this modification on the hardware of the control unit.

5.2   In a practical computer the shift instructions accommodate multiple shifts. Use the address field of SHR and SHL to specify the number of shifts. How can you accommodate this modification by (a) hardware changes only (b) changes to microprograms only?

5.3   Write microinstruction sequences for the following new instructions:

JSR: Subroutine jump; use memory location 0 for storing the return address.
RET: Return from subroutine.
SUB Z: $ACC \leftarrow Z - ACC$, where Z is a memory address.

5.4   Design a single-bus structure for ASC.

5.5   Discuss how you can accommodate more than one input/output device on ASC. Specify the hardware modifications needed.

5.6   Design the μCU for ASC.

5.7   Rewrite the microprogram sequence for HLT instruction, if the JSR and RET instructions of problem 5.3 are implemented by extending the HLT opcode. That is, use the unused bits of the HLT instruction to signify JSR and RET.

5.8   Complete the HDL description of ASC given in Section 5.11.

5.9   Describe the serial 2s complementer circuit of Chapter 2, using the HDL.

5.10 We have assumed single level of indirect addressing for ASC. What changes are needed to extend this to multiple levels whereby the indirection is performed until the most significant bit of the memory word, addressed at the current level, is non-zero.

5.11 Change the ASC instruction format to accommodate both preindexed and postindexed indirect addressing. Rewrite the microcode to accommodate those operations.

5.12 Use a 16-bit up-counter as the PC for ASC. What changes are needed for the control unit hardware? Does it alter the operation of any of the instructions?

5.13 Replace the core memory of ASC with a semiconductor memory with an access time equal to the slowest register transfer time in ASC. How does this affect the control unit hardware and the microprogram?

5.14 Design a paged-addressing mechanism for ASC. Assume that the 2 most significant bits of the 9-bit direct address are used to select one of the four 9-bit segment registers. The contents of a segment register concatenated with the least significant 7 bits of the address field forms the 16-bit address. Show the hardware details. What is the effect of this address scheme on indirect and index address computations?

5.15 Assume that the ASC memory is organized as 8 bits per word. That means each single-address instruction now occupies two words and zero-address instructions occupy one word each. The ASC bus structure remains the same. MBR is now 8 bits long and is connected to the least significant 8 bits of the bus structure. Rewrite the fetch microprogram.

5.16 Include four general-purpose registers into ASC structure to replace the accumulator and index registers. Each register can be used either as an accumulator or as an index register. Expand ASC instruction set to utilize these registers. Assume the same set of operations as are now available on ASC. Is there any merit in including register-to-register operations in the instruction set? Design the new instruction format.

Chapter 6

Practical Architectures

The objective of the previous chapter was to illustrate the design of a simple but complete computer (ASC). Simplicity was our main consideration, and so architectural alternatives possible at each stage in the design cycle were not presented. This chapter describes the architectural features of commercially available machines as enhancements to the basic architecture of ASC. The majority of examples are taken from manufacturers' manuals of the following machines:

Digital Equipment Corporation's (DEC) PDP-11 — a 16-bit minicomputer.

International Business Machine's (IBM) 370 — a 32-bit large-scale machine.

Intel Corporation's 8080 — an 8-bit microprocessor.

MOS Technology's 6502 (M6502) — also an 8-bit microprocessor.

Architectural features of other machines are also included in the chapter as needed to illustrate concepts. We will use the machine architectures as examples rather than provide a complete system view of any of the commercially available machines.

Details of the instruction set, processor structure and memory, control unit, and ALU enhancements will be provided as practical architectural modifications to ASC. Enhancements to the input/output subsystem along with a few system structures are described in Chapter 7. We will first distinguish between the three popular types of computer systems now available.

6.1   Types of Computer Systems

A modern-day computer system can be a large-scale machine, a mini-computer, or a microcomputer. It would be difficult to produce sets of characteristics that would definitively place a system in one of these three categories today; original distinctions are becoming blurred with advances in hardware technology. A microcomputer of the eighties, for example, can provide roughly the same processing capability as that of a large-scale computer of the sixties. The physical size of a computer system probably is its most distinguishing feature. The central processing unit (CPU) of a large-scale machine requires a wheelbarrow to move it from one place to another, while that of a minicomputer can be carried without any mechanical help, and a microcomputer can be fitted easily on an 8- by 12-inch board and carried in one hand. Table 6.1 lists some of the characteristics of the three types of computer systems. As can be noted, there is a considerable amount of overlap in their characteristics. Architectural features found in large-scale machines eventually appear in "mini" and "micro" computer systems; hence, the features discussed in this chapter are assumed to apply equally well to all three classes.

6.2   Instruction Set

The selection of a set of instructions for a machine is influenced heavily by the application for which the machine is intended. If the machine is for general-purpose data processing, then the basic arithmetic and logic operations must be included in the instruction set. Some machines such as the IBM 370 have separate instructions for binary and decimal (BCD) arithmetic, making them suitable for both scientific and business-oriented processing, respectively. Some processors (such as M6502) can operate in either binary or decimal mode; that is, the same instruction operates on either type of data. The logical operations AND, OR, NOT, and EXCLUSIVE-OR and the SHIFT and CIRCULATE operations are needed to access the data at bit and byte levels and to implement other arithmetic operations such as multiply and divide and floating-point arithmetic. Some control instructions for branching (conditional and unconditional), halt, and subroutine call and return are also required. Input/output (I/O) can be performed using dedicated instructions for input and output (INTEL 8080, IBM 370) or a memory-mapped I/O (DEC PDP-11, M6502) where the I/O devices are treated as memory locations and hence all the operations using memory are also applicable to I/O.

Table 6.1 Characteristics of contemporary computers

Characteristic	Large-scale computer	Minicomputer	Microcomputer
Size of the CPU	Usually not easily portable	About 19″ × 3′ Equipment rack	40-pin DIP; 8″ × 12″ board for a typical system
Basic cost (for a minimum system)	Above $100,000	$15,000–$90,000	$50–$500
Word size	32–60 bits	16–32 bits	4, 8, 16 bits, new 32 bits
Typical processor cycle time	0.058–0.75 μs	0.2–1 μs	1 μs
Application	General purpose (high-volume data processing)	Most dedicated, some general purpose	Specialized (dedicated controllers)

The current trend in instruction set design is to provide a set of powerful instructions that can accommodate high-level language constructs such as loop controls and multiple branches as one instruction rather than as a series of assembly-level instructions. Digital Equipment Corporation's VAX-11 series of machines provides such high-level constructs at the assembly language level. Since hardware has become less expensive and the implementation of complex functions using hardware is now cost effective, the instruction sets of present-day microcomputers are as elaborate and as powerful as those of the large-scale machines of the seventies.

As the instruction set becomes larger, the complexity of the control unit increases. During the SSI and MSI (small scale and medium scale integrated circuit) era the instruction sets were kept small to limit the hardware complexity. As hardware technology advanced to LSI and VLSI (large scale and very large scale integration), hardware complexity and cost were not the limiting factors and hence larger instruction sets with powerful macroinstructions were designed. A study of application programs in any language reveals that only a few of the instructions in a large instruction set are used frequently; hence, a small instruction set with the most often used instructions will serve equally well while limiting hardware complexity. This observation has had great effect on microprocessor architectures, because the silicon area on an IC chip saved by using a small instruction set has been used to implement more powerful hardware operators and greater word lengths. Such designs produce *reduced instruction set computers* (RISC).

In general, an instruction set can be classified according to the type of operand used by each instruction. The operand is located either in a register or in a memory location. The typical classes of instructions are

1. Memory-to-memory instructions. Both operands are in memory.
2. Memory-to-register instructions. One of the operands is in memory, the other in a register.
3. Register-reference instructions. The operation is performed on the contents of one or more registers.
4. Memory-reference instructions. The operation is performed on contents of memory locations.
5. Control instructions. These are branching, halt, pause, and the like.
6. Input/output instructions.
7. Macroinstructions. These are equivalent to a set of (more than one) instructions of the types 1 through 6.

Note that the arithmetic and logic instructions are a subset of the memory and register reference instructions.

6.2.1 Instruction Length

The length of an instruction is a function of the number of addresses in the instruction. Typically, a certain number of bits are needed for the opcode; register references do not require a large number of bits, while memory references consume the major portion of an instruction. Hence, memory-reference and memory-to-memory instructions will be longer than the other types of instructions. A variable-length format can be used with these to conserve the amount of memory occupied by the program, but this increases the complexity of the control unit.

The number of memory addresses in an instruction dictates the speed of execution of the instruction, in addition to increasing the instruction length. Each memory address requires a memory read or write access that is slower than the corresponding load or store operation on a register. Based on the number of addresses (operands), the following instruction organizations can be envisioned:

1. Three-address.
2. Two-address.
3. One-address.
4. Zero-address.

Typical instruction sets required to accomplish the four basic arithmetic operations for each of the above instruction organizations are:

Three-address machine.

ADD	A,B,C	$M[C] \leftarrow M[A] + M[B]$
SUB	A,B,C	$M[C] \leftarrow M[A] - M[B]$
MPY	A,B,C	$M[C] \leftarrow M[A] * M[B]$
DIV	A,B,C	$M[C] \leftarrow M[A] / M[B]$

A, B, and C are memory locations.

Each of the above instructions requires three memory accesses for execution, thereby increasing the execution time. In practice, the majority of operations are based on two operands with the result occupying the position of one of the operands. Thus, instruction lengths are reduced and execution speed is increased by using a two-address format:

Two-address machine.

ADD	A,B	$M[A] \leftarrow M[A] + M[B]$
SUB	A,B	$M[A] \leftarrow M[A] - M[B]$
MPY	A,B	$M[A] \leftarrow M[A] * M[B]$
DIV	A,B	$M[A] \leftarrow M[A] / M[B]$

The first operand is lost after the operation.

If one of the operands can be retained in a register, the execution speeds of the above instructions can be increased. Further, if the operand register is implied by the opcode, a second operand field is not required in the instruction, thus reducing the instruction length:

One-address machine.

ADD	A	$ACC \leftarrow ACC + M[A]$
SUB	A	$ACC \leftarrow ACC - M[A]$
MPY	A	$ACC \leftarrow ACC * M[A]$
DIV	A	$ACC \leftarrow ACC / M[A]$
LOAD	A	$ACC \leftarrow M[A]$
STORE	A	$M[A] \leftarrow ACC$

"ACC" is an accumulator or any other register implied by the instruction. (An accumulator is required here). If both the operands can be held in registers, the execution time is decreased. Further, if the opcode implies the two registers, instructions can be of zero-address type:

Zero-address machine.

ADD		$SL \leftarrow SL + TL$, POP
SUB		$SL \leftarrow SL - TL$, POP
MPY		$SL \leftarrow SL * TL$, POP
DIV		$SL \leftarrow SL\ /\ TL$, POP
LOAD	*A*	PUSH, $TL \leftarrow M[A]$
STORE	*A*	$M[A] \leftarrow TL$, POP

SL and *TL* are the second level and top level of a last-in, first-out (LIFO) stack of registers. A LIFO stack is simply a set of storage locations or registers organized in a LIFO manner. A coin box (shown below) is the most popular example of a LIFO stack. Coins are inserted and retrieved from the same end (top) of the coin box. PUSHing a coin moves the stack of coins down one level, the new coin occupying the top level (TL). POPing the coin box retrieves the coin on the top level. The second level (SL) coin becomes the new top level after the POP.

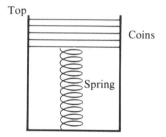

In a LIFO stack (or simply "stack"):

PUSH implies	all the levels move down by one;
	TL ← data, and
POP implies	pops out ← TL,
	TL ← SL;
	all other levels move up.

We will defer the details of stack implementation until section 6.3. In a zero-address machine all the arithmetic operations are on the top two levels of a stack, so no explicit addresses are needed as part of the instruction. However, some memory-reference (one-address) instructions such as LOAD and STORE are required.

Assuming *n* bits for an address representation and *m* bits for the opcode, the instruction lengths in the above four organizations are:

Three-address: $m + 3n$ bits.
Two-address: $m + 2n$ bits.
One-address: $m + n$ bits.
Zero-address: n bits.

Figure 6.1 offers programs to compute the function $F = A * B + C * D$ using each of the above instruction sets. Here A, B, C, D, and F are memory locations. Contents of A, B, C, and D are assumed to be integer values and the results are assumed to fit in one memory word. Program sizes and execution times can be easily computed from benchmark programs of the type presented in Figure 6.1, using the typical set of operations performed in an application environment. Results of such benchmark studies can be used in selecting an instruction set and instruction format.

In IBM 370, the instructions are 2, 4, or 6 bytes long; DEC PDP-11 employs an innovative addressing scheme to represent both single and double operand instructions in two bytes. An instruction in INTEL 8080

Figure 6.1 Programs to compute $F = A * B + C * D$

Program	Program length
Three-address	
MPY A,B,A	
MPY C,D,C	$3(m + 3n)$ bits.
ADD A,C,F	
Two-address	
MPY A,B	
MPY C,D	
ADD A,C	$4(m + 3n)$ bits assuming a MOVE instruction.
SUB F,F } MOVE F,A	
ADD F,A	
One-address	
LOAD A	
MPY B	
STORE F	
LOAD C	$7(m + n)$ bits.
MPY D	
ADD F	
STORE F	
Zero-address	
LOAD A	
LOAD B	
MPY	
LOAD C	
LOAD D	$3m + 5(m + n)$ bits.
MPY	
ADD	
STORE F	

is either 1, 2, or 3 bytes long. The instruction formats are discussed later in this section.

6.2.2 Opcode Selection

Assignment of opcode for instructions in an instruction set can significantly influence the efficiency of the decoding process at the execute phase of the instruction cycle. (ASC opcodes have been arbitrarily assigned.) Two opcode assignments are generally followed:

1. Reserved opcode method.
2. Class code method.

In the reserved opcode method, each instruction would have its own opcode. This method is suitable for instruction sets with fewer instructions. In the class code method, the opcode consists of two parts: a class code part and an operation part. The class code identifies the type or class of instruction and the remaining bits in the opcode (operation part) identify a particular operation in that class. This method is suitable for larger instruction sets and for instruction sets with variable instruction lengths. Class codes provide a convenient means of distinguishing between various classes of instructions in the instruction set. The two opcode assignment modes are illustrated here:

Reserved opcode instruction

Class code instruction

In practice, it may not be possible to identify a class code pattern in an instruction set. When the instructions are of fixed length and the bits of the opcode always completely decoded, there may not be any advantage to assigning opcodes in a class code form. For example, the INTEL 8080 instruction set does not exhibit a class code form; in IBM 370, the first 2 bits of the opcode distinguish between 2-, 4-, and 6-byte instructions. MOSTEK 6502 uses a class code in the sense that part of the opcode distinguishes between the allowed addressing modes of the same instruction. For example, the "add memory to accumulator with carry" instruction (ADC) of MOSTEK 6502 has the following opcode (hexadecimal) variations:

Addressing mode	Opcode (H)
Immediate mode	69
Zero page	65
Zero page, index X	75
Nonzero page	6D
Nonzero page, index X	7D
Nonzero page, index Y	79
Preindexed-indirect	61
Postindexed-indirect	71

We will describe the paged addressing mode later in this chapter.

6.2.3 Instruction Formats

The majority of machines use a fixed-field format within the instruction while varying the length of the instruction to accommodate a varying number of addresses. Some machines vary even the field format within an instruction. In such cases, a specific field of the instruction defines the instruction format. Samples of instruction formats follow.

M6502.

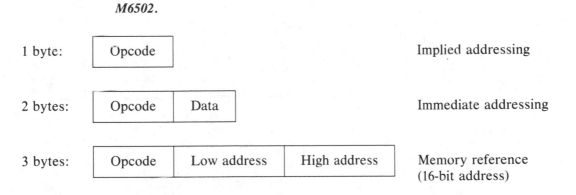

PDP-11. *Single-operand instruction*

Double-operand instruction

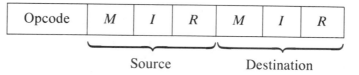

Here, R indicates one of the eight general-purpose *registers*, I refers to the *direct-indirect flag*, and M indicates *mode* of the register — operand, auto increment pointer, auto decrement pointer, or index.

Branch instructions

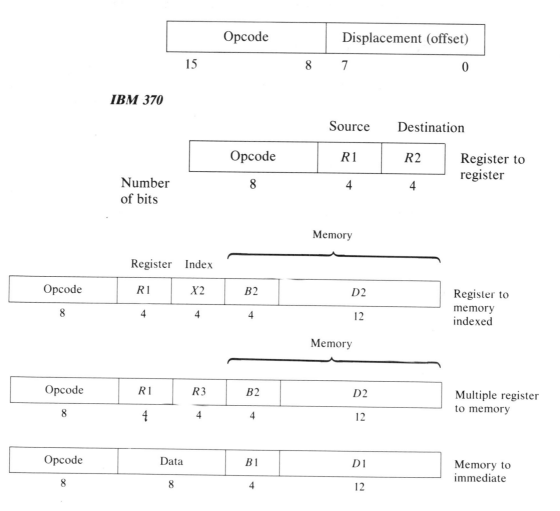

IBM 370

Opcode	L1	L2	B1	D1	B2	D1	Memory to memory
8	4	4	4	12	4	12	

Here, $R1$, $R2$, and $R3$ each stand for one of the sixteen general-purpose *registers* (GPRs), $B1$ and $B2$ are *base* register designations (one of the sixteen GPRs), Data indicates immediate data, $D1$ and $D2$ refer to 12-bit *displacement*, and $L1$ and $L2$ indicate *lengths* of data in bytes. The base-displacement addressing mode is described later in this chapter.

6.3 Stack Implementation

A LIFO stack is used for address and data manipulation, return-address storage and parameter passing during subroutine call and return, and arithmetic operations. It is a versatile structure useful in a variety of operations in a computer system. Two popular implementations of "stack" are

1. RAM-based implementation.
2. Shift-register-based implementation.

In a RAM-based implementation, a special register called a *stack pointer* (SP) is used to hold the address of the top level of the stack. The stack is built in a reserved area in the memory. The PUSH operation then corresponds to

$$SP \leftarrow SP + 1.$$

$$MBR \leftarrow data.$$

$$MAR \leftarrow SP.$$

$$WRITE\ MEMORY.$$

The POP operation corresponds to

$$MAR \leftarrow SP.$$

$$READ\ MEMORY.$$

$$Output \leftarrow MBR.$$

$$SP \leftarrow SP - 1.$$

In this implementation, the stack grows toward higher address memory locations as items are PUSHed into it. There is no actual movement of data between the levels during PUSH and POP operations.

Figure 6.2 A shift-register-based stack

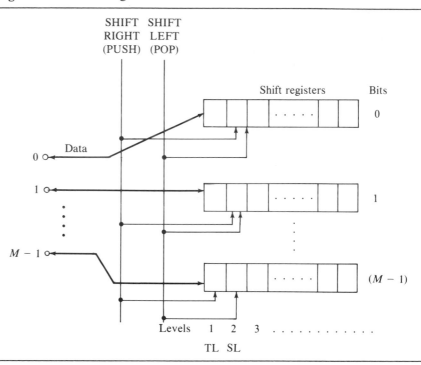

Figure 6.2 portrays the shift-register-based implementation of an n-level stack. Each stack level can hold an m-bit datum. Data are PUSHed into stack by using a SHIFT RIGHT signal and POPed out of stack by using a SHIFT LEFT signal. There is movement of data between levels in this implementation.

Shift-register-based implementations are faster than RAM-based stacks because no memory access is needed. RAM-based implementations are popular because no additional hardware is needed (other than SP) to implement a stack. Instructions to PUSH and POP registers and memory locations must be added to the instruction set once a stack is included in the design.

6.4 Registers

Each of the registers in ASC is designed to be a special-purpose register (accumulator, index register, program counter, etc.). The assignment of functions limits the utility of these registers, but such machines are simpler to design. As the hardware technology has advanced, yielding lower cost hardware, the number of registers in the CPU has increased. The majority of registers are now designed as general-purpose registers and hence can be used as accumulators, index registers, or pointer registers (that is, registers whose content is an address pointing to a memory location).

The *program status word* (or condition code register) is a common facility that was not incorporated in ASC. All information regarding CPU activity, including the type of results (positive, zero, overflow, etc.) from an arithmetic operation and the interrupt status, are continually saved in this register. A representative list of register structures follows.

M6502. (See Figure 6.3.)

Accumulator, index register X, and index register Y — each 8 bits long.
Program counter — 16 bits.
Stack pointer — 16 bits (the high-order byte is always 0000 0001).
Processor status register:

N	V	1	B	D	I	Z	C	8 bits.

N is negative, V is overflow, 1 is not used, B is break command, D is decimal, I is interrupt disable, Z is zero, and C is carry flag.
Instruction register — 8 bits.
(Interrupt processing is discussed in Chapter 7).

INTEL 8080 (See Figure 6.4.)

Register pairs B,C and D,E — each register 8 bits long; 8-bit operands utilize individual registers and 16-bit operands utilize register pairs.
Register pair H,L — usually used for address storage.
Stack pointer — 16 bits.
Program counter — 16 bits.
Accumulator — 8 bits.
Buffer registers to store ALU operands — two, 8 bits long.
Status flag register:

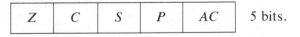

Z	C	S	P	AC	5 bits.

Z is zero, C is carry, S is sign, P is parity, and AC is auxiliary carry (for decimal arithmetic).

Figure 6.3 M6502 structure (courtesy of MOS Technology Inc.)

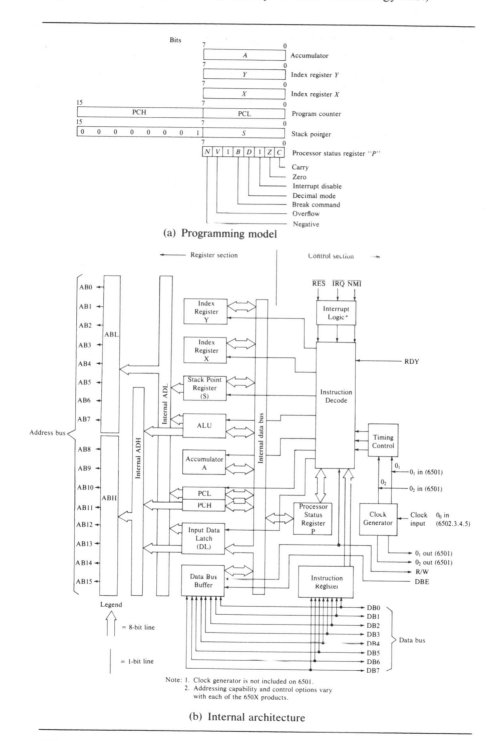

(a) Programming model

(b) Internal architecture

Note: 1. Clock generator is not included on 6501.
2. Addressing capability and control options vary
with each of the 650X products.

252

Figure 6.3 (Continued)

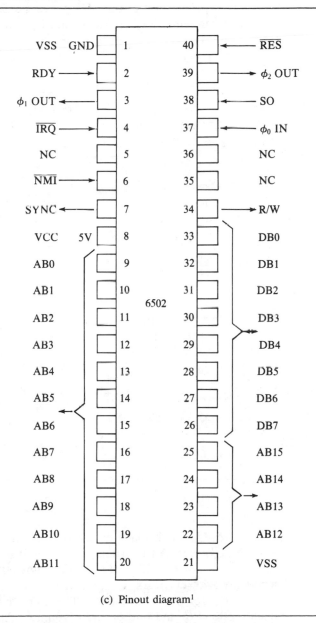

(c) Pinout diagram[1]

[1] Address bus (AB0-AB15); data bus (DB0-DB7); power (VSS, V_{CC}); clock (ϕ_0 IN, ϕ_1 OUT, ϕ_2 OUT); interrupt ($\overline{IRQ}$, $\overline{NMI}$); reset ($\overline{RES}$); synchronize (SYNC); read-write (R/W); ready (RDY); set overflow (S.O.); no connection (N.C.).

Figure 6.4 INTEL 8080 functional block diagram (Reprinted by permission of Intel Corporation, Copyright 1977. All mnemonics copyright Intel Corporation 1977.)

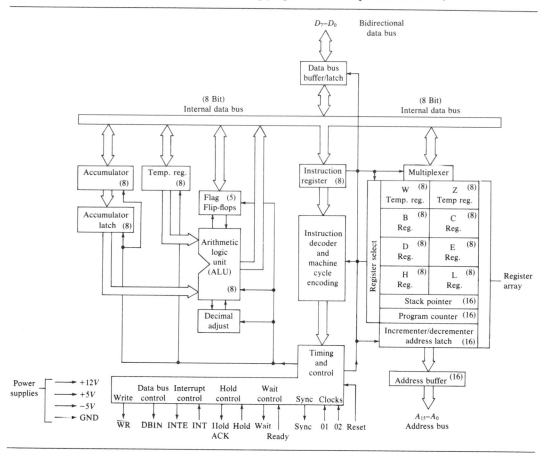

DEC PDP-11. This machine can operate in three modes: *user, supervisory,* and *kernel.* All instructions are valid in kernel mode, but certain instructions (such as HALT) are not allowed in the other two modes. There are two sets of six registers each (*R0–R5*): set 0 is for the user mode and set 1 is for the other modes. There are three stack pointers, one for each mode (*R6*) and one program counter. All registers can be used in operand (contain data), pointer (contain address), and indexed modes. The processor status word has the following format:

Current mode	Previous mode		Not used	Priority	T	N	Z	V	C
15 14	13 12	11	10 9 8 7	6 5	4	3	2	1	0

Register set 0 or set 1

CPU (can operate on eight priority levels; refer to Chapter 7)

Condition codes:
T: trap
N: negative
Z: zero
V: overflow
C: carry

IBM 370. This is a 32-bit machine. There are sixteen general-purpose registers, each 32 bits long. They can be used as base registers, index registers, or operand registers. There are four 64-bit floating-point registers. The program status word has the following format:

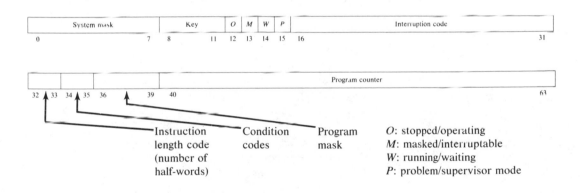

System mask	Key	O	M	W	P	Interruption code
0 7	8 11	12	13	14	15	16 31

			Program counter
32 33 34 35 36		39 40	63

Instruction length code (number of half-words)

Condition codes

Program mask

O: stopped/operating
M: masked/interruptable
W: running/waiting
P: problem/supervisor mode

6.5   Addressing Modes

The direct, indexed, and indirect addressing modes are the most common. Some machines allow preindexed-indirect, some allow postindexed-indirect, and some machines allow both modes. There are three other addressing modes that are popular. They are described below.

6.5.1   Immediate Addressing

In this mode, the operand is a part of the instruction. The address field is used to represent the operand itself rather than the address of the operand. From a programmer's point of view, this mode is equivalent to the literal addressing used in ASC. The literal addressing was converted into a direct address by the ASC assembler. In practice, to accommodate an immediate addressing mode, the instruction contains a data field and an opcode. This addressing mode makes operations with constant operands faster since the operand can be accessed without another memory fetch.

6.5.2 Paged Addressing

When this mode of addressing is allowed, the memory is assumed to consist of several equal-sized blocks or *pages*. The memory address can then be treated as having a page number and a location address (offset) within the page. Figure 6.5 shows a paged memory in which each page is 256 bytes long. The instruction format in such an environment will have a *page bit* and enough additional bits to address the largest offset (that is, the size of the page). Usually the "zero page" of the memory is used for the storage of the most often used data and pointers. The page bit specifies whether the address corresponds to the zero page or the "current page" (i.e., the page in which the instruction is located). Address modifiers (to indicate indexing, indirect, etc.) are also included in the instruction format, as shown below:

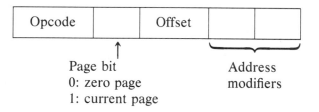

If the pages are large enough, the majority of the memory references by the program will be within the same page and those locations are addressed with fewer bits in the address field than in the case of the direct-addressing scheme. If the referenced location is beyond the page, an extra memory cycle may be needed to access it.

MOSTEK 6502 uses such an addressing scheme. The 16-bit address is divided into an 8-bit page address and an 8-bit offset within the page (of 256 bytes). Further, the processor has unique opcodes for zero-page mode instructions. These instructions are assembled into 2 bytes, the higher byte of the address being zero, while the non-zero page instructions need 3 bytes to represent the opcode and a 16-bit address.

Paged memory schemes are also useful in organizing virtual memory systems, as described in Section 6.8.

Figure 6.5 Paged memory

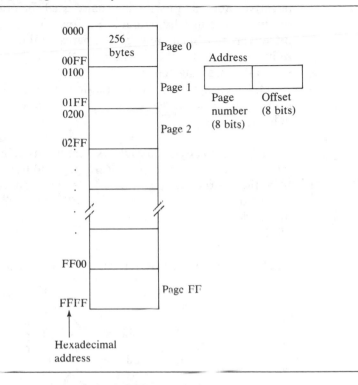

6.5.3 Base-Register Addressing

In some machines, one of the CPU registers is used as a *base register*. The beginning address of the program is loaded into this register as a first step in program execution. Each address referenced in the program is an offset (displacement) with respect to the contents of the base register. Only the base register identification and the displacement are represented in the instruction format, thus conserving bits. Since the set of instructions to load the base register is part of the program, relocation of the programs is automatic. IBM 370 series machines use this scheme; any of the general-purpose registers can be designated as a base register by the programmer.

6.5.4 Relative Addressing

In this mode of addressing, an offset (or displacement) is provided as part of the instruction. This offset is added to the current value of PC during execution to find an effective address. The offset can be either positive or negative. Such addressing is usually used for branch instructions. Since the jumps are usually within a few locations of the current address, the offset can be a small number compared to the actual jump address, thus reducing the bits in the instruction. DEC PDP-11 and MOSTEK 6502 use such an addressing scheme.

Implementation of the addressing modes varies from processor to processor. Addressing modes of some practical machines are listed below.

M6502.   MOSTEK 6502 allows direct, preindexed-indirect, and post-indexed-indirect addressing. Zero-page addressing is employed to reduce the instruction length by 1 byte. The addresses are 2 bytes long. A typical absolute address instruction uses 3 bytes. A zero-page address instruction uses only 2 bytes. Table 6.2 shows the instruction set of the 6502.

Table 6.2 M6502 instruction set (Courtesy of MOS Technology, Inc.)

Object code	Instruction		Object code	Instruction	
00	BRK		30 pp	BMI	disp
01 pp	ORA	(addr,X)	31 pp	AND	(addr),Y
05 pp	ORA	addr	35 pp	AND	addr,X
06 pp	ASL	addr	36 pp	ROL	addr,X
08	PHP		38	SEC	
09 pp	ORA	data	39 ppqq	AND	addr16,Y
0A	ASL	A	3D ppqq	AND	addr16,X
0D ppqq	ORA	addr16	3E ppqq	ROL	addr16,X
0E ppqq	ASL	addr16	40	RTI	
10 pp	BPL	disp	41 pp	EOR	(addr,X)
11 pp	ORA	(addr),Y	45 pp	EOR	addr
15 pp	ORA	addr,X	46 pp	LSR	addr
16 pp	ASL	addr,X	48	PHA	
18	CLC		49 pp	EOR	data
19 ppqq	ORA	addr16,Y	4A	LSR	A
1D ppqq	ORA	addr16,X	4C ppqq	JMP	label
1E ppqq	ASL	addr16,X	4D ppqq	EOR	addr16
20 ppqq	JSR	label	4E ppqq	LSR	addr16
21 pp	AND	(addr,X)	50 pp	BVC	disp
24 pp	BIT	addr	51 pp	EOR	(addr),Y
25 pp	AND	addr	55 pp	EOR	addr,X
26 pp	ROL	addr	56 pp	LSR	addr,X
28	PLP		58	CLI	
29 pp	AND	data	59 ppqq	EOR	addr16,Y
2A	ROL	A	5D ppqq	EOR	addr16,X
2C ppqq	BIT	addr16	5E ppqq	LSR	addr16,X
2D ppqq	AND	addr16	60	RTS	
2E ppqq	ROL	addr16	61 pp	ADC	(addr,X)

Table 6.2 (Continued)

Object code	Instruction		Object code	Instruction	
65 pp	ADC	addr	B4 pp	LDY	addr,X
66 pp	ROR	addr	B5 pp	LDA	addr,X
68	PLA		B6 pp	LDX	addr,Y
69 pp	ADC	data	B8	CLV	
6A	ROR	A	B9 ppqq	LDA	addr16,Y
6C ppqq	JMP	(label)	BA	TSX	
6D ppqq	ADC	addr16	BC ppqq	LDY	addr16,X
6E ppqq	ROR	addr16	BD ppqq	LDA	addr16,X
70 pp	BVS	disp	BE ppqq	LDX	addr16,Y
71 pp	ADC	(addr),Y	C0 pp	CPY	data
75 pp	ADC	addr,X	C1 pp	CMP	(addr,X)
76 pp	ROR	addr,X	C4 pp	CPY	addr
78	SEI		C5 pp	CMP	addr
79 ppqq	ADC	addr16,Y	C6 pp	DEC	addr
7D ppqq	ADC	addr16,X	C8	INY	
7E ppqq	ROR	addr16,X	C9 pp	CMP	data
81 pp	STA	(addr,X)	CA	DEX	
84 pp	STY	addr	CC ppqq	CPY	addr16
85 pp	STA	addr	CD ppqq	CMP	addr16
86 pp	STX	addr	CE ppqq	DEC	addr16
88	DEY		D0 pp	BNE	disp
8A	TXA		D1 pp	CMP	(addr),Y
8C ppqq	STY	addr16	D5 pp	CMP	addr,X
8D ppqq	STA	addr16	D6 pp	DEC	addr,X
8E ppqq	STX	addr16	D8	CLD	
90 pp	BCC	disp	D9 ppqq	CMP	addr16,Y
91 pp	STA	(addr),Y	DD ppqq	CMP	addr16,X
94 pp	STY	addr,X	DE ppqq	DEC	addr16,X
95 pp	STA	addr,X	E0 pp	CPX	data
96 pp	STX	addr,Y	E1 pp	SBC	(addr,X)
98	TYA		E4 pp	CPX	addr
99 ppqq	STA	addr16,Y	E5 pp	SBC	addr
9A	TXS		E6 pp	INC	addr
9D ppqq	STA	addr16,X	E8	INX	
A0 pp	LDY	data	E9 pp	SBC	data
A1 pp	LDA	(addr,X)	EA	NOP	
A2 pp	LDX	data	EC ppqq	CPX	addr16
A4 pp	LDY	addr	ED ppqq	SBC	addr16
A5 pp	LDA	addr	EE ppqq	INC	addr16
A6 pp	LDX	addr	F0 pp	BEQ	disp
A8	TAY		F1 pp	SBC	(addr),Y
A9 pp	LDA	data	F5 pp	SBC	addr,X
AA	TAX		F6 pp	INC	addr,X
AC ppqq	LDY	addr16	F8	SED	
AD ppqq	LDA	addr16	F9 ppqq	SBC	addr16,Y
AE ppqq	LDX	addr16	FD ppqq	SBC	addr16,X
B0 pp	BCS	disp	FE ppqq	INC	addr16,X
B1 pp	LDA	(addr),Y			

INTEL 8080. The majority of the memory references for INTEL 8080 are based on the contents of register pair H, L. These registers are loaded, incremented, and decremented under program control. The instructions are thus only 1 byte long and imply indirect addressing through the H, L register pair. Some instructions have the 2-byte address as part of them (direct addressing). There are also single-byte instructions operating in an implied addressing mode. Table 6.3 shows the INTEL 8080 instruction set.

DEC PDP-11. The two instruction formats of PDP-11 shown earlier in this chapter provide a versatile addressing capability. Mode (M) bits allow the contents of the referenced register to be (1) an operand, (2) a pointer to a memory location that is incremented (auto increment) or decremented (auto decrement) automatically after accessing that memory location, or (3) an index. In the index mode the instructions are two words long. The content of the second word is an address and is indexed by the referenced register. The indirect bit (*I*) allows direct and indirect addressing in all the four register modes. In addition, PDP-11 allows PC-relative addressing, in which an offset is provided as part of the instruction and added to the current PC value to find the effective address of the operand. Some examples are shown below:

Mnemonic	Octal opcode	Comments
CLR	0050 *nn*	Clear word, *nn* is the register reference.
CLRB	1050 *nn*	Clear byte.
ADD	06 *nn mm*	Add, *nn* = source, *mm* = destination.
ADD *R2, R4*	06 02 04	$R4 \leftarrow R2 + R4$.
CLR (*R5*)+	0050 25	Auto increment pointer, clear $R5 \leftarrow 0$, $R5 \leftarrow R5 + 1$.
ADD @*X(R2),R1*	06 72 01 ⌉	@ indicates indirect; *X* indicates indexing.
	Address ⌋	$R1 \leftarrow M[M[\text{Address} + R2]] + R1$ immediate.
ADD #10, R0	062700 ⌉ 000010 ⌋	$R0 \leftarrow 10$.
INC Offset	005267 ⌉ Offset ⌋	$M[PC + \text{Offset}] \leftarrow M[PC + \text{Offset}] + 1$.

IBM 370. Any of the 16 general-purpose registers can be used as an index register, an operand register, or a base register. The 12-bit displacement field allows 4K bytes of displacement from the contents of the base register. A new base register is needed if the reference exceeds the 4K range. Immediate addressing is allowed. In decimal arithmetic where the

Table 6.3 INTEL 8080 instruction set (Reprinted by permission of Intel Corporation, Copyright 1977. All mnemonics copyright Intel Corporation 1977.)

Mnemonic	Description	Instruction code[1]								Clock[2] cycles
		D_7	D_6	D_5	D_4	D_3	D_2	D_1	D_0	
ACI	Add immediate to A with carry	1	1	0	0	1	1	1	0	7
ADC M	Add memory to A with carry	1	0	0	0	1	1	1	0	7
ADC r	Add register to A with carry	1	0	0	0	1	S	S	S	4
ADD M	Add memory to A	1	0	0	0	0	1	1	0	7
ADD r	Add register to A	1	0	0	0	0	S	S	S	4
ADI	Add immediate to A	1	1	0	0	0	1	1	0	7
ANA M	And memory with A	1	0	1	0	0	1	1	0	7
ANA r	And register with A	1	0	1	0	0	S	S	S	4
ANI	And immediate with A	1	1	1	0	0	1	1	0	7
CALL	Call unconditional	1	1	0	0	1	1	0	1	17
CC	Call on carry	1	1	0	1	1	1	0	0	11/17
CM	Call on minus	1	1	1	1	1	1	0	0	11/17
CMA	Compliment A	0	0	1	0	1	1	1	1	4
CMC	Compliment carry	0	0	1	1	1	1	1	1	4
CMP M	Compare memory with A	1	0	1	1	1	1	1	0	7
CMP r	Compare register with A	1	0	1	1	1	S	S	S	4
CNC	Call on no carry	1	1	0	1	0	1	0	0	11/17
CNZ	Call on no zero	1	1	0	0	0	1	0	0	11/17
CP	Call on positive	1	1	1	1	0	1	0	0	11/17
CPE	Call on parity even	1	1	1	0	1	1	0	0	11/17
CPI	Compare immediate with A	1	1	1	1	1	1	1	0	7
CPO	Call on parity odd	1	1	1	0	0	1	0	0	11/17
CZ	Call on zero	1	1	0	0	1	1	0	0	11/17
DAA	Decimal adjust A	0	0	1	0	0	1	1	1	4
DAD B	Add B & C to H & L	0	0	0	0	1	0	0	1	10
DAD D	Add D & E to H & L	0	0	0	1	1	0	0	1	10
DAD H	Add H & L to H & L	0	0	1	0	1	0	0	1	10
DAD SP	Add stack pointer to H & L	0	0	1	1	1	0	0	1	10
DCR M	Decrement memory	0	0	1	1	0	1	0	1	10
DCR r	Decrement register	0	0	D	D	D	1	0	1	5
DCX B	Decrement B & C	0	0	0	0	1	0	1	1	5
DCX D	Decrement D & E	0	0	0	1	1	0	1	1	5
DCX H	Decrement H & L	0	0	1	0	1	0	1	1	5

Table 6.3 (Continued)

Mnemonic	Description	D_7	D_6	D_5	D_4	D_3	D_2	D_1	D_0	Clock[2] cycles
DCX SP	Decrement stack pointer	0	0	1	1	1	0	1	1	5
DI	Disable Interrupt	1	1	1	1	0	0	1	1	4
EI	Enable Interrupts	1	1	1	1	1	0	1	1	4
HLT	Halt	0	1	1	1	0	1	1	0	7
IN	Input	1	1	0	1	1	0	1	1	10
INR M	Increment memory	0	0	1	1	0	1	0	0	10
INR r	Increment register	0	0	D	D	D	1	0	0	5
INX B	Increment B & C registers	0	0	0	0	0	0	1	1	5
INX D	Increment D & E registers	0	0	0	1	0	0	1	1	5
INX H	Increment H & L registers	0	0	1	0	0	0	1	1	5
INX SP	Increment stack pointer	0	0	1	1	0	0	1	1	5
JC	Jump on carry	1	1	0	1	1	0	1	0	10
JM	Jump on minus	1	1	1	1	1	0	1	0	10
JMP	Jump unconditional	1	1	0	0	0	0	1	1	10
JNC	Jump on no carry	1	1	0	1	0	0	1	0	10
JNZ	Jump on no zero	1	1	0	0	0	0	1	0	10
JP	Jump on positive	1	1	1	1	0	0	1	0	10
JPE	Jump on parity even	1	1	1	0	1	0	1	0	10
JPO	Jump on parity odd	1	1	1	0	0	0	1	0	10
JZ	Jump on zero	1	1	0	0	1	0	1	0	10
LDA	Load A direct	0	0	1	1	1	0	1	0	13
LDAX B	Load A indirect	0	0	0	0	1	0	1	0	7
LDAX D	Load A indirect	0	0	0	1	1	0	1	0	7
LHLD	Load H & L direct	0	0	1	0	1	0	1	0	16
LXI B	Load immediate register Pair B & C	0	0	0	0	0	0	0	1	10
LXI D	Load immediate register Pair D & E	0	0	0	1	0	0	0	1	10
LXI H	Load immediate register Pair H & L	0	0	1	0	0	0	0	1	10
LXI SP	Load immediate stack pointer	0	0	1	1	0	0	0	1	10
MVI M	Move immediate memory	0	0	1	1	0	1	1	0	10
MVI r	Move immediate register	0	0	D	D	D	1	1	0	7
MOV M, r	Move register to memory	0	1	1	1	0	S	S	S	7
MOV r, M	Move memory to register	0	1	D	D	D	1	1	0	7
MOV r1,r2	Move register to register	0	1	D	D	D	S	S	S	5
NOP	No-operation	0	0	0	0	0	0	0	0	4
ORA M	Or memory with A	1	0	1	1	0	1	1	0	7
ORA r	Or register with A	1	0	1	1	0	S	S	S	4
ORI	Or immediate with A	1	1	1	1	0	1	1	0	7

Instruction code[1]

Mnemonic	D7	D6	D5	D4	D3	D2	D1	D0	Output	Clock Cycles
OUT	1	1	0	1	0	0	1	1		10
PCHL	1	1	1	0	1	0	0	1	H & L to program counter	5
POP B	1	1	0	0	0	0	0	1	Pop register pair B & C off stack	10
POP D	1	1	0	1	0	0	0	1	Pop register pair D & E off stack	10
POP H	1	1	1	0	0	0	0	1	Pop register pair H & L off stack	10
POP PSW	1	1	1	1	0	0	0	1	Pop A and Flags off stack	10
PUSH B	1	1	0	0	0	1	0	1	Push register Pair B & C on stack	11
PUSH D	1	1	0	1	0	1	0	1	Push register Pair D & E on stack	11
PUSH H	1	1	1	0	0	1	0	1	Push register Pair H & L on stack	11
PUSH PSW	1	1	1	1	0	1	0	1	Push A and Flags on stack	11
RAL	0	0	0	1	0	1	1	1	Rotate A left through carry	4
RAR	0	0	0	1	1	1	1	1	Rotate A right through carry	4
RC	1	1	0	1	1	0	0	0	Return on carry	5/11
RET	1	1	0	0	1	0	0	1	Return	10
RLC	0	0	0	0	0	1	1	1	Rotate A left	4
RM	1	1	1	1	1	0	0	0	Return on minus	5/11
RNC	1	1	0	1	0	0	0	0	Return on no carry	5/11
RNZ	1	1	0	0	0	0	0	0	Return on no zero	5/11
RP	1	1	1	1	0	0	0	0	Return on positive	5/11
RPE	1	1	1	0	1	0	0	0	Return on parity even	5/11
RPO	1	1	1	0	0	0	0	0	Return on parity odd	5/11
RRC	0	0	0	0	1	1	1	1	Rotate A right	4
RST	1	1	A	A	A	1	1	1	Restart	11
RZ	1	1	0	0	1	0	0	0	Return on zero	5/11
SBB M	1	0	0	1	1	1	1	0	Subtract memory from A with borrow	7
SBB r	1	0	0	1	1	S	S	S	Subtract register from A with borrow	4
SBI	1	1	0	1	1	1	1	0	Subtract immediate from A with borrow	7
SHLD	0	0	1	0	0	0	1	0	Store H & L direct	16
SPHL	1	1	1	1	1	0	0	1	H & L to stack pointer	5
STA	0	0	1	1	0	0	1	0	Store A direct	13
STAX B	0	0	0	0	0	0	1	0	Store A indirect	7
STAX D	0	0	0	1	0	0	1	0	Store A indirect	7
STC	0	0	1	1	0	1	1	1	Set carry	4
SUB M	1	0	0	1	0	1	1	0	Subtract memory from A	7
SUB r	1	0	0	1	0	S	S	S	Subtract register from A	4
SUI	1	1	0	1	0	1	1	0	Subtract immediate from A	7
XCHG	1	1	1	0	1	0	1	1	Exchange D & E, H & L Registers	4
XRA M	1	0	1	0	1	1	1	0	Exclusive Or memory with A	7
XRA r	1	0	1	0	1	S	S	S	Exclusive Or register with A	4
XRI	1	1	1	0	1	1	1	0	Exclusive Or immediate with A	7
XTHL	1	1	1	0	0	0	1	1	Exchange top of stack, H & L	18

[1] DDD or SSS — 000 B — 001 C — 010 D — 011 E — 100 H — 101 L — 110 Memory — 111 A.

[2] Two possible cycle times, (5/11) indicate instruction cycles dependent on condition flags.

memory-to-memory operations are used (6-byte instructions), the lengths of the operands are also specified, thus allowing variable-length operands. Indirect addressing is not allowed.

6.6 Data Formats

Data representation differs from machine to machine. The data format depends on the word size, code used (ASCII and EBCDIC are the most popular codes), and arithmetic mode (1s or 2s complement, binary or decimal) employed by the machine. The fixed-point binary number (integer) representation is common to all the machines and is shown below for an n-bit machine:

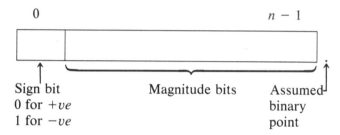

Sign bit
0 for $+ve$
1 for $-ve$ Magnitude bits   Assumed
                                                                binary
                                                                point

Negative numbers are represented either as 2s complements (PDP-11, MOSTEK 6502) or as 1s complements (Univac 1100 series, Data General ECLIPSE).

6.6.1 Decimal Data

Machines that allow decimal (BCD) arithmetic mode use 4 bits per decimal digit and pack as many digits as possible into the machine word. Either a separate set of instructions is used to operate on such data (as in IBM 370) or the arithmetic is changed from one mode to the other (as in MOSTEK 6502) by an instruction provided for that purpose, so that the same instruction can be used to operate on either type of data. A BCD digit occupies 4 bits and hence two decimal (BCD) digits can be packed into 1 byte as shown below:

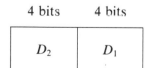

INTEL 8080 and
MOSTEK 6502 representation

IBM 370 allows the decimal numbers to be of variable length (from one to sixteen digits). The length is specified (or implied) as part of the instruction. Two digits are *packed* into 1 byte. Zeros are padded on the most significant end if needed. A typical data format is shown below:

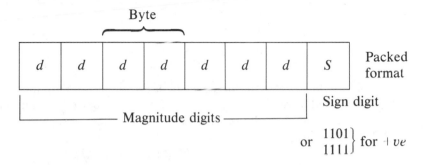

In the *unpacked* form, IBM 370 uses 1 byte for each decimal digit: the upper 4 bits is the *zone* field and contains 1111 and the lower 4 bits have the decimal digit.

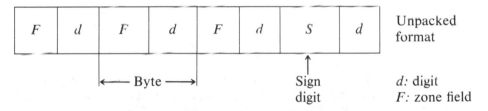

All the arithmetic operations are on packed numbers; the unpacked format is useful for input/output since the IBM 370 uses EBCDIC code (1 byte per character).

6.6.2 Character Strings

These are represented 1 byte per character, using either ASCII or EBCDIC code. The maximum length of the character string is a design parameter of the particular machine.

6.6.3 Floating-Point Numbers

We have so far used only integer arithmetic in this book. In practice, floating-point (real) numbers are used in computations and are represented as shown below:

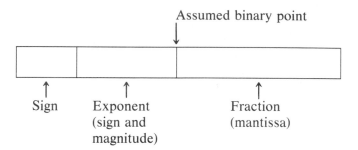

Assumed binary point

Sign   Exponent   Fraction
        (sign and   (mantissa)
        magnitude)

The representation consists of the sign of the number, an exponent field, and a fraction field. For example, consider the real number $(23.5)_{10}$. This number can be represented as:

$$(23.5)_{10} = (10111.1)_2$$
$$= 0.101111 \times 2^5$$

and hence the representation is

0	0101	101111
Sign	Exponent	Fraction

In the above example, the most significant bit of the fraction is 1. When the fraction consists of 1 or more zero bits at the most significant end, it is usually shifted left until the most significant bit is non-zero and the exponent is adjusted accordingly. This process is called *normalization* of a fraction. Since in practice there will be only a limited number of bits to represent the fraction, normalization enables more bits to be retained, thus increasing accuracy. Two floating-point representations are described below.

IBM 370

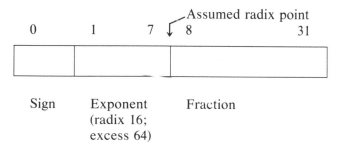

Assumed radix point

0   1   7   8   31

Sign   Exponent   Fraction
        (radix 16;
        excess 64)

The fraction is represented using either 24 bits (single precision) or 56 bits (double precision). The exponent is a radix-16 exponent and is expressed as an excess-64 number (that is, a 64 is added to the true exponent so that the exponent representation ranges from 0 through 127 rather than -64 to 63).

IEEE Standard. The Institute of Electrical and Electronic Engineers' (IEEE) standard for floating-point representation is shown below:

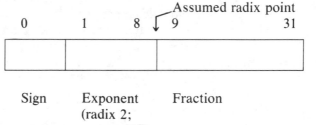

A "1" is assumed to the left of the radix point in this representation, to gain an extra bit of accuracy in representing fractions.

Example 6.1 The number $(23.5)_{10}$ is shown below in both of the representations:

$$(23.5)_{10} = (10111.1)_2 = (0.101111) \times (2)^5$$

$$= (0001\ 0111.1)_2$$

$$= 0.(0001\ 0111\ 1)_2 \times (16)^2$$

0	1000010	0001 0111 1000 0000 0000 0000	IBM
Sign	Exponent	Fraction	

0	1000 0100	0111 1000 0000 0000 0000 000	IEEE standard
Sign	Exponent	Fraction	

6.7 CPU Structures

ASC used a multibus architecture. If a single-bus structure were designed for ASC, it would necessitate buffer registers in the ALU to hold one of the operands when an ALU operation requires two operands. Since there would be only one data transfer path, one of the two operands would be first transferred to the ALU buffer and the operation performed with the second operand on the bus during a subsequent time frame, thus making the CPU slower. Both single and multiple bus structures have been used in practice.

The data transfer paths in the CPU of large, mini, and micro computers are parallel buses. If faster operating speeds are not required, serial bus architecture can be employed, as usually is the case with the processor ICs used to build calculators. The design goal in fabricating a calculator IC is to pack as many functions into one IC as possible. By using a serial-transfer scheme, silicon area on the IC is conserved and can be used for implementing other complex functions. Some representative bus structures are shown in Figures 6.3(b), 6.4, and 6.6.

MOSTEK 6502 structure, shown in Figure 6.3(b), uses an 8-bit data bus and two 8-bit address buses (ADH for the higher order 8 bits and ADL for the lower order 8 bits of the 16-bit address). Since the 6502 is an 8-bit machine with 16-bit addresses, all address manipulations are performed in two parts (high and low parts) each containing 8 bits. These two parts are stored in ABL and ABH buffers, which are connected to the 16-bit address bus. The CPU provides an 8-bit bidirectional data bus for external transfer.

INTEL 8080 uses an 8-bit internal data bus for all register transfers (refer to Figure 6.4). The arithmetic unit operates on two 8-bit operands residing in the temporary register (TEMP REG) and the accumulator latch. The CPU provides an 8-bit bidirectional data bus, a 16-bit address bus, and a set of control signals. These are used in building a complete microcomputer system.

Figure 6.6(a) shows the structure of PDP-11/45 CPU. All data paths within the CPU are 16 bits wide. There are two processor blocks (an arithmetic-logic processor and a floating-point processor), sixteen general-purpose registers, and a program status register. The memory management unit allows the use of *solid-state* (semiconductor) and *core* memory blocks simultaneously in the system. The CPU is configured as a device connected to the *unibus* (universal bus) along with memory and peripheral devices.

The unibus *priority arbitration logic* resolves the relative priorities of the devices requesting the bus. The CPU can be programmed to operate on eight levels of priority. Once the bus is granted, the requesting device becomes the bus master to transfer data to another device (*slave*). A second unibus (unibus B) is configured as a memory bus to which semiconductor memory blocks are connected. A typical system structure is shown in Figure 6.6(b). The unibus is the communicating path between

Figure 6.6 PDP-11/45 structure (Copyright, Digital Equipment
Corporation, 1978. All Rights Reserved.)

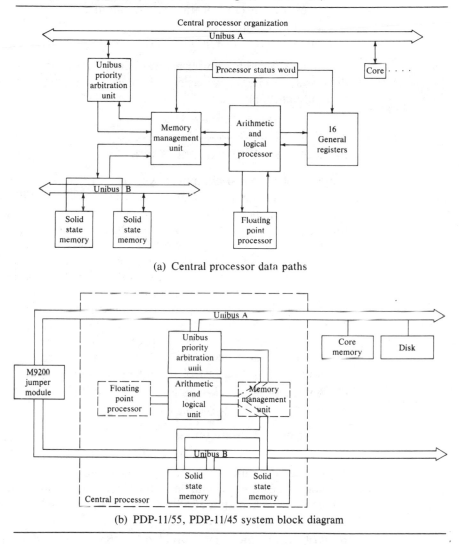

(a) Central processor data paths

(b) PDP-11/55, PDP-11/45 system block diagram

the CPU, memory, and peripheral devices. It is an asynchronous bus
capable of transferring one 16-bit word every 400 nanoseconds. There are
56 lines in the unibus:

18 address lines (256K byte or 128K word address space).
16 data lines plus 2 parity lines.

2 lines for type of transfer (data in, data out, data in pause, data out byte).

8 lines for bus control, timing, and status.

5 bus request lines.

5 unidirectional bus grant lines.

The unibus provides uniform interfacing characteristics for all devices, thus making interfacing easier. Chapter 7 gives further details on unibus structure and operation.

6.8 Memory System Enhancement

Memory of practical computer systems is organized into a hierarchy of cache, primary, and secondary memories as discussed in Chapter 3. This hierarchical organization enables a faster memory access and enhances the capacity of the memory system while maintaining a low cost.

Traditionally, memory cycle times have been much longer than CPU cycle times. This speed gap between the memory and the CPU means that the CPU must wait for memory to respond to an access request. With the advances in hardware technology, semiconductor memories are now competitive (cost effective) and are replacing magnetic core memories as primary memory devices. Even with the availability of these fast memories, the CPU-memory speed gap exists. Several techniques have been used to reduce this speed gap and to increase the memory system capacity while optimizing the cost of the memory system. We will discuss some popular enhancement techniques used in actual machines, next.

6.8.1 Speed Enhancement

The obvious method of increasing the memory access speed is to use a higher speed memory technology. Once the technology is selected, the memory access speeds can be further increased by judicious use of decoding and access techniques. Six such techniques are described below:

Banking. The memory is divided into physically independent blocks or *banks*. Each bank has its own MAR and MBR, thus allowing a simultaneous access of more than one bank. Supposing that the program and data are stored in different banks, the instruction fetched from one bank can be rewritten (assuming a core memory) while the data are fetched from the other bank, thus increasing the execution speed. This is a natural method of speed enhancement, since the expansions to the memory are usually in blocks of some fixed size. The primary memory address in this organiza-

Figure 6.7 Memory banking

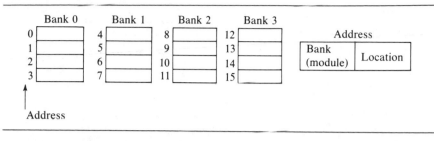

tion consists of two parts, the bank number and the location or displacement within the bank, as shown in Figure 6.7. The decoding is similar to a 2½-D decoding scheme. The bank bits in the address select (enable) one of the banks while the remaining address bits select a word in that bank.

Interleaving. The addressing scheme used above organizes the memory such that the subsequent memory locations are in the same bank. The advantage of this arrangement is that even if a memory bank fails, the other banks provide continuous memory space. Since sequential program execution requires that subsequent locations of the same bank be accessed, the instruction fetch speed is not enhanced. "Interleaving" the memory blocks is a technique to spread the subsequent addresses to separate physical memory blocks. This is done by using the low-order bits of the address to select the bank, as shown in Figure 6.8. A disadvantage of this organization is that if one of the memory banks fails, the "interleaved" memory system becomes inoperative.

An alternative organization is to interleave the memory to create several interleaved subsystems. This is done by using a combination of high-order and low-order address bits for selecting the memory banks, as shown in Figure 6.9.

Figure 6.8 Memory interleaving

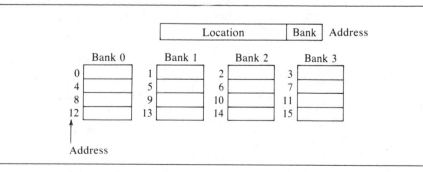

Figure 6.9 Memory with interleaved subsystems

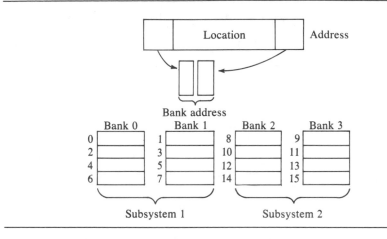

There is no general guideline to select one addressing scheme over the other among the three described above. Each computer system uses its own scheme. The basic aim of these schemes is to spread subsequent memory references over several physical banks so that faster accessing is possible.

DEC PDP-11/45 interleaves memory blocks in pairs of 8K word banks. If the two banks are magnetic core memories, the memory cycle time averages 650 nanoseconds compared to the 850-nanosecond individual cycle time.

Primary memory in Control Data Corporation's (CDC) CDC 6600 is organized into 131,072 words, each 60 bits long in thirty-two banks of 4,096 words per bank. These banks are arranged in an interleaved fashion, which provides a high degree of random-access overlap and block transfer speed. Each word in the primary memory is identified by an 18-bit address. The least significant 5 bits of the address are used to select one of the thirty-two banks and the remaining bits to select a word within the bank. Consecutive addresses, therefore, lie in separate physical memory blocks.

Multiport Memories. Multiple-port (multiport) memories are available in which each port corresponds to an MAR and an MBR. Independent accesses to the memory can be made from each port. The memory system resolves the conflicts between the ports on a priority basis. Multiport memories are useful in an environment where more than one device accesses the memory. Examples of such systems are a single processor system with a direct-memory access (DMA), I/O controller (see Chapter 7), and a multiprocessor system with more than one CPU (see Chapter 8).

Wider Word Fetch.   IBM 370 fetches 64 bits (two words) in each memory access. This enhances execution speed, because the second word fetched most likely contains the next instruction to be executed, thus saving a "wait" for the fetch. If the second word does not contain the required instruction (during a jump, for example) a new fetch is required. This scheme was also used in the IBM 7094, a machine designed in the early sixties.

Instruction Buffer.   Providing a first-in, first-out (FIFO) buffer (or queue) between the CPU and the primary memory enhances the instruction fetch speed. Instructions from the primary memory are fed into the buffer (queue) at one end and the CPU fetches the instructions from the other end, as shown in Figure 6.10. As long as the instruction execution is sequential, the two operations of filling the buffer (prefetching) and fetching from the buffer into CPU can go on simultaneously. But when a jump (conditional or unconditional) instruction is executed, the next instruction to be executed may or may not be in the buffer. If the required instruction is not in the buffer, the fetch operation must be directed to the primary memory and the buffer is refilled from the new memory address. If the buffer is large enough, the complete range of the jump (or loop) may be accommodated in the buffer. In such cases, the CPU can signal the buffer to FREEZE, thereby stopping the prefetch operation. Once the loop or jump is satisfied, both FETCH operations can continue normally.

The buffer management requires hardware components to manage the queue (e.g., check for queue full or queue empty) and mechanisms to

Figure 6.10 Instruction buffer

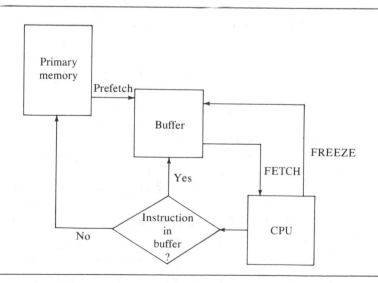

identify the address range in the buffer and to freeze and unfreeze the buffer.

CDC 6600 uses an instruction buffer that can store eight 60-bit words, that is, 16 to 32 instructions, since the instructions are either 15 or 30 bits long. Figure 6.11 shows the instruction buffer organization. Instructions from main memory are brought into the buffer through a buffer register. The lowest level of the buffer is transferred to the instruction register for execution purposes while the contents of the buffer move up one position. A new set of instructions (60 bits) enters the buffer through the buffer register. When a branch instruction is encountered, if the address of the branch is within the range of the buffer, the next instruction is retrieved from it. If not, instructions are fetched from the new memory address.

Cache Memory. A cache memory is a small but fast memory block inserted between the CPU and the primary memory. CPU fetches data and instructions from the cache. Since cache is about ten times faster than the primary memory, the CPU-memory speed gap is considerably reduced.

In this speed enhancement scheme, the primary memory and cache are usually divided into equal-sized pages. Required pages from the primary memory are first transferred into the cache and execution of the program begins with the CPU fetching data and instructions from the cache. If the address of the instruction to be executed or the data to be fetched is not in the cache (i.e., a miss), an appropriate page from the primary memory is transferred into the cache. If the address is in the cache (i.e., a hit), the execution of instructions from the cache continues.

Figure 6.11 CDC 6600 instruction buffer

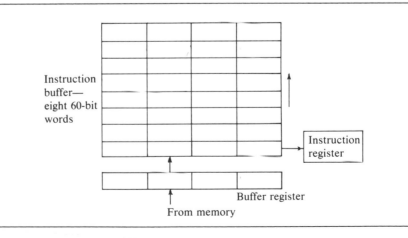

Writing data into a primary memory location using the cache scheme is usually done in two ways. In the first method, the data to be written are entered both into cache and into the corresponding page in the primary memory. In the second method, a tag is associated with each cache page. The tag indicates whether a page is altered or not due to a memory "write" operation. If not altered, the page is discarded and another required page is brought into the cache. A virtual-memory management scheme similar to the one described in the next subsection is needed to manage the cache-primary memory interactions.

IBM 360 model 85 employs a user-transparent cache to match the 80 nanosecond CPU with the 1 microsecond cycle time of the core memory. The cache is a 16K-byte fast storage. The effect of the cache is equivalent to having a primary memory with 100-nanosecond cycle time.

Data General Corporation's ECLIPSE minicomputer system has a 64-word, 200-nanosecond cache. The main memory is a 700-nanosecond semiconductor memory, four-way interleaved. Each reference to the memory retrieves a block of four words into the cache. The cache is divided into sixteen pages of four words each. The least recently used (LRU) block in the cache is replaced by the next block of words retrieved from the primary memory.

6.8.2   Size Enhancement

The main memory of a machine usually is not large enough to serve as the sole storage medium for all the programs and data. Disks and drums are used to increase capacity. However, the program must be in the main memory when it is executed. Mechanisms to transfer programs from secondary to main storage as needed during the execution of the program are thus required. In earlier systems, programs were divided into smaller segments and the segments were loaded manually into the main memory as they were needed. Since this program-loading operation would be complex in a large-system environment, automatic means of transferring segments of programs in and out of the primary memory were devised. With these mechanisms, transfer operations are visible to the user. The user can further assume that the size of the memory available for programs during execution is the combined capacities of primary and secondary storage. This combined main memory and disk storage hierarchy is called the *virtual storage*. In a virtual storage environment, programs are divided into equal size segments known as *pages* and only the pages required for execution at any time are brought into the main memory.

Consider the memory system shown in Figure 6.12. The primary memory is 2^p pages long; the secondary memory has the capacity to store 2^q pages where $q > p$, and each page has 2^d words. The user assumes that

Figure 6.12 Virtual memory system

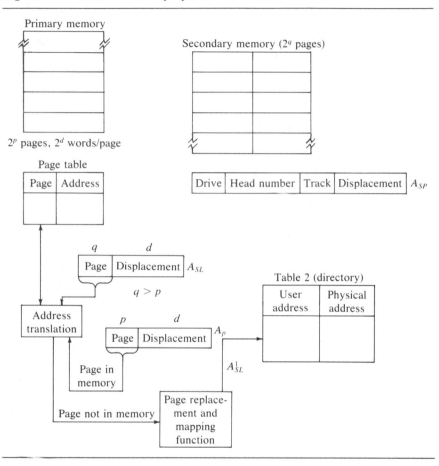

the total memory capacity available for programs is 2^q pages. The user-logical address format (A_{SL}) can address a page and a memory location within a page. In this scheme, when a page is residing on the disk, the physical address of a word in the page has the components shown in A_{SP} (drive number, head number, track number, and displacement or word number within the track). Table 2 in Figure 6.12 is a directory of A_{SL}-to-A_{SP} transformation. At any time there can be 2^p pages in the primary memory. For the pages in the primary memory, A_{SL} must be translated into the primary address A_P. The page table provides information indicating which of the *virtual* (or secondary) *pages* are residing in which *real* (or primary) *page*. If the program during execution refers to an address A_{SL}, the address translation hardware converts it into A_p if that page is primary memory resident (a hit). If not (a miss), the page replacement hardware moves one of the required pages from the secondary memory to replace a real page that is not needed immediately. The virtual memory operation thus requires the following mechanisms:

1. Address translation: determines whether the referenced page is in real memory or not and keeps track of the page movements in both memories.
2. Mapping function: determines where the pages are to be located in the secondary memory.
3. Page replacement algorithm: decides which of the real pages are to be replaced.

The page table is maintained in an associative memory (in IBM 370) for faster search and address translation. The page-replacement algorithms are based on the usage statistics of the real pages. The least recently used (LRU) page is usually replaced because, due to the "local" nature of the address references in a program, if a page is not recently referenced it is not likely that it will be needed immediately. Mapping functions compress the secondary storage into smaller real memory. Direct mapping assumes a fixed real-page slot for each virtual page, while associative mapping schemes either assign a set of virtual pages to a real-page slot (set associative) or allow any virtual page to occupy any real-page slot (fully associative).

Virtual memory schemes have been used in almost all large-scale computer systems. Virtual memory mechanisms can be implemented in software (as part of the operating system function) or by using specially designed hardware. Some microprocessor families and minicomputers use a special-purpose support circuit called *memory management unit* (MMU).

6.9 Control-Unit Enhancement

Two popular methods of designing the control unit were discussed in Chapter 5. This section lists some of the features found in actual machines that enhance the performance of the control unit.

6.9.1 Hardwired Control Units

The control unit for the ASC has the simplest synchronous hardwired configuration. Each *major cycle* consists of four *minor cycles,* and as many major cycles as required are used for the execution of an instruction. A majority of actual control units are synchronous control units that are enhanced versions of the ASC control unit. For example, it is not necessary to use up a complete major cycle if the microoperations corresponding to an instruction execution (or fetch or defer) can be completed in a part of the major cycle. The only optimization performed in the ASC control unit was to reduce the number of major cycles needed to execute certain instructions (SHR, SHL) by not entering an execute cycle, since all the required microoperations to implement those instructions could be completed in one major cycle. Further optimization is possible. For example, the microoperations corresponding to the execution of each branch instruction (BRU, BIP, BIN) could all be completed in one minor cycle rather than in a complete major cycle as they are in the ASC control unit. Thus, three minor cycles could be saved in the execution of branch instructions by returning to fetch cycle after the first minor cycle in the execute cycle. When such enhancements are implemented, the state-change circuitry of the control unit becomes more complex but the execution speed increases.

INTEL 8080 has a synchronous control unit operating with a major cycle (machine cycle) consisting of three, four, or five minor cycles (states). An instruction cycle consists of one to five major cycles, depending on the type of instruction. The machine cycles are controlled by a two-phase nonoverlapping clock, as shown in Figure 6.13(a). "SYNC" identifies the beginning of a machine cycle. There are ten types of machine cycles: fetch, memory read, memory write, stack read, stack write, input, output, interrupt acknowledge, halt acknowledge, and interrupt acknowledge while halt. Figure 6.13(b) shows the pinout diagram of INTEL 8080. The signals shown are described below.

A_{15-0}	Address bus.
D_{7-0}	Data bus.
SYNC	System synchronize signal.
READY	Used to indicate if data are ready on the data bus (used to interface slow memory).
WAIT	Puts the processor into wait state (required when using slow memories).
DBIN	Data bus in (i.e., data accepted by CPU).
$\overline{WR}$	Read/write mode (CPU is in write mode when $\overline{WR}$ is 0).
RESET	Input to CPU to initialize CPU status.
HOLD	Input signal to request CPU to release data and address buses for DMA operation (see Chapter 7).
HLDA	Hold acknowledge (response of CPU to HOLD).
INT	Interrupt CPU (see Chapter 7 for details).
INTE	Interrupt enable (CPU is ready to accept interrupts).

Instructions in the 8080 contain 1 to 3 bytes. Each instruction requires from one to five machine or memory cycles for fetching and execution.

Machine cycles are called M1, M2, M3, M4, and M5. Each machine cycle requires from three to five states, T1, T2, T3, T4, and T5, for its completion. Each state has the duration of one clock period (0.5 microseconds). There are three other states (WAIT, HOLD, and HALT), which last from one to an indefinite number of clock periods, as controlled by external signals. Machine cycle M1 is always operation-code fetch

Figure 6.13 INTEL 8080 (Reprinted by permission of Intel Corporation, Copyright 1981. All mnemonics copyright Intel Corporation 1981.)

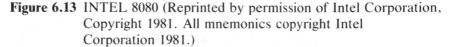

First state of every machine cycle

$\phi 1$

$\phi 2$

SYNC

(a) Nonoverlapping clock

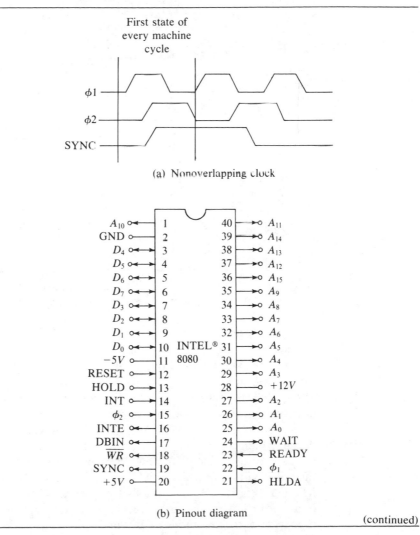

A_{10}	1	40	A_{11}
GND	2	39	A_{14}
D_4	3	38	A_{13}
D_5	4	37	A_{12}
D_6	5	36	A_{15}
D_7	6	35	A_9
D_3	7	34	A_8
D_2	8	33	A_7
D_1	9	32	A_6
D_0	10 INTEL®	31	A_5
$-5V$	11 8080	30	A_4
RESET	12	29	A_3
HOLD	13	28	$+12V$
INT	14	27	A_2
ϕ_2	15	26	A_1
INTE	16	25	A_0
DBIN	17	24	WAIT
$\overline{WR}$	18	23	READY
SYNC	19	22	ϕ_1
$+5V$	20	21	HLDA

(b) Pinout diagram

(continued)

Figure 6.13 (Continued)

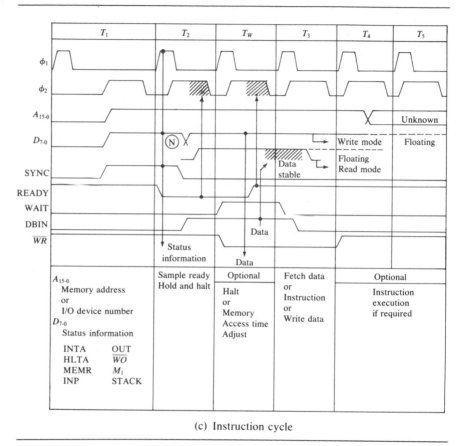

(c) Instruction cycle

cycle and lasts four or five clock periods. Machine cycles M2, M3, M4, and M5 normally last three clock periods each.

To further understand the basic timing operation of the INTEL 8080, refer to the state diagram shown in Figure 6.13(c). During T1, the content of the program counter is sent to the address bus, SYNC is true, and the data bus contains the status information pertaining to the cycle that is currently being initiated. T1 is always followed by another state, T2, during which the condition of the READY, HOLD, and HALT acknowledge signals are tested. If READY is true, T3 can be entered; otherwise, the CPU will go into the WAIT state (T_w) and stays there for as long as READY is false. READY thus allows the CPU speed to be synchronized to a memory with any access time or to any input device. The user, by properly controlling the READY line, can single-step through a program.

During T3, the data coming from memory are available on the data bus and are transferred into the instruction register (during M1 only). The instruction decoder and control sections then generate the basic signals to control the internal data transfer, the timing, and the machine cycle requirements of the instruction.

At the end of T4 (if the cycle is complete) or at the end of T5 (if it is not), the 8080 goes back to T1 and enters machine cycle M2, unless the instruction required only one machine cycle for its execution. In such cases, a new M1 cycle is entered. The loop is repeated for as many cycles and states as may be required by the instruction.

Instruction-state requirements range from a minimum of four states for nonmemory referencing instructions (such as register and accumulator arithmetic instructions) and up to eighteen states for the most complex instructions (such as instructions to exchange the contents of registers H and L with the contents of the two top locations of the stack). At the maximum clock frequency of 2 megahertz, this means that all instructions will be executed in intervals from 2 to 9 microseconds. If a HALT instruction is executed, the processor enters a WAIT state and remains there until an interrupt is received. Chapter 7 provides details of interrupt processing.

Figure 6.14 shows the microoperation sequences of nine instructions (one column for each instruction). Refer to the complete instruction

Figure 6.14 INTEL 8080 microinstructions (Reprinted by permission of Intel Corporation, copyright 1981. All mnemonics copyright Intel Corporation 1981.)

Mnemonic		JMP adrs	CALL adrs
Opcode ($D_7 - D_0$)		1100 0011	1100 1101
M1[1]	T4[3]	X	SP ← SP − 1
	T5		
M2	T1	PC OUT, STATUS[5]	PC OUT, STATUS[5]
	T2[2]	PC ← PC + 1	PC ← PC + 1
	T3	Z ← B2[4]	Z ← B2
M3	T1	PC OUT, STATUS[5]	PC OUT, STATUS[5]
	T2[2]	PC ← PC + 1	PC ← PC + 1
	T3	W ← B3[4]	W ← B3

(continued)

Figure 6.14 (Continued)

Mnemonic		JMP adrs	CALL adrs
Opcode $(D_7 - D_0)$		1100 0011	1100 1101
M4	T1		SP OUT, STATUS[9]
	T2[2]		Data bus ← PCH
	T3		SP ← SP − 1
M5	T1		SP OUT, STATUS[9]
	T2[2]		Data bus ← PCL
	T3		
	T4[3]		
	T5		
During the fetch of next instruction		WZ OUT, STATUS[8] PC ← WZ + 1	WZ OUT, STATUS[8] PC ← WZ + 1

Mnemonic		MOV r1, r2	XCHG	ADD r	ADD M
Opcode $(D_7 - D_0)$		01 DDD SSS	1110 1011	1000 0SSS	1000 0110
M1[1]	T4[3]	TMP ← SSS	HL ↔ DE	TMP ← SS ACT ← A	ACT ← A
	T5	DDD ← TM			
M2	T1			[7]	HL OUT STATUS[5]
	T2[2]			A ← ACT + TMP	TMP ← DATA
	T3				
M3	T1				[7]
	T2[2]				A ← TMP + ACT
	T3				

Figure 6.14 (Continued)

Mnemonic		MVI M, data	INR M	SHLD adrs
Opcode $D_7 - D_0$		0011 0110	0011 0100	0010 0010
M1[1]	T4[3]	X	X	X
	T5			
M2	T1	PC OUT, STATUS[5]	HL OUT, STATUS[5]	PC OUT, STATUS[5]
	T2[2] T3	TMP ← B2	TMP ← DATA ALU ← TMP + 1	PC ← PC + 1 Z ← B2
M3	T1	HL OUT, STATUS[6]	HL OUT, STATUS[6]	PC OUT, STATUS[5]
	T2[2] T3	Data bus ← TMP	Data bus ← ALU	PC ← PC + 1 WZ ← B3
M4	T1			WZ OUT, STATUS[6]
	T2[2] T3			Data bus ← L WZ ← WZ + 1
M5	T1			WZ OUT, STATUS[6]
	T2[2] T3			Data bus ← H
	T4[3] T5			

[1] The first memory cycle ($M1$) is always an instruction fetch; the first (or only) byte, containing the opcode, is fetched during this cycle.

[2] *Fetch cycle* (M1): T1: Address bus ← PC; status signals on data bus. T2: PC ← PC + 1. T3: TMP/IR ← INSTRUCTION.

[3] States T4 and T5 are present, as required, for operations that are completely internal to the CPU. The contents of the internal bus during T4 and T5 are available at the data bus; this is designed for testing purposes only. An "X" denotes that the state is present but is only used for such internal operations as instruction decoding.

[4] Instruction bytes are designated B1, B2, and B3. *SSS* is the source register. *DDD* is the destination register. M memory location is pointed to by *HL* registers. r_1 and r_2 are registers.

[5] Memory read subcycles; an instruction or data word will be read.

[6] Memory write subcycle.

[7] The results of these arithmetic, logical, or rotate instructions are not moved into the accumulator (A) until state T2 of the next instruction cycle. That is, A is loaded while the next instruction is being fetched; this overlapping of operations allows for faster processing.

[8] This represents the first subcycle (the instruction fetch) of the next instruction cycle.

[9] Stack write subcycle.

set of Table 6.2 and the register structure of Figure 6.4 for details. The first three states (T_1, T_2, and T_3) of the fetch machine cycle (M1) are the same for all instructions. Note that for instructions such as ADD *r,* once the memory operand is fetched into the CPU, addition is performed while the CPU is fetching the next instruction in sequence from the memory. This overlap of instruction fetching and execution increases the speed of program execution.

Figure 6.15 shows the structure of INTEL 8086, a 16-bit microprocessor. This microprocessor is partitioned into two parts: the *execution unit* (EU) that fetches instructions from a six-instruction-long instruction buffer (queue) and executes them, and the *bus interface unit* (BIU) that generates the instruction address and transfers instructions from memory

Figure 6.15 INTEL 8086 elementary block diagram (Reprinted by permission of Intel Corporation, copyright 1981. All mnemonics copyright Intel Corporation 1981.)

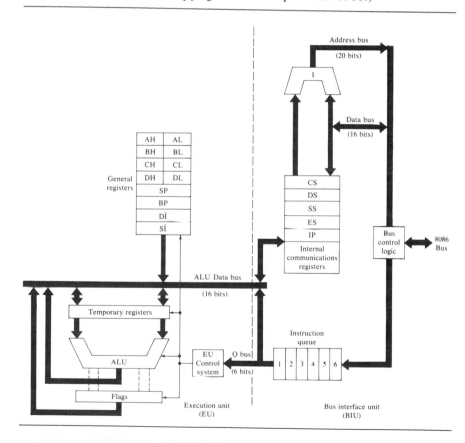

to the instruction queue. EU and BIU are two independent units working concurrently, thus increasing the instruction processing speed. As long as the instructions are fetched from sequential locations, the instruction queue remains filled and the EU and BIU operations remain smooth. When the EU refers to an instruction address beyond the range of the instruction queue (as may happen during jump instructions), the instruction queue is refilled from the new address.

Instruction buffers, cache memories, and wider word fetch schemes discussed in Section 6.8 are also considered as enhancements to the control unit.

6.9.2 Microprogrammed Control Units

The execution time for an instruction is proportional to the number of microoperations required and hence the length of microprogram sequence for the instruction. Since a microprogrammed control unit (MPCU) starts fetching the next instruction once the last microoperation of the current instruction microprogram is executed, MPCU can be treated as an asynchronous control unit. An MPCU is slower than the hardwired control unit because of the addition of CROM access time to the register transfer time. But it is more flexible than hardwired CU and requires minimum changes in hardware if the instruction set is to be modified or enhanced.

The size of the CROM is one of the design parameters. Although the price of ROM circuits is decreasing, the associated data paths required within the control unit add to the cost. Hence, the number of bits per CROM word is to be minimized. If the word size is reduced, encoding of control signals into groups (as in the ASC MPCU design) is required. This adds decoding circuitry to generate control signals. Alternatively, more than one word of the CROM may be used to represent one microinstruction. This would necessitate a judicious partitioning and assignment of control signals to CROM bits. The encoded form of the microinstruction format used in the ASC MPCU is called *vertical* microinstruction while the unpacked form (1 bit per control signal) is called *horizontal* microinstruction. The horizontal and vertical designations also are used to denote the partitioning of the total set of control signals into that of a set of independent functions such as adder control, shifter control, and register transfer control. The use of a microinstruction for the identification of the simultaneous use of multiple functional units is also a horizontal microinstruction format. In this context, the vertical microinstruction treats the complete control as one function. Figure 6.16 shows several formats for microinstructions.

Figure 6.17 shows the structure of Nanodata Corporation's QM-1. QM-1 has two levels of microprogram control; each microinstruction in-

Figure 6.16 Example microinstruction formats

Instruction	Jump address

Instruction	Test	Jump address

Instruction	Test	Test true jump address	Test false jump address

1	Instruction	
0	Test	Jump address

Figure 6.17 Nanodata QM-1 structure

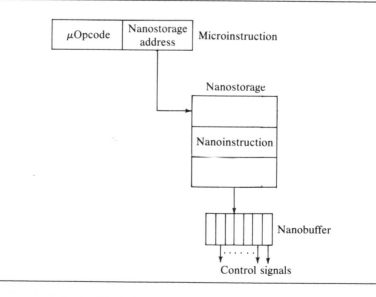

vokes a nanoinstruction sequence. The nanocontrol unit is a hardwired control unit. The major application of QM-1 is the emulation of other architectures. The two-level control unit provides a flexible emulation capability ("emulation" is the process of making the host machine interpret the target machine instructions by microprogramming the host).

Some machines are designed with a *writable control store*. The system programmers can load a microprogram into the control store (RAM or ROM) on the machine to emulate a target machine or to implement a new instruction on the host. Machines such as the Nanodata QM-1 are called "soft machines," since they do not have an instruction set of their own,

Figure 6.18 DEC VAX-11/750 microarchitecture (Copyright, Digital Equipment Corporation, 1979. All Rights Reserved.)

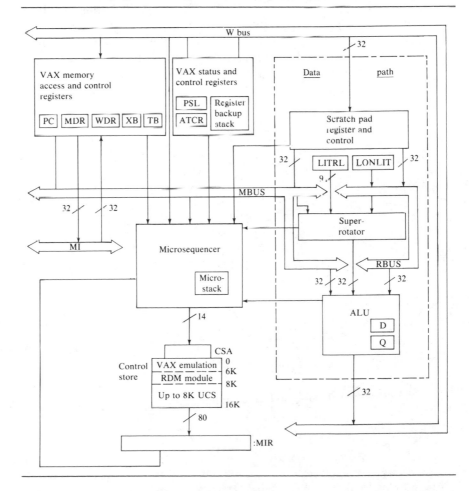

but an instruction set required for an application can be devised by micro-programming these machines.

Figures 6.18 and 6.19 depict Digital Equipment Corporation's VAX-11/750 microarchitecture and microinstruction fields. There are three internal buses in the DEC VAX-11/750: the *WBUS, MBUS,* and *RBUS.* The output of the ALU, unless inhibited, goes on the *WBUS.* Data to be written into memory and data to be written into the scratch pad registers are taken from the *WBUS.* States and control information is passed to or from the particular registers via the *WBUS.*

The *MBUS* and *RBUS* provide a source for the super-rotator and the ALU. Data on the *MBUS* are primarily taken from the main-memory interface registers and from the *M* scratch pad registers. Data on the *RBUS* are from the *R* scratch pad registers and the long literal register. The ALU can perform 2s complement arithmetic, BCD arithmetic, and logical operations. The output of the ALU can be shifted or rotated. There are fifty-six scratch pad registers. The super-rotator can barrel-shift a 64-bit data element, extract a desired field from a given piece of data, and construct a 32-bit data element according to a variety of specifications. This provides VAX-11/750 with a very efficient bit-manipulation

Figure 6.19 DEC VAX-11/750 microinstruction fields (Copyright, Digital Equipment Corporation, 1979. All Rights Reserved.)

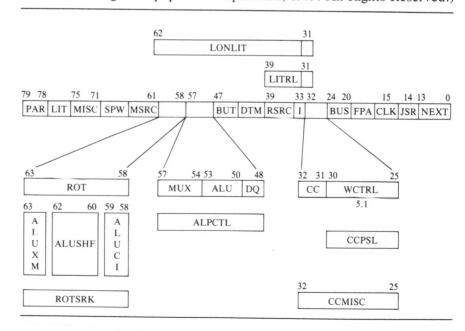

capability. Different components or elements are controlled by the bits in microinstruction fields.

The control store is a 16K, 80-bit word memory. Of this, the low-order 6K words are required to emulate VAX and the next 2K words are required for the remote diagnostic module (RDM). This leaves 8K 80-bit words of address space for user control store (UCS) or writable control store of which 1K is actually available as part of the control store.

VAX uses the microarchitecture primarily to emulate the VAX computer exceptions and interrupt mechanism. Emulation starts with branch on microtest (BUT) bits in the microinstruction.

6.9.3 Instruction Execution Overlap

INTEL 8080 uses the overlap concept in instruction execution to increase the processing speed. The overlap is limited to executing a set of microoperations of the previous instruction during the fetch cycle of the current instruction. In general, the control unit can be envisioned as a device with three subfunctions: fetch, decode (or address computation), and execute. If the control unit is designed in a modular form, one module for each of the above functions, it is possible to overlap the instruction processing.

Figure 6.20 introduces the concept of an instruction processing *pipeline*. The control unit has three modules. The processing sequence is shown in (b). Any time after t_2, the first module will be fetching instruction ($I + 1$), the second module will be decoding instruction "I," while

Figure 6.20 Pipelined instruction processing

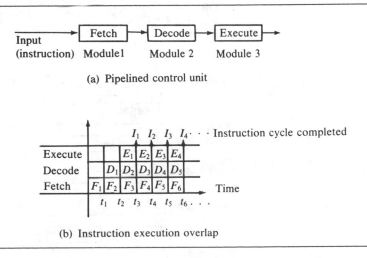

(a) Pipelined control unit

(b) Instruction execution overlap

the third module is executing instruction $(I - 1)$. From time t_3 onwards, the throughput of the pipeline is one instruction per time slot.

For simplicity of representation, each module is shown to take an equal amount of processing time. If such equal time partition of the processing time cannot be made, intermediate registers to hold the results and flags to indicate the completion of one task and to begin the next task are needed. Such instruction execution overlap is used in all machines to a certain extent. The "pipelined" architecture is used wherever such over-lapped processing is possible. We will discuss a pipeline for arithmetic operations in the next section.

6.10   Arithmetic-Logic Unit Enhancement

The ASC arithmetic-logic unit (ALU) was designed to perform addition, complementation, and shift operations on 16-bit binary data, in parallel. The four basic arithmetic operations can be performed using this ALU and appropriate software routines as described in Chapter 4. A number of enhancements that make the ASC ALU resemble a practical ALU are described in this section.

6.10.1   Logical Operations

In addition to simple "shift right" or "shift left" operations, ALUs can perform the following set of logical operations. (See instruction sets in Tables 6.2 and 6.3 for typical operations.)

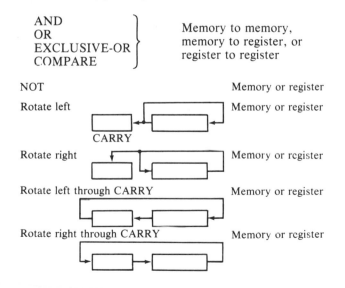

Multiple-Bit Shift. ASC ALU is designed for one bit shift at a time. It is desirable to have the capability of performing multiple shifts using one instruction. Since the address field in the ASC instruction format for shift instructions is not used, it may represent the number of shifts. The control unit must be changed to recognize the shift count in the address field and perform the appropriate number of shifts.

6.10.2 Addition and Subtraction

The pseudo-parallel adder used in the ASC ALU is slow; the addition is complete only after the CARRY has rippled through the most significant bit. There are several techniques to increase the speed of addition. We will discuss one such technique (CARRY LOOK-AHEAD) below.

Consider the ith stage of the pseudo-parallel adder with inputs a_i, b_i, and C_{i-1} (CARRY IN) and the outputs s_i and C_i (CARRY OUT) shown here:

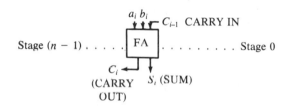

We define two functions;

$$\text{Generate:} \quad G_i = a_i \cdot b_i. \qquad (6\text{--}1)$$

$$\text{Propagate:} \quad P_i = a_i \oplus b_i. \qquad (6\text{--}2)$$

These functions imply that the stage i generates a CARRY if $(a_i \cdot b_i) = 1$ and the CARRY C_{i-1} is propagated to C_i if $(a_i \oplus b_i) = 1$. Substituting G_i and P_i into the equations for the SUM and CARRY functions of the full adder, we get:

$$\text{SUM:} \quad S_i = a_i \oplus b_i \oplus C_{i-1}$$

$$= P_i \oplus C_{i-1} \qquad (6\text{--}3)$$

$$\text{CARRY:} \ C_i = a_i \cdot b_i \cdot \overline{C}_{i-1} + \overline{a}_i \cdot b_i \cdot C_{i-1} + a_i \cdot \overline{b}_i \cdot C_{i-1} + a_i \cdot b_i \cdot C_{i-1}$$

$$= a_i b_i + (\overline{a}_i b_i + a_i \overline{b}_i) C_{i-1}$$

$$= a_i b_i + (a_i \oplus b_i) C_{i-1}$$

$$= G_i + P_i C_{i-1} \qquad (6\text{--}4)$$

G_i and P_i can be generated simultaneously since a_i and b_i are available. Equation (6.3) implies that S_i can be simultaneously generated if all CARRY IN (C_{i-1}) signals are available. From equation (6–4),

$$C_0 = G_0 + P_0 C_{-1} \qquad\qquad (C_{-1} \text{ is CARRY IN to the right-most bit.})$$

$$C_1 = G_1 + C_0 P_0$$
$$= G_1 + G_0 P_1 + C_{-1} P_0 P_1$$

$$.$$
$$.$$
$$.$$

$$C_i = G_i + G_{i-1} P_i + G_{i-2} P_{i-1} P_i + \cdots\cdots$$
$$+ G_0 P_1 P_2 \ldots . P_i + C_{-1} P_0 P_1 \ldots . P_i. \qquad\qquad (6\text{–}5)$$

From equation (6–5) it is seen that C_i is a function of only Gs and Ps of the ith and earlier stages. All C_is can be simultaneously generated because Gs and Ps are available. Figure 6.21 shows a 4-bit CARRY LOOK-AHEAD adder (CLA) schematic and the detailed circuitry. This adder is faster than the ripple-carry adder since the delay is independent of the number of stages in the adder and equal to the delay of the three stages of circuitry in Figure 6.21 (that is, about six gate delays). Four-bit and 8-bit off-the-

Figure 6.21 CARRY LOOK-AHEAD adder (CLA)

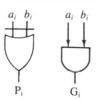

(a) Propagate, CARRY generate

(b) SUM

Figure 6.21 (Continued)

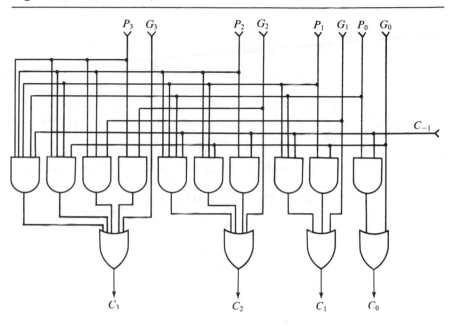

(c) CLA circuitry (4 bit)

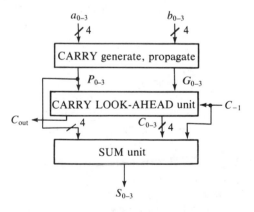

(d) CLA schematic

shelf CLA units are available in TTL. It is possible to connect several such units to form larger adders.

6.10.3 Multiplication

Multiplication can be performed by repeated addition of the multiplicand to itself multiplier number of times. In the binary system, multiplication by a power of 2 corresponds to shifting the multiplicand left by one position and hence multiplication can be performed by a series of shift and add operations.

Example 6.2   Consider the multiplication of two 4-bit numbers:

Multiplicand   1011
(D) $\times$ 1101   Multiplier $D = d_{n-1}, \ldots, d_1 d_0$
              1011   (R)
              0000 $R = r_{n-1}, \ldots, r_1 r_0$
            1011   Partial products
          1011
        10001111   Product

Note that each nonzero partial product above is the multiplicand shifted left an appropriate number of bits. Since the product of two n-bit numbers is $2n$ bits long, we can start off with a $2n$-bit accumulator containing all 0s and obtain the product by the following algorithm:

1. Perform the following step n times ($i = 0$ through $n - 1$):
2. Test the multiplier bit r_i.

    If $r_i = 0$, shift accumulator right 1 bit;
    If $r_i = 1$, add multiplicand (D) to the most significant end of the accumulator and shift the accumulator right 1 bit.

Figure 6.22(a) shows a set of registers that can be used for multiplying two 4-bit numbers. In general, for multiplying two n-bit numbers, R and D registers are each n bits long and the accumulator (A) is (n + 1) bits long. The concatenation of registers A and R (that is, $A \, ¢ \, R$) will be used to store the product. The extra bit in A can be used for representing the sign of the product. We will see from the multiplication example shown in Figure 6.22(c) that the extra bit is needed to store the carry during partial product computation. The multiplication algorithm is shown in Figure 6.22(b).

Various multiplication algorithms that perform multiplication faster than in the above example are available. Hardware multipliers are also

Figure 6.22 Multiplication

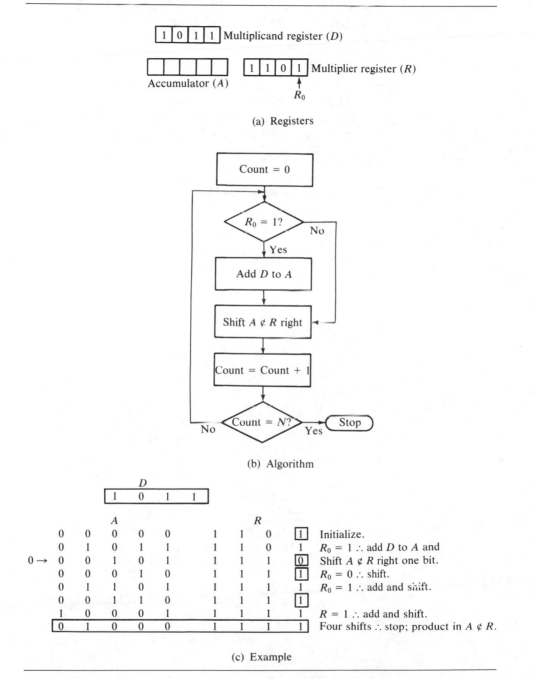

(a) Registers

(b) Algorithm

(c) Example

available as off-the-shelf units. One such multiplier is described later in this section. The book by Hwang listed as a reference at the end of this chapter provides details of multiplication algorithms and hardware.

6.10.4 Division

Division can be performed by repeated subtraction. We will describe two division algorithms that utilize shift and add operations in this section. We will assume that an n-bit integer X (dividend) is divided by another n-bit integer Y (divisor) to obtain an n-bit quotient Q and a remainder R, where

$$\frac{X}{Y} = Q + \frac{R}{Y} \tag{6-6}$$

and

$$0 \le R < Y.$$

The first algorithm corresponds to the usual trial-and-error procedure for division and is illustrated with the following example. Let

$$X = 1011 \text{ (i.e., } n = 4),$$

and

$$Y = 0011,$$

$$Q = q_3 q_2 q_1 q_0.$$

Example 6.3

0011 ⎰ 000 1011	Expand X with $(n-1)$ zeros.
−001 1	Subtract $2^{n-1}y$.
111 0011	Result is negative $\therefore q_{n-1} = 0$.
+001 1	Restore by adding $2^{n-1}y$ back.
000 1011	
− 00 11	Subtract $2^{n-2}y$.
111 1111	Result is negative $\therefore q_{n-2} = 0$.
+001 1	Restore by adding $2^{n-2}y$.
000 1011	
− 0 011	Subtract $2^{n-3}y$.
000 0101	Result is positive $\therefore q_{n-3} = 1$.
−0011	Subtract $2^{n-4}y$.
000 0010	Result is positive $\therefore q_{n-4} = 1$.
	Stop, after n steps.

$\therefore$ remainder = (0010), quotient = (0011).

This is called a *restoring division* algorithm, since the dividend is restored to its previous value if the result of the subtraction at any step is negative. If numbers are expressed in complement form, subtraction can be replaced by addition. The algorithms for an n-bit division are generalized below:

1. Assume initial value of dividend D is $(n - 1)$ zeros concatenated with X.
2. Perform the following step for $i = (n - 1)$ through 0: Subtract $2^i \cdot y$ from D. If the result is negative, $q_i = 0$ and restore D by adding $2^i \cdot y$; if the result is positive, $q_i = 1$.
3. Collect q_i to form the quotient Q; the value of D after the last step is the remainder.

The second division algorithm is the *nonrestoring division* method. Example 6.4 illustrates this method.

Example 6.4 Let $X = 1011$, $Y = 0110$.

$$
\begin{array}{r|l}
0110 \; \overline{\;|\; 000\ 1011} & \text{Trial dividend.} \\
\underline{-011\ 0} & \text{Subtract } 2^{n-1} \cdot Y. \\
101\ 1011 & \text{Negative result } \therefore q_3 = 0. \\
\underline{+\ 01\ 10} & \text{Add } 2^{n-2} \cdot Y. \\
111\ 0011 & \text{Negative result } \therefore q_2 = 0. \\
\underline{+\ \ 0\ 110} & \text{Add } 2^{n-3} \cdot Y. \\
111\ 1111 & \text{Negative result } \therefore q_1 = 0. \\
\underline{+\ \ \ \ 0110} & \text{Add } 2^{n-4} \cdot Y. \\
000\ 0101 & \text{Positive result } \therefore q_0 = 1.
\end{array}
$$

$\therefore$ quotient $= 0001$, remainder $= 0101$

This method can be generalized into the following steps:

1. Assume initial value of dividend d is $(n - 1)$ zeros concatenated with X; set $i = n - 1$.
2. Subtract $2^i \cdot Y$ from D.
3. If the result is negative, $q_i = 0$; if the result is positive, $q_i = 1$, $i = i - 1$; if $i = 0$, go to step 5; otherwise, go to step 4.
4. If the result is negative, add $2^i \cdot Y$ to the result; otherwise, subtract $2^i \cdot Y$ from the result to form new D; go to step 3.
5. If the final result is negative, $q_0 = 0$; otherwise $q_0 = 1$. If the final result is negative, correct the remainder by adding $2^0 \cdot Y$ to it.

The multiplication and division algorithms discussed above assume the operands are positive and no provision is made for a sign bit, although the most significant bit of the result in division algorithms can be treated as a sign bit. Direct methods for multiplication and division of numbers represented in 1s and 2s complement forms are available.

The hardware implementation of multiply and divide is usually an optional feature on smaller machines. Multiply and divide algorithms can be implemented either in hardware or in firmware by developing microprograms to implement these algorithms or by using software routines, as in Chapter 4. Figure 6.23 shows the register usage for binary multiply-divide operations on IBM 370.

6.10.5 Off-the-Shelf ALUs

An ALU can be built using off-the-shelf ICs. For example, the SN 74181 shown in Figure 6.24 is a multifunction ALU. It can perform sixteen binary arithmetic operations on two 4-bit operands A and B. The function to be performed is selected by pins S0, S1, S2, and S3 and include addition, subtraction, decrement, and straight transfer, as shown in Figure 6.23(b). C_n is the CARRY INPUT and C_{n+4} is the CARRY OUTPUT if the IC is used as a 4-bit ripple-carry adder. The IC can also be used with a look-ahead carry generator (74182) to build high-speed adders of multiple stages forming 4, 8, 12, and 16-bit adders.

Figure 6.23 Register usage for fixed-point multiply and divide on IBM 370

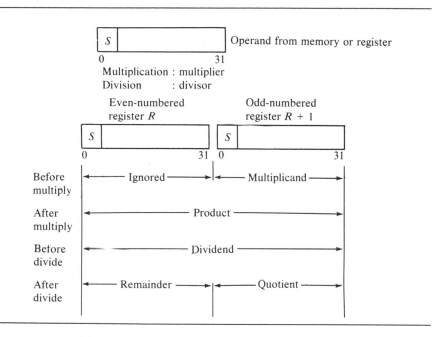

Figure 6.24 An ALU (Courtesy of Texas Instruments Incorporated)

74181
Arithmetic logic units/
function generators

16 Arithmetic operations
16 Logic functions

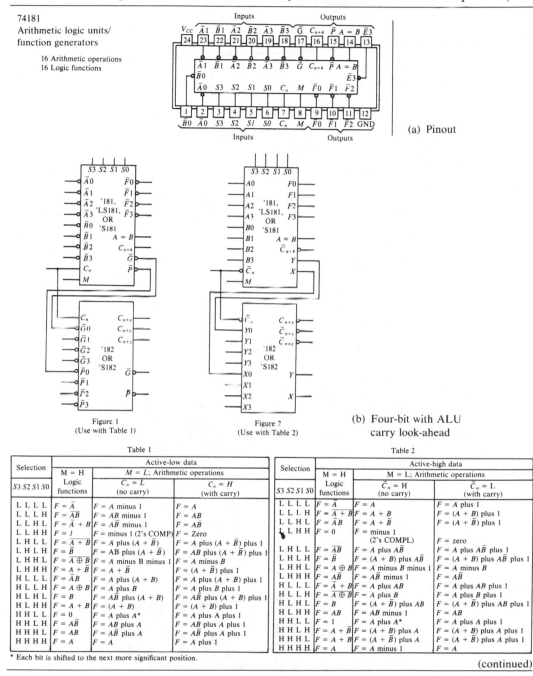

(a) Pinout

Figure 1
(Use with Table 1)

Figure 2
(Use with Table 2)

(b) Four-bit with ALU
carry look-ahead

Table 1

| Selection | M = H | M = L; Arithmetic operations | |
S3 S2 S1 S0	Logic functions	$C_n = L$ (no carry)	$C_n = H$ (with carry)
L L L L	$F = \bar{A}$	$F = A$ minus 1	$F = A$
L L L H	$F = \bar{A}\bar{B}$	$F = AB$ minus 1	$F = AB$
L L H L	$F = \bar{A} + B$	$F = A\bar{B}$ minus 1	$F = A\bar{B}$
L L H H	$F = 1$	$F =$ minus 1 (2's COMP)	$F =$ Zero
L H L L	$F = \bar{A} + \bar{B}$	$F = A$ plus $(A + \bar{B})$	$F = A$ plus $(A + \bar{B})$ plus 1
L H L H	$F = \bar{B}$	$F = AB$ plus $(A + \bar{B})$	$F = AB$ plus $(A + \bar{B})$ plus 1
L H H L	$F = \overline{A \oplus B}$	$F = A$ minus B minus 1	$F = A$ minus B
L H H H	$F = A + \bar{B}$	$F = A + \bar{B}$	$F = (A + \bar{B})$ plus 1
H L L L	$F = \bar{A}B$	$F = A$ plus $(A + B)$	$F = A$ plus $(A + B)$ plus 1
H L L H	$F = A \oplus B$	$F = A$ plus B	$F = A$ plus B plus 1
H L H L	$F = B$	$F = A\bar{B}$ plus $(A + B)$	$F = A\bar{B}$ plus $(A + B)$ plus 1
H L H H	$F = A + B$	$F = (A + B)$	$F = (A + B)$ plus 1
H H L L	$F = 0$	$F = A$ plus A*	$F = A$ plus A plus 1
H H L H	$F = A\bar{B}$	$F = AB$ plus A	$F = AB$ plus A plus 1
H H H L	$F = AB$	$F = A\bar{B}$ plus A	$F = A\bar{B}$ plus A plus 1
H H H H	$F = A$	$F = A$	$F = A$ plus 1

* Each bit is shifted to the next more significant position.

Table 2

| Selection | M = H | M = L; Arithmetic operations | |
S3 S2 S1 S0	Logic functions	$\bar{C}_n = H$ (no carry)	$\bar{C}_n = L$ (with carry)
L L L L	$F = \bar{A}$	$F = A$	$F = A$ plus 1
L L L H	$F = \overline{A + B}$	$F = A + B$	$F = (A + B)$ plus 1
L L H L	$F = \bar{A}B$	$F = A + \bar{B}$	$F = (A + \bar{B})$ plus 1
L L H H	$F = 0$	$F =$ minus 1 (2's COMPL)	$F =$ zero
L H L L	$F = \overline{AB}$	$F = A$ plus $A\bar{B}$	$F = A$ plus $A\bar{B}$ plus 1
L H L H	$F = \bar{B}$	$F = (A + B)$ plus $A\bar{B}$	$F = (A + B)$ plus $A\bar{B}$ plus 1
L H H L	$F = A \oplus B$	$F = A$ minus B minus 1	$F = A$ minus B
L H H H	$F = A\bar{B}$	$F = A\bar{B}$ minus 1	$F = A\bar{B}$
H L L L	$F = \bar{A} + B$	$F = A$ plus AB	$F = A$ plus AB plus 1
H L L H	$F = \overline{A \oplus B}$	$F = A$ plus B	$F = A$ plus B plus 1
H L H L	$F = B$	$F = (A + \bar{B})$ plus AB	$F = (A + \bar{B})$ plus AB plus 1
H L H H	$F = AB$	$F = AB$ minus 1	$F = AB$
H H L L	$F = 1$	$F = A$ plus A*	$F = A$ plus A plus 1
H H L H	$F = A + \bar{B}$	$F = (A + \bar{B})$ plus A	$F = (A + \bar{B})$ plus A plus 1
H H H L	$F = A + B$	$F = (A + \bar{B})$ plus A	$F = (A + \bar{B})$ plus A plus 1
H H H H	$F = A$	$F = A$ minus 1	$F = A$

(continued)

Figure 6.24 (Continued)

74182
Look-ahead carry generators

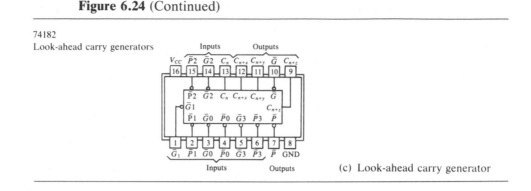

(c) Look-ahead carry generator

Figure 6.25 shows an 8-by-8-bit *parallel multiplier* (Texas Instruments SBP 9708). It provides a 16-bit product as the output. It is designed to be used as a microcomputer system component either as a single-stage multiplier or as a stage of a pipelined (see next section for a description of a pipeline) multiplier. In the transparent mode, the multiplier-multiplicand latches accept the two operands and the 16-bit product bypasses the output latches and is available in two of the multiplier array bytes directly from the 8-bit, 4-to-1 multiplexer. This mode is best selected when the need is for fast, isolated multiply occurrences. In the latched mode, during the first write cycle, the multiplier latch accepts new data and the

Figure 6.25 An 8-by-8-bit multiplier (Courtesy of Texas Instruments Incorporated)

16-Pin Dip
SBP 9708C . . . J or N Package
SBP 9708 E,M . . . J Package

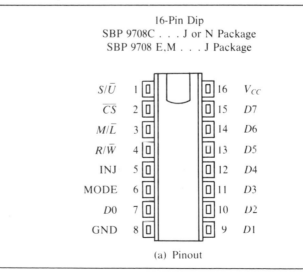

(a) Pinout

Figure 6.25 (Continued)

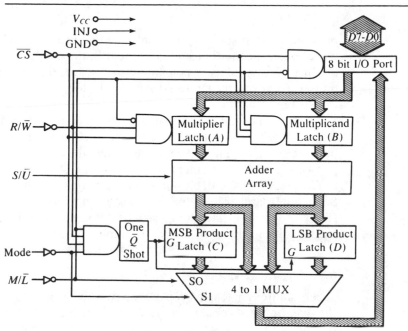

(b) Functional logic

Mode	Input				Function
	$\overline{CS}$	R/$\overline{W}$	M/$\overline{L}$	Mode	
Transparent multiply	H	X	X	X	I/O disabled.
	L	L	L	H	Load multiplier latch.
	L	L	H	H	Load multiplicand latch.
	L	H	L	H	Read LSB product from adder array.
	L	H	H	H	Read MSB product from adder array.
Latched multiply	L	L	L	L	Load multiplier, latch, strobe adder array data into product latches.
	L	L	H	L	Load multiplicand latch.
	L	H	L	L	Read LSB product latch.
	L	H	H	L	Read MSB product latch.

(c) Control function table

$S/\overline{U}$	I/O Significance
L	Unsigned byte multiply
H	Signed byte multiply

(d) Sign-bit selection function table

301

previous array result is strobed into the two product latches. On the next write cycle, the multiplicand is latched. In this mode, designed for multiply-intensive systems, pipelining allows sequential multiplication operations carried out at a rate 50 percent faster than that achieved in the transparent mode.

In addition to single line controls for operating mode (MODE) and sign-bit handling (S/$\overline{\text{U}}$), active-low chip-select ($\overline{\text{CS}}$) and read-write (R/$\overline{\text{W}}$) inputs are configured to make the multiplier addressable from hardware and software as either a memory-mapped or an I/O-mapped peripheral (refer to Chapter 7 for the definition of memory and I/O mapped peripherals). Sequential parallel byte loading (write) and result output (reading) are steered to or from the storage latches by a single most significant byte/least significant byte (M/$\overline{\text{L}}$) control input.

6.10.6   Stack ALUs

A zero-address machine uses the top two levels of a stack as operands for the majority of its operations. The result of the operation is pushed onto the top of the stack while the two operands are discarded from the stack (refer to Section 6.2). Figure 6.26 shows the model of a stack. The data from the input register enter the top level of the stack when PUSH is activated. Contents of the top level of the stack are always available at the top level output. POP when activated pops the stack. When an empty stack is popped, an underflow status is generated while an attempt to push into a full stack generates an overflow.

Figure 6.27 shows a stack-based ALU. To perform an operation on the top two levels of the stack, the following microoperation sequence must be performed:

Operation	Comments
POP	OUTPUT ← Top level; i.e., first operand (X); Top level ← Second level (Y); other levels move up.
ALU operation	$Z \leftarrow f(X, Y)$ based on the ALU control signal.
	OUTPUT ← Second level; i.e., POP second operand.
INPUT Z	Top level ← Z; i.e., PUSH the result.

Figure 6.26 Stack model

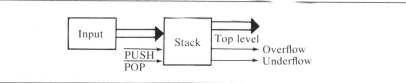

Figure 6.27 Stack ALU

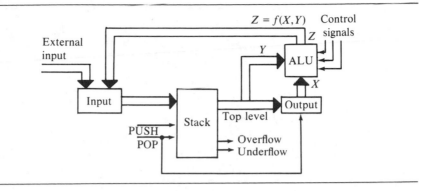

For the stack ALU to be fast, the stack must be implemented in hardware (as shown in Figure 6.2). Off-the-shelf stack ICs are also available.

Stack architectures have the following advantages:

1. The majority of operations are on the top two levels of the stack; hence, faster execution times are possible because address decoding and data fetch are not excessive.
2. Intermediate results in a computation usually can be left on the stack, thereby reducing the memory access needed and increasing the throughput.
3. Program lengths are reduced, since zero-address instructions are shorter compared to one-, two-, and three-address instructions.

6.10.7 Pipelining

Instructions are executed in an overlapped manner to increase the execution speed of the CPU, as discussed in Section 6.9. This overlapped instruction processing is made possible by a three-stage control unit design. Each of these stages performs its own sequence of operations on the instructions. At the end of this sequence the instruction is moved to the next stage while the current stage begins its processing on the next instruction. This is the concept of *pipelined* architecture. A pipelined arithmetic unit can be used to enhance the arithmetic processing speed.

Example 6.5 The addition of two floating-point numbers is shown below:

$$(0.5 \times 10^{-3}) + (0.75 \times 10^{-2})$$

$$= 0.05 \times 10^{-2} + 0.75 \times 10^{-2} \qquad \text{Equalize exponents.}$$

$$= 0.80 \times 10^{-2} \qquad\qquad\qquad \text{Add mantissa.}$$

Figure 6.28 Floating-point add pipeline

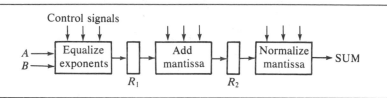

Note: A and B are the floating-point numbers to be added. R_1, R_2 are holding registers.

If the mantissa of the sum is greater than 1, the exponent needs to be adjusted to make the mantissa less than 1 as in the following:

$$0.5 \times 10^{-3} + 0.75 \times 10^{-3}$$

$$= 0.5 \times 10^{-3} + 0.75 \times 10^{-3} \qquad \text{Equalize exponents.}$$

$$= 1.25 \times 10^{-3} \qquad\qquad\qquad \text{Add mantissa.}$$

$$= 0.125 \times 10^{-2} \qquad\qquad\quad \text{Normalize mantissa.}$$

These three steps involved in the floating-point addition can be used to design a three-stage pipeline as shown in Figure 6.28. Each stage receives its own control signals. R_1 and R_2 are holding registers to hold the data between stages. These buffer registers especially are needed when the processing times for stages are not equal. In addition to the data-holding registers, some flag bits to indicate the completion of processing may be needed at the output of each stage.

Figure 6.29 shows a pipeline scheme to add two 4-bit binary numbers.

Figure 6.29 Floating-point binary adder

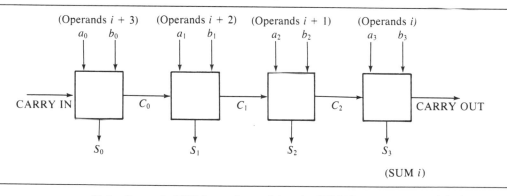

Note: Operands i SUM complete at i, but the SUM bits were generated during i, $i - 1$, $i - 2$, and $i - 3$.

Here the carries propagate along the pipeline while the data bits to be added are input through the lateral inputs of the stages. Note that once the pipeline is full, each stage will be performing an addition. At any time, four sets of operands are being processed. The addition of the operands entering the pipeline at time t will be complete at time $(t + 4\Delta)$ where Δ is the processing time of each stage. It is necessary to store the sum bits produced during four time slots to get the sum of a set of operands.

CDC STAR-100 (STring ARray) uses pipelined processors to perform bit, byte, 32-bit, or 64-bit floating-point operations in scalar or vector mode. The pipeline organization enables it to produce 100 million floating-point results per second. Chapter 8 describes the structure of this machine in more detail.

6.10.8 Multiple Processors

An obvious method of increasing the throughput of the CPU is to duplicate the processors (ALUs). Each processor can be a general-purpose processor or dedicated to certain processing functions. The control unit of such a CPU will be complex because it must schedule the processing activities on multiple processors and coordinate their simultaneous operation.

CDC 6600 architecture comprises ten functional units: one add, one double-precision add, two multiplies, one divide, two incrementers, one shifter, one Boolean, and one branch unit. A set of operand registers is connected to a functional unit when it is activated by the control unit. As many functional units as possible are simultaneously activated, thus increasing the throughput of the machine. A description of the CDC 6600 architecture is given in Chapter 8.

6.10.9 Decimal Arithmetic

Some ALUs allow decimal arithmetic. In this mode, 4 bits are used to represent a decimal (BCD) digit and the arithmetic can be performed in two modes, *bit serial* and *digit serial*.

Example 6.6 Figure 6.30 shows the addition of two decimal digits. In case 1, the sum results in a valid digit. In cases 2 and 3 the sum exceeds the highest valid digit 9 and hence a 6 is added to the sum to bring it to the proper decimal value. Thus the "ADD 6" correction is needed when the sum of the digits is between $(A)_{16}$ and $(F)_{16}$.

Figure 6.31(a) shows a digit serial (bit parallel) decimal adder. A bit serial adder is shown in (b). The bit serial adder is similar to the serial

Figure 6.30 BCD addition

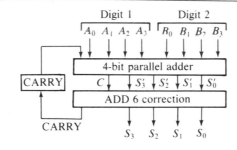

	Case 1	Case 2	Case 3	
	5	6	7	Decimal
	+ 3	4	5	
	8	A	C	← Hexadecimal
Correction	0	+ 6	+ 6	← Decimal
	8	10	12	← Decimal

Figure 6.31 Decimal adder

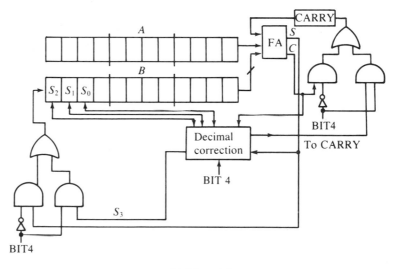

(a) Digit serial (bit parallel)

(b) Bit serial

Note: S = SUM and C = CARRY.

adder discussed in Chapter 2, except for the ADD 6 correction circuit. The sum bits enter the B register from the left-hand input. At BIT 4, the decimal correction circuit examines sum bits S_0, S_1, S_2, and S_3 and returns the corrected sum to the B register while generating an appropriate carry for the next digit.

Some processors use separate instructions for decimal arithmetic, while others use special instructions to switch the ALU between decimal and binary arithmetic modes. In the latter case, the same set of instructions operate both on decimal and binary data. MOSTEK 6502 uses a decimal instruction to enter decimal mode and clear decimal instruction to return to binary mode. The arithmetic is performed in digit serial mode. Hewlett-Packard 35 system uses a serial arithmetic on 13-digit (52-bit) floating-point decimal numbers. Chapter 7 gives further details on this calculator system.

6.10.10 Serial versus Parallel ALUs

The majority of processors use parallel ALUs. It is possible to use serial arithmetic where slow operations are acceptable. For example, in a calculator IC, serial arithmetic is adequate due to the slow nature of human interaction with the calculator. A considerable amount of silicon "real estate" can be conserved by using serial arithmetic in the design of an IC. The silicon area thus saved can be used in implementing other complex operations that may be required.

6.11 Summary

Enhancements to the memory, control unit, and ALU subsystems of ASC were described in this chapter. All the architectural features described here have appeared in actual machines. The reader is referred to manufacturers' manuals for further details of any of the machine examples given in this chapter. Chapter 7 describes enhancements to the input/output subsystem and provides details of selected system architectures.

References

Chu, Y. *Digital Computer Design Fundamentals.* New York, N.Y.: McGraw-Hill, 1962.

Foster, C. C. *Computer Architecture.* New York, N.Y.: Van Nostrand Reinhold, 1970.

Gear, C. W. *Computer Organization and Programming.* New York, N.Y.: McGraw-Hill, 1974.

6502 Hardware Manual. Norristown, Pa.: MOS Technology, Inc., 1976.

Hwang, K. *Computer Arithmetic.* New York, N.Y.: John Wiley, 1979.

IBM System/370 Principles of Operation. GA22-7000. IBM Corporation, 1973.

INTEL 8080 Microcomputer Systems Users Manual. Santa Clara, Calif.: Intel Corporation, 1977.

PDP-11 Processor Hand Book. Maynard, Mass.: Digital Equipment Corporation, 1978.

Pooch, V. A., and R. Chattergy. *Minicomputers: Hardware, Software and Selection.* St. Paul, Minn.: West, 1980.

QM-1 Hardware Level User's Manual. Buffalo, N.Y.: Nanodata Corporation, 1972.

Stone, H. S. *Introduction to Computer Architecture.* 2d ed. Chicago, Ill.: Science Research Associates, 1980.

The Bipolar Microcomputer Components Data Book. Dallas, Tex.: Texas Instruments, Inc., 1978.

The TTL Data Book. Dallas, Tex.: Texas Instruments, Inc., 1976.

VAX Hardware Handbook. Maynard, Mass.: Digital Equipment Corporation, 1979.

Whitney, T. M. "Introduction to Calculators," in *Introduction to Computer Architecture.* Edited by H. S. Stone, 1st ed. Ch. 3, pp. 76–135. Chicago, Ill.: Science Research Associates, 1975.

Whitney, T. M., F. Rode, and C. Tung. "The Powerful Pocketful: An Electronic Calculator Challenges the Slide Rule." *Hewlett-Packard Journal,* June 1972, pp. 2–9.

Problems

6.1 List the architectural features of the computer system you have access to, with reference to the characteristics described in this chapter.

6.2 Design an appropriate program status register for ASC.

6.3 Represent the following numbers in IBM and IEEE standard floating-point notation:

$$46.24 \times 10^{-3}$$

$$2.46 \times 10^{2}$$

6.4 Design a 4-bit-per-level, eight-level stack using shift registers. In addition to allowing PUSH and POP operations, the stack must generate an "overflow" signal when an attempt to PUSH into a full stack is made and an "underflow" signal when an empty stack is popped.

6.5 Design the stack of Problem 6.4 using a RAM.

6.6 Assume that ASC has a stack pointer register (SP) that is initialized to 0 when power is turned on. There are also two instructions LSP and SSP for loading and storing the SP from and into a memory location, respectively. The following operations are required:

     a. PUSH: TL ← ACC.
     b. POP: ACC ← TL.
     c. ADD: SL ← TL + SL; POP

Write subroutines for these operations using the ASC instrucion set.

6.7   Assume that ASC memory is two-way interleaved (i.e., two 32K word banks are arranged such that consecutive locations lie in separate physical blocks). Rewrite the microinstruction sequences for LDA and TCA instructions to efficiently utilize the interleaved memory.

6.8   Give an algorithm to generate the sum of two numbers in excess-3 representation (i.e., each digit of the number corresponds to 4 bits, in excess-3 format). Design the circuit for the adder, similar to that given in Figure 6.31.

6.9   Given that

$$F = M + N + P * (Q - R * S)/(T + V),$$

where $F, M, \ldots, V$ each represent a memory location, generate code for

    a. A stack machine.
    b. A one-address machine.
    c. A two-address machine.
    d. Assume 8 bits for opcode and 16 bits for an address and compute the length of the program in each of the above cases.
    e. How many memory cycles are needed to execute the above programs? Assume that the stack is ten levels deep. What is the effect on the program in (a) if the stack is restricted to four levels?

6.10 Design detailed block diagrams for each of the stages in the pipeline of Figure 6.28. Assume IEEE standard format for floating-point numbers.

6.11 List the changes needed to convert ASC control unit to include three modules — fetch, defer, and execute — working in a pipelined mode. Assume that only LDA, STA, SHR, LDX, TCA, and HLT instructions are required.

6.12 A hardware stack is used to evaluate arithmetic expressions. The expression can contain both REAL and INTEGER operands. The data representation contains a TAG bit with each operand. TAG bit is 1 for REAL and 0 for INTEGER. Assume that two hardware blocks are available: one to convert from REAL to INTEGER and the other to convert from INTEGER to REAL format. Design an appropriate stack mechanism. List the control signals required to perform addition and subtraction on the top two levels of stack.

6.13 Assume that ASC memory is built using eight interleaved blocks of 8K words each. Include an instruction buffer 8 words long into the ASC control unit. Develop the microoperations needed to manage this buffer. Assume that the buffer will be refilled (as a block) when the last instruction in the buffer is fetched or when a jump is to an address beyond the address range in the buffer.

6.14 Assume the memory banking configuration of Figure 6.7 and develop the microoperations needed, for Problem 6.13.

6.15 An example of a macroinstruction is a TRANSLATE instruction. This instruction replaces an operand with a translated version of itself, the translated version being derived from a table stored in a specified memory location. Assume that in ASC the operand is located in the accumulator and the beginning address of the table is located in the second word of the instruction (i.e., the instruction is 2 words long). The accumulator content thus provides the offset into the table. Write a microprogram for TRANSLATE.

Chapter 7

Input/Output (I/O)

In the design of ASC we assumed one input device and one output device transferring data in and out of the accumulator using a programmed input/output (I/O) mode. An actual computer system, however, consists of several input and output devices, or *peripherals*. Although the programmed I/O mode can be used in such an environment, it is slow and may not be suitable, especially when the machine is used as a real-time processor responding to irregular changes in the external environment. Consider the example of a processor used to monitor the condition of a patient in a hospital. Although the majority of its patient data gathering operations can be performed in a programmed I/O mode, alarming conditions such as abnormal blood pressure or temperature occur irregularly and detection of such events requires that the processor be interrupted by the event from its regular activity. We will discuss the general concept of interrupt processing and interrupt-driven I/O in this chapter.

The transfer of information between the processor and a peripheral consists of the following steps:

1. Selection of the device and checking the device for readiness.
2. Transfer initiation, when the device is ready.
3. Information transfer.
4. Conclusion.

These steps can be controlled by the processor or the peripheral or both. Contingent upon where the transfer control is located, three modes of input/output are possible. They are

1. Programmed I/O.
2. Interrupt mode I/O.
3. Direct memory access (DMA).

We will discuss each of these modes in detail following a discussion of a general I/O model and the I/O problem.

Pertinent details of some mini, micro, and large-scale computer system structures also will be provided to complete the description of architectures given as examples.

7.1 General I/O Model

ASC communicates with its peripherals through *data input lines* (DIL), *data output lines* (DOL), and the *data flip-flop*. We can generalize this I/O structure to include several peripheral devices, as shown in Figure 7.1. The *I/O bus* consists of data input and output lines, *control lines* (e.g., lines carrying the INPUT or OUTPUT command from the processor to devices, lines from each device to the processor to set or reset the data flip-flop) and device selection lines (DSL) or *address lines,* which address the device involved in the data transfer at any time.

To address multiple devices, a device number is required. The unused bits in input (RWD) and output (WWD) instruction representation can be used for the device address. In Figure 7.2, the least significant 4 bits are treated as device selection bits during an I/O operation and thus can address sixteen devices. The central processing unit (CPU) or the processor transmits this address on device selection lines or the address bus and

Figure 7.1. Multiple I/O devices

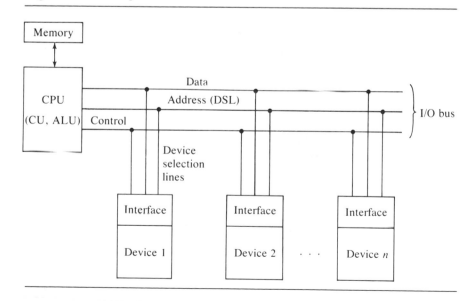

Figure 7.2 Changes required to accommodate multiple devices

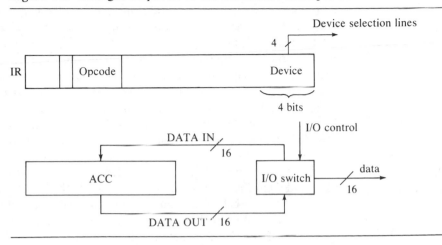

each device decodes this address. Only the device that corresponds to the address responds to the I/O request. The control and data lines are used by the selected device until the data transfer is complete.

Figure 7.3 shows the functional details of a *device interface*. A device interface is unique to a particular device since each device is itself unique with respect to its data representation and read-write operational characteristics. The device interface consists of a device controller that receives commands from the CPU and reports the status of the device to the CPU. Device selection (address decoding) is also shown as a part of the controller. If the device is, for example, a paper tape reader, typical commands

Figure 7.3 Device interface

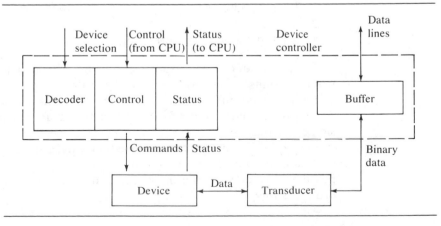

from the CPU to the controller are: IS DEVICE BUSY?, ADVANCE TAPE, READ, REWIND TAPE, and the like. Typical status signals sent to the CPU by the device controller are: DEVICE BUSY, NOT BUSY, DATA READY, DEVICE NOT OPERABLE, and so on. The transducer converts the data represented on the I/O medium (paper tape, cards, etc.) into binary format and stores it in the data buffer, if the device is an input device. In the case of an output device, the CPU sends the data into the buffer and the transducer converts this binary data into a format suitable for output onto the external medium (i.e., hole, no-hole pattern onto a paper tape punch, 0/1 bit write format onto a magnetic tape unit, and so on).

Figure 7.4 shows the functional details of an interface between the CPU and a card reader. When the CPU sends the device address on DSL and sets the INPUT command, the address decoder activates the *select-device card reader* mechanism by resetting the *device-ready flip-flop*. The $\bar{Q}$ output of the flip-flop acts as the *advance card* to the next column signal. The card advance mechanism is assumed to be capable of moving the card to the next column position and raising the CARD ON COLUMN signal, thereby setting the device-ready flip-flop; setting the DATA READY signal; and gating the outputs of photocells (one for each row of the card) into the data *buffer*. The data are now available on data input lines (DIL). This is a very much simplified description of the interface.

7.2 The I/O Problem

The major functions of a device interface are

1. Timing and control.
2. Data conversion.
3. Error detection and correction.

The timing and control aspects correspond to the manipulation of control and status signals to bring about the data transfer. In addition, the operating speed difference between the CPU and the device (see Table 7.1) must be compensated for by the interface. In general, data conversion from one code to the other is needed, since each device (or the medium on which data are represented) may use a different code to represent data. Errors occur during transmission and must be detected and if possible corrected by the interface. A discussion of each of these I/O problems follows.

Figure 7.4 Card reader interface

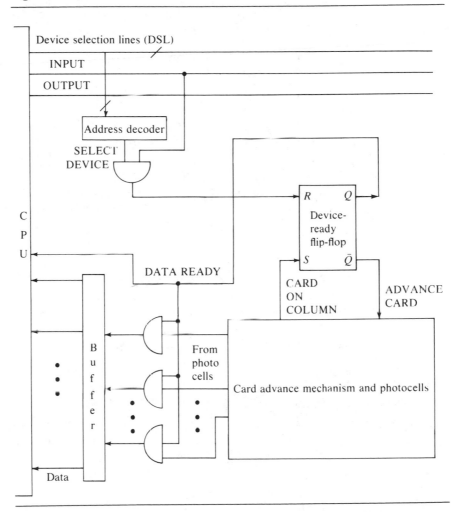

7.2.1 Timing and Control

Peripheral devices operate in an asynchronous mode with respect to the CPU because they are not usually controlled by the same clock that controls the CPU. Therefore, the data transfer between the CPU and the device must be synchronized. In a card reader interface, for example, if the data buffer is large enough to hold one character, this character must be transmitted into the CPU before the next character is read by the reader; otherwise, the character in the buffer might be lost.

Table 7.1 Typical operating speeds

Device	Rate (characters/second)
Man	5
Communication modems	40–1200
Teleprinters	10–120
CRT	10–960
Paper tape readers	10–1000
Paper tape punches	10–150
Card readers	80–3000 (100–2000 cards/minute)
Card punches	80–400
Line printers	100–80,000 (60–40,000 lines/minute)
Magnetic tapes	15,000–320,000
Magnetic disks	30,000–1.5×10^6
CPU to memory	(0.5–4 million words/second)
CPU register transfer	(1–15 million transfers/second)

Note: A character usually corresponds to an 8-bit byte.

The data transfer is completely controlled by the CPU in the programmed I/O. A typical sequence of events (*protocol* or *handshake*) for the data transfer in this I/O mode is shown below. We have combined the protocols for both INPUT and OUTPUT. A device will be either in the input or the output mode at any time:

Processor	Device controller
1. Selects the device and checks the status of the device.	
	2. Signals the processor that it is ready or not ready.
3. (If device not ready, go to step 1; if ready, go to step 4.)	
4. Signals the device to initiate data transfer (send data or accept data); if OUTPUT, gates data onto data lines and sets output control line.	
	5. If OUTPUT, signals the processor that the data are accepted; if INPUT, gathers data and signals CPU that the data are ready on data lines.
6. If INPUT, accepts the data; if OUTPUT, removes data from data lines.	
7. Disconnects the device (i.e., removes the device address from address lines).	

This sequence repeats for each transfer. The speed difference between the CPU and the device renders this mode of I/O inefficient.

An alternative is to distribute part of the control activities to the device controller. Now, the CPU sends a command to the device controller to input or output data and continues its processing activity. The controller collects the data from (or sends data to) the device and "interrupts" the CPU. The CPU disconnects the device after the data transfer is complete (that is, the CPU services the interrupt) and returns to the mainline processing from which it was interrupted. A typical sequence of events during an *interrupt-mode I/O* is:

Processor	Device controller
1. Selects the device; if OUTPUT, puts the data on data lines and sets output control line; if INPUT, sets input command line.	
2. Continues the processing activity.	
	3. If OUTPUT, collects data from data lines and transmits to the medium; if INPUT, collects data from the medium into the data buffer.
	4. Interrupts the processor.
5. Processor recognizes the interrupt and saves its processing status; if OUTPUT, removes data from data lines; if INPUT, gates data into accumulator.	
6. Disconnects the device.	
7. Restores the processing status and returns to processing activity.	

The protocol assumes that the CPU always initiates the data transfer. In practice, a peripheral device may first interrupt the CPU and the type of transfer (input or output) is determined during the CPU-peripheral handshake. The data input need not be initiated only by the CPU. The causes of interrupt and the popular interrupt structures are discussed in the next section. Interrupt mode I/O reduces the CPU wait time (for the slow device) but requires a more complex device controller than in the programmed I/O mode.

In addition to the above protocols, other control and timing issues are introduced by the characteristics of the *link* (that is, the data line or lines that connect the device and the CPU). The data link can be *simplex* (unidirectional), *half-duplex* (either direction, one way at a time), *full-duplex* (both directions simultaneously), *serial,* or *parallel.* Serial transmission requires that a constant clock rate be maintained throughout data transmission to avoid synchronization problems; in parallel transmission, care must be taken to avoid data "skewing" (i.e., data arriving at different times on the bus lines due to different electrical characteristics of individual bit lines).

7.2.2 Data Conversion

The data representation on the I/O medium is unique to each medium. For example, a magnetic tape uses either ASCII or EBCDIC codes to represent data; punched cards use Hollerith code to represent one character per card column (see Appendix A). Internally, the CPU might use a binary or BCD (decimal) representation. In addition, the interface link might be organized as serial-by-bit, serial-by-character (quasi-parallel), or serial-by-word (fully parallel). Thus, two levels of data conversion are to be accomplished by the interface: conversion from peripheral to link format and from link to CPU format.

7.2.3 Error Detection and Correction

Errors may occur whenever data are transmitted between two devices. One or more extra bits known as *parity bits* are used as part of the data representation to facilitate error detection and correction. Such parity bits, if not already present in the data, are included into the data stream by the interface before transmission and checked at the destination. Depending on the number of parity bits, various levels of error detection and correction are possible. Error detection and correction are particularly important in I/O because the peripheral devices exposed to the external environment are error prone. Errors may be due to mechanical wear, temperature and humidity variations, mismounted storage media, circuit drift, incorrect data transfer sequences (protocols), and the like.

Figure 7.5(a) shows a parity bit included into a data stream of 8 bits. The parity bit P is 1 if *odd parity* is used (the total number of 1s is odd) and 0 if *even parity* is used (the total number of 1s is even). When this 9-bit data word is transmitted, the receiver of the data computes the parity bit. If P matches the computed parity, there is no error in transmission; if an error is detected, the data can be retransmitted.

Figure 7.5(b) shows a parity scheme for a magnetic tape. An extra track (track 8) is added to the tape format. The parity track stores the parity bit for each character represented on the eight tracks of the tape. At the end of a record, a longitudinal parity character consisting of a parity bit for each track is added. More elaborate error detection and correction schemes are often used; references listed at the end of this chapter provide details of those schemes.

Figure 7.5 Parity bits for error detection on a magnetic tape

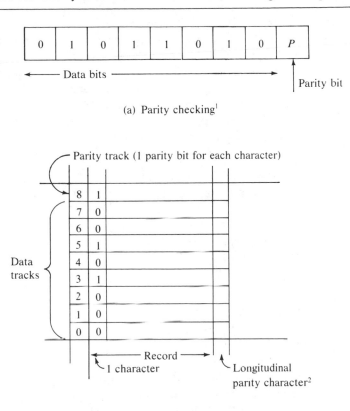

(a) Parity checking[1]

(b) Magnetic tape data representation

[1]$P = 1$ for odd parity (total number of 1s is odd); $P = 0$ for even parity (total number of 1s is even).
[2]One bit for each track; parity check for the complete record.

7.3 Interrupts

In a number of conditions the processor may be interrupted from its normal processing activity. Some of these conditions are

1. Power failure as detected by a sensor.
2. Arithmetic conditions such as overflow and underflow.
3. Illegal data or illegal instruction code.
4. Errors in data transmission and storage.
5. Software-generated interrupts (as intended by the user).

In each of these conditions the processor must discontinue its processing activity, attend to the interrupting condition, and (if possible) resume the processing activity from where it had been when the interrupt occurred. In order for the processor to be able to resume normal processing after servicing the interrupt, it is essential to at least save the address of the instruction to be executed just before entering the interrupt service mode. In addition, contents of the accumulator and all other registers must be saved. Typically, when an interrupt is received, the processor completes the current instruction and jumps to an *interrupt service routine*. An interrupt service routine is a program preloaded into the machine memory that performs the following functions:

1. Disables further interrupts temporarily.
2. Saves the processor status (all registers).
3. Enables further interrupts.
4. Determines the cause of interrupt.
5. Services the interrupt.
6. Restores the processor status.
7. Returns from interrupt.

The processor disables further interrupts just long enough to save the status, since a proper return from interrupt service routine is not possible if the status is not completely saved. The processor status usually comprises the contents of all the registers, including the program counter and the program status word. "Servicing" the interrupt simply means taking care of the interrupt condition: in the case of an I/O interrupt, it corresponds to data transfer; in case of power failure, it is the saving of registers and status for a normal resumption of processing when the power is back; during an arithmetic condition, it is checking the previous operation or simply setting a flag to indicate the arithmetic error.

7.3.1 Interrupt Mechanism for ASC

An interrupt may occur at any time. The processor recognizes interrupts only at the end of the execution of the current instruction. If the interrupt needs to be recognized earlier (say, at the end of a fetch, before execution), a more complex design is needed because the processor status has to be rolled back to the end of the execution of the previous instruction. Assuming the simpler case for ASC, the fetch microsequence must be altered to recognize the interrupt. Let us assume that there is an interrupt input (INT) into the control unit. The interrupt signal stays ON until it is recognized by the control unit. Reserve memory locations 0 through 4 for saving registers (PC, ACC, and index registers) before entering the interrupt service routine located in memory locations 5 and onwards (see Figure 7.6).

Figure 7.6 Interrupt software (memory map)

Address	Contents	

Address   Contents

0	(PC)	Reserved for return address
1	(ACC)	⎫
2	(INDEX 1)	⎬ Reserved locations
3	(INDEX 2)	
4	(INDEX 3)	⎭
5	Disable interrupt	
6	STA 1	⎫
7	STX 2, 1	⎬ Save registers
8	STX 3, 2	
9	STX 4, 3	⎭
10	Enable interrupt	

    .
    .
    .

> Poll for
> interrupting device
>
> Interrupt service
> routines

    .

Disable interrupt
LDX 2, 1 ⎫
LDX 3, 2 ⎬ Resave registers
LDX 4, 3 ⎭
LDA 1
Enable interrupt
JMP * 0   Return from interrupt

The fetch sequence now looks like the following:

T_1:   IF INT = 1 THEN MAR ← 0 ELSE MAR ← PC, READ.
T_2:   IF INT = 1 THEN MBR ← PC, WRITE ELSE PC ← PC + 1.
T_3:   IF INT = 1 THEN PC ← 5 ELSE IR ← MBR, WRITE.
T_4:   IF INT = 1 THEN STATE ← F ELSE (as before).

If INT is "high," one machine cycle is used for entering the interrupt service routine (i.e., stores *PC* in location 0; sets *PC* = 5). The first part of the service routine (in Figure 7.6) stores all the registers. The devices are then *polled,* as discussed later in this section, to find the interrupting device. The interrupt is serviced and the registers are restored before returning from the interrupt.

This interrupt handling scheme requires that the INT line be at 1 during the fetch cycle. That is, although the INT line can go to 1 any time, it has to stay at 1 until the end of the next fetch cycle in order to be recognized by the CPU. Further, it must go to 0 at the end of T_4. Otherwise, another fetch cycle in the interrupt mode is invoked. This timing requirement on the INT line can be simplified by including an *interrupt-enable* flip-flop and an *interrupt flip-flop* (INTF) into the control unit and gating the INT line into INTF at T_1, as shown in Figure 7.7. The fetch sequence to accommodate these changes is shown here:

T_1: IF INTF = 1 THEN MAR ← 0 ELSE MAR ← PC, READ.
T_2: IF INTF = 1 THEN MBR ← PC, WRITE ELSE PC ← PC + 1.
T_3: IF INTF = 1 THEN PC ← 6 ELSE IR ← MBR, WRITE.
T_4: INTF = 1 THEN STATE ← F, DISABLE INT,
               RESET INT, ACKNOWLEDGE ELSE (as before).

Note that the interrupt sequence now disables interrupts in T_4 thereby not requiring the DISABLE interrupt instruction at location 5 in Figure 7.6. The interrupt service routine execution then starts at location 6. An ENABLE interrupt instruction is required. This instruction sets the interrupt-enable flip-flop and allows further interrupt. Note also that an interrupt acknowledge signal is generated by the CPU during T_4 to indicate to the external devices that the interrupt has been recognized. In this scheme, the interrupt line must be held high until the next fetch cycle

Figure 7.7 Interrupt hardware

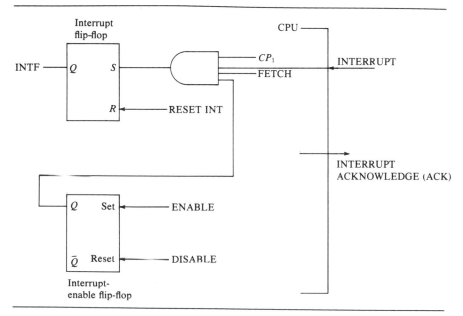

(i.e., one instruction cycle at the worst case) for the interrupt to be recognized. Once an interrupt is recognized, no further interrupts are allowed unless interrupts are enabled.

7.3.2 Multiple Interrupts

In the interrupt scheme, if a second interrupt occurs while the processor is executing the interrupt service routine, memory locations 0 through 5 are overwritten, thereby destroying the status information needed to return from the first interrupt. In practice, it is possible that another interrupt may occur while an interrupt is being serviced. If the processor status is saved on a stack rather than in dedicated memory locations as in the above scheme, multiple interrupts can be serviced: at the first interrupt, status 1 is pushed onto the stack; at the second interrupt, status 2 is pushed onto the top of the stack. When the second interrupt service is complete, status 2 is popped from the stack, thus leaving status 1 on stack intact for the return from the first interrupt. A stack thus allows the "nesting" of multiple interrupts.

7.3.3 Polling

Once an interrupt is recognized, the CPU must invoke the appropriate interrupt service routine for each interrupt condition. In an interrupt-mode I/O scheme, CPU polls each device to identify the interrupting device. Polling can be implemented in either software or hardware. In the software implementation, the polling routine addresses each I/O device in turn and reads its status. If the status indicates an interrupting condition, the service routine corresponding to that device is executed. Polling thus incorporates a priority among devices since the highest priority device is addressed first followed by lower priority devices.

Figure 7.8 shows a hardware polling scheme. The binary counter contains the address of the first device initially and counts up at each clock pulse if the CPU is in the polling mode. When the count reaches the address of the interrupting device, the interrupt request flip-flop is set, thereby preventing the clock from incrementing the binary counter. The address of the interrupting device is then in the binary counter.

7.3.4 Vectored Interrupts

An alternative to polling as a means of recognizing the interrupting device is to use a vectored interrupt structure like the one shown in Figure 7.9. Here the CPU generates an acknowledge (ACK) signal in response to an

Figure 7.8 Polling hardware (eight devices)

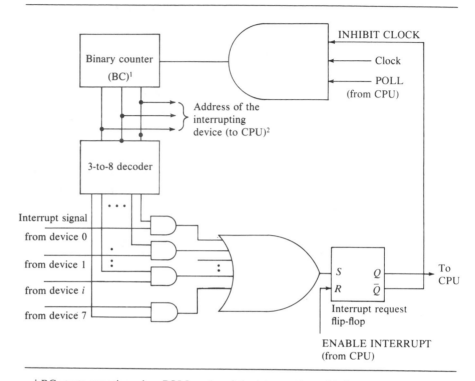

[1] BC starts counting when POLL = 1 and the interrupt is enabled.
[2] Interrupting device (D_i), sets INT request flip-flop, and BC is stopped at i ($i = 0$ through 7). CPU receives i as an address.

interrupt. If a device is interrupting (that is, interrupt flip-flop is set), the ACK flip-flop in the device interface is set by the ACK signal and the device sends its address (vector) onto DSL. The CPU then reads DSL to identify the device. In the structure of Figure 7.9, all interrupting devices send vectors onto DSL simultaneously. To prevent this and to isolate the vector of a single device, the I/O devices are usually connected in a *daisy chain* structure in which the highest priority device receives the ACK first, followed by lower priority devices. The first interrupting device in the chain inhibits the propagation of the ACK signal further. Figure 7.10 shows a typical daisy chain interface. Figure 7.11 shows another daisy chain scheme, in which the interrupt signal of a higher priority device prevents the interrupt signal of lower priority devices from reaching the CPU.

Figure 7.9 Vectored interrupt structure

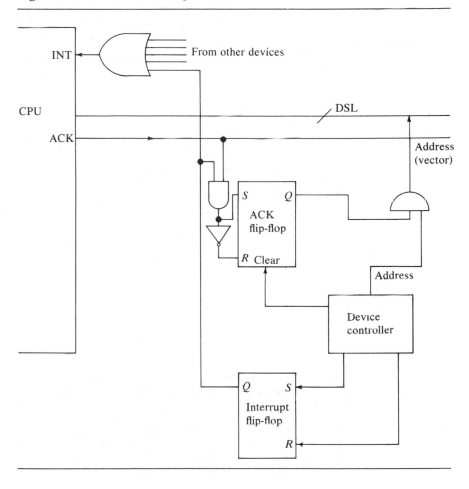

7.3.5   Types of Interrupt Structures

In the interrupt structure shown in Figure 7.9, interrupt lines of all the devices are ORed together and hence any device can interrupt the CPU. This is called a *single-priority* structure because all devices are equal (in importance) as far as interrupting the CPU is concerned. Single-priority structures can adopt either polling or vectoring to identify the interrupting device. A *single-priority polled* structure is the least complex interrupt structure, since polling is usually done by software, and the slowest because of polling. In a *single-priority vectored* structure, the CPU sends

Figure 7.10 Daisy chain interface

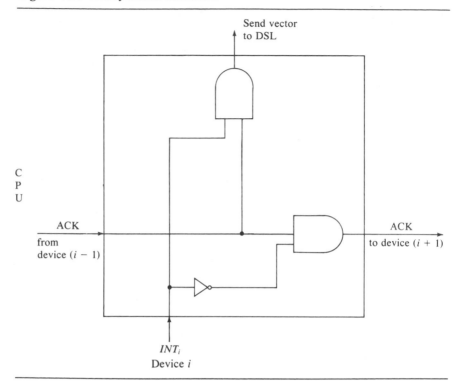

Send vector
to DSL

CPU

ACK
from
device $(i - 1)$

ACK
to device $(i + 1)$

INT_i
Device i

Note: Device $(i - 1)$ has a higher priority than device (i); etc.

out an ACK signal in response to an interrupt and the interrupting device returns a vector that is used by the CPU to execute the appropriate service routine. This structure operates faster than the polled structure but requires a more complex device controller.

The forward daisy chain structure of Figure 7.11 is a *multipriority* structure, since interrupting the CPU depends on the priority of the device. The highest priority device can always interrupt the CPU in this structure. A higher priority device can interrupt the CPU while the CPU is servicing an interrupt from a lower priority device. An interrupt from a lower priority device is prohibited from reaching the CPU when it is servicing a higher priority device. Once an interrupt is recognized by the CPU, the recognition of the interrupting device is done either by polling or by using vectors. The *multipriority vectored* structure is the fastest and most complex of the interrupt structures. Table 7.2 summarizes the characteristics of these interrupt structures.

In actual systems more than one interrupt input line will be provided at

Figure 7.11 Daisy chaining

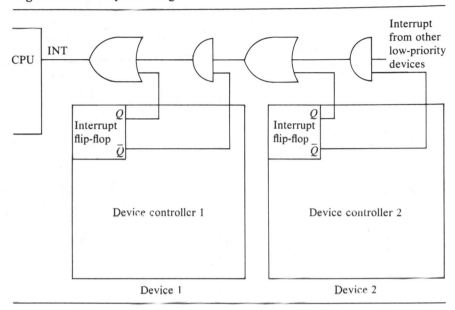

the CPU so that a hardware multilevel structure is possible. Within each level, devices can be daisy chained and each level assigned a priority. The priorities may also be dynamically changed (changed during the system operation). Figure 7.12 shows a masking scheme for such dynamic priority operations. The MASK register is set by the CPU to represent the levels that are permitted to interrupt (levels 2 and 3 are masked out and levels 1 and 4 are enabled). An INT signal is generated only if the enabled levels interrupt; that is, the levels that are masked out cannot interrupt the CPU. Note that in this scheme a device can be connected to more than one level (D_1 is connected to levels 1 and 2).

Table 7.2 Characteristics of interrupt structures

Structure	Response time	Complexity
Single-priority		
Polled	Slowest	Lowest
Vectored	Fast	Medium
Multipriority		
Polled	Slow	Low
Vectored	Fastest	Highest

Figure 7.12 Masking interrupts

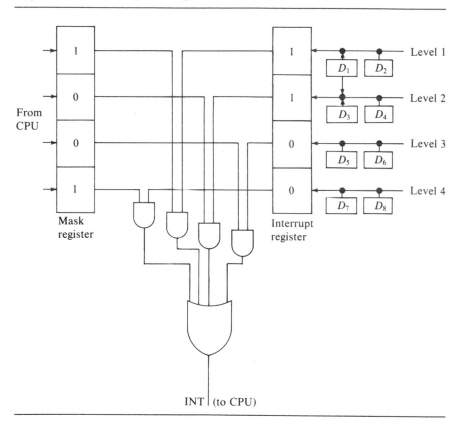

INT (to CPU)

7.4   Direct Memory Access

The programmed and interrupt mode I/O structures transfer data from the device into or out of a CPU register (accumulator in ASC). If the amount of data to be transferred is large, these schemes would overload the CPU. Data are normally required to be in the memory, especially when voluminous, and some complex computations are to be performed on them. A *direct memory access* (DMA) scheme enables a device controller to transfer data directly into or from machine memory. The majority of data transfer control operations are now performed by a device controller. CPU initiates the transfer by commanding the DMA device to transfer the data and then continues with its processing activities. The DMA device completes the data transfer and interrupts the CPU only when it is completed.

Figure 7.13 shows a DMA transfer structure. The DMA device (either a DMA *controller* or a DMA *channel*) is a limited-capability processor. It will have a word-count register, an address register, and a data buffer register. To start a transfer, the CPU initializes the address register (AR) of the DMA channel with the memory address from (or to) which the data must be transferred and the word-count register (WCR) with the number of units of data (words, or bytes) to be transferred. Note that the data bus

Figure 7.13 DMA transfer structure

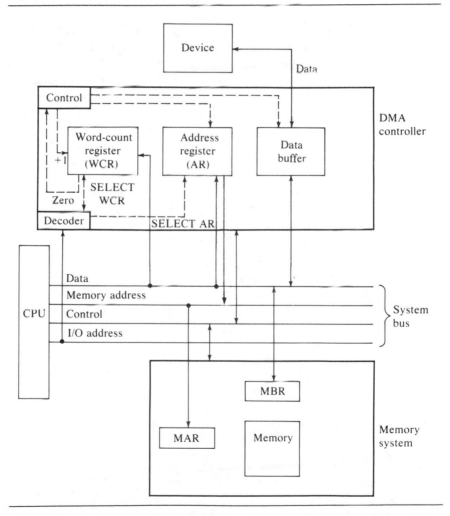

Note: Memory and I/O ADDRESS buses are shown separately for clarity; a single-address bus with a control line indicating memory or I/O operation is an alternative.

is connected to these two registers. Usually, these registers are addressed by the CPU as output devices; using DSL or address bus, the initial values are transferred into them via the data bus. The DMA controller can decrement WCR and increment AR for each word transferred. Assuming an input transfer, the DMA controller starts the input device and acquires the data in its buffer register. This word is then transferred into the memory location addressed by AR; that is,

$$\text{MAR} \leftarrow \text{AR}.$$
$$\text{MBR} \leftarrow \text{Data buffer, WRITE MEMORY.}$$

These transfers are done using the address and data buses.

In this scheme, the CPU and the DMA device controller both try to access the memory through MAR and MBR. Since the memory cannot be simultaneously accessed both by the DMA and the CPU, a priority scheme is used to prohibit CPU from accessing the memory during a DMA operation. That is, a memory cycle is assigned to the DMA device for the transfer of data during which the CPU is prevented from accessing memory. This is called *cycle stealing,* since the DMA device "steals" a memory cycle from the CPU when it is required to access the memory. Once the transfer is complete, the CPU can access the memory. The DMA controller decrements the WCR and increments AR in preparation for the next transfer. When WCR reaches 0, a transfer-complete interrupt is sent to the CPU by the DMA controller. Figure 7.14 shows the sequence of events during a DMA transfer.

Figure 7.14 DMA transfer

CPU	DMA controller
1. Initializes AR, WCR; commands DMA controller to start data transmission; continues processing.	
	2. If WCR $\neq$ 0, gathers data; holds CPU (i.e., "steals" a memory cycle); if WCR = 0, sends transfer-complete interrupt to CPU.
3. CPU continues with any processing that does not need a memory access; if memory access is needed, tries to acquire a memory cycle if DMA is not accessing the memory.	
	4. DMA transfers data; releases the memory; decrements WCR; increments AR; goes to step 2.

DMA devices always have higher priority than the CPU for memory access because the data available in the device buffer may be lost if not transferred immediately. Hence, if an I/O device connected via DMA is fast enough, it can steal several consecutive memory cycles, thus "holding" back the CPU from accessing the memory for several cycles. If not, the CPU will access the memory in between each DMA transfer cycle.

DMA controllers can be either dedicated to one device or shared among several input/output devices. Figure 7.15 shows a bus structure that enables such a sharing. This bus structure is called *compatible I/O bus structure* because an I/O device is configured to perform both programmed and DMA transfers. DMA channels are shared by all the I/O devices. The I/O device may be transferring data at any time through either programmed or DMA paths. Some computer systems use a multiple-bus structure in which some I/O devices are connected to the DMA bus while others communicate with the CPU in a programmed I/O mode.

7.5 Channels

A channel is a more sophisticated I/O controller than a DMA device but performs I/O transfers in a DMA mode. It is a limited-capability processor that can perform all operations a DMA system can. In addition, a channel is configured to interface several I/O devices to the memory while a DMA controller is usually connected to one device. A channel performs extensive error detection and correction, data formatting, and code conversion. Unlike DMA, the channel can interrupt CPU under any error condition. There are two types of channels: *multiplexer* and *selector*.

Figure 7.15 Compatible I/O bus structure

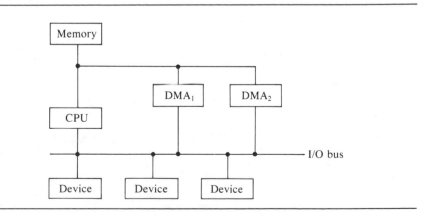

A *multiplexer channel* is connected to several low- and medium-speed devices (card readers, paper tape readers, etc.). The channel scans these devices in turn and collects data into a buffer. Each unit of data is also tagged by the channel to indicate the device it came from (in an input mode). When these data are transferred into the memory, the tags are used to identify the memory buffer areas reserved for each device. A multiplexer channel handles all the operations needed for such transfers from multiple devices after it has been initialized by the CPU. It interrupts the CPU when the transfer is complete. Two types of multiplexer channels are common: (1) character multiplexers, which transfer one character (usually one byte) from each device, and (2) block multiplexers, which transfer a block of data from each device connected to them.

A *selector channel* interfaces high-speed devices such as magnetic tapes and disks to the memory. These devices can keep a channel busy because of their high data-transfer rates. Although several devices are connected to each selector channel, the channel stays with one device until the data transfer from that device is complete.

Figure 7.16 A typical computer system

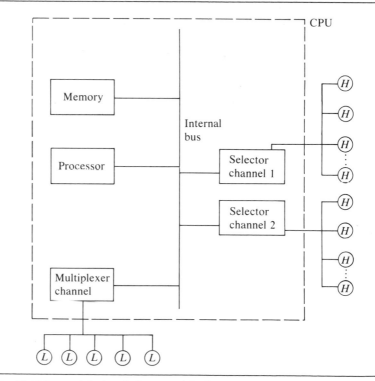

Note: *H:* high speed device; *L:* low speed device.

Figure 7.16 shows a typical computer system structure with several channels. Each device is assigned to one channel. It is possible to connect a device to more than one channel through a multichannel switching interface. Channels are normally treated as a part of the CPU in conventional computer architecture; that is, channels are CPU-resident I/O processors.

7.6 Front-End Processors

Channels and interrupt structures perform the majority of I/O operations and control, thus freeing the central processor for internal data processing. This enhances the throughput of the computer system. A further step in this direction of distributing the I/O processing functions to peripherals is to make channels more versatile, like full-fledged processors. Such I/O processors are called *peripheral* or *front-end processors* (FEP). With the advent of microprocessors and the availability of less expensive hardware devices, it is now possible to make the front-end processor versatile enough while keeping the cost low. A large-scale computer system uses several minicomputers as FEPs while a minicomputer might use another mini or a microcomputer for the FEP. Since FEPs are programmable, they serve as flexible I/O device controllers, to enable easier interfacing of a variety of I/O devices to the CPU. They also perform as much processing on the data as possible (source processing) before they are transferred into the memory. If the FEP has a writable control store (i.e., the control ROM is field-programmable), the microprogram can be changed to reflect the device interface needed. Some of the currently available computer systems (Systems Engineering Laboratories' SEL 32, Hewlett-Packard's HP 1000) provide such microprogrammed I/O controllers as FEPs.

The coupling between the FEP and the central processor is either through a disk system or through the shared memory (Figure 7.17). In a *disk-coupled* system, the FEP stores data on the disk unit, which in turn is processed by the central processor. During the output, the central processor stores data on the disk and provides the required control information to FEP to enable data output. This system is easier than other systems to implement even when the two processors (FEP and CPU) are not identical because timing and control aspects of the processor-disk interface are essentially independent.

In the shared-memory system, each processor acts as a DMA device with respect to the shared memory. Hence, a complex handshake is needed, especially when the two processors are not identical. This system will generally be faster, however, since an intermediate direct-access device is not used. Figure 7.17 shows the two FEP-CPU coupling schemes.

Figure 7.17 Front-end processors

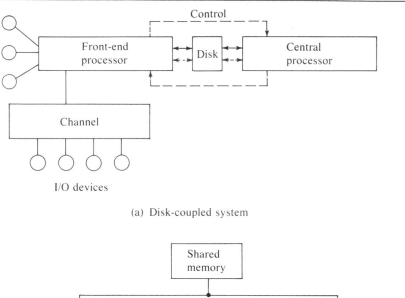

(a) Disk-coupled system

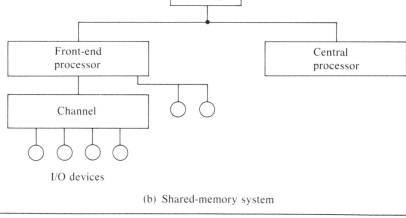

(b) Shared-memory system

7.7   Serial I/O

We assumed a parallel data bus transferring a unit of data (word or byte) between the CPU memory and the I/O device in the earlier sections of this chapter. Devices such as low-data-rate terminals and teletype use a serial mode of data transfer containing a single line in either direction of transfer. The transmission usually is in the form of an asynchronous stream of characters. That is, there is no fixed time interval between the

Figure 7.18 Serial data format

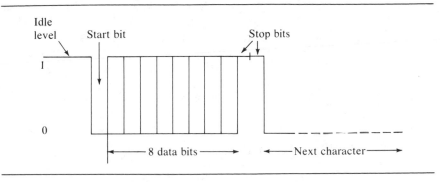

two adjacent characters. Figure 7.18 shows the format of an 8-bit character for asynchronous serial transmission. The transmission line is assumed to stay at 1 during the idle state, in which there is no character being transmitted. A transition from 1 to 0 indicates the beginning of transmission (*start* bit). The start bit is followed by 8 data bits and 2 *stop* bits terminate the character. Each bit is allotted a fixed time slot and hence the receiver can decode the 11-bit pattern into the proper 8-bit character code.

Figure 7.19 shows a serial transmission controller. The CPU transfers data to be output into the interface buffer. The interface controller generates the state bit, shifts the data in the buffer 1 bit at a time onto output lines, and terminates with 2 stop bits. During an input, the start and stop

Figure 7.19 Serial data controller

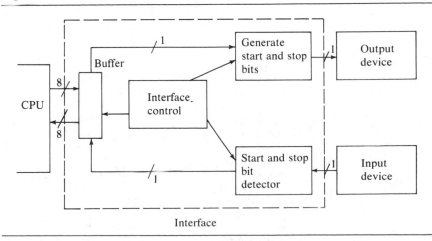

bits are removed from the input stream and the data bits are shifted into the buffer and in turn transferred into the CPU. The electrical characteristics of this asynchronous serial interface have been standardized by the Electronic Industries Association, and it is called EIA RS232C.

The data transfer rate is measured in bits per second or "baud" rate. For a 10-character-per-second transmission, for example, the baud rate is 110 (that is, 10 characters per second by 11 bits per character) and the time slot for each bit in the character is thus 9.09 milliseconds.

7.8 Common I/O Devices

A variety of input/output devices are used to communicate with computers. We will briefly describe the important characteristics of the most common devices. We will classify these I/O devices in the following categories:

1. Online devices that communicate with the machine in an interactive mode such as teletype and display terminals.
2. Offline devices that communicate in a noninteractive mode, such as card reader and punch, paper tape reader and punch, and printers.
3. Real-time data acquisition devices such as analog-to-digital (A/D) and digital-to-analog (D/A) converters.
4. Backup storage devices that can also be classified as I/O devices, such as magnetic tapes and disks.

We will now list the important characteristics of some of these devices. Table 7.3 shows the data transfer rates for some common devices.

Table 7.3 Data transfer rates of I/O devices

Device	Transfer rate
Teletype	10–60 characters/second
Display terminals	10–240 characters/second
Card reader	60–2000 cards/minute
Card punch	100–250 cards/minute
Paper tape reader	10–1000 characters/second
Paper tape punch	10–200 characters/second
Impact printers	100–3000 lines/minute
Nonimpact printers	100–40,000 lines/minute
A/D and D/A converters	Up to 50,000 samples/second
Magnetic tape	15,000–30,000 characters/second
Cassette tape	10–400 characters/second
Hard disk	30,000–2×10^6 characters/second
Floppy disk	25,000 characters/second

7.8.1 Teletype

This is the most common I/O device and consists of a keyboard and a printer. It usually also has a paper tape reader and punch. Keyboard and printer are used in an interactive mode, although the two are independent devices in the sense that the keyboard can be used to input data while the printer is printing the output data. It is also possible to "echo" what is typed on the keyboard onto the printer.

Each key stroke on the keyboard is converted into an 11-bit pattern consisting of a sync character (0), 8-bit ASCII code corresponding to the key, and 2 stop bits (1s) and transmitted on a serial line to the CPU. A 10-character-per-second transfer rate is the most common.

The paper tape punch mechanism could be used to generate a paper tape offline, for a later data or program input activity. The CPU can also output data onto the paper tape.

7.8.2 Display Terminals

Several types of terminals are now available. The trend has been to use a monitor or a cathode ray tube (CRT) in place of the printer on the teletype, thereby achieving better speeds and reliability. The teletype keyboard is also replaced with office typewriter-like keyboards in modern input/output terminals. An independent printer is used along with these terminals if a hard copy of the output information is needed.

A terminal can be classified either as a *dumb* or an *intelligent* device based on its capabilities. An intelligent terminal is usually microprocessor-based and can perform some amount of processing such as code conversion, format conversion, and editing locally, whereas a dumb terminal simply is an input/output device and the CPU handles all I/O-oriented tasks.

Terminals are usually interfaced to the CPU through serial lines and standard interfaces of which EIA RS232C is the most common. Terminals transfer data at the rate of 300 to 9,600 bits per second. When terminals are at a remote site from the CPU, telephone lines are used to connect the two. In this environment, a *modem* (modulator-demodulator) is used to convert the digital information into carrier (telephone line) signals at the transmitter and another modem used at the receiver reconverts the carrier signals into digital information.

Display technology is experiencing a rapid change. Newer capabilities are being added to displays almost daily. Sophisticated alphanumeric and graphic displays are now commonly available. Various devices such as the light pen and joystick to help the user work with displays have been developed. These devices enable the user to designate a point directly on the display, thereby working as input devices.

7.8.3 Card Reader and Punch

The 80-column card is the most popular input medium, especially in a batch-processing environment. Each column on the card represents a character. Hollerith code (see Appendix A) is used to represent characters. Card-reader speeds range from 60 to 2,000 cards per minute. Although card punches have been popular, the current trend is to use magnetic tapes or disks as output devices rather than card punches.

7.8.4 Paper Tape Reader and Punch

The paper tape uses the track (channel) format similar to that of a magnetic tape for character storage. Eight-channel paper tapes are the most common. A character is represented by a line consisting of a pattern of eight holes and no holes, one on each channel. In addition to these data channels, a track of sprocket holes is placed on the paper tape to enable tape movement. The sprocket holes are 0.1 inch apart. Teletype punches punch at the rate of 10 characters per second. Faster punches that can punch around 300 characters per second are also available.

Paper tape has been a popular input/output medium. It is inexpensive compared to magnetic tape or cards. The disadvantages of paper tapes are slow speed, inflexibility, and tendency to tear easily. The majority of operations for which the paper tape was used earlier are now utilizing magnetic tapes, magnetic cassette tapes, or floppy-disk units. The paper tape punch and readers are thus almost obsolete now.

7.8.5 Printers

Two types of printers are available: *character printers,* which print one character at a time, very much like the office typewriter, and *line printers,* which print one line at a time. Line printers have one print head for each position on the line (usually a maximum of 132 characters per line) and are faster than character printers.

Based on the mechanism for printing, printers can be classified as either *impact* or *nonimpact* printers. Impact printers print by mechanical means; nonimpact printers print by using an ink jet, by pressing heated dots on special thermal paper to form characters, or by blowing carbon dust on the paper in a dot matrix for each character. With the popularity of microprocessors and personal computer systems, printers of a very wide speed and price range are now available.

7.8.6 A/D and D/A Converters

Figure 7.20 shows a digital processor controlling an analog device. Real-time and process-control environments, monitoring laboratory instru-

Figure 7.20 Controlling an analog device

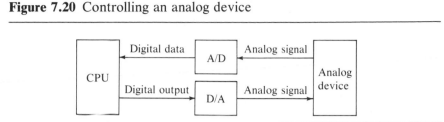

ments, fall into the application mode shown in the figure. Here the analog signal produced by the device is converted into a digital bit pattern by the A/D converter. The processor outputs the data in digital form, which is converted into analog form by the D/A converter. D/A converters are resistor-ladder networks that convert the input n-bit digital information into the corresponding analog voltage level.

A/D converters normally use a counter along with a D/A converter. The contents of the counter are incremented, converted into analog signals, and compared to the incoming analog signal. When the counter value corresponds to a voltage equivalent to the input analog voltage, the counter is stopped from incrementing further. The contents of the counter, then, correspond to the equivalent digital signal.

Secondary storage devices such as magnetic tapes (reel to reel and cassette), disks (hard and floppy) described in Chapter 3 are also used as input/output devices.

This survey of I/O devices and their characteristics is very brief. The reader is referred to manufacturers' literature for further information on I/O devices.

7.9   System Structures

Figures 7.15 and 7.16 showed two bus structures for a general computer system. Many large systems are configured around a multiple-bus structure (memory bus, I/O buses). Minicomputer systems use either a multiple-bus structure or a compatible I/O bus structure. There is no general baseline structure for a system; each system is unique. We will briefly describe the system structures of a minicomputer (DEC PDP-11), a microcomputer system (INTEL 8080), a calculator system (Hewlett-Packard 35) and two large-scale systems (IBM 360 and CDC 6600). Further details on these machines can be obtained from the manufacturers' manuals.

7.9.1   DEC PDP-11 System

The PDP-11 system (Figure 7.21) structure is based on the 56-line *unibus*. This bus connects the I/O devices, CPU, and memory. The devices can

Figure 7.21 PDP-11 system (Copyright, Digital Equipment Corporation, 1978. All Rights Reserved.)

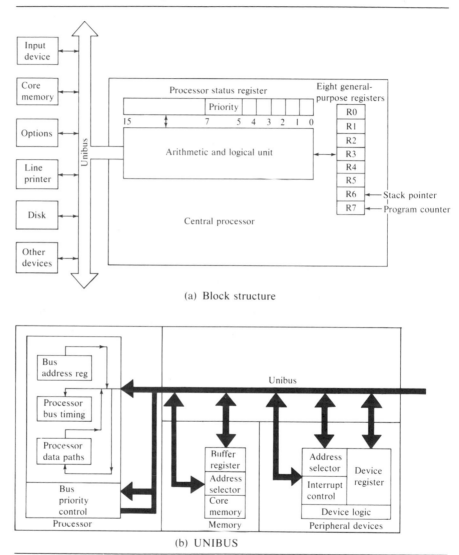

(a) Block structure

(b) UNIBUS

send, receive, or exchange data without processor intervention and without intermediate data buffering in the memory. The unibus makes the peripheral interfacing requirements uniform and hence has made the PDP-11 family of computers popular. Several unibus-compatible peripheral controllers and interfaces are available from non-DEC sources.

PDP-11 architecture takes advantage of the unibus in its method of addressing peripheral devices. Memory elements, such as the main core memory or any read-only or solid-state memories, have ascending addresses starting at zero, while registers that store I/O data or the status of individual peripheral devices have addresses in the highest 4K words of addressing space. Two memory words are normally reserved for each peripheral device (one for data, one for control). Some devices, such as magnetic tape and disk units, use up to 6 words.

Communication between any two devices on the bus is performed in a master-slave mode. During any bus operation, one device, the bus master, controls the bus when communicating with another device on the bus, the slave. For example, the processor as master can fetch an instruction from the memory, which is always a slave; or the disk as master can transfer data to the memory as slave. Master-slave relationships are dynamic; that is, the processor may, for example, pass bus control to a disk at which point the disk may become master and communicate with slave memory, and so on.

When two or more devices try to obtain control of the bus at one time, priority circuits decide among them. Devices have unique priority levels, fixed at system installation. A unit with a high priority level always takes precedence over one with a low priority level; in the case of units with equal priority levels, the one closest to the processor on the bus takes precedence over those further away (daisy chain).

Suppose the processor has control of the bus when three devices, all of higher priority than the processor, request bus control. If the requesting devices are of different priority, the processor will grant use of the bus to the one with the highest priority. If they are all of the same priority, all three signals come to the processor along the same bus line and the processor sees only one request signal. Its reply, granting priority, travels down the bus to the nearest requesting device, passing through any intervening nonrequesting device. The requesting device takes control of the bus, executes a single bus cycle of a few hundred nanoseconds, and relinquishes the bus. Then the request grant sequence occurs again, this time going to the second device down the line, which has been in wait mode. When all higher priority requests have been granted, control of the bus returns to the lowest priority device.

The processor usually has the lowest priority because in general it can stop whatever it is doing without serious consequences. Peripheral devices may be involved with some kind of mechanical motion or may be connected to a real-time process, either of which requires immediate attention to a request to avoid data loss.

The priority arbitration takes place asynchronously in parallel with data transfer. Every device on the bus except memory is capable of becoming a bus master. Communication is interlocked, so that each control signal issued by the master must be acknowledged by a response from the slave to complete the transfer. This simplifies the device interface because timing is no longer critical. The maximum typical transfer rate on the unibus is one 16-bit word every 400 nanoseconds, or about 2.5 million 16-bit words per second.

Bus Control. There are two ways of requesting bus control: nonprocessor request (NPR) or bus request (BR). An NPR is issued when a device needs to perform a data transaction with another device and does not use the CPU. Therefore, the CPU can relinquish bus control while an instruction is being executed. A BR is issued when a device needs to interrupt the CPU for service and hence an interrupt is not serviced until the processor has finished executing its current instruction. The following protocol is used to request the bus (BR):

1. The device makes a bus request by asserting the BR line.
2. Bus arbitrator recognizes the request by issuing a bus grant (BG). This bus grant is issued only if the priority of the device is greater than the priority currently assigned to the processor.
3. The device acknowledges the bus grant and inhibits further grants by asserting SELECTION ACKNOWLEDGE (SACK). The device also clears BR.
4. Bus arbitrator receives SACK and clears BG.
5. The device asserts BUS BUSY (BBSY) and clears SACK.
6. The device asserts BUS INTERRUPT (INTR) and sends its address vector.
7. The processor enters an interrupt service routine corresponding to the device, based on the address vector.

The following protocol is used for NPR data transfer requests:

1. The device makes a nonprocessor request by asserting NPR.
2. Bus arbitrator recognizes the request by issuing a nonprocessor grant or NPG.
3. The device acknowledges the grant and inhibits further grants by asserting SACK; device also clears NPR.
4. Bus arbitrator receives SACK and clears NPG.
5. The device asserts BUS BUSY (BBSY) and clears SACK. (Once a device's bus request has been honored, it becomes bus master as soon as the current bus master relinquishes control.)
6. Current bus master relinquishes bus control by clearing BBSY.
7. New device assumes bus control by setting BBSY and starts its data transfer to the slave device.

Interrupt Structure. Figure 7.22 shows the interrupt structure of PDP-11. There are five levels of priority: NPR, BR7, BR6, BR5, and BR4. NPR has the highest priority and BR4 has the lowest. In addition, there are interrupt levels 0 through 3 for software interrupts. The CPU itself can operate at any of the priority levels 0 through 7. The CPU releases the bus to a requesting device if the device priority is higher than the CPU priority at that time. There can be several devices connected to same priority level. Within each level, the devices are daisy chained.

There are two lines associated with each BR (BR7, BR6, BR5, or BR4) and the bus grant BG (BG7, BG6, BG5, or BG4). Because there are only five vertical priority levels, it is often necessary to connect more than one device to a single level.

The grant line for the NPR level (NPG) is connected to all the devices on that level in a daisy chain arrangement. When an NPG is issued, it first goes to the device closest to the CPU. If that device did not make the request, it permits the NPG to travel to the next device. Whenever the NPG reaches a device that has made a request, that device captures the

Figure 7.22 Priority control in PDP-11 (Copyright, Digital Equipment Corporation, 1978. All Rights Reserved.)

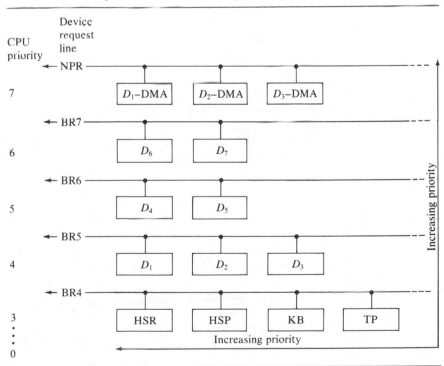

grant and prevents it from passing to any subsequent device in the chain. BR chaining is identical to NPR chaining in function. However, each BR level has its own BG chain.

The CPU can be set to any one of eight priority levels. Priority is not fixed; it can be raised or lowered by software. The CPU priority is elevated from level 4 to level 6 when the CPU stops servicing a BR4 device and starts servicing a BR6 device. This programmable priority feature permits masking of bus requests. The CPU can hold off servicing lower priority devices until more critical functions are completed.

Interrupt Service.   The interrupting device first gains the bus control and sends its vector to the CPU. The vector points to the two memory locations reserved for the device. The first of these memory words contains the address of the interrupt service routine (the new program counter value) and the second contains the new program status word (PS). The CPU pushes the current PC and PS contents onto a stack and loads the new PC and PS values, to enter the interrupt service routine. At the end of service, the return from interrupt instruction pops two words (PC and PS) into the corresponding CPU registers.

7.9.2   INTEL 8080

Figure 7.23 shows the details of a microcomputer system based on IN- TEL 8080. The structure shown here is typical of any microcomputer system. Several RAM and ROM modules are interfaced via the 16-bit address bus and the 8-bit data bus. The placement of RAM and ROM modules in the address range allowed by the microprocessor is done by decoding the address bus appropriately and enabling the required module. Special devices are available to interface I/O devices to the CPU. The I/O can be either memory-mapped or isolated (using input and output commands). If the memory-mapped I/O is used, a memory address is reserved for the I/O device. In the isolated I/O mode, each I/O instruction is 2 bytes long. The second byte is the address of one of the 256 devices that can be connected to the CPU. The control bus carries the following signals at the minimum: MEMORY READ-WRITE, I/O READ-WRITE, and INTERRUPT ACK.

Interrupts are recognized by the processor when the external device drives the interrupt line (INT) high. The interrupt may occur at any time, but it is recognized only after the instruction currently being executed is completed. When the interrupt is acknowledged by the processor on INTA line, the external device "jams" a RESTART (RST) instruction onto the data bus. This is equivalent in effect to fetching the RST instruc-

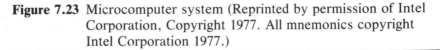

Figure 7.23 Microcomputer system (Reprinted by permission of Intel Corporation, Copyright 1977. All mnemonics copyright Intel Corporation 1977.)

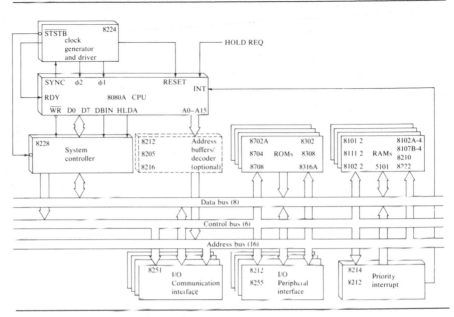

tion. RST is a 1-byte instruction, 3 bits of which are for device identification. RST becomes a CALL instruction to memory locations 0, 8, 16, 24, 32, 40, 48, or 56, depending on these 3 bits. These locations designate the beginning of interrupt service routines. RST also pushes the current value of PC onto the stack (return address).

Special devices are available to build an external priority structure among the interrupting devices (8214, 8259), direct memory access (8257), or I/O communication interface (8251). These devices are supplied by the manufacturer and are compatible with the bus structure of the 8080 system. Other support circuits are available from the manufacturer to aid system design. Typical of these support devices are I/O ports, bus drivers, priority interrupt controllers, peripheral interface adapters, communication interface, disk and CRT controllers, and DMA controllers. We will briefly describe the characteristics of two such devices (a DMA controller and a priority interrupt controller) used in building INTEL 8080-based microcomputer systems.

Figure 7.24 shows the details of a *DMA controller* (8257). The 8257 is a programmable, four-channel DMA device which, when coupled with a single Intel 8212 I/O port device, provides a complete four-channel DMA

Figure 7.24 DMA controller (Reprinted by permission of Intel Corporation, Copyright 1977. All mnemonics copyright Intel Corporation 1977.)

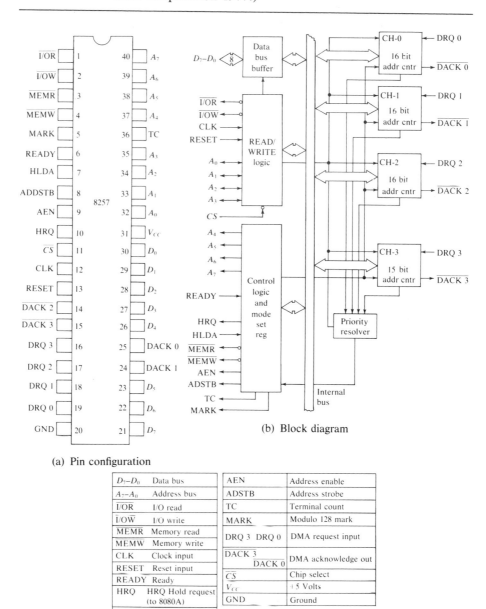

(a) Pin configuration

(b) Block diagram

D_7-D_0	Data bus		AEN	Address enable
A_7-A_0	Address bus		ADSTB	Address strobe
$\overline{I/OR}$	I/O read		TC	Terminal count
$\overline{I/OW}$	I/O write		MARK	Modulo 128 mark
$\overline{MEMR}$	Memory read		DRQ 3 DRQ 0	DMA request input
$\overline{MEMW}$	Memory write			
CLK	Clock input		$\overline{DACK\ 3}$	DMA acknowledge out
RESET	Reset input		$\overline{DACK\ 0}$	
READY	Ready		$\overline{CS}$	Chip select
HRQ	HRQ Hold request		V_{cc}	+5 Volts
	(to 8080A)		GND	Ground
HLDA	Hold acknowledge			
	(from 8080A)			

(c) Pin names

controller for use in Intel microcomputer systems. After being initialized by software, the 8257 can transfer a block of data containing up to 16,384 bytes between memory and a peripheral device directly, without further intervention required of the CPU. Upon receiving a DMA transfer request from an enabled peripheral, the 8257:

1. Acquires control of the system bus.
2. Acknowledges the peripheral that is connected to the highest priority channel.
3. Outputs the least significant 8 bits of the memory address onto system address lines A_0–A_7 and outputs the most significant 8 bits of the memory address to the 8212 I/O port via the data bus (the 8212 places these address bits on lines A_8–A_{15}).
4. Generates the appropriate memory and I/O read-write control signals that cause the peripheral to receive or deposit a data byte directly from or to the addressed location in memory.

The 8257 obtains the control of the system bus and repeats the transfer sequence as long as a peripheral maintains its DMA request. Thus, the 8257 can transfer a block of data to or from a high-speed peripheral (for example, a sector of data on a floppy disk) in a single "burst." When the specified number of data bytes has been transferred, the 8257 activates its terminal count (TC) output, informing the CPU that the operation is complete.

The 8257 offers three different modes of operation: (1) *DMA read*, which causes data to be transferred from memory to a peripheral; (2) *DMA write*, which causes data to be transferred from a peripheral to memory; and (3) *DMA verify*, which does not actually involve the transfer of data, but is used in verifying the newly acquired data.

The 8257 provides four separate DMA channels (CH-0 to CH-3). Each channel includes two 16-bit registers: a DMA address register and a terminal count register. Both registers must be initialized before a channel is enabled. The DMA address register is loaded with the address of the first memory location to be accessed. The value loaded into the low-order 14 bits of the terminal count register specifies the number of DMA cycles minus one before the terminal count (TC) output is activated. The most significant 2 bits of the terminal count register specify the type of DMA operation for that channel. These 2 bits are not modified during a DMA cycle but can be changed between DMA blocks.

Each channel accepts a DMA request (DRQ*n*) input and provides a DMA acknowledge (DACK*n*) output. DRQ0–DRQ3 are individual asynchronous channel request inputs used by the peripherals to obtain a DMA cycle. DRQ0 has the highest priority and DRQ3 has the lowest. A request can be generated by raising the request line and holding it high until DMA acknowledges. For multiple DMA cycles (burst mode), the request line is held high until the DMA acknowledge of the last cycle arrives. A rotating priority mode of operation is also possible in which the DMA ACK signals (DAK0–DAK3) inform the peripheral connected to that channel that it has been selected for a DMA cycle.

The three-state, bidirectional, 8-bit data bus buffer interfaces the 8257 to the system data bus. When the 8257 is being programmed by the CPU, 8 bits of data for a DMA address register, a terminal count register, or the mode set register are received on the data bus (D_0–D_7). When the CPU reads a DMA address register, a terminal count register, or the status register, the data are sent to the CPU over the data bus. During DMA cycles (when the 8257 is the bus master), the 8257 will output the most significant 8 bits of the memory address (from one of the DMA address registers) to the 8212 latch via the data bus. These address bits will be transferred at the beginning of the DMA cycle; the bus will then be released to handle the memory data transfer during the balance of the DMA cycle.

When the CPU is programming or reading one of the 8257's registers (i.e., when the 8257 is a slave device on the system bus), the read-write logic accepts the ($\overline{I/OR}$) or ($\overline{I/OW}$) signal, decodes the least significant 4 address bits (A_0–A_3), and either writes the contents of the data bus into the addressed register (if $\overline{I/OW}$ is true) or places the contents of the addressed register onto the data bus (if $\overline{I/OR}$ is true).

During DMA cycles (when the 8257 is the bus "master"), the read-write logic generates the I/O READ and memory WRITE (DMA write cycle) or I/O WRITE and memory READ (DMA read cycle) signals that control the data link with the peripheral that has been granted the DMA cycle. During DMA transfers, non-DMA I/O devices should be disabled using "AEN" signal to inhibit I/O device decoding of the memory address as an erroneous device address.

The I/OR input allows the 8-bit status register or the upper-lower byte of a 16-bit DMA address register or terminal-count register to be read in the slave mode. In the master mode, I/OR is a control output which is used to access data from a peripheral during the DMA write cycle.

The I/OW signal allows the contents of the data bus to be loaded into the 8-bit mode set register or the upper-lower byte of a 16-bit DMA address register or terminal-count register in the slave mode. In the master mode, I/OW is a control output which allows data to be output to a peripheral during a DMA read cycle.

The least significant 4 address lines (A_0–A_3) are bidirectional. In the slave mode they are inputs that select one of the registers to be read or programmed. In the master mode they are outputs which constitute the least significant 4 bits of the 16-bit memory address generated by the 8257.

The CHIP SELECT signal (CS) enables the I/O READ or I/O WRITE input when the 8257 is being read or programmed in the slave mode. In the master mode, CS is automatically disabled to prevent the chip from selecting itself while performing the DMA function.

The HOLD REQUEST (HRQ) output requests control of the system bus. HRQ is connected to the HOLD input on the CPU.

The HOLD ACKNOWLEDGE (HLDA) input from the CPU indicates that the 8257 has acquired control of the system bus.

MEMORY READ (MEMR) output is used to read data from the addressed memory location during DMA read cycles.

Terminal-count (TC) output notifies the currently selected peripheral that the present DMA cycle should be the last cycle for this data block. If the TC STOP bit in the mode set register is set, the selected channel will be automatically disabled at the end of that DMA cycle. TC is activated when the 14-bit value in the selected channel's terminal count register equals zero.

Modulo 128 MARK output notifies the selected peripheral that the current DMA cycle is the 128th cycle since the previous MARK output. MARK always occurs at 128 (and all multiples of 128) cycles from the end of the data block.

There are four pairs of "channel registers," each pair consisting of a 16-bit terminal count register (one pair for each channel). The 8257 also includes two "general registers": one 8-bit mode set register and one 8-bit status register. The registers are loaded or read when the CPU executes a WRITE or READ instruction that addresses the 8257 device and the appropriate register within the 8257. The contents of all these registers are established by the CPU before issuing a DMA request. Each of these registers appears as a memory location to the CPU.

When the 8257 is not executing a DMA cycle, it is in the idle state. A DMA cycle begins when one or more DMA request (DRQn) lines become active. The 8257 then sends a HOLD REQUEST (HRQ) to the CPU and waits for the CPU to return a HOLD ACKNOWLEDGE (HLDA). When HLDA is received, the DMA ACK ($\overline{\text{DACK}n}$) line for the highest priority requesting channel is activated, thus selecting that channel and its peripheral for the DMA cycle. The DMA request (DRQn) input should remain high until either $\overline{\text{DACK}n}$ is received for a single DMA cycle service or both the $\overline{\text{DACK}n}$ and TC outputs are received when transferring an entire data block in a "burst" mode. If the 8257 should lose control of the system bus (i.e., if HSDA goes false), the DMA acknowledge will be removed after the current DMA cycle is completed and no more DMA cycles will occur until the 8257 again acquires control of the system bus.

During DMA write cycles, the I/O READ (I/OR) output is generated followed by the MEMORY WRITE (MEMW) output. During DMA read cycles, the MEMORY READ (MEMR) output is generated followed by the I/O WRITE (I/OW) output. No read or write control signals are generated during DMA verify cycles. Figure 7.25 shows a typical system structure with four disk units interfaced through the DMA controller.

Figure 7.26 shows the *programmable interrupt controller* (8259). It is a 28-pin DIP that can handle up to eight vectored priority interrupts for the CPU and is cascadable for up to 64 vectored interrupt levels. It is programmed by the system's software as an I/O peripheral. A selection of priority modes is available to the programmer so that the manner in which the requests are processed by the 8259 can be configured to match his system requirements. The priority modes can be changed or reconfigured dynamically at any time during the main program execution. This means that the complete interrupt structure can be defined as required based on the total system environment.

The interrupts at the IR input lines (0–7) are handled by two registers in cascade, the interrupt request register (IRR) and the in-service register (ISR). The IRR is used to store all interrupt levels that are requesting service and the ISR is used to store all interrupt levels that are being serviced. The priority resolver logic block determines the priorities of the bits set in the IRR. The highest priority is selected and stored into the corresponding bit of the ISR during INTA pulse.

Figure 7.25 DMA as disk controller (Reprinted by permission of Intel Corporation, Copyright 1977. All mnemonics copyright Intel Corporation 1977.)

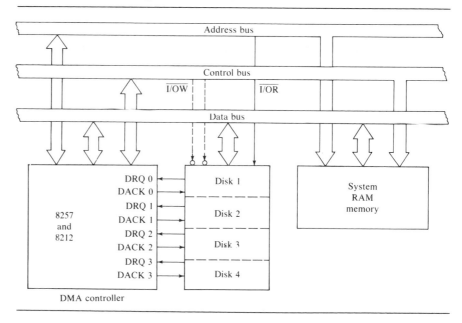

Figure 7.26 Programmable interrupt controller (Reprinted by permission of Intel Corporation, Copyright 1977. All mnemonics copyright Intel Corporation 1977.)

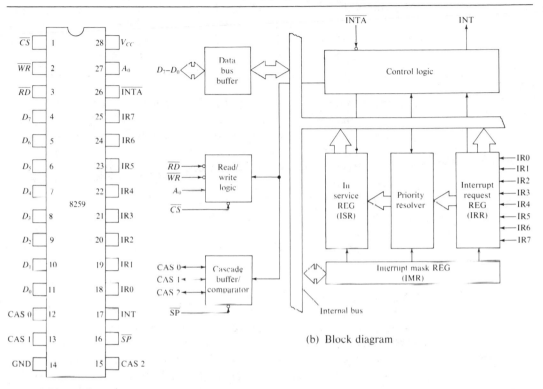

(a) Pin configuration

(b) Block diagram

D_7–D_0	Data bus (bi-directional)
$\overline{RD}$	Read input
$\overline{WR}$	Write input
A_0	Command select address
$\overline{CS}$	Chip select
CAS1–CAS0	Cascade lines
$\overline{SP}$	Slave program input
INT	Interrupt output
$\overline{INTA}$	Interrupt acknowledge input
IR0–IR7	Interrupt request inputs

(c) Pin names

The interrupt (INT) output goes directly to the CPU interrupt input. Three interrupt acknowledge ($\overline{INTA}$) pulses will cause the 8259 to release a 3-byte CALL instruction onto the data bus. The interrupt mask register (IMR) stores the bits of the interrupt lines to be masked. The IMR operates on the ISR. Masking of a higher priority input will not affect the interrupt request lines of lower priority.

The cascade buffer-comparator is employed when more than one 8259 is used in the system. The 8259 interacts with the CPU as follows:

1. One or more of the interrupt request lines (IR_{7-0}) are raised high, setting the corresponding IRR bit(s).
2. The 8259 accepts these requests, resolves the priorities, and sends an INT to the CPU.
3. The CPU acknowledges the INT and responds with an $\overline{INTA}$ pulse.
4. Upon receiving an $\overline{INTA}$ from the CPU, the highest priority ISR bit is set and the corresponding IRR bit is reset. The 8259 will also release a CALL instruction code (11001101) onto the 8-bit data bus through its D_{7-0} pins.
5. This CALL instruction will initiate two more $\overline{INTA}$ pulses to be sent to the 8259 from the CPU.
6. These two $\overline{INTA}$ pulses allow the 8259 to release its preprogrammed subroutine address onto the data bus. The lower 8-bit address is released at the first $\overline{INTA}$ pulse and the higher 8-bit address is released at the second $\overline{INTA}$ pulse.
7. This completes the 3-byte CALL instruction released by the 8259. ISR bit is not reset until the end of the subroutine when an EOI (end of interrupt) command is issued to the 8259.

Figure 7.27 shows a typical system structure using an Intel 8259. The 8259 requires programming by the CPU before normal operation can begin. The initialization and operation command words are provided by the CPU as a part of this programming. The reader is referred to the appropriate Intel manuals for further details on these devices.

The MOSTEK 6502 uses a system structure very similar to that of the 8080. It allows only memory-mapped I/O. There are three interrupt pins on the processor: IRQ, NMI, and RESET. IRQ is the interrupt request line. I/O interrupts are connected to IRQ. The interrupts on this pin can be disabled or enabled by the programmer. The non-maskable interrupt (NMI) is always enabled. Critical interrupts (power failure, for example) are connected to the NMI level. RESET is for system reset. The highest addressed 6 bytes of the memory are reserved for interrupt processing, 2 bytes for each interrupt level. During an interrupt, the processor fetches the 2-byte address of the corresponding interrupt service routine from

Figure 7.27 8259 interface to standard system bus (Reprinted by permission of Intel Corporation, Copyright 1977. All mnemonics copyright Intel Corporation 1977.)

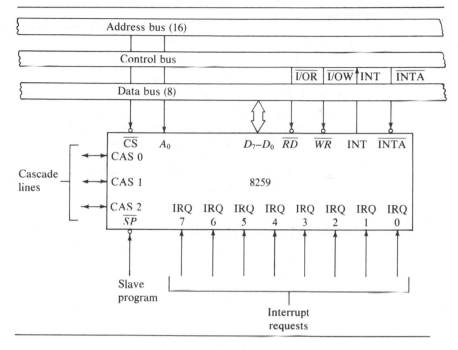

these locations. The system designer must initialize these locations with proper addresses as part of the system design.

7.9.3 Hewlett-Packard 35 System

HP 35 is a set of basic devices from which several HP advanced calculators are designed. The main reason for selecting it as an example is its serial architecture. A minimum calculator system configuration is shown in Figure 7.28(a). The system consists of a control and timing circuit (a 28-pin DIP), an arithmetic and register circuit (a 16-pin DIP), three 256- by 10-bit ROMs, and keyboard and display interfaces. Up to eight ROMs can be configured into the system.

The calculator can perform the four basic arithmetic operations and several transcendental functions such as logarithms, trigonometric functions, and square root. ROMs store programs for each of these functions. HP 35 is a 56-bit machine. Each register is 56 bits long and can store 14 BCD (decimal) digits. All operations are in BCD. The data format is shown:

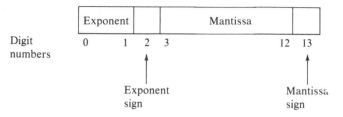

All operations are bit serial and are based on a 56-bit word cycle. The instruction bus (I_s) and the address bus (I_A) are single-line buses. The SYNC signal synchronizes the system components. It will be high during 10-bit times for a word cycle in which I_s will have a valid instruction. Figure 7.28(b) shows the timing relationships of SYNC, I_s, and I_A. The

Figure 7.28 HP 35 system (Courtesy of Hewlett-Packard Corporation)

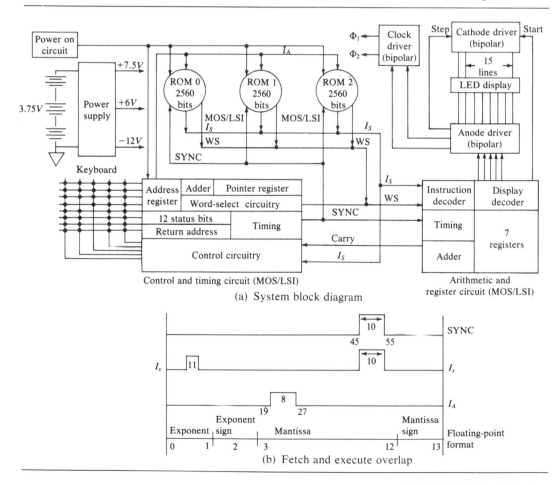

(a) System block diagram

(b) Fetch and execute overlap

Figure 7.28 (Continued)

Type	Fields
Jump routine	8 | Subroutine Address | 0 1 |
Conditional branch	8 | Branch Address | 1 1 |
Arithmetic	5 3 | Operations | Word select | 1 0 |
Status register	4 2 | Bit | Operation 0 1 0 0 |
Pointer register	4 2 | Digit | Operation 1 1 0 0 |
Load constant, stack operations	6 | X X X X X X 1 0 0 0 |
Miscellaneous ROM select, subroutine return, external entry, no operation, etc.	6 | X X X X X X 0 0 0 0 |

(c) Instruction set

(continued)

word select (WS) signal is generated in the ROM or in the control and timing circuit and enables the arithmetic unit to perform different operations on the fields of the 56-bit word (that is, the exponents are manipulated during the first eight time slots, the exponent sign during the next four time slots, and so on).

Each keystroke on the keyboard invokes a program stored in ROM. The instructions in ROMs are 10 bits long. Figure 7.28(c) gives their formats. The 8-bit address selects one of the ROM words. There is a separate ROM SELECT signal for enabling each ROM unit. The selected ROM sends an instruction on I_s. The next instruction address is on I_A during the execution of current instruction.

The control and timing circuit is a microprogrammed control unit that scans the keyboard and generates the ROM address and the timing corresponding to each keystroke. In Figure 7.28(d), the 12-bit status register is the program status word. The address circuitry generates the 8-bit ROM address and the ROM select signal.

Figure 7.28 (Continued)

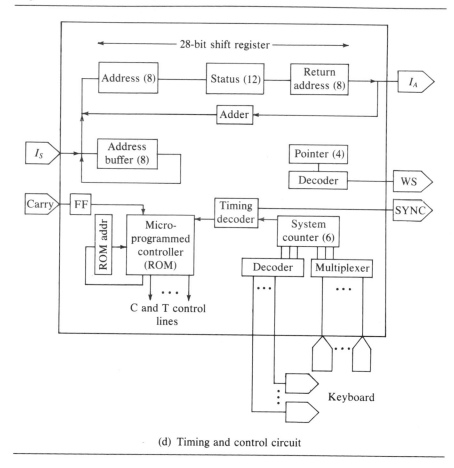

(d) Timing and control circuit

Figure 7.28(e) shows the details of the arithmetic and register circuit. There are seven 56-bit registers: working registers A, B, and C; a four-level stack C, D, E, and F; and a memory register M. A has an additional 4 bits to allow a left-shift operation. Register C communicates with external memory through the BCD line. The interconnections (serial by bit) of these registers allow operations such as transfer and exchange.

The digit-serial BCD adder-subtractor circuit performs operations on two single-digit operands, as guided by the instruction code on I_s and the WS signal. The keyboard is arranged as a five-column-by-eight-row matrix. The display consists of fourteen seven-segment displays and fourteen decimal points.

Figure 7.28 (Continued)

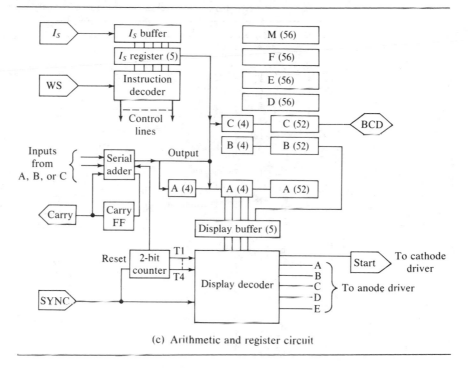

(c) Arithmetic and register circuit

7.9.4 IBM 360 System

The IBM 360 (System/360) is the name given to a third-generation series of large-scale computers. More recent than the 360 is the IBM system 370, which has been followed by cost-reduced implementations in the series 3030 and series 4300, which constitute the current primary product line. We will briefly describe the System/360 characteristics.

System/360 is distinguished by a design orientation toward very large memories and a hierarchy of memory speeds, a broad spectrum of manipulative functions, and a uniform treatment of I/O functions that facilitate communication with a diversity of I/O devices. The IBM System/360 structure shown in Figure 7.29 is used in at least seven announced models. Even though the allowable channels or storage capacity may vary from model to model, the logical structure can be discussed without reference to specific models.

Direct communication with a large number of low-speed terminals and other I/O devices is provided through a special multiplexer channel unit.

Figure 7.29 Functional schematic of IBM 360 system (Courtesy of International Business Machines Corporation)

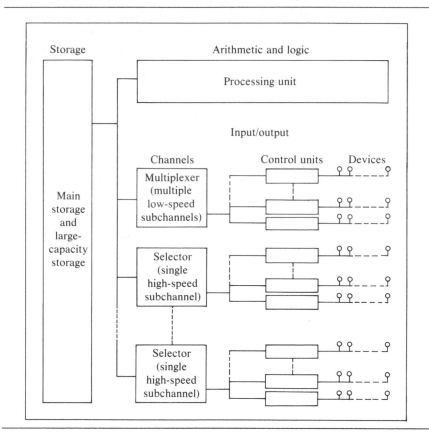

Communication with high-speed I/O devices is accomplished by the SE-LECTOR channel units. Conceptually, the I/O system acts as a set of subchannels that operate concurrently with one another and the processing unit. Each subchannel, instructed by its own control word sequence, can govern a data transfer operation between storage and a selected I/O device. A multiplexer channel can function either as one or as many subchannels. A selector channel always functions as a single subchannel. The control unit of each I/O device attaches to the channels via a standard interface.

The processing unit has sixteen general-purpose 32-bit registers used for addressing, indexing, and accumulating. Four 64-bit floating-point accumulators are optionally available. The inclusion of multiple registers permits effective use to be made of small high-speed memories. Four distinct types of processing are provided: logical manipulation of individual bits, character strings, and fixed words; decimal arithmetic; fixed-point binary arithmetic; and floating-point arithmetic. Figure 7.30 shows the registers and data paths.

An *input/output interrupt* signals the CPU that an I/O channel is free, that a specific channel or control unit activity has been completed, or that a special condition has arisen. The address of the I/O channel and control unit associated with the interruption are stored in bits 16–31 of the old PSW. Additional information on the nature of the interruption is saved in a channel status word that is stored when the interrupt is accepted by the CPU. I/O interrupt can be masked off with bits 0–6 of the PSW and with a control register.

A *program interrupt* arises from an improper specification of computer facilities, an illegal use of an instruction or data, or a request for system monitoring.

The purpose of the *supervisor call interrupt* is to provide a means of switching from the problem state to the supervisor state. It is initiated by the supervisor call instruction.

The *external interrupt* allows the CPU to respond to the timer, an interrupt key on the operator's console, or to one of six signals in lines to the CPU. The signal in lines may be part of a direct control feature that allows inter-CPU communications.

A *machine check interrupt* results from a system malfunction (hardware malfunction).

Figure 7.30 Schematic of basic registers and data paths (Courtesy of International Business Machines Corporation)

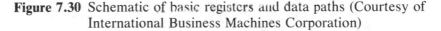

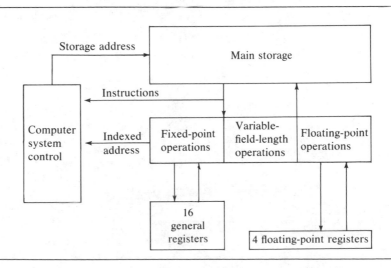

Interrupt requests are honored between instruction executions. When several requests occur during execution of an instruction, the *priorities* are honored in the following order:

1. Machine check.
2. Program or supervisor call.
3. External.
4. Input/output.

The program call and supervisor call are mutually exclusive.

If a machine-check interrupt occurs, no other interrupts can be taken until machine check is fully processed. Otherwise, the execution of the CPU program is delayed while PSWs are appropriately stored and fetched for each interrupt.

7.9.5   Control Data 6600

The CDC 6600 first announced in 1964 was designed for two types of use: large-scale scientific processing and time-sharing of smaller problems. To accommodate large-scale scientific processing, a high-speed, floating-point, multifunctional CPU was used. The peripheral activity was separated from CPU activity by providing twelve input/output channels

Figure 7.31 CDC 6600 system structure (Courtesy of Control Data Corporation)

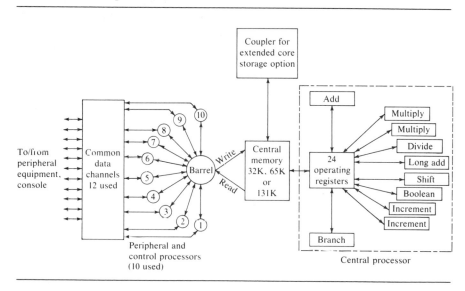

controlled by ten peripheral processors. Figure 7.31 shows the system structure.

The ten peripheral processors have access to central memory. One of these processors acts as a control processor for the system while the others are performing I/O tasks. Each of these processors has its own memory, used for storing programs and for data buffering. The peripheral processors access the central memory in a time-shared memory for 100 nanoseconds, once every 1000 nanoseconds, by a register barrel mecha-

Figure 7.32 Central processor operating registers of CDC 6600 (Courtesy of Control Data Corporation)

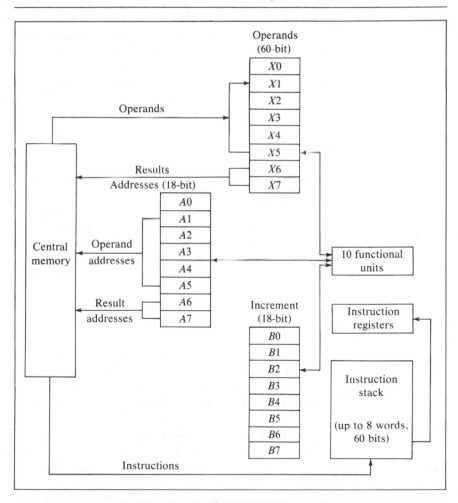

nism. I/O channels are bidirectional 12-bit paths. One 12-bit word can be transferred into or out of the memory every 1000 nanoseconds by each channel.

The central processor obtains its programs and data from the central memory. It can be interrupted by a peripheral processor. There are 10 functional units in the central processor that can operate in parallel on one or two 60-bit operands to produce a 60-bit result. The operands and results are provided in the operating registers. A functional unit is activated by the control unit as soon as the operands are available in the operating registers. Since the functional units work concurrently, a number of arithmetic operations can be performed in parallel.

There are 24 operating registers: eight 18-bit index registers, eight 18-bit address registers, and eight 60-bit floating-point registers. Figure 7.32 shows the data and address paths. Instructions are either 15 bits or 30 bits long. An instruction stack capable of holding 32 instructions enhances instruction execution speed (refer to Chapter 6).

The control unit maintains a *scoreboard,* which is a running file of the status of all registers and functional units and their allocation. As new instructions are fetched, resources are allocated to execute them by referring to the scoreboard. Instructions are queued for later processing if resources can not be allocated.

Central memory is organized in 32 banks of 4K words. Each consecutive address calls for a different bank. Five memory trunks are provided between memory and five floating-point registers. An instruction calling for an address register implicitly initiates a memory reference on its trunk. An overlapped memory access and arithmetic operation is thus possible. The concurrent operation of functional units, high transfer rates between registers and memory, and separation of peripheral activity from the processing activity make CDC 6600 a fast machine.

7.10 Summary

Various modes of data transfer between the I/O devices and the CPU were discussed in this chapter. The advances in hardware technology and dropping prices of hardware have made it possible to implement various cost-effective and versatile I/O structures. The system structures described in this chapter are representative of commercially available machines although each system is unique in its structure. Interfacing I/O devices to the CPU is usually a major task. But recent efforts toward standardizing the communication protocols between the devices and the CPU have resulted in several standards such as the EIA S-100 and the IEEE-488 bus standards; it is now possible to interface an I/O device or a

CPU made by one manufacturer with a compatible device by another manufacturer with much ease. The trend of distributing the processing to I/O processors from the CPU has continued over the past few years. The current architectures connect several general-purpose processors to form a distributed processing network. Newer and more intelligent I/O devices are being introduced almost daily. A list of the major characteristics of such devices would quickly become obsolete. The magazines listed as references at the end of this chapter provide up-to-date information on such devices.

Several techniques used in practical architectures to enhance the system performance were listed in Chapters 6 and 7. Each system will have its own unique architectural features. A detailed study of the particular architecture is needed to understand such features. The concepts discussed here provide a baseline set of features. In practice, the architecture of a machine evolves over several years and the machine designer tries to maintain an upward compatibility in terms of processing characteristics as the system evolves. Tracing a family of machines to gather the changing architectural characteristics and to distinguish the influence of advances in hardware and software technology on the system architecture would be an interesting and instructive project.

References

Baer, J. L. *Computer Systems Architecture*. Rockville, Md.: Computer Sciences Press, 1980.

Computer Design. Littleton, Mass.: Computer Design Publishing Corp. Published monthly.

Digital Design. Boston, Mass.: Benwill Publishing Corp. Published monthly.

Hewlett-Packard 35 Manual. Corvallis, Oreg.: Hewlett-Packard Co., 1976.

High Technology. Garden City, N.Y.: United Technical Publications. Published monthly.

Knoblock, D. E., D. C. Loughry, and C. A. Visser. "Insight into Interfacing." *IEEE Spectrum,* May 1975, pp. 50–57.

MCS6500 Microcomputer Family Hardware Manual. Norristown, Pa.: MOS Technology, Inc., 1976.

MCS-80 User's Manual. Santa Clara, Calif.: Intel Corporation, 1977.

Morrow, G., and H. Fullmer. "Proposed Standard for S-100 bus." *IEEE Computer,* May 1978, pp. 84–89.

Pooch, V. W., and R. Chattergy. *Minicomputers: Hardware, Software and Selection*. New York, N.Y.: West, 1980.

Siewiorek, D. P., C. G. Bell, and A. Newell. *Computer Structures: Principles and Examples*. New York, N.Y.: McGraw-Hill, 1982.

Sloan, M. E. *Computer Hardware and Organization: An Introduction.* Palo Alto, Calif.: Science Research Associates, 1976.

Stone, H. S. *Introduction to Computer Architecture.* 2d ed. Chicago, Ill.: Science Research Associates, 1980.

System/360 Principles of Operation. Armonk, N.Y.: IBM Corporation, 1976.

System/360 System Summary. Armonk, N.Y.: IBM Corporation, 1976.

Problems

7.1   Design the hardware required to interface several I/O devices to ASC, assuming the least significant 4 bits of I/O instruction to be the address, without changing the current ASC structure and the microprogram.

7.2   Assume that there is a serial output line connected to the LSB of the accumulator. The contents of the accumulator are to be output on this line. It is required that a start bit of 0 and 2 stop bits (1) delimit the data bits. Write an assembly language program on ASC to accomplish the data output. What changes in hardware are needed to perform this transfer?

7.3   Rewrite the fetch microinstruction sequence for ASC, assuming that the processor status is saved on a stack before entering interrupt service. Include a stack pointer register.

7.4   Rewrite the sequence in Problem 7.3, assuming a vectored interrupt mode. Assume that the device sends its address as the vector.

7.5   Design the complete hardware for a "daisy chained" interrupt structure where a higher priority device prevents the lower priority device from interrupting the CPU. The device should also provide a vector to the CPU.

7.6   Write microprograms to describe the handshake between the peripheral and CPU during (a) interrupt mode I/O and (b) DMA. Use the HDL structure common to ASC microprograms to describe these asynchronous operations.

7.7   Develop a complete hardware block diagram of a multiplexer channel. List the microoperations of each block in the diagram.

7.8   Repeat Problem 7.7 for a selector channel.

7.9   Develop a schematic for a printer controller. Assume that one character (8 bits) is transferred to the printer at a time, in a programmed I/O mode.

7.10 Repeat Problem 7.9, assuming that the printer has a buffer that can hold 80 characters. Printing is activated only when the buffer is full.

7.11 Design a bus controller to resolve the memory-access requests by the CPU and a DMA device.

7.12 The structure of Figure 7.8 polls the peripheral devices in the order of the device numbers. Design a structure in which the order of polling (i.e., priorities) can be specified. (Hint: Use a buffer to store the priorities).

7.13 Design a set of instructions to program the DMA controller. Specify the instruction formats, assuming ASC as the CPU.

7.14 A cassette recorder-player needs to be interfaced to ASC. Assume that the cassette unit has a buffer to store 1 character and the cassette logic can read or record a character into or out of this buffer. What other control lines are needed for the interface? Generate the interface protocol.

7.15 Compare the timing characteristics of programmed input mode with that of the vector-mode, interrupt-driven input scheme, on ASC. Use the major cycles needed to perform the input as the unit of time.

Chapter 8

Advanced Architectures

Up to this point, we have considered processors that have essentially a single instruction stream operating upon a single data stream. We have described various enhancements such as memory interleaving, pipelined arithmetic units, and instruction fetch-execute overlap to increase the processing speed of these machines. Faster technologies have been employed wherever possible (semiconductor memories versus core, for example) in the implementation of these machines in an effort to increase the system throughput.

There are applications, especially in real-time processing, that make the machine throughput inadequate even with all these enhancements. It has thus been necessary to develop newer architectures with higher degrees of parallelism than the above schemes provide, to circumvent the limits of technology and to accommodate faster processing. A great deal of research and development has been devoted to the development of newer architectures and several supercomputers have evolved as a result. In this chapter, we will first provide a classification of architectures, followed by a description of representative supercomputer architectures. We will end the chapter with a discussion of current architectural trends: high-level-language machines, data-flow machines, computer networking, and distributed processing. Coverage of these topics is necessarily a brief overview; the references at the end of the chapter provide further details on these topics.

366

8.1   Classes of Architectures

Flynn divided computer architectures into four main classes, based on the number of instruction and data streams:

1. Single instruction stream, single data stream (SISD) machines, which are uniprocessors such as ASC, PDP-11, and INTEL 8080.
2. Single instruction stream, multiple data stream (SIMD) architectures, which are systems with multiple arithmetic-logic processors and a control processor. Each arithmetic-logic processor processes a data stream of its own, as directed by the single control processor. They are also called array processors or vector processors.
3. Multiple instruction stream, single data stream (MISD) machines, in which the single data stream is simultaneously acted upon by a multiple instruction stream. A system with a pipelined ALU can be considered an MISD, although that extends the definition of a data stream somewhat.
4. Multiple instruction stream, multiple data stream (MIMD) machines, which contain multiple processors, each executing its own instruction stream to process the data stream allocated to it. A computer system with one processor and an I/O channel working in parallel is the simplest example of an MIMD.

Almost all the machines used as examples in previous chapters are SISD machines; an exception is the CDC 6600, which is an MIMD with independent instruction streams, one for each active functional unit operating on multiple data streams. We will now provide models for the last three of the above-listed classifications followed by a brief description of several popular architectures. We will call the last three architecture classes *supercomputers*.

8.1.1   SIMD

Figure 8.1 shows the structure of an SIMD. There are n arithmetic-logic processors ($P1$–Pn), each with its own memory block ($M1$–Mn). The individual memory blocks combined constitute the system memory. The memory bus is used to transfer instructions and data to the control processor (CP). The control processor decodes instructions and sends control signals to processors $P1$–Pn. The processor interconnection network enables data exchange between the processors.

The control processor, in practice, is a full-fledged uniprocessor. It retrieves instructions from memory, sends arithmetic-logic instructions to processors, and executes control (branch, stop, etc.) instructions itself. Processors $P1$–Pn execute the same instruction at any time, each on its

Figure 8.1 SIMD structure

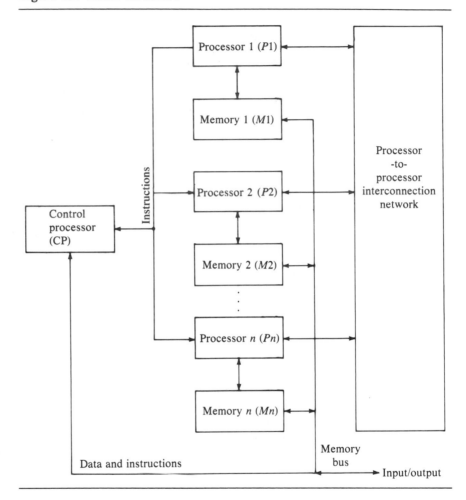

own data stream. Based on the arithmetic-logic conditions, some of the processors may be deactivated during certain operations. Such activation and deactivation of processors is handled by the control processor.

SIMDs are special purpose machines, suitable for array or vector processing. For example, in computing the sum of the column elements of a matrix, each column of the matrix can be assigned to a processor of an SIMD. The column sums can then be computed in N steps for an $N \times N$ matrix ($N \le n$), rather than in N^2 steps required on an SISD. Thus, SIMDs can provide a high throughput, as long as the processing algorithm exhibits a high degree of parallelism at the instruction level.

8.1.2 MISD

Figure 8.2 shows the organization of an MISD machine. There are n processors (or processing stations) arranged in a pipeline. The data stream from the memory enters the pipeline at processor 1 and moves from station to station through processor n, and the resulting data stream enters the memory. The control unit of the machine is shown to have n subunits, one for each processor. Thus, there will be at any time n independent instruction streams. Note that the concept of data stream in this model is somewhat broad; each data unit is viewed as a data stream, although those units of data belong to one data stream.

Assuming that a unit of data stays with each station for x seconds, the total processing time per unit of data is $(n \cdot x)$ seconds. But, once the pipeline is full, there will be an output from the pipeline every x seconds, thereby achieving a very high throughput.

8.1.3 MIMD

Figure 8.3 shows an MIMD structure consisting of p memory blocks, n processing elements, and m input/output channels. The processor-to-memory interconnection network enables the connection of a processor to any of the memory blocks. In addition to establishing the processor-memory connections, the network should also have a memory-mapping

Figure 8.2 MISD structure

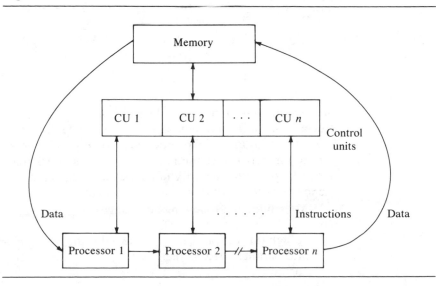

Figure 8.3 MIMD structure

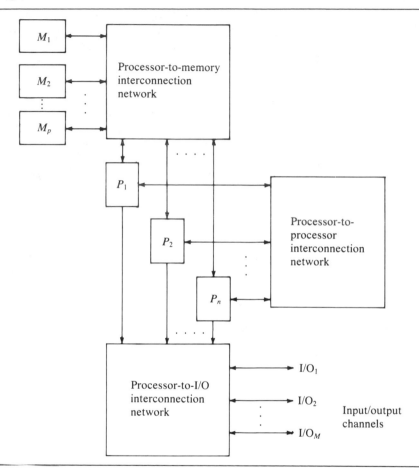

mechanism that performs a logical-to-physical address mapping. The processor-to-I/O interconnection network enables the connection of an I/O channel to any of the processors. The processor-to-processor interconnection network is more of an interrupt network than a data exchange network, since the majority of data exchanges can be performed through the memory-to-processor interconnection.

MIMDs offer the following advantages:

1. A high throughput can be achieved if the processing can be broken into parallel streams thereby keeping all the processors active concurrently.

2. Since the processors and memory blocks are general-purpose resources, a faulty resource can be easily switched out, thereby achieving better fault tolerance.
3. A dynamic reconfiguration of resources is possible, to accommodate the processing loads.

MIMDs are more general-purpose in application than are SIMDs. The processors are not in synchronization instruction-by-instruction as in SIMD. But, it is required that the processing algorithms exhibit a high degree of parallelism, so that several processors are active concurrently at any time.

Some of the issues of concern in the design of an MIMD system are

1. Processor scheduling: efficient allocation of processors to processing needs in a dynamic fashion as the computation progresses.
2. Processor synchronization: prevention of processors trying to change a unit of data simultaneously; and obeying the precedence constraints in data manipulation.
3. Interconnection network design: the processor-to-memory or processor-to-peripheral interconnection network is still probably the most expensive element of the system and can become a bottleneck.
4. Overhead: ideally an n processor system should provide n times the throughput of a uniprocessor. This is not true in practice because of the overhead processing required to coordinate the activities between the various processors.
5. Partitioning: identifying parallelism in processing algorithms to invoke concurrent processing streams is not a trivial problem.

8.2 Supercomputers

Several supercomputer architectures have been attempted since the sixties to overcome the SISD throughput bottleneck. The majority of these architectures have been implemented in quantities of one or two. Nevertheless, these research and development efforts have contributed immensely to the area of computer architecture. We will briefly describe the following supercomputer architectures, concentrating mainly on architectural details rather than the application areas for these machines:

SIMD: ILLIAC-IV and STARAN.
MISD: CDC STAR-100 and Texas Instruments ASC.
MIMD: Carnegie-Mellon University's C· mmp and Cm*.

We will also discuss Cray Research Inc.'s CRAY-1, a system that can be classified under all the above three categories.

8.2.1 ILLIAC-IV

The ILLIAC-IV project was started in 1966 at the University of Illinois. The objective was to build a parallel machine capable of executing 10^9 instructions per second. To achieve this speed, a system with 256 processors controlled by a control processor was envisioned. The set of processors was divided into four quadrants of 64 processors each, each quadrant to be controlled by one control unit. Only one quadrant was built and it achieved a speed of 2×10^8 instructions per second.

Figure 8.4 shows the ILLIAC-IV system structure. The system is controlled by a Burroughs B-6500 processor. This machine compiles the ILLIAC-IV programs, schedules array programs, controls the array configurations, and manages the disk file transfers and peripherals. The disk file unit acts as the backup memory for the system.

Figure 8.5 shows the configuration of a quadrant. The control unit provides the control signals for all processing elements ($PE_0–PE_{63}$),

Figure 8.4 ILLIAC-IV system structure

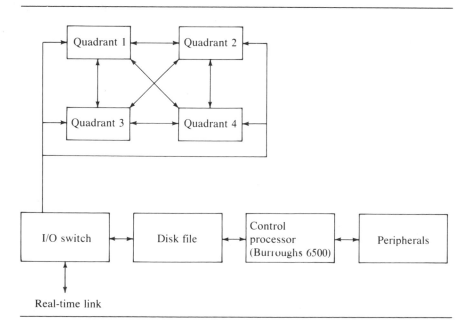

which work in an instruction-by-instruction lock-step mode. The control unit (CU) executes all program control instructions and transfers processing instructions to PEs. The CU and the PE array execute in parallel. In addition, the CU generates and broadcasts the addresses of operands that are common to all PEs, receives status signals from PEs, from the internal I/O operations, and from B-6500 and performs the appropriate control function.

Each PE has four 64-bit registers (accumulator, operand register, data-routing register, and general storage register), an arithmetic-logic unit, a 16-bit local index register, and an 8-bit mode register that stores the processor status and provides the PE enable-disable information. Each processing element memory (PEM) block consists of a 250-nanosecond cycle-time memory with 2K 64-bit words.

The PE-to-PE routing network connects each PE to four of its neigh-

Figure 8.5 A quadrant of ILLIAC-IV

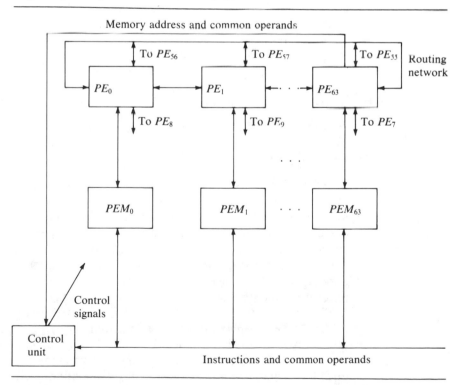

Note: PE_i is connected to PE_{i+1}, PE_{i-1}, PE_{i+8}, and PE_{i-8}; $0 \leq i \leq 63$.

bors (i.e., PE_i to PE_{i+1}, PE_{i-1}, PE_{i+8}, and PE_{i-8}). The PE array is arranged as an 8×8 matrix with end-around connections. Interprocessor data communication of arbitrary distances is accomplished by a sequence of routings over the routing network.

The processing array is basically 64-bit-computation oriented. But, it can be configured to perform as a 128 32-bit subprocessor array or a 512 8-bit subprocessor array. The subprocessor arrays are not completely independent because of the common index register in each PE and the 64-bit data routing path.

The applications envisioned for ILLIAC-IV were

1. Manipulation of large matrices.
2. Computations of solutions for large sets of difference equations for weather-prediction purposes.
3. Fast data correlation for fast-response, phased-array radar systems.

Two high-level languages have evolved over the years for programming ILLIAC-IV: A FORTRAN-like language (CFD) oriented towards computational fluid dynamics and an ALGOL-like language, GLYPNIR. A compiler that extracts parallelism from a regular FORTRAN program and converts it into a parallel FORTRAN (IVTRAN) has also been attempted. There is no operating system. ILLIAC-IV, being an experimental machine, did not offer a software library or a set of software tools, thereby making it difficult to program. The ILLIAC-IV is now located at the NASA Ames Center and is not operational.

8.2.2 STARAN

STARAN is an associative processor. Consider the associative memory shown in Figure 8.6. At each associative memory word an arithmetic-logic unit (ALU) is shown. The associative memory block is similar to the one discussed in Chapter 3. A search through the associative memory for specified data results in the selection of words that match the data (i.e., corresponding result register bits are set to 1). Using the result register as a mask, the ALU corresponding to each respondent can be activated to perform an update processing of the selected fields in the selected associative memory words. The processing is performed in a bit-serial mode if each ALU is a single-bit ALU or in a byte- or word-serial mode if the ALU allows it. The latter mode results in a very high hardware cost since one such ALU is required at each associative memory word. Note that once the memory words are selected, the updating operation can be performed simultaneously on all the memory words. Further, by using a

Figure 8.6 An associative processor

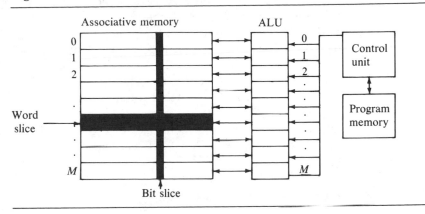

common control unit to drive the ALUs in a lock-step mode, an SIMD mode of processing is possible.

STARAN, developed by Good Year Aerospace Corporation, is an SIMD and an associative processor with applications in real-time processing involving a wide variety of sensors, signal processors, displays, stor-

Figure 8.7 STARAN/645 system structure

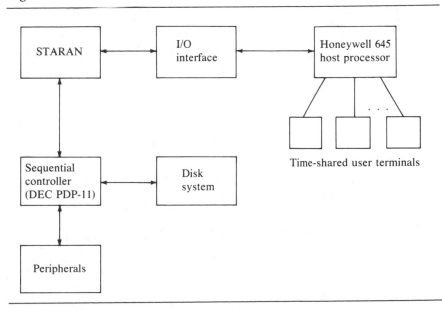

age devices, and so on. Figure 8.7 shows the system structure of a STARAN/645 system at Rome Air Development Center (RADC). STARAN is configured as a peripheral for the host machine (Honeywell 645), the two interfaced with a versatile I/O interface. The function of the sequential controller (DEC PDP-11) is to interface the system peripherals, disk system, and operator to the STARAN.

Figure 8.8 shows the STARAN organization. The control memory consists of all the application program equivalents to drive the array controller. The array controller controls up to 32 modules of 256- by 256-bit associative memory arrays. Each associative memory array is a multidi-

Figure 8.8 STARAN organization

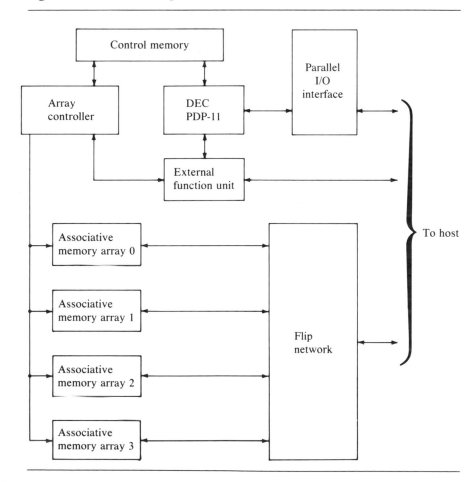

mensional access (MDA) array. The array can be accessed in a *bit-slice mode* (corresponding bit from each of the 256 words) for processing or in a *word-slice mode* (one 256-bit word at a time) for input/output operations. A number of other access modes are allowed.

The *flip network* is an interconnection network that allows the permutation of operands selected from the memory, the ALU registers of the arrays, or the external I/O units, thereby enabling a software reconfiguration of the arrays.

There are three 256-bit registers in each array: the M register contains the write mask for a parallel memory write; the X register along with its logic can perform various logical operations between its own contents and the output of the flip network; the Y register acts as a mask for operations on X register contents.

The first production configuration of STARAN was used in 1972 for onsite tests of air traffic control. Such real-time, massive data-base-oriented processing is the application for which associative processors are suitable.

Several manufacturers have developed associative processing equipment. The cost of associative memories prohibited the wide use of such machines. With the reduction in cost of semiconductor memories, however, there are several associative memory systems now available that can be used as special-purpose peripherals attached to any general-purpose processor.

8.2.3 CDC STAR-100

STAR-100, developed by Control Data Corporation, is an MISD machine. It has two arithmetic pipelines and a string processing unit (Figure 8.9). The arithmetic pipelines process 64-bit data while the string processor handles 16-bit data. Pipeline 1 can perform floating-point addition and multiplication and address computations. Pipeline 2 can perform floating-point addition and nonpipelined floating-point division. It also has a multifunction unit that can perform both floating-point multiplication and division. Once full, a 64-bit result is output by the pipeline every 40 nanoseconds. The 64-bit pipeline can be split into two 32-bit pipelines, working in parallel and yielding a result every 20 nanoseconds.

Figure 8.10 shows the details of a pipeline. P_1, P_2, . . . , P_M are processors and R_1, R_2, . . . , R_{M-1} are registers provided between stages for holding the data. Each processor performs a specific step in the overall processing. In the floating-point add pipeline the operations of compare exponent, align mantissa, add mantissa, normalize, and output are each performed by a processor P_i in the pipeline.

Figure 8.9 CDC STAR-100 structure

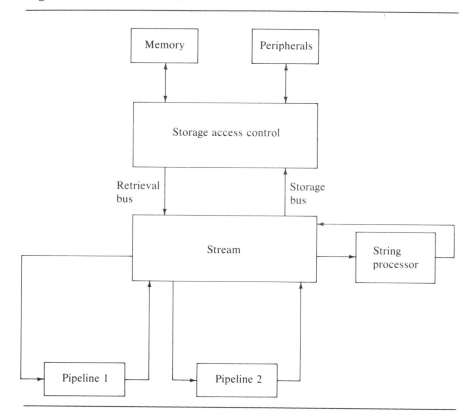

8.2.4 Texas Instruments ASC

The Texas Instruments Advanced Scientific Computer (TI ASC) is a pipelined machine. The purpose of building the machine was to support seismic processing. An ASC system consists of an eight-way interleaved memory communicating with eight subsystems through an 8-by-8 crossbar. Four of the eight memory parts are used by the central processor and each of the other four are used by a peripheral processor, a disk storage unit, a data communications unit, and peripherals. The peripheral processor acts as a control unit for the system.

A typical ASC configuration consists of an instruction processing unit, one to four pipelined arithmetic units (or pipes), and one to four memory buffer units, as shown in Figure 8.11. The instruction processing unit is also configured as a four-stage pipeline performing instruction fetch, decode, effective address calculation, and register operand fetch operations.

Figure 8.10 Pipeline of CDC STAR-100

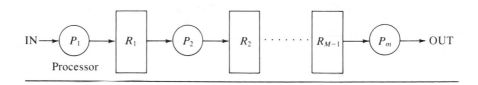

The memory buffer unit interfaces the central memory and the arithmetic unit. It has three double buffers X, Y, and Z with 8 words per buffer. X and Y are for input and Z is for the output data. The double buffer arrangement enhances the pipeline processing speed.

Figure 8.12 shows the eight stages of an arithmetic pipeline. The lines show the configuration of this pipeline for two operations: floating-point add and fixed-point multiply. The pipeline provides a result every 60 nanoseconds.

Figure 8.11 TI ASC central processor

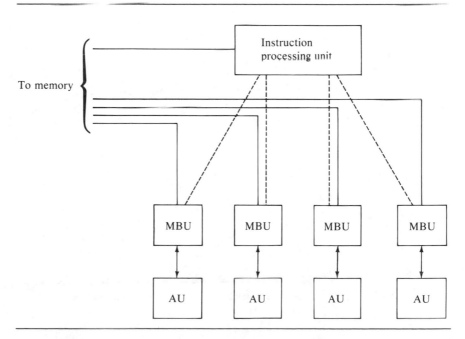

Note: MBU: memory buffer unit; AU: arithmetic unit.

Figure 8.12 TI ASC pipeline

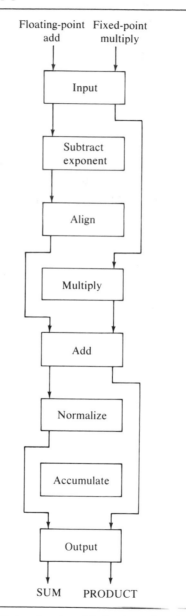

Note: The ''Accumulate'' stage is not used in floating-point add and multiply operations.

8.2.5 C· mmp

C· mmp (a "multiminiprocessor") is an MIMD system developed by Carnegie-Mellon University during the years 1971–1978. The goal of this project was to build a multiprocessor that would support a general-purpose time-shared environment. The machine would be symmetric (i.e., no master-slave relationship among processors) and use as much commercially available hardware as possible.

Figure 8.13 shows the structure of C· mmp. There are 16 memory blocks (M_0–M_{15}) connected to 16 processors (P_0–P_{15}) through a 16-by-16 crossbar network. An interprocessor bus connects the processors to provide common clock information and handles interprocessor interrupts. Each processor has a local memory block (M_{local}), a disk unit, and other peripherals.

The primary memory consists of 1.4M bytes of core memory (eleven parts) and 1.3M bytes of MOS memory (five parts). The core memory at each part consists of eight modules of 16K bytes each, thereby providing an eight-way interleaving. The MOS memory is configured as four 65K-byte modules per part. These modules are not interleaved. The local (nonshared) memory of each processor is an 8K-byte core memory.

The processors are PDP-11/40s and PDP-11/20s, selected because of the uniform interfacing characteristics of the unibus. Some modifications were required to make these processors suitable for the multiprocessing environment and to provide software protection. For example, HALT, WAIT, and RESET instructions were prohibited from user programs; instructions such as RETURN FROM INTERRUPT that modify processor status word were also prohibited to facilitate appropriate relocation of programs in the multiprocessing environment.

A crossbar to connect peripheral devices to processors was first envisioned but was not built due to cost considerations. The peripheral devices are connected to each processor through the standard unibus interface. Zero-latency paging disk units and CMU-designed graphic display units are attached to each processor.

The DMAP unit maps the 18-bit address on the unibus into the 25-bit address required for primary memory access. Four of the 25 bits of the primary memory address are used to select one of the sixteen parts and the remaining 21 bits to select a location within the memory block attached to the part. All references to shared memory are first checked against the contents of the 2K-byte cache. If the data are available in the cache, the primary memory is by-passed. Thus, cache is employed to reduce the memory contention rather than to speed up the memory access. Only one prototype cache has been built.

The crossbar switch allows the maximum concurrency of sixteen paths

Figure 8.13 Structure of C· mmp

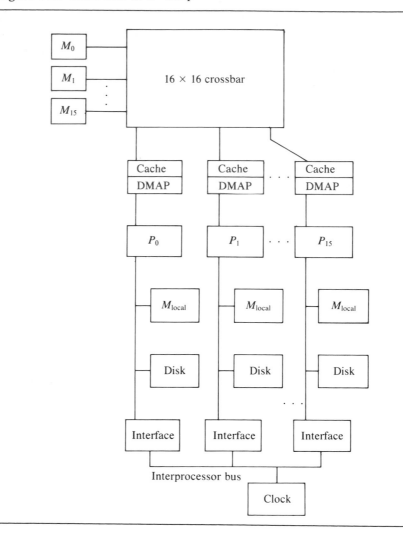

when all processors request different memory parts. It also resolves the memory contention when more than one processor requires the same memory part.

The C· mmp system is controlled by the Hydra operating system. The system has been used as a testbed and has contributed to the better understanding of memory contention, crossbar design, reliability, and software recovery problems.

8.2.6   Cm*

The Cm* (a "multimicroprocessor") is an MIMD designed and built by the Department of Computer Science at Carnegie-Mellon University. The goals of the Cm* were to investigate new interconnection structures for multiprocessors and to provide a vehicle for exploring software issues in distributed multiprocessing systems. The Cm* uses a *packet switched* interconnection scheme. (Packet switching is a mode of data transfer in which the data is broken up into smaller packets and transmitted over the interconnection network. There is no dedicated physical path for packet transfer; rather, the packet travels from node to node in the interconnection network until it reaches the destination. All the register transfer schemes we have seen so far employ a dedicated physical path between the source and the destination, until the transfer is complete. This is the *circuit switching* mode.) The principal connecting elements in Cm* are buses shared by a large number of processing elements. The processing elements communicate with each other by sending and receiving messages. Specialized processors control the routing and buffering of messages. With such an interconnection structure, one would be tempted to view Cm* as a network rather than as a multiprocessor. One crucial feature of Cm*, however, marks it unambiguously as a multiprocessor: there is a single systemwide physical address space and every processor can access all the memory in the system.

A unique feature of Cm* is the great flexibility of its address structure. It was recognized in the early stages of design that no one knew what kind of address structure was best suited for a large multiprocessor with a connection scheme like that of Cm*. Consequently, the address structure of Cm* is left in the hands of the operating system designer and embodied by him in microcode.

Another distinguishing feature of Cm* is the nature and number of processors that it comprises. Most MIMD systems are made up of a small number of processors (two to eight, generally; sixteen in the case of C·mmp) and each processor is usually a mainframe computer. Cm*, on the other hand, is built out of microcomputers. In its present implementation it has fifty processors, but it can be expanded further in a straightforward way.

The basic processing element in Cm* is a computer module (Cm) that is basically a modified version of an LSI-11 microcomputer. (LSI-11 is a low-cost, low-performance version of PDP-11.) A Cm consists of an LSI-11 bus to which are attached a processor, up to 128K bytes of memory, and some peripheral devices (see Figure 8.14). Also present on this bus is a local switch called *Slocal*, which connects this Cm to the rest of Cm*. The major distinguishing characteristic of the Cm* architecture is this Slocal (local switch). The Slocal performs two mapping functions:

1. It decides whether a processor-generated address is to be routed to local memory or a peripheral in this Cm, or should be passed up to the Kmap.
2. On the basis of this decision, it either maps the 16-bit address to an 18-bit LSI-11 bus address or passes on the 16-bit address to the Kmap to which it is attached.

Figure 8.15 shows the next level in the Cm* interconnection hierarchy. Up to 14 Cms are connected together by a common bus called the *map bus,* resulting in a structure called a *cluster.* Attached to the map bus is a Kmap, which is a sophisticated switching controller. It has the control of the map bus and handles the routing and buffering of messages between Cms. The Kmap also acts as the gateway to its cluster and interfaces it to the rest of the system.

The Kmap plays a key role in the Cm*'s interconnection scheme and its address structure. A subset of the memory references generated within a Cm is passed by the Cm's Slocal to the Kmap. Each Cm in a cluster has a 4-bit identifier called the Cm number and this identifier is prefixed to all references passed by a Slocal to its Kmap. The Kmap maps this reference using tables stored in the memory of the Cm.

The Kmap decides on one of two courses of action, depending on whether the mapping yields an address within this cluster or an address in another cluster. If the resulting address is within the cluster, the Kmap constructs a request containing the appropriate Cm number, the 18-bit physical address, and a code indicating the requested operation, and puts this request on the map bus. The Slocal of the Cm referred to in the request performs the appropriate action at the specified address. The data

Figure 8.14 A computer module (Cm)

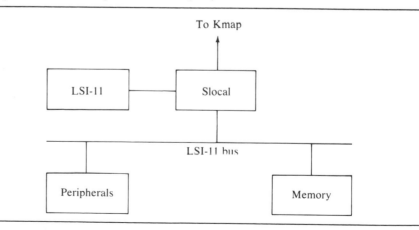

Figure 8.15 A Cm* cluster

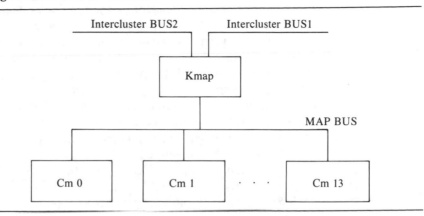

involved in the reference (read or write) is directly passed between the invoking and responding Cms.

If the address produced after the Kmap mapping lies in another cluster, the Kmap at the requesting cluster sends a request to the Kmap at the destination cluster via one of the intercluster buses. The latter Kmap performs the requested operation on the appropriate Cm in its cluster and returns an indication of this fact to the former Kmap. The data involved in the access form part of the requests and responses.

Many clusters are connected together via intercluster buses to form a complete Cm* system. Each cluster is connected to two intercluster buses so that a single bus failure will not isolate a cluster. Figure 8.16 illustrates these interconnections.

Figure 8.16 A Cm* system with four clusters

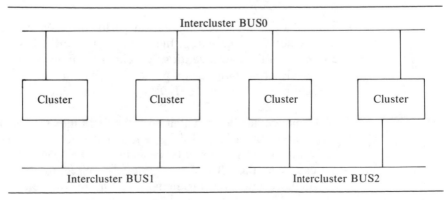

Performance improvement in Cm* due to additional processors in a cluster is very much dependent on the specific application chosen. When configured as a network, the addition of processors improves performance only to a limited extent. In fact, beyond a certain point, a performance loss rather than a gain is noted because of the heavy loading of the interconnection buses. If the processing activity is partitioned such that it is local in a computer module or concentrated in a cluster, thereby reducing the traffic on the intercluster bus, the performance stays high.

Another factor that limits the number of modules in a cluster is reliability. To avoid the occurrence of map bus failures, the maximum number of modules in a cluster is limited to fourteen.

Any Cm can initiate the I/O device attached to any other Cm. However, interrupts can still be handled only by the Cm to which the I/O device is attached. From an error-recovery point of view, this is undesirable, since if a Cm is lost, all I/O attached to it is lost. This is one respect in which Cm* fails to be a robust system.

One of the positive features of Cm* is its extensive use of the microcoded Kmaps for a variety of purposes. The microcoded Kmap facilitates experimentation and permits a wider range of operating system design for Cm* than would be possible otherwise. The Kmap implements many functions that would normally be implemented by the operating system. For example, the message system and the synchronization mechanism are implemented in Kmap microcode very inexpensively. The importance of this fact is apparent if one realizes that, in the decomposition of many applications into units that may be executed in parallel, the cost of interaction between these units dominates computation costs within each unit.

Cm* is an experimental system and has contributed much to the understanding of multiprocessor interconnection, software design, and distributed processing problems.

8.2.7 CRAY-1

The CRAY-1, a second-generation vector processor designed and manufactured by Cray Research, Inc., has been described as the most powerful computer of the late seventies. Benchmark studies show that the CRAY-1 is capable of sustaining computational rates of 138 million floating-point operations per second (MFLOPS) over long periods of time and attaining speeds of up to 250 MFLOPS in short bursts. The CRAY-1 processor's performance has been evaluated to be five times that of the CDC 7600 or fifteen times that of an IBM System/370 Model 168. With only scalar units active, the CRAY-1 is still twice as fast as the CDC 7600. These statistics indicate that the CRAY-1 is uniquely suited to the solution of computationally intensive problems encountered in fields such as weather forecasting, aircraft design, nuclear research, geophysical research, and seismic analysis.

The basic configuration of CRAY-1 consists of a CPU, power and cooling equipment, a maintenance control unit (MCU), a mass storage (disk) subsystem, and one or more front-end computers that are usually used as job-entry stations.

The CPU includes a computation section, a memory section, and an I/O section. The computation section holds the operating and support registers (a total of 4,888 bytes of storage with an access time of 6 nanoseconds), twelve independent functional units that perform the actual arithmetic and logic operations on the data, and four instruction buffers, each consisting of sixty-four 16-bit registers. The memory section consists of 1,048,576 72-bit words, arranged in sixteen banks. A word has 64 data bits and 8 check bits enabling a single-bit error correction and double-bit error detection. Input/output is via twenty-four I/O channels, twelve each for input and output. Any number of channels may be active at a given time. For a 16-bit channel, transfer rates of 20M bytes per second are possible.

The computation section of the CPU is shown in Figure 8.17. There are five types of operating registers:

8 24-bit address (A) registers.
64 24-bit address-save (B) registers.
8 64-bit scalar (S) registers.
64 64-bit scalar save (T) registers.
8 64-element vector (V) registers (each element containing 64 bits).

The functional units take operands from and store results into the A, S, and V registers. The B and T registers are used as fast-access backup storage areas that significantly reduce memory accesses. Scalar values can be stored into and read back from the B and T registers in two clock cycles by the A and B registers, respectively. The scalar performance of the CRAY-1 benefits greatly from these buffer storage areas.

The eight 24-bit A registers ($A0$–$A7$) serve a number of purposes. They are mainly used as address registers for memory references and as index registers. However, they can also be used to count loops, to provide shift counts, and for channel I/O operations. In address applications, they are used to index base addresses for scalar memory references and to provide both base and index addresses for vector memory references. A register values can be modified (by adding, subtracting, and multiplying register values) in the address function unit. The results of these operations are returned to A registers. The A registers can be loaded directly from memory or through the B registers. Data transfer is also possible between the

Figure 8.17 CRAY-1 computation section (Courtesy of Cray Research, Inc.)

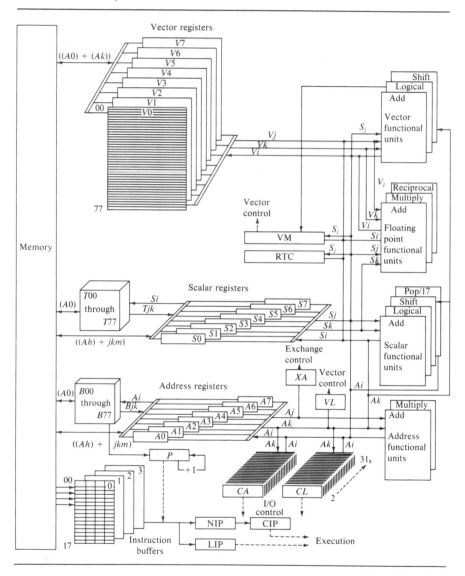

A and B registers and between the A register and the vector-length registers.

The sixty-four B registers (B0–B77 octal) are used as buffer storage for the A registers. Transfer between an A and a B register requires only one clock cycle. A block transfer mechanism between B registers and main memory at the rate of one register transfer per clock cycle is available. It is thus possible to save and restore the entire contents of the B registers when calling and exiting subroutines.

The eight S registers ($S0$–$S7$) serve as accumulators for all scalar operations. Both source and destination for scalar arithmetic and logic operations are S registers. In addition, scalar operands for vector operations are held in the S registers. Logical, shift, fixed-point and floating-point arithmetic can be performed on S register operands.

The sixty-four T registers ($T0$–T 77 octal) serve as buffer storage for the S registers. A transfer between an S and a T register is completed in one memory cycle. Block transfer of T registers to or from memory is possible at the rate of one word per clock period.

The 64-element V registers ($V0$–$V7$) serve as source operands for and receive results from the vector functional units (logical, shift, and add units). Operand or result transfer can take place at the rate of one per clock cycle. Each vector element is 64 bits wide, and when successive elements of the V register contain associated data, the register is said to contain a vector. Two support registers control operations on vector registers. The vector mask (VM) register is used to perform operations on individual elements of vector registers. The vector length (VL) register contains the number of elements to be processed by the functional units. Thus, between 0 and 64 elements can be processed by an instruction.

The VL register is a 7-bit register that specifies the vector length of the operation to be performed. The VM register is used to control the vector merge and test operations. Each bit of the 64-bit VM register corresponds to an element in a V register.

The 24-bit P register specifies the parcel address of the current program address in memory. The high-order 22 bits supply a memory address and the low-order 2 bits specify a parcel number within the word. The address capability of the CRAY-1 is therefore 4 megawords.

The 18-bit BA register contains the upper 18 bits of a memory address, the lower 4 bits being considered 0s. Absolute memory addresses are formed by adding 16 to the relative memory address specified by the program instructions.

The LA register holds the upper 18 bits of a 22-bit memory address, the lower 4 bits of which are considered to be 0s. Each time a program executes, the LA register is loaded with the upper 18 bits of the absolute address one greater than the highest address referenced by the program.

The 8-bit XA register contains the upper 8 bits of a 12-bit memory address, the lower 4 bits of which are 0s. The BA register specifies the first word of a 16-word set of memory addresses. Two-hundred fifty-six such sets can be specified using the 8 bits of the XA register. The 16-word sets, called *exchange packages,* contain the context information necessary for operations following an interrupt or a context switch. An exchange package saves the A, S, P, and V registers and the supporting registers BA, LA, XA, M, and F.

The 9-bit F register contains flags, which when set indicate interrupt conditions that cause initiation of an exchange sequence. The interrupt conditions are normal exit, error exit, I/O interrupt, uncorrected memory error, program range error, operand range error, floating-point overflow, real-time clock interrupt, and console interrupt. The 3-bit M register is used to enable or disable certain kinds of interrupts. The 64-bit programmable real-time clock (RTC) provides 100-nanosecond time periods.

There are twelve independent functional units, each of which is a specialized unit implementing algorithms for a portion of the instructions. Several functional units can be concurrently active. A functional unit receives operands from registers and delivers the result to a register. No information is retained in the functional units for use in subsequent instructions. The units operate in the three-address mode, with source and destination addressing limited to register designators. The time elapsed between the delivery of the operands to a functional unit and the completion of the operation is called "functional unit time" and is measured in 12.5-nanosecond clock periods. All functional units are fully pipelined into single clock-period segments. Information arriving at or moving within a functional unit is captured and held in a register at the end of every clock period. Therefore, an unrelated computation with a new set of operands can be initiated every clock cycle. Once the pipeline is full, each functional unit can be driven at the resultant rate of one per clock period.

The twelve functional units can be organized into four groups: address, scalar, vector, and floating-point. The address add and address multiply functional units provide 24-bit results to the A registers. Four units, the scalar add and the scalar population count units, provide 64-bit results to the S registers. Three functional units, the vector add, vector shift, and vector logical units, supply 64-bit results to the V registers. Finally, three functional units, the floating-point add, the floating-point multiply, and the reciprocal approximation units provide 64-bit results to either V or S registers.

Integer arithmetic is performed in 24-bit or 64-bit 2s complement form. Floating-point quantities have signed magnitude representation with a 49-bit signed binary fraction and a 15-bit biased binary integer exponent.

The instruction set on the CRAY-1 provided floating-point addition, subtraction, multiplication, and reciprocal approximation. Fixed-point instructions include integer addition, integer subtraction, and integer multiplication. Instructions for Boolean operations such as OR, AND, and EXCLUSIVE-OR are provided along with a mask-controlled merge operation. There are 128 opcodes classified either as one-parcel or two-parcel instructions, where a parcel consists of 16 bits.

All instructions on the CRAY-1 are executed from one of four instruction buffers. Each instruction buffer consists of sixty-four 16-bit parcels so that a total of between 128 and 256 instructions are held in the four buffers. The buffers can contain nonconsecutive program segments. A base address register, which contains the upper 18 bits of the addresses held in the buffer, is associated with each buffer. The base address register is scanned every clock period. If the high-order 18 bits of the P register match one of the buffer base address registers, the corresponding instruction is moved into the next instruction parcel (NIP) register. The instruction is moved to the current instruction parcel (CIP) register for execution. The second parcel of a two-parcel instruction resides in the NIP register when the instruction issues. The P register points to the next instruction to exit from the buffers. Prior to issue, instructions may be held in the NIP, lower instruction parcel (LIP), or CIP registers. When the upper 18 bits of the P register do not match any base address register, an out-of-buffer condition occurs and instructions have to be read in from memory into an instruction buffer.

Vector instructions can be classified into four types. In type 1 vector instruction, the operands are obtained from two vector registers (V_j and V_k) and the result enters a vector register (V_i). Each clock period, operand pairs from V_j and V_k are transmitted to the functional unit and the corresponding results are available n clock cycles later at V_i, where n is the functional unit time of the given functional unit. Type 2 vector instruction uses one operand from an S register (scalar) and one from a V_j register (vector). A copy of the S register is transmitted to the functional unit with each V register operand. The resulting vector enters a V_i register set. The last two types of vector instructions transfer data between memory and the V register set.

When a vector instruction is issued, the functional unit and operand registers used in the instruction are reserved for a number of clock periods determined by the length of the vector instruction. A subsequent vector instruction that requires the same functional unit or operand registers cannot be issued until the reservations are released. Two independent vector instructions (i.e., those that use different functional units, and operand registers) can be issued in subsequent clock cycles.

The main memory is organized in 16 banks with 72 modules per bank. Each module contributes 1 bit to a 64-bit word with an 8-bit check byte. A bank can hold 64K words, so that the total main memory is 1 megaword. The memory is sixteen-way interleaved. The bank cycle time (time required to insert or remove an element of data in memory) is four clock periods (50 nanoseconds). When there is no memory conflict (due to I/O), transfers can take place at the rate of 1 word for every two clock periods to S registers or 1 word every clock cycle to B, T, or V registers.

The I/O section consists of 24 channels, 12 for input and 12 for output. Each input channel is provided with a 64-bit assembly register while each output channel has a 64-bit disassembly register. Additionally, both input and output channels consist of a data bus (16 data bits and 3 control lines), a current address (CA) register, and a channel-limit (CL) register. The channels are divided into four groups, each group sharing a common link with the main memory; a group is polled every four cycles for pending memory requests. Within the same group, priority for memory access is given to the channel with the lowest number.

A 16-bit minicomputer serves as the maintenance control unit (MCU). The MCU performs system initialization and basic recovery of the operating system. The MCU can also be used to monitor CRAY-1 performance or as a job-entry station. The Data General Eclipse S-200 is a typical MCU.

A minimum of at least one 16-bit minicomputer is required by CRAY-1 as a front-end system. The front-end system serves as a job-entry station to submit jobs to CRAY-1, processes output, or serves as a data concentrator and multiplexer for remote stations or terminals. The front-end system operates asynchronously with respect to CRAY-1 under the control of its own operating system.

Mass storage on CRAY-1 consists of two or more disk controllers and multiple-disk storage units.

The most remarkable feature of the CRAY-1 is its implementation. Since a high-speed computer must keep signal runs as short as possible, a cylindrical shape was chosen for the CRAY-1. Only four chip types were used in the design. Special cooling techniques have been used to handle the acute cooling problems because of high component density.

CRAY-1 thus is a very high performance computer. The main reasons for its high performance are

1. Parallel operation of the twelve functional units.
2. Pipelining of these functional units.
3. Presence of vector processing units.
4. Chaining of results from unit to unit.
5. Extremely fast cycle time of 12.5 nanoseconds.

8.3   High-Level-Language Architectures

When high-level languages (HLL) are used for programming computers, the programs must be converted into the object code (or machine language program) before the program execution begins. In conventional architectures, the translation from source to machine language is per-

Figure 8.18 Evolution of high-level-language architectures

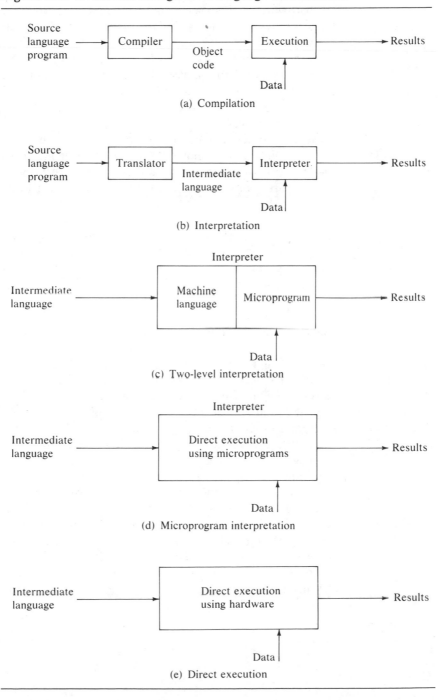

(a) Compilation

(b) Interpretation

(c) Two-level interpretation

(d) Microprogram interpretation

(e) Direct execution

formed by software means (compilers) and the execution is performed by the hardware. To help speed up the compilation process, block-structured languages were developed and the machine hardware supported the translation process by stack organizations. As the hardware costs came down with the improvements in hardware technology, more complex instructions were added to the assembly language instruction sets to provide a more direct translation capability. Stack architectures of Burroughs 5500 and 6700 series, and more recently DEC VAX-11/780 are examples of such architectures.

Several other modes of program translation and execution have evolved. Figure 8.18 shows the evolution starting from the compilation mode in (a). In the interpretive mode of Figure 8.18(b), the source program is first converted into an intermediate form (a set of tables, or a reverse polish notation) and the intermediate language program is interpreted by the hardware. Two variations of this mode are shown in (c) and (d). In (c), the intermediate language constructs are first converted into machine language and then interpreted by the microprograms. In (d), the microprograms are designed to interpret the intermediate language programs directly. This mode of interpretation is called *direct execution language (DEL) architecture*.

In a DEL architecture, the microprograms interpret high-level language constructs rather than machine-language constructs, as they do in conventional machines. As such, microprograms to interpret each HLL must be designed individually. A well-known DEL architecture is that of the EULER machine, in which a subset of ALGOL-60 constructs were directly executed by microprogramming an IBM 360. The intermediate language used was the reverse polish string. Other FORTRAN, ALGOL, APL, and Pascal architectures exist.

In DEL architectures, the translation from source HLL to intermediate language is performed by the software. In an HLL architecture like the one shown in (e), the hardware is specifically designed for translating and subsequently executing the source HLL program. A well-known architecture of this type is the SYMBOL machine developed at Iowa State University in 1971, to execute a high-level language called Symbol Programming Language. The advantage of HLL architectures is a very high translate-load-execute speed. The disadvantage is that only one source language for which the machine is designed can be used in programming the machine.

8.4   Data-Flow Architectures

Data-flow architectures tend to maximize the concurrency of operations (parallelism) by breaking the processing activity into sets of the most primitive operations possible. Further, the computations in a data-flow machine are data-driven. That is, an operation is performed as and when its operands are available. This is unlike the machines we have described so far, where the required data are gathered when an instruction needs them. The sequence of operations in a data-flow machine obey the precedence constraint imposed by the algorithm used rather than by the control

Figure 8.19 A data-flow graph

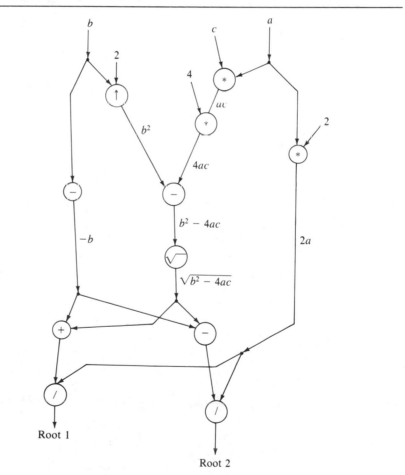

statements in the program. A data-flow architecture assumes that a number of functional units are available, that as many of these functional units as possible are invoked at any given time, and that these functional units are purely functional in the sense that they induce no side effects on either the data or the computation sequence.

The data-flow diagram of Figure 8.19 shows the computation of the roots of a quadratic equation. Assuming that a, b, and c values are available, $(-b)$, (b^2) (ac), and $(2a)$ can be computed immediately, followed by the computation of $(4ac)$, $(b^2 - 4ac)$, and $\sqrt{(b^2 - 4ac)}$, in that order. After this, $(-b + \sqrt{b^2 - 4ac})$ and $(-b - \sqrt{b^2 - 4ac})$ can be simultaneously computed followed by the simultaneous computation of the two roots. Note that the only requirement is that the operands be ready before an operation can be invoked. No other time or sequence constraints are imposed.

Figure 8.20 A data-flow machine

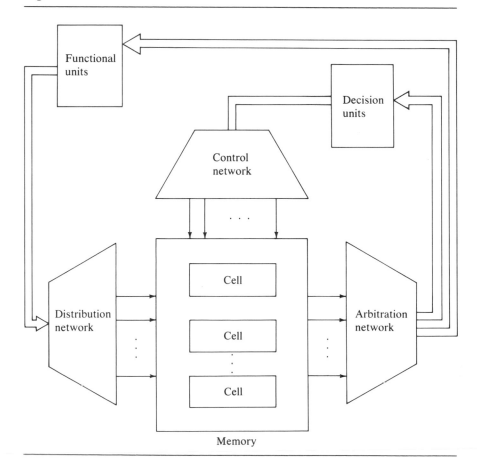

Figure 8.20 shows a schematic view of a data-flow machine. The machine memory consists of a series of cells where each cell contains an opcode and two operands. When both operands are ready, the cell is presented to the arbitration network that assigns the cell to either a functional unit (for operations) or a decision unit (for predicates). The outputs of functional units are presented to the distribution network, which stores the result in appropriate cells as directed by the control network. A very high throughput can be achieved if the algorithms are represented with the maximum degree of concurrency possible and the three networks of the processor are designed to bring about fast communication between the memory and functional and decision units.

Two experimental data-flow machines (at the University of Utah and in Toulouse, France) have been built. The data-flow project at Massachusetts Institute of Technology has concentrated on the design of languages and representation techniques and feasibility evaluation of data-flow concepts through simulation.

8.5 Computer Networks and Distributed Processing

In an MIMD, several processors are connected with each other and the shared memory through the interconnection network, in a tightly coupled manner. The shared-memory interconnection of two or more computers discussed in Chapter 5 is another example of tightly coupled processors. A computer network, on the other hand, is a set of computer systems loosely coupled through a communication network. Figure 8.21 shows a model for a computer network. Each computer system in the network is a host. Each host is connected to a node in the communication network that transmits messages from and to the hosts connected to it. In a network, most of the processing is done by the local host at each site (node). If a resource (compiler, data base, etc.) is not available at the local host, a node calls upon a host that holds the resource through the communication network.

With the introduction of microprocessors, local networks have become very popular because this system architecture provides a dedicated processor for local processing while providing the possibilities of sharing the resources with other nodes. Various networks have been built using large-scale machines, minicomputers, and microcomputers. A number of topologies for communication networks exist.

In a computer network, if a node fails, the resources at that node are no longer available. If, on the other hand, each node in a network is made a general-purpose resource, the processing can continue even if a node fails, although at a reduced rate. A *distributed processing* system is one in which the processing, the data base, and the control are distributed. That

Figure 8.21 A computer network

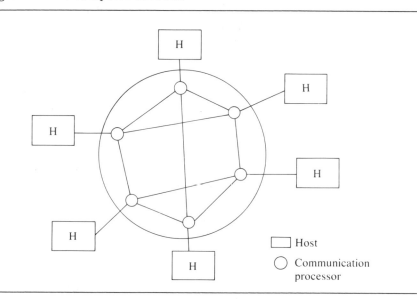

is, there are several general-purpose processors distributed geographically; no one processor will be a master controller at any time and there is no central data base; rather it is a combination of all the subdatabases on all the machines. Although no such processing system exists to the author's knowledge, systems that adopt the distributed processing concepts to various degrees exist.

The advantages of distributed processing systems are

1. Efficient processing, since each node performs the processing for which it is most suited.
2. Dynamic reconfiguration of the system architecture to suit the processing loads.
3. Graceful degradation of the system in case of failure of a node, and redundancy if needed.

8.6   Impact of VLSI on Architecture

As hardware technology moved into the large-scale integrated circuit (LSI) era, more functions were implemented in hardware. Larger instruction sets, complex control units, a large number of general-purpose registers, larger memories, and corresponding memory-management units, became common. But the basic architecture remained that of a von

Neumann machine. The other major impact was on the economics of the computer market, due to the reduction in hardware costs.

It has been possible to implement a sophisticated 16-bit processor on a chip. Some of the 16-bit architectures on a chip have internal 32-bit organizations. As we move into the VLSI era, 32-bit processors with memory and input/output support will be available on a chip. In addition, it will be possible to implement SIMD and MIMD architectures on a chip.

VLSI, with its capability to implement an enormous number of devices on a chip, has also brought in problems with respect to conquering the complexity. Computer-aided design methodologies and design systems have not kept pace with the growth of technology and a school of thought exists that the computer industry may not be able to make full use of VLSI capabilities due to the lack of design tools. It is observed that the design of a sophisticated VLSI chip requires 5 to 6 years of team effort, yet it faces the possibility of becoming obsolete within a year or two of its introduction due to the emergence of ever more sophisticated chips.

One solution in the direction of conquering the complexity of a VLSI chip is to use regular structures (patterns) as in memory chips, as much as possible, thereby reducing the design complexity. This observation has resulted in trends towards regular architectures that use identical patterns in an iterative fashion, and newer computational algorithms that translate into regular patterns in hardware are being devised.

8.7 Summary

We have provided a brief look at major supercomputer architectures and classifications. As can be seen, there are machines that fall into more than one architectural classification. Developments in both software and hardware technology have influenced computer design and architecture. More and more software concepts are being implemented in hardware toward the evolution of high-level-language architectures. Availability of low-cost, fast hardware and reduction in communication costs have given birth to computer networks and the distributed processing concept. The VLSI era, although it has given us the capability to fabricate a complex system on a chip, has also introduced new problems in terms of managing the complexity of the system and chip fabrication.

References

Baer, J. L. *Computer Systems Architecture*. Rockville, Md.: Computer Science Press, 1980.

Barnes, G. H., R. M. Brown, M. Kato, D. J. Kuck, D. L. Slotnick, and R. A. Stokes. "The ILLIAC-IV Computer." *IEEE Transactions on Computers,* Vol. C-17, August 1968, pp. 746–757.

Batcher, K. E. "The Multidimensional Access Memory in STARAN." *IEEE Transactions on Computers,* Vol. C-26, February 1977, pp. 174–178.

Batcher, K. E. "STARAN Series E." *Proceedings of the International Conference on Parallel Processing,* 1977, pp. 140–143.

Chu, Y. (ed.). *High-Level Language Computer Architecture.* New York, N.Y.: Academic Press, 1975.

Control Data STAR-100 Computer Hardware Reference Manual. Minneapolis, Minn: Control Data Corporation, 1972.

CRAY-1 Computer System Hardware Reference Manual. Minneapolis, Minn: Cray Research, Inc., 1977.

Enslow, P. H., Jr. *Multiprocessor and Parallel Processing.* New York, N.Y.: Wiley Interscience, 1974.

Dennis, J. B. "First Version of a Data Flow Procedure Language," in *Lecture Notes in Computer Science.* Berlin: Springer Verlag, 1974, pp. 362–376.

Dennis, J. B., and D. P. Misunas. "A Preliminary Data Flow Architecture for a Basic Data Flow Processor." *Proceedings of the Second Symposium on Computer Architecture,* 1975, pp. 126–376.

Enslow, P. H., Jr. "Multiprocessor Organization." *Computing Surveys,* Vol. 9, March 1977, pp. 103–129.

Faggin, F. "How VLSI Impacts Computer Architecture." *IEEE Spectrum,* Vol. 15. May 1978, pp. 28–31.

Flynn, M. J. "Very High Speed Computing Systems." *Proceedings of IEEE,* Vol. 54. December 1966, pp. 1901–1909.

Hord, R. M. *The ILLIAC-IV: The First Supercomputer.* Rockville, Md.: Computer Science Press, 1983.

Kartashev, S. P., and S. I. Kartashev (ed.) *Designing and Programming Modern Computers and Systems: LSI Modular Computer Systems.* Vol. 1. Englewood Cliffs, N.J.: Prentice Hall, 1982.

Moore, G. "VLSI: Some Fundamental Challenges." *IEEE Spectrum,* Vol. 16, April 1979, pp. 30–37.

Myers, G. J. *Advances in Computer Architecture.* New York, N.Y.: John Wiley, 1982.

Oleinick, P. N. "The Implementation and Evaluation of Parallel Algorithms on C· mmp." Ph.D. dissertation, Carnegie-Mellon University, 1978.

Ramamoorthy, C. V., and H. F. Li. "Pipeline Architectures." *Computing Surveys,* 9, March 1977, pp. 61–102.

Rice, R., and W. R. Smith. "SYMBOL — A Major Departure from Classical Software Dominated von Neumann Computing Systems." *Proceedings of the American Federation of Information Processing Societies 1971 Spring Joint Computer Conference.* Vol. 38. Montvale, N.J.: AFIPS Press, 1971, pp. 575–587.

Rudolf, J. A. "A Production Implementation of an Associative Array Processor STARAN." *Proceedings of AFIPS 1972 Fall Joint Computer Conference.* Vol. 41. Montvale, N.J.: AFIPS Press, 1972, pp. 229–241.

Russel, R. M. "The Cray-1 Computer System." *Communications of the ACM.* Vol. 21, January 1978, pp. 63–72.

Sutherland, I. E., and C. A. Mead. "Microelectronics and Computer Science." *Scientific American,* Vol. 237, 1977, pp. 210–229.

Siewiorek, D. P., C. G. Bell, and A. Newell. *Computer Structures: Principles and Examples*. New York, N.Y.: McGraw-Hill, 1982.

Stone, H. S., (ed.). *Introduction to Computer Architecture*. 2d ed. Chicago, Ill: Science Research Associates, 1980.

Swan, R. J., A. Bechtholsheim, K. W. Lai, and J. K. Ousterhout. "The Implementation of the Cm* Multimicroprocessor." *Proceedings of the AFIPS 1977 National Computer Conference,* Vol. 46. Montvale, N.J.: AFIPS Press, 1977, pp. 645–655.

Swan, R. J., S. H. Fuller, and I. P. Siewiorek. "Cm*: A Modular Multimicroprocessor." *Proceedings of the AFIPS 1977 National Computer Conference.* Vol. 46. Montvale, N.J.: AFIPS Press, 1977, p. 637–644.

Texas Instruments, Inc. *A Description of the Advanced Scientic Computer System.* Austin, Tex., 1972.

Wulf, W. A., and C. G. Bell. "C· mmp: A Multimini Processor." *Proc. AFIPS 1972 Fall Joint Comp. Conf.* Vol. 41. Montvale, N.J.: AFIPS Press, 1972, pp. 765–777.

Yau, S. S., and H. S. Fung. "Associative Architecture — A Survey." *Computing Surveys*. Vol. 9. March 1977, pp. 3–28.

Appendix A

Number Systems and Codes

Number systems and computer codes are reviewed in this appendix. The books listed as references provide further details on these topics.

A number system consists of a set of symbols called *digits* and a set of relations defining the addition (+), subtraction (−), multiplication (×), and division (÷) of the digits. The total number of digits is the *radix* (or *base*) of the number system. In the "positional notation" of a number, the *radix point* separates the integer portion of the number from its fraction portion and if there is no fraction portion, the radix point is also omitted from the representation. Further, in this notation, each position has a weight equivalent to a power of the base. The power starts with 0 and increases by 1 as we move each position to the left of the radix point, and decreases by 1 as we move to the right. A typical number in decimal system is shown in Example A.1.

Example A.1

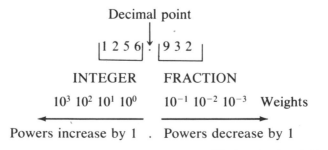

This number also can be represented as the polynomial

$$1 \times 10^3 + 2 \times 10^2 + 5 \times 10^1 + 6 \times 10^0$$
$$+ 9 \times 10^{-1} + 3 \times 10^{-2} + 2 \times 10^{-3}.$$

A general positional representation of a number N is

$$N = (a_n \ldots a_3 a_2 a_1 a_0 \cdot a_{-1} a_{-2} a_{-3} \ldots a_{-m})_r. \qquad \text{(A–1)}$$

Where r is the radix of the number system, a_{-1}, a_0, a_1, a_2, etc. are digits such that $0 \leq a \leq (r - 1)$ for all i; a_n is the most significant digit (MSD) and a_{-m} is the least significant digit (LSD). The polynomial representation of the above number is

$$N = \sum_{i=-m}^{n} a_i r^i. \qquad \text{(A–2)}$$

The largest integer that can be represented with n digits is $(r^n - 1)$. Table A.1 lists the first few numbers in various systems. We will discuss

Table A.1 Number systems

Decimal $r = 10$	Binary $r = 2$	Ternary $r = 3$	Quaternary $r = 4$	Octal $r = 8$	Hexadecimal $r = 16$
0	0	0	0	0	0
1	1	1	1	1	1
2	10	2	2	2	2
3	11	10	3	3	3
4	100	11	10	4	4
5	101	12	11	5	5
6	110	20	12	6	6
7	111	21	13	7	7
8	1000	22	20	10	8
9	1001	100	21	11	9
10	1010	101	22	12	A
11	1011	102	23	13	B
12	1100	110	30	14	C
13	1101	111	31	15	D
14	1110	112	32	16	E
15	1111	120	33	17	F
16	10000	121	100	20	10
17	10001	122	101	21	11
18	10010	200	102	22	12
19	10011	201	103	23	13
20	10100	202	110	24	14

binary, octal, and hexadecimal number systems. Digital computers employ the binary system, but octal and hexadecimal systems are useful in representing binary information in a shorthand form.

A.1   Binary System

In this system, radix (r) is 2 and the allowed *bi*nary dig*its* (bits) are 0 and 1. A typical number is shown below in the positional notation.

Example A.2

$$N = (11010 \quad . \quad 1101)_2$$

$2^4 2^3 2^2 2^1 2^0$. $2^{-1} 2^{-2} 2^{-3} 2^{-4}$	Weights
16 8 4 2 1 . ½ ¼ ⅛ ¹⁄₁₆	Weights in decimal

Weights double for each move   .   Weights are halved for each
to left from binary point.   move to right from binary
                                      point.

In polynomial form, the above number is

$$N = 1 \times 2^4 + 1 \times 2^3 + 0 \times 2^2 + 1 \times 2^1 + 0 \times 2^0$$

$$+ 1 \times 2^{-1} + 1 \times 2^{-2} + 0 \times 2^{-3} + 1 \times 2^{-4}$$

$$= 16 + 8 + 0 + 4 + 0 + ½ + ¼ + 0 + ¹⁄₁₆ \qquad \text{Decimal}$$

$$= 28 + ½ + ¼ + ¹⁄₁₆ \qquad \text{Decimal}$$

$$= (28 ^{13}⁄_{16})_{10}.$$

Thus, to convert a number from binary to decimal, we can simply accumulate the weights corresponding to each nonzero bit of the binary number.

Each bit can take the value of a 0 or a 1. With 2 bits, we can derive four (2^2) distinct combinations: 00, 01, 10, and 11. The decimal values of these patterns range from 0 to 3 (i.e., $2^2 - 1$). In general, with n bits it is possible to have 2^n combinations of 0s and 1s and these combinations, when viewed as binary numbers, take values from 0 to $(2^n - 1)_{10}$. Table A.2 shows some binary numbers. A procedure for writing all the combinations of 0s and 1s for any n follows.

With n bits, 2^n combinations are possible. The first combination contains n 0s and the last contains n 1s. To generate the other combinations, note that in Table A.2, in the bit position i ($0 \le i \le n - 1$), the 0s and 1s

Table A.2 Binary numbers

$n = 2$	$n = 3$	$n = 4$

| 1 | 0 | | 2 | 1 | 0 | | 3 | 2 | 1 | 0 | ←Bit position |

00	000	0000
01	001	0001
10	010	0010
11	011	0011
	100	0100
	101	0101
	110	0110
	111	0111
		1000
		1001
		1010
		1011
		1100
		1101
		1110
		1111

alternate every 2^i rows as we move from row to row. The least significant bit (LSB) corresponds to $i = 0$ and the most significant bit (MSB) corresponds to $i = n - 1$. That is, starting with a 0 in the first row, in the LSB position ($i = 0$), the values of bits alternate every row ($2^i = 2^0 = 1$); the values in bit position 1 ($i = 1$), alternate every two rows, etc. This procedure is repeated through the MSB ($i = n - 1$) position, to generate all the 2^n combinations.

A.2   Octal System

In this system, $r = 8$ and the allowed digits are 0, 1, 2, 3, 4, 5, 6, and 7. A typical number is shown below in positional notation.

Example A.3

$$N = (4\,5\,2\,6\,.\,2\,3)_8$$

$$= 8^3 8^2 8^1 8^0\,.\,8^{-1} 8^{-2} \qquad \text{Weights}$$

$$= 4 \times 8^3 + 5 \times 8^2 + 2 \times 8^1 + 6 \times 8^0 + 2 \times 8^{-1} + 3 \times 8^{-2} \longleftarrow$$

$$\qquad\qquad\qquad\qquad\qquad\qquad\qquad\qquad \text{Polynomial form}$$

$$= 2048 + 320 + 16 + 6 + 2/8 + 3/64 \qquad \text{Decimal}$$

$$= (2390\,19/64)_{10}$$

A.3 Hexadecimal System

In this system, r = 16, and the allowed digits are 0, 1, 2, 3, 4, 5, 6, 7, 8, 9, A, B, C, D, E, and F. Digits A through F correspond to decimal values 10 through 15. A typical number is shown in Example A.4.

Example A.4

$$N = (A\ 1\ F\ .\ 1\ C)_{16}$$
$$= 16^2 16^1 16^0\ .\ 16^{-1} 16^{-2} \qquad\qquad \text{Weights}$$
$$= A \times 16^2 + 1 \times 16^1 + F \times 16^0 + 1 \times 16^{-1} + C \times 16^{-2}$$

Polynomial form

$$= 10 \times 16^2 + 1 \times 16^1 + 15 \times 16^0 + 1 \times 16^{-1} + 12 \times 16^{-2} \quad \text{Decimal}$$
$$= (2591 {}^{28}\!/_{256})_{10}$$

A.4 Conversion

To convert numbers from any system to decimal, we simply expand the given number as a polynomial and evaluate the polynomial using decimal arithmetic, as we have seen in Examples A.1 through A.4.

To convert an integer number in decimal to any other system, we use the *radix divide* technique. This technique requires the following steps:

1. Divide the given number successively by the required base, noting the remainders at each step; the quotient at each step becomes the new dividend for subsequent division. Stop division when the quotient reaches 0.
2. Collect the remainders from each step (last to first) and place them left to right to form the required number.

This procedure is illustrated by the following examples.

Example A.5 $(245)_{10} = (?)_2$ (i.e., convert $(245)_{10}$ to binary).

$$
\begin{array}{r|ll}
2 & 245 & \text{Remainders} \\
\text{Required}\quad 2 & 122 & 1 \\
\text{base}\qquad 2 & 61 & 0 \\
2 & 30 & 1 \\
2 & 15 & 0 \\
2 & 7 & 1 \\
2 & 3 & 1 \\
2 & 1 & 1 \\
& 0 & 1 \quad = (1111\ 0101)_2
\end{array}
$$

Example A.6 $(245)_{10} = (?)_8$.

$$
\begin{array}{r|ll}
8 & 245 & \\
8 & 30 & 5 \\
8 & 3 & 6 \\
& 0 & 3 \quad = (365)_8
\end{array}
$$

Example A.7 $(245)_{10} - (?)_{16}$.

$$
\begin{array}{r|ll}
16 & 245 & \\
16 & 15 & 5 - 5, \\
& 0 & 15 = F \quad = (F5)_{16}
\end{array}
$$

To convert a fraction in decimal to any other system, the *radix multiply* technique is used. The steps in this method are as follows:

1. Successively multiply the given fraction by the required base, noting the integer portion of the product at each step. Use the fractional part of the product as the multiplicand for subsequent steps. Stop when the fraction either reaches 0 or recurs.
2. Collect the integer digits at each step from first to last and arrange them left to right.

It is not possible to represent a given decimal fraction in binary exactly if the radix multiplication process does not converge to 0. The accuracy, then, depends on the number of bits used to represent the fraction. Some examples follow.

Example A.8 $(0.250)_{10} = (?)_2$.

$$
\begin{array}{r}
0.25 \\
\times\ 2 \\
\hline
0.50 \\
\times\ 2 \\
\hline
1.00 \quad = (0.01)_2
\end{array}
$$

Example A.9 $(0.345)_{10} = (?)_2$.

$$
\begin{array}{r}
0.345 \\
\times\ 2 \\
\hline
0.690 \\
\times\ 2 \\
\hline
1.280 \\
\times\ 2 \\
\hline
0.560 \quad \text{Multiply fractions only.} \\
\times\ 2 \\
\hline
1.120 \\
\times\ 2 \\
\hline
0.240 \\
\times\ 2 \\
\hline
0.480
\end{array}
$$

$$= (0.010100)_2$$

The fraction may never reach zero; stop when the required number of fraction digits are obtained, the fraction will not be accurate.

Example A.10 $(0.345)_{10} = (?)_8$.

$$
\begin{array}{r}
0.345 \\
\times\ 8 \\
\hline
2.760 \\
\times\ 8 \\
\hline
6.080 \\
\times\ 8 \\
\hline
0.640 \\
\times\ 8 \\
\hline
5.120 \quad = (0.2605)_8
\end{array}
$$

Example A.11 $(242.45)_{10} = (?)_2$.

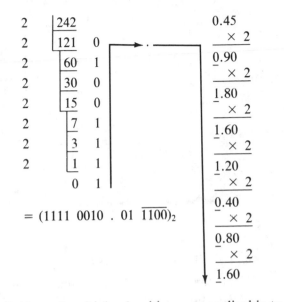

$$= (1111\ 0010\ .\ 01\ \overline{1100})_2$$

The radix divide and multiply algorithms are applicable to the conversion of numbers from any base to any other base. In converting a number from base p to base q, the number in base p is divided (or multiplied) by q in *base p arithmetic*. These methods are convenient when p is 10 because of our familiarity with decimal arithmetic. In general, it is easier to convert a base p number to base q ($p \neq 10$, $q \neq 10$) by first converting the number to decimal from base p and then converting this decimal number into base q; that is, $(N)_p \rightarrow (?)_{10} \rightarrow (?)_q$, as shown by Example A.12.

Example A.12 $(25.34)_8 = (?)_5$.

Convert to base 10

$$(25.34)_8 = 2 \times 8^1 + 5 \times 8^0 + 3 \times 8^{-1} + 4 \times 8^{-2} \quad \text{Decimal}$$

$$= 16 + 5 + \tfrac{3}{8} + \tfrac{4}{64} \quad \text{Decimal}$$

$$= (21\tfrac{28}{64})_{10}$$

$$= (21.4375)_{10}$$

Convert to base 5

$$
\begin{array}{ll}
5\lfloor 21 & \quad 0.4375 \\
\;5\lfloor 4\;1 & \quad\quad \times\;5 \\
\;\;\;\;0\;4 & \quad 2.1875 \\
& \quad\quad \times\;5 \\
& \quad 0.9375 \\
& \quad\quad \times\;5 \\
& \quad 4.6875 \\
& \quad\quad \times\;5 \\
& \quad 3.4375 \\
& \quad\quad \times\;5 \\
& \quad 2.1875 \quad\quad\text{*Repeats}
\end{array}
$$

$$= (41.\overline{2043})_5 .$$

A.4.1 Base 2^k Conversion

When converting a number from base p to base q, if p and q are both powers of 2 an easier conversion procedure may be used. Here, the number in base p is first converted into binary, which number is then converted into base q. This is called *base 2^k conversion*.

Let $p = 2^{k_1}$. In base 2^k conversion, each digit of the number in base p is first expanded into a k_1-bit binary number. The bits of the number thus obtained are regrouped into groups of k_2 bits; each such group is equivalent to a digit in base q ($q = 2^{k_2}$). The grouping starts at the radix point and proceeds in either direction. Some examples follow.

Example A.13 $(4\,2\,A\,5\,6\,.\,F\,1)_{16} = (?)_8 .$

$$p = 16 = 2^4 \quad\quad q = 8 = 2^3$$

$$k_1 = 4 \quad\quad\quad\quad k_2 = 3$$

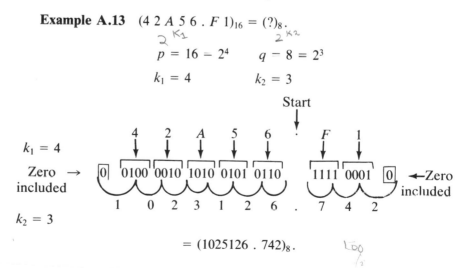

$$= (1025126\,.\,742)_8 .$$

Example A.14 $(AF5.2C)_{16} = (?)_4$.

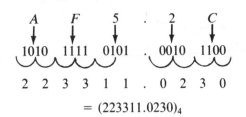

Base 16 = 2^4 ∴ $k_1 = 4$

Base 4 = 2^2 ∴ $k_2 = 2$

$$= (223311.0230)_4$$

Example A.15 $(565.23)_8 = (?)_{16}$.

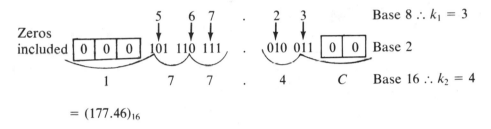

$$= (177.46)_{16}$$

A.5   Arithmetic

This section provides a review of binary, octal, and hexadecimal arithmetics. Arithmetic in any number system is similar to that in the decimal system. Binary arithmetic is easier to perform (and understand) than decimal arithmetic since only two digits are involved. Arithmetic in octal and hexadecimal systems is more complex and may require practice if we are unfamiliar with those systems.

A.5.1   Binary Arithmetic

Table A.3 shows the rules for binary addition, subtraction, and multiplication.

Addition.   From Table A.3(a), note that $0 + 0 = 0, 0 + 1 = 1, 1 + 0 = 1$, and $1 + 1 = 10$. Thus the addition of two 1s results in a SUM of 0 and a CARRY of 1. This CARRY is used in the addition of bits in the next most significant position in the addition of two binary numbers, as shown by Example A.16.

Table A.3 Binary arithmetic

$A + B$	0	A 1		$A - B$	0	A 1		$A \times B$	0	A 1
B 0	0	1		B 0	0	1		B 0	0	0
1	1	10		1	11	0		1	0	1

CARRY SUM   BORROW DIFFERENCE

(a) Addition   (b) Subtraction   (c) Multiplication

Example A.16

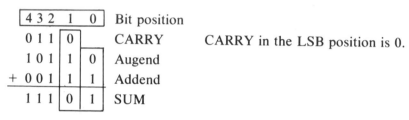

4 3 2	1	0	Bit position
0 1 1	0		CARRY
1 0 1	1	0	Augend
+ 0 0 1	1	1	Addend
1 1 1	0	1	SUM

CARRY in the LSB position is 0.

Here, bits in the LSB (bit position 0) position are first added to generate a SUM bit of 1 and a CARRY bit of 0. This CARRY is used in the addition of bits in position 1. This process is repeated through the MSB (bit position 4).

In general, addition of two n-bit numbers results in a SUM containing a maximum of $(n + 1)$ bits. If the arithmetic has to be confined to n bits, care should be taken to see that the two numbers are small enough so that their SUM does not exceed n bits. Another example of addition follows.

Example A.17

```
1 1 1 1 1 1 0     CARRY
  1 0 1 1 0 1 0   Augend
  0 1 1 0 1 1 1   Addend
1 0 0 1 0 0 0 1   SUM
```

Subtraction.   From Table A.3(b), $0 - 0 = 0$, $1 - 0 = 1$, $1 - 1 = 0$, and $0 - 1 = 1$ with a BORROW of 1. Subtraction of two binary numbers is performed starting from LSB toward MSB one stage at a time. Subtracting a 1 from a 0 results in a 1 with a BORROW of 1 from the next (more significant) stage. Some examples follow.

Example A.18

5	4	3	2	1	0

Bit position

```
    0           0
    ꝉ  0  1  ꝉ | 0 | 1 |   Minuend
  - 0  1  1  0 | 1 | 0 |   Subtrahend
    ─────────────────────
       1  0  0 | 1 | 1 |   DIFFERENCE
```

Bit position 1 requires a borrow from bit position 2. Due to this borrow, minuend bit 2 is a 0. The subtraction continues through the MSB.

Example A.19

7	6	5	4	3	2	1	0

Bit position

```
  0  0           0
  ꝉ  ꝉ  0  0  ꝉ  0  1  0    Minuend
        1  1
- 0  1  1  0  1  1  1  1    Subtrahend
  ──────────────────────
  0  1  0  1  1  1  0  1    DIFFERENCE
```

Bit 2 requires a borrow from bit 3; after this borrow, minuend bit 3 is 0. Then, bit 3 requires a borrow. Since bits 4 and 5 of the minuend are 0s, borrowing is from bit 6. In this process, the intermediate minuend bits 4 and 5 each attain a value of 1 (compare this with the decimal subtraction). The subtraction continues through the MSB.

Multiplication. The multiplication is similar to decimal multiplication. From Table A.3(c), $0 \times 0 = 0$, $0 \times 1 = 0$, $1 \times 0 = 0$, and $1 \times 1 = 1$. An example follows.

Example A.20

```
      1011        Multiplicand
   ×  1100        Multiplier                          ┌─Multiplier bits
                                                      ↓
      0000                      (1011) × 0
      0000                      (1011) × 0
      1011                      (1011) × 1
      1011                      (1011) × 1
   ─────────
   10000100       PRODUCT
```

In general, the PRODUCT of two n-bit numbers is $(2n)$ bits long. To multiply two n-bit numbers A and B, where $B = (b_{n-1}b_{n-2} \ldots b_1 b_0)$, the following procedure can be used:

1. Start with a $2n$-bit PRODUCT with a zero value (all 0s).
2. For each $b_i (0 < i < n - 1) \neq 0$: shift A, i positions to the left and add to the PRODUCT.

Thus, binary multiplication can be performed by repeated shifting and addition of the multiplicand to the partial product, to obtain the PRODUCT.

Division. Division is the repeated subtraction of the divisor from the dividend. The longhand procedure of decimal division can also be used in binary.

Example A.21 $110101 \div 111.$

```
                 0111    Quotient
    111  | 110,101                   110 < 111 ∴ q₁ = 0
           -000
            1101                      1101 > 111 ∴ q₂ = 1
          -  111
            1100                      1100 > 111 ∴ q₃ = 1
          -  111
            1011                      1011 > 111 ∴ q₄ = 1
          -  111
             100    Remainder
```

$110 < 111 \therefore q_1 = 0$

$1101 > 111 \therefore q_2 = 1$

$1100 > 111 \therefore q_3 = 1$

$1011 > 111 \therefore q_4 = 1$

Note that the division is repeated subtraction of the divisor from the dividend.

References listed at the end of this chapter provide the details of several other binary multiplication and division algorithms. Hardware implementation of binary addition and subtraction is discussed in Chapter 1 of this book and several multiplication and division algorithms are given in Chapter 6.

Shifting.   In general, shifting a base r number left by one position (and inserting a 0 into the vacant LSD position) is equivalent to multiplying the number by r; and shifting the number right by one position (inserting a 0 into the vacant MSD position) is equivalent to dividing the number by r.

In the binary system, each left shift multiplies the number by 2 and each right shift divides the number by 2, as shown by Example A.22.

Example A.22

	Binary	Decimal
N	01011.11	11-3/4
$2 * N$	10111.1 $\boxed{0}$ INSERT	23-1/2
$N \div 2$ INSERT $\boxed{0}$ 0101.11		5-3/4

(Inaccurate, since only 2-bit accuracy is retained.)

If the MSB of an n-bit number is not 0, shifting left would result in a number larger than the magnitude that can be accommodated in n bits and the 1 shifted out of MSB can not be discarded; if nonzero bits shifted out of LSB bit during a right shift are discarded, the accuracy is lost.

A.5.2 Octal Arithmetic

Table A.4 shows the addition and multiplication tables for octal arithmetic. The following examples illustrate the four arithmetic operations and their similarity to decimal arithmetic.

Example A.23 *Addition.*

```
    1 1 1   ← Carries
    1 4 7 6
  + 3 5 5 4
    5 2 5 2   SUM
```

Scratch pad

$$
\begin{array}{r}
6 \\
+ \ 4 \\
\hline
(10)_{10} = (12)_8
\end{array}
$$

$$
\begin{array}{r}
1 \\
+ \ 7 \\
+ \ 5 \\
\hline
(13)_{10} = (15)_8
\end{array}
$$

$$
\begin{array}{r}
1 \\
+ \ 4 \\
+ \ 5 \\
\hline
(10)_{10} = (12)_8
\end{array}
$$

$$
\begin{array}{r}
1 \\
+ \ 1 \\
+ \ 3 \\
\hline
(5)_{10} = (5)_8
\end{array}
$$

Table A.4 Octal arithmetic

					A			
$A + B$	0	1	2	3	4	5	6	7
0	0	1	2	3	4	5	6	7
1	1	2	3	4	5	6	7	10
2	2	3	4	5	6	7	10	11
B 3	3	4	5	6	7	10	11	12
4	4	5	6	7	10	11	12	13
5	5	6	7	10	11	12	13	14
6	6	7	10	11	12	13	14	15
7	7	10	11	12	13	14	15	16

(a) Addition

					A			
$A \times B$	0	1	2	3	4	5	6	7
0	0	0	0	0	0	0	0	0
1	0	1	2	3	4	5	6	7
2	0	2	4	6	10	12	14	16
B 3	0	3	6	11	14	17	22	25
4	0	4	10	14	20	24	30	34
5	0	5	12	17	24	31	36	43
6	0	6	14	22	30	36	44	52
7	0	7	16	25	34	43	52	61

(b) Multiplication

Example A.24 *Subtraction.*

```
   4 14
   5  4 7 5      Digit position 2
  -3  7 6 4      Borrow from position 3.
  ----------          ∴     Octal      Decimal
   1  5 1 1                  14₈          12
                            - 7₈        - 7
                            ------      -------
                             5₈        5₁₀ = 5₈
```

$$14_8 - 7_8 = 5_8$$
$$5_{10} = 5_8$$

Example A.25

```
      3 7 7
   5  4 0 0 4 5
 - 3  2 5 6 5 4
 --------------
   2  1 2 1 7 1
```

The intermediate 0s become $(r - 1)$ or 7 when borrowed.

Example A.26 *Multiplication.*

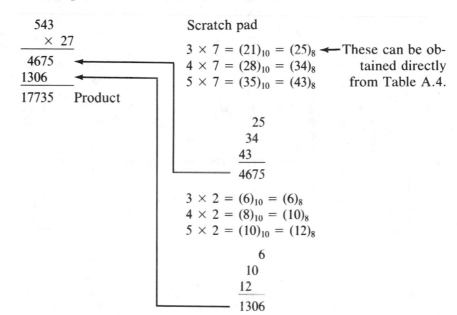

```
543
× 27
─────
4675
1306
─────
17735    Product
```

Scratch pad

$3 \times 7 = (21)_{10} = (25)_8$ ← These can be ob-
$4 \times 7 = (28)_{10} = (34)_8$ tained directly
$5 \times 7 = (35)_{10} = (43)_8$ from Table A.4.

```
 25
 34
 43
────
4675
```

$3 \times 2 = (6)_{10} = (6)_8$
$4 \times 2 = (8)_{10} = (10)_8$
$5 \times 2 = (10)_{10} = (12)_8$

```
 6
10
12
────
1306
```

Example A.27 *Division.* $543 \div 7$.

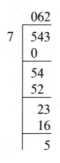

```
        062
    ┌──────
  7 │ 543
    │ 0
    ├──────
    │ 54
    │ 52
    ├──────
    │ 23
    │ 16
    ├──────
    │  5
```

Use the multiplication table of Table A.4 to derive the quotient digit (by trial and error).

A.5.3   Hexadecimal Arithmetic

Table A.5 provides the addition and multiplication tables for hexadecimal arithmetic. The following examples illustrate the arithmetic.

Table A.5 Hexadecimal arithmetic

+	0	1	2	3	4	5	6	7	8	9	A	B	C	D	E	F
0	0	1	2	3	4	5	6	7	8	9	A	B	C	D	E	F
1	1	2	3	4	5	6	7	8	9	A	B	C	D	E	F	10
2	2	3	4	5	6	7	8	9	A	B	C	D	E	F	10	11
3	3	4	5	6	7	8	9	A	B	C	D	E	F	10	11	12
4	4	5	6	7	8	9	A	B	C	D	E	F	10	11	12	13
5	5	6	7	8	9	A	B	C	D	E	F	10	11	12	13	14
6	6	7	8	9	A	B	C	D	E	F	10	11	12	13	14	15
7	7	8	9	A	B	C	D	E	F	10	11	12	13	14	15	16
8	8	9	A	B	C	D	E	F	10	11	12	13	14	15	16	17
9	9	A	B	C	D	E	F	10	11	12	13	14	15	16	17	18
A	A	B	C	D	E	F	10	11	12	13	14	15	16	17	18	19
B	B	C	D	E	F	10	11	12	13	14	15	16	17	18	19	1A
C	C	D	E	F	10	11	12	13	14	15	16	17	18	19	1A	1B
D	D	E	F	10	11	12	13	14	15	16	17	18	19	1A	1B	1C
E	E	F	10	11	12	13	14	15	16	17	18	19	1A	1B	1C	1D
F	F	10	11	12	13	14	15	16	17	18	19	1A	1B	1C	1D	1E

(a) Addition

×	0	1	2	3	4	5	6	7	8	9	A	B	C	D	E	F
0	0	0	0	0	0	0	0	0	0	0	0	0	0	0	0	0
1	0	1	2	3	4	5	6	7	8	9	A	B	C	D	E	F
2	0	2	4	6	8	A	C	E	10	12	14	16	18	1A	1C	1E
3	0	3	6	9	C	F	12	15	18	1B	1E	21	24	27	2A	2D
4	0	4	8	C	10	14	18	1C	20	24	28	2C	30	34	38	3C
5	0	5	A	F	14	19	1E	23	28	2D	32	37	3C	41	46	4B
6	0	6	C	12	18	1E	24	2A	30	36	3C	42	48	4E	54	5A
7	0	7	E	15	1C	23	2A	31	38	3F	46	4D	54	5B	62	69
8	0	8	10	18	20	28	30	38	40	48	50	58	60	68	70	78
9	0	9	12	1B	24	2D	36	3F	48	51	5A	63	6C	75	7E	87
A	0	A	14	1E	28	32	3C	46	50	5A	64	6E	78	82	8C	96
B	0	B	16	21	2C	37	42	4D	58	63	6E	79	84	8F	9A	A5
C	0	C	18	24	30	3C	48	54	60	6C	78	84	90	9C	A8	B4
D	0	D	1A	27	34	41	4E	5B	68	75	82	8F	9C	A9	B6	C3
E	0	E	1C	2A	38	46	54	62	70	7E	8C	9A	A8	B6	C4	D2
F	0	F	1E	2D	3C	4B	5A	69	78	87	96	A5	B4	C3	D2	E1

(b) Multiplication

Example A.28 *Addition.*

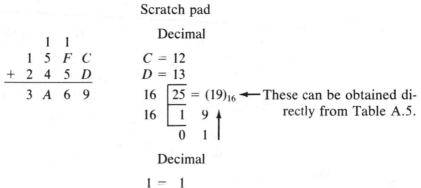

Scratch pad

Decimal

$$
\begin{array}{cccc}
 & 1 & 1 & \\
1 & 5 & F & C \\
+ \; 2 & 4 & 5 & D \\
\hline
3 & A & 6 & 9
\end{array}
$$

$C = 12$
$D = 13$

16 $\boxed{25}$ = $(19)_{16}$ ◀— These can be obtained di-
16 $\boxed{1}$ 9 ↑   rectly from Table A.5.
    0   1 |

Decimal

$$
\begin{array}{rl}
1 = & 1 \\
F = & 15 \\
5 = & \underline{5} \\
21 = & (15)_{16}
\end{array}
$$

Example A.29 *Subtraction.*

Scratch pad

Decimal

$$
\begin{array}{cccc}
1 & 13 & 15 & \\
 & 3 & & \\
\cancel{2} & 4 & \cancel{5} & D \quad \text{Minuend} \\
- \; 1 & 5 & F & C \quad \text{Subtrahend} \\
\hline
0 & E & 6 & 1 \quad \text{Difference}
\end{array}
$$

$(15)_{16} = 21$

$-(F)_{16} - \dfrac{-15}{6} = (6)_{16}$

$(13)_{16} = 19$

$-(5)_{16} = \dfrac{-5}{14} = (E)_{16}$

Example A.30 *Multiplication.*

$$
\begin{array}{r}
1\ E\ 4\ A \\
\times\ FA2 \\
\hline
3 \\
0\ 3\ C\ 9\ 4 \qquad P_1 \\
+\ 1\ 2\ E\ E\ 4 \qquad P_2 \\
+\ 2\ 2\ 6\ 5\ 6 \qquad P_3 \\
\hline
2\ 3\ 9\ 8\ 0\ D\ 4
\end{array}
$$

Scratch pad

Decimal	Hexadecimal
$A \times 2 = 20 =$	$1\ 4$
$4 \times 2 = 8 =$	$0\ 8$
$E \times 2 = 28 =$	$1\ C$
$1 \times 2 = 2 =$	$0\ 2$
	$0\ 3\ C\ 9\ 4\ = P_1$
$A \times A = 100 =$	$6\ 4$
$4 \times A = 40 =$	$2\ 8$
$E \times A = 140 =$	$8\ C$
$1 \times A = 10 =$	A
	$1\ 2\ E\ E\ 4\ = P_2$
$A \times F = 150 =$	$9\ 6$
$4 \times F = 60 =$	$3\ C$
$E \times F = 120 =$	$1\ 3\ 2$
$1 \times F = 15 =$	$O\ F$
	$2\ 2\ 6\ 5\ 6 = P_2$

Example A.31 *Division.* $1\ A\ F\ 3 \div E.$

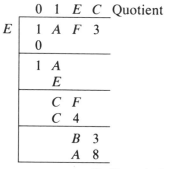

$$
\begin{array}{r|rrrrl}
 & 0 & 1 & E & C & \text{Quotient} \\
\hline
E & 1 & A & F & 3 \\
 & 0 \\
\hline
 & 1 & A \\
 & & E \\
\hline
 & & C & F \\
 & & C & 4 \\
\hline
 & & & B & 3 \\
 & & & A & 8 \\
\hline
 & & & B & & \text{Remainder}
\end{array}
$$

A.6 Sign-Magnitude Representation

In this representation, the MSD of the number represents the sign. It is 0 for positive numbers and $(r - 1)$ for negative numbers, where r is the base of the number system. Some representation examples follow.

Example A.32

$$(+25)_{10} = 0,0025$$
$$(-25)_{10} = 9,0025$$
$$(+2)_2 = 0,0010$$
$$(-2)_2 = 1,0010$$
$$(+56)_8 = 0,0056$$
$$(-56)_8 = 7,0056$$
$$(+1F)_{16} = 0,001F$$
$$(-1F)_{16} = E,001F$$

Sign, magnitude

All numbers are shown as five-digit numbers. In arithmetic with sign-magnitude numbers, the magnitude and sign are treated separately.

A.7 Complement Number Systems

Consider the subtraction of a number A from a number B. This is equivalent to adding $(-A)$ to B. The complement number system provides a convenient way of representing negative numbers (that is, complements of positive numbers), thus converting the subtraction to an addition. Since multiplication and division correspond to repeated addition and subtraction, respectively, it is possible to perform the four basic arithmetic operations using only the hardware for addition when negative numbers are represented in complement form. There are two popular complement number systems, (1) *radix complement* and (2) *diminished radix complement*.

A.7.1 Radix Complement System

This system is called either 2s complement or 10s complement system, depending on whether the base of the number is 2 or 10. We will discuss the 2s complement system. The 10s complement system also displays the same characteristics as the 2s complement system.

The radix complement of a number $(N)_r$ is defined as

$$[N]_r = r^n - (N)_r \qquad\qquad (A-3)$$

where $[N]_r$ is the radix complement of $(N)_r$ and n is the number of digits in $(N)_r$.

Example A.33   The 2s complement of $(01010)_2$ is $2^5 - (01010)_2$; $N = 5$, $r = 2$.

$$= 100000 - 01010$$

$$= 10110$$

$$\therefore [01010]_2 = (10110)_2.$$

There are two other methods for obtaining the 2s complement of a number.

Method 1

$[01010]_2 = ?$

10101   ←Complement each bit (i.e., change each 0 to 1 and 1 to 0).

 + 1   ←Add 1 to the LSB to get the 2s complement.
───────
10110

Method 2

$[010\,|\,10]_2 = ?$

           |10   ←Copy the bits from LSB until and including the first nonzero bit.

101 | ←Complement the remaining bits through MSB to get the 2s complement.
──────────
101 | 10

Twos Complement Arithmetic. In the 2s complement system, positive numbers remain in their normal form while the negative numbers are represented in the 2s complement form. Some examples using a 5-bit (4-magnitude, 1-sign) representation are presented.

Example A.34

	Sign Magnitude	
+5	0, 0101	
−5	1, 1011	2s complement of +5
+4	0, 0100	
−4	1, 1100	

Examples of arithmetic using these 5-bit 2s complement numbers are shown in the examples.

Example A.35

	Sign-magnitude	2s complement	
5	0, 0101	0, 0101	
−4	1, 0100	1, 1100	(2s complement of +4)

CARRY from sign position 10, 0001   SUM
$$= +(0001)_2$$

There is a CARRY from the MSB (sign bit in this case) indicating that the result is positive (+1); CARRY is discarded.

Example A.36

	Sign-magnitude	2s complement
4	0, 0100	0, 0100
−5	1, 0101	1, 1011

1, 1111   SUM
No CARRY
$$= -(0001)_2$$

There is no CARRY from MSB. Hence, the result is negative and must be 2s complemented to find its value, that is, $-(0001)_2$ or -1.

To summarize, in 2s complement addition if the MSB generates a CARRY, it is ignored and the result is treated as positive; if there is no CARRY, the result is negative and is in the 2s complement format. Note that in this arithmetic the sign bit is treated as though it is one of the magnitude bits.

Shifting.   Shifting a 2s complement number left or right by one bit is equivalent to multiplying it by 2 or dividing it by 2, respectively. The sign bit is copied into the vacant position during a right shift and 0 is inserted into LSB during a left shift. An example follows.

Example A.37

| 1 | 0 0 1 0 1 0 0 0   0 |

1   1 0 0 1 0 1 0 0   0   Right shift (copy sign bit.)

1   1 1 0 0 1 0 1 0   0   Right shift (copy sign bit.)

1   1 0 0 1 0 1 0 0 | 0 | Left shift (Insert 0.)

1   0 0 1 0 1 0 0 0 | 0 | Left shift (Insert 0.)

Change in the value of the sign bit during a left shift indicates that there is an overflow (i.e., the result is too large).

A.7.2   Diminished Radix Complement

The diminished radix complement $[N]_{r-1}$ of a number $(N)_r$ is defined as

$$[N]_{r-1} = r^n - (N)_r - 1 \qquad\qquad (A-4)$$

where n is the number of digits in $(N)_r$. Note that

$$[N]_r = [N]_{r-1} + 1. \qquad\qquad (A-5)$$

The diminished radix complement is called 1s complement or 9s complement, depending on whether the base of the system is 2 or 10, respectively.

Since $(2^n - 1)$ is an n-bit binary number with all of its bits equal to 1, the 1s complement of a number is obtained by subtracting each of its bits by 1. This is the same as complementing each bit. As an example, the 1s complement of $(10110)_2$ is $(01001)_2$. The 9s complement of a decimal number is obtained by subtracting each of its digits from 9.

Addition. In the 1s complement number system, the positive numbers remain in their true binary form while the negative numbers are represented in the 1s complement form. The following examples illustrate the arithmetic in this system using a 5-bit (4-magnitude, 1-sign) representation.

Example A.38

	Sign-magnitude	1s complement
5	0, 0101	0, 0101
−4	1, 0100	1, 1011
		1 0, 0000　SUM

Add the CARRY end-around → ⌐───→1

　　　　　　　　　　　　　　　　0, 0001

The CARRY generated from MSB during the addition is added (end-around) to the LSB to obtain the correct SUM; the result is positive.

Example A.39

	Sign-magnitude	1s complement
4	0, 0100	0, 0100
−5	1, 0101	1, 1010
		1, 1110　SUM

No CARRY

∴ Complement and the result is −(0001).

If there is no CARRY from the MSB, the result is negative and is in the 1s complement form.

Shifting. While shifting 1s complement numbers right, the sign bit is copied into the vacant positions on the left (as in the 2s complement system); during a left shift, sign bit is copied into the vacant positions on the right.

Table A.6 summarizes the operations in both complement systems. Some digital systems use a 2s complement system while others employ 1s complement.

Table A.6 Complement number systems

Operation	CARRY from MSB	1s complement	2s complement	Sign of the result
ADD	0	Result is in 1s complement	Result is in 2s complement	Negative
	1	Add 1 to LSB of the result	Neglect the CARRY	Positive
Shift left		Copy sign bit on the right	Copy 0s on the right	
Shift right		Copy sign bit on the left	Copy sign bit on the left	

A.8 Codes

A digital system requires that all its information be in binary form. But the external world uses the alphabetic characters, decimal digits, and special characters (e.g., periods, commas, plus and minus signs) to represent information. A unique pattern of 0s and 1s is used to represent each required character. This pattern is the "code" corresponding to that character. We will list several codes that are commonly used in digital systems.

A.8.1 Binary Coded Decimal (BCD)

BCD is one of the popular codes used to represent numeric information. Each decimal digit is coded into 4 bits:

$$
\begin{array}{ll}
0 \quad 0000 & 5 \quad 0101 \\
1 \quad 0001 & 6 \quad 0110 \\
2 \quad 0010 & 7 \quad 0111 \\
3 \quad 0011 & 8 \quad 1000 \\
4 \quad 0100 & 9 \quad 1001
\end{array}
$$

Only ten of the possible sixteen (2^4) patterns of 4 bits are used. As an example, the number $(432)_{10}$ would be represented as

$$
\underset{4 \qquad 3 \qquad 2}{(0100 \quad 0011 \quad 0010)_{BCD}}
$$

When the data are represented in BCD, the arithmetic can also be done on each digit, as in decimal arithmetic.

A.8.2 Excess-3

Excess-3 is also a 4-bit code. The code for each decimal digit is obtained by adding 3 to the corresponding BCD code:

0	0011	5	1000
1	0100	6	1011
2	0101	7	1010
3	0110	8	1011
4	0111	9	1100

Excess-3 code enables simpler BCD arithmetic hardware. For example, the 9s complement of any digit can be obtained simply by taking the 1s complement of the corresponding code.

Consider the addition of two decimal digits. In BCD, when the SUM exceeds 9, a 6 is added to bring the resulting digit into the range 0–9. A CARRY is generated in this process that is used in the addition of digits in the next stage.

In Excess-3 it is not necessary to check to see if the SUM exceeds 9 or not since the correction can be done just by checking to see if the addition has resulted in a CARRY or not. The correction is either add 3 to or subtract 3 from the result, as shown by Example A.40.

Example A.40

Decimal	BCD	Excess-3
3	0011	0110
+2	0010	0101
5	0101	[0] 1011
	SUM < 9: No	CARRY = 0
	correction	∴ Subtract 0011
	needed.	3 1000
5	0101	1000
+ 6	0110	1001
11	1011	10001
	SUM > 9:	CARRY = 1
	∴ Add 6: 0110	∴ Add 3: 0011
	1,0001	1,0100

A.8.3 Two-Out-of-Five Code

This code uses 5 bits to represent each decimal digit. As the name implies, 2 bits out of the 5 bits are 1s in each code word:

0	11000	5	01010
1	00011	6	01100
2	00101	7	10001
3	00110	8	10010
4	01001	9	10100

With 5 bits, 32 code words are possible. Only 10 of them are used, but the code provides an automatic error detection capability since the number of 1s in the code word must always be two.

This code uses a simple "parity" scheme. Since the number of 1s is always even, it is called "even parity." In general, one or more parity bits are included into the code word to facilitate error detection and correction. Even and odd parity schemes are the simplest ones. Several other schemes are used to generate parity bits where a higher degree of error detection and correction is needed.

A.8.4 Alphanumeric Codes

When alphabetic characters, numeric digits, and special characters are used in representing the information to be processed by the digital system, an alphanumeric code is used. Two popular alphanumeric codes are

Figure A.1 An 80-column (Hollerith) card

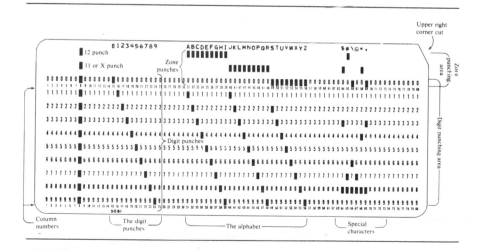

Extended BCD Interchange Code (EBCDIC) and American Standard Code for Information Interchange (ASCII). These codes are shown in Table A.7. This table also shows the codes used in representing alphanumeric information on cards. On an 80-column card (shown in Figure A.1), each column can represent a character. The card has twelve rows: numeric rows 0 through 9 and rows 11 and 12. Rows 0, 11, and 12 are called *zone punch* rows. Table A.7 shows the pattern of punches for each alphanumeric character.

Table A.7 Alphanumeric codes

Character	EBCDIC code	ASCII code	BCD cards	EBCDIC cards
blank	0100 0000	0100 0000	No punch	No punch
.	0100 1011	0100 1110	12,8,3	12,8,3
(	0100 1101	0100 1000	0,8,4	12,8,5
+	0100 1110	0100 1011	12	12,8,6
$	0101 1011	0100 0100	11,8,3	11,8,3
*	0101 1100	0100 1010	11,8,4	11,8,4
)	0101 1101	0100 1001	12,8,4	11,8,5
—	0110 0000	0100 1101	11	11
/	0110 0001	0100 1100	0,1	0,1
,	0110 1011	0100 1111	0,8,3	0,8,3
;	0111 1101	0100 0111	4,8	8,5
=	0111 1110	0101 1101	3,8	8,6
A	1100 0001	1010 0001	12,1	12,1
B	1100 0010	1010 0010	12,2	12,2
C	1100 0011	1010 0011	12,3	12,3
D	1100 0100	1010 0100	12,4	12,4
E	1100 0101	1010 0101	12,5	12,5
F	1100 0110	1010 0110	12,6	12,6
G	1100 0111	1010 0111	12,7	12,7
H	1100 1000	1010 1000	12,8	12,8
I	1100 1001	1010 1001	12,9	12,9
J	1101 0001	1010 1010	11,1	11,1
K	1101 0010	1010 1011	11,2	11,2
L	1101 0011	1010 1100	11,3	11,3
M	1101 0100	1010 1101	11,4	11,4
N	1101 0101	1010 1110	11,5	11,5
O	1101 0110	1010 1111	11,6	11,6
P	1101 0111	1011 0000	11,7	11,7
Q	1101 1000	1011 0001	11,8	11,8
R	1101 1001	1011 0010	11,9	11,9
S	1110 0010	1011 0011	0,2	0,2
T	1110 0011	1011 0100	0,3	0,3
U	1110 0100	1011 0101	0,4	0,4

(continued)

Table A.7 (Continued)

Character	EBCDIC code	ASCII code	BCD cards	EBCDIC cards
V	1110 0101	1011 0110	0,5	0,5
W	1110 0110	1011 0111	0,6	0,6
X	1110 0111	1011 1000	0,7	0,7
Y	1110 1000	1011 1001	0,8	0,8
Z	1110 1001	1011 1010	0,9	0,9
0	1111 0000	0101 0000	0	0
1	1111 0001	0101 0001	1	1
2	1111 0010	0101 0010	2	2
3	1111 0011	0101 0011	3	3
4	1111 0100	0101 0100	4	4
5	1111 0101	0101 0101	5	5
6	1111 0110	0101 0110	6	6
7	1111 0111	0101 0111	7	7
8	1111 1000	0101 1000	8	8
9	1111 1001	0101 1001	9	9

If the cards are used for inputting information into a digital computer that uses EBCDIC code internally, each character read from the card (i.e., a 12-bit pattern of 0s and 1s) is converted into an 8-bit EBCDIC code word. When the processed information is to be listed on a line printer, the internal EBCDIC code must be converted into a code used by the printer.

References

Chu, Y. *Digital Computer Design Fundamentals*. New York, N.Y.: McGraw-Hill, 1962.

Feingold, C. *Introduction to Data Processing*. Dubuque, Iowa: Wm. C. Brown, 1975.

Gear, C. W. *Computer Organization and Programming*. New York, N.Y.: McGraw-Hill, 1974.

Nagle, H. T., J. D. Irwin, and B. D. Carroll. *Introduction to Computer Logic*. Englewood Cliffs, N.J.: Prentice-Hall, 1975.

Appendix B

Minimization of Boolean Functions

We used the theorems and postulates of Boolean algebra to simplify Boolean functions in Chapter 1. A minimized function yields a less complex circuit than a nonminimized function. In general, the complexity of a gate increases as the number of inputs increases. Hence, a reduction in the number of literals in a Boolean function reduces the complexity of the complete circuit. In designing integrated circuits (IC), there are other considerations, such as the area taken up by the circuit on the silicon wafer used to fabricate the IC and the regularity of the structure of the circuit from a fabrication point of view. For example, a programmable logic array (PLA) implementation (see Chapter 3) of the circuit yields a more regular structure than the random logic (i.e., using gates) implementation. Minimizing the number of literals in the function may not yield a less complex PLA implementation. However, if some product terms in the SOP form can be completely eliminated from the function, the PLA size can be reduced.

Minimization using theorems and postulates is tedious. Two other popular minimization methods are (1) using Karnaugh maps (K-maps), and (2) the Quine-McCluskey procedure. These two methods are described in this appendix.

B.1 Venn Diagrams

Truth tables and canonical forms were used in Chapter 1 to represent Boolean functions. Another method of representing a function is by using Venn diagrams. The variables are represented as circles in a "universe"

431

that is a rectangle. The universe corresponds to 1 (everything), and 0 corresponds to null (nothing). Figures B.1 and B.2 show typical logic operations using Venn diagrams. In these diagrams, the NOT operation is identified by the area "NOT belonging" to the particular variable; the OR operation is the "union" of two areas (that is, the area that belongs to either or both) corresponding to the two operands; and the AND operation is the "intersection" of the two areas (that is, the area that is common to both) corresponding to the two operands. The unshaded area is the area in which the expression is 0. Note that all the combinations shown in the truth tables can also be shown in the Venn diagrams. Figure B.3 shows all the combinations corresponding to two- and three-variable functions.

B.2   Karnaugh Maps

Karnaugh maps (K-maps) are modified Venn diagrams. Consider the two-variable Venn diagram shown in Figure B.4(a). All four combinations of the two variables are shown. The four areas are identified by the four minterms in (b), and (c) shows the Venn diagram rearranged such that the four areas are equal. Also note that the two right-hand blocks of the diagram correspond to A (m_2 and m_3), and the two blocks at the bottom (m_1 and m_3) correspond to B. Figure B.4(d) marks the areas A, $\bar{A}$, B, and $\bar{B}$ explicitly, and (e) is the usual form for a K-map of two variables. The

Figure B.1 Logic operations using Venn diagrams

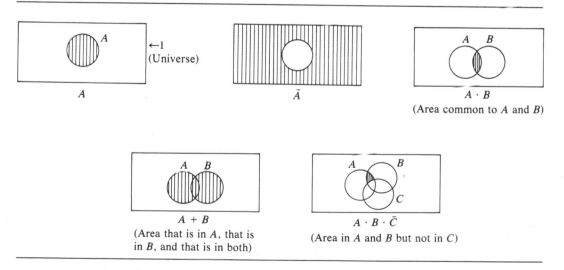

Figure B.2 Representation of $A\bar{B} + B\bar{C}$ using Venn diagrams

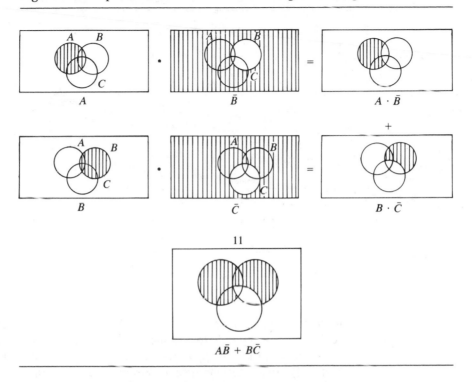

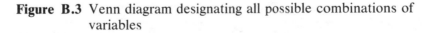

two variables A and B are distributed such that the values of A are along the top and those of B are along the side.

Figure B.5 shows a three-variable K-map. Since there are 2^3 or 8 combinations of three variables, we will need eight blocks. The blocks are arranged such that the two right-hand columns correspond to A, the two

Figure B.3 Venn diagram designating all possible combinations of variables

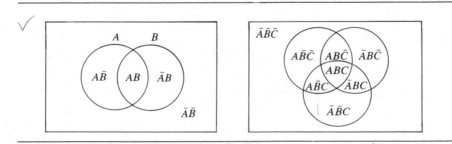

Figure B.4 Two-variable Karnaugh map

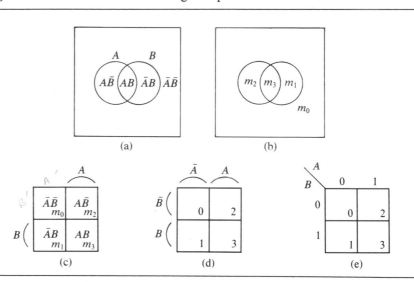

Note: m_0, m_1, m_2, and m_3 are minterms.

middle columns correspond to B, and the bottom row corresponds to C. Each block corresponds to a minterm. For example, the block named m_6 corresponds to the area in A and B but not in C. That is the area $AB\bar{C}$, which is 110 in minterm code and is minterm m_6. The first two variables A and B are represented by the four combinations along the top and the third variable C along the side as in Figure B.5(b). Note that the area A consists of the blocks where A has a value of 1 (blocks 4, 5, 6, and 7), irrespective of B and C; similarly, B is 1 in blocks 2, 3, 6, and 7 and C is 1 in 1, 3, 5, and 7. Once the variable values are listed along the top and side, it is very easy to identify the minterm corresponding to each block. For example, the

Figure B.5 Three-variable Karnaugh map

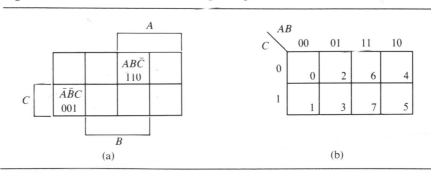

Figure B.6 Four-variable Karnaugh map

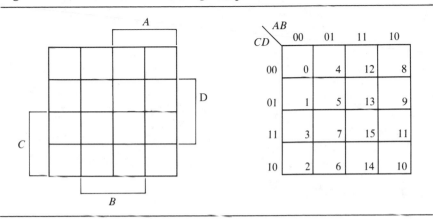

left-hand, top-corner block corresponds to $A = 0$, $B = 0$, and $C = 0$; that is, $ABC = 000 = m_0$.

A four-variable Karnaugh map is shown in Figure B.6. The areas and minterms are also identified.

B.2.1 Representation of Functions on K-maps

We represented functions on Venn diagrams by shading the areas. On Karnaugh maps, each block is given a value of a 0 or 1 depending on the value of the function. Each block corresponding to a minterm will have a value of 1; all other blocks will have 0s as shown in Examples B.1 and B.2.

Example B.1 $f(X,Y,Z) = \Sigma m(0,1,4)$. Place a 1 corresponding to each minterm.

Z \ XY	00	01	11	10
0	1 _0_	0 _2_	0 _6_	1 _4_
1	1 _1_	0 _3_	0 _7_	0 _5_

Example B.2 $f(A,B,C,D) = \Pi_M(1,4,9,10,14)$. Place a 0 corresponding to each maxterm.

CD \ AB	00	01	11	10
00	1 _0_	0 _4_	1 _12_	1 _8_
01	0 _1_	1 _5_	1 _13_	0 _9_
11	1 _3_	1 _7_	1 _15_	1 _11_
10	1 _2_	1 _6_	0 _14_	0 _10_

Usually 0s are not shown explicitly on the K-map. Only 1s are shown and a blank block corresponds to a 0.

B.2.2 Plotting Sum of Products Form

When the function is given in the sum of products (SOP) form, the equivalent minterm list can be derived by the method given in Chapter 1 and the minterms can be plotted on the K-map. An alternative and faster method is to intersect the area on the K-map corresponding to each product term as illustrated in Example B.3.

Example B.3 $F(X,Y,Z) = X\bar{Y} + \bar{Y}\bar{Z}$.

Z \ XY	00	01	11	10
0	_0_	_2_	_6_	_4_
1	_1_	_3_	_7_	_5_

X corresponds to blocks 4,5,6,7 (all the blocks where X is 1); $\bar{Y}$ corresponds to blocks 0,1,4,5 (all the blocks where $\bar{Y}$ is 1); $X\bar{Y}$ corresponds to their intersection; that is, $X\bar{Y} = \underline{\underline{4,5}}$. Similarly,

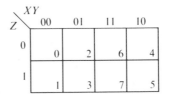

$$\bar{Y} = 0,1,4,5$$

$$\bar{Z} = 0,2,4,6 \qquad \therefore \bar{Y}\bar{Z} = \underline{\underline{0,4}}.$$

Therefore, the K-map will have 1 in the union of (4,5) and (0,4), which is (0,4,5):

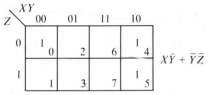

$$X\bar{Y} + \bar{Y}\bar{Z}$$

Alternatively, $X\bar{Y}$ corresponds to the area where $X = 1$ *and* $Y = 0$, which is the last column; XZ corresponds to the area where both $Y = 0$ and $Z = 0$, which is blocks 0 and 4. Hence the union of the two corresponds to blocks 0,4,5.

Note also that in this three-variable K-map, if a product term has two variables missing (as in Y), we use four 1s corresponding to the four minterms that can be generated out of a single-variable product term in the representation. In general, a product term with n missing variables will be represented by 2^n 1s on the K-map. An example follows.

Example B.4 $P(A,B,C,D) = A\bar{B} + \bar{A}BC + \bar{C}\bar{D}$.

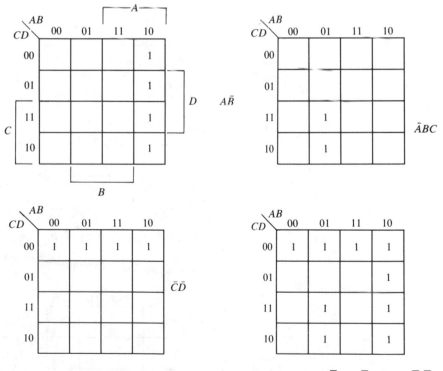

$$P(A,B,C,D) = A\bar{B} + \bar{A}BC + \bar{C}\bar{D}.$$

B.2.3   Plotting Product of Sums Form

The procedure for plotting a product of sums (POS) expression is similar to that for the SOP form, except that 0s are used instead of 1s.

Example B.5 $F(X,Y,Z) = (X + \bar{Y})(\bar{Y} + \bar{Z})$.

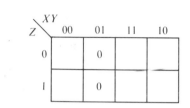

$(X + \bar{Y}) = 0$ only if $X = 0$ and $\bar{Y} = 0$; that is, $X = 0$ and $Y = 1$ or the area $(\bar{X}Y)$.

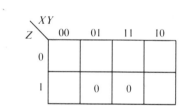

$(\bar{Y} + \bar{Z}) = 0$ only if $\bar{Y} = 0$ and $\bar{Z} = 0$; that is, $Y = 1$ and $Z = 1$ or the area (YZ)

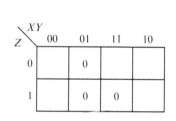

$F(X,Y,Z)$ is 0 when either $(X + \bar{Y})$ is 0 or $(\bar{Y} + \bar{Z}) = 0$ or the area $(\bar{X}Y) + (YZ)$.

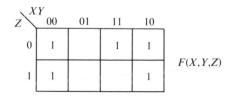

B.2.4 Minimization

Note that the combination of variable values represented by any block on a K-map differs from that of its adjacent block only in one variable, that variable being complemented in one block and true (or uncomplemented) in the other. For example, consider blocks 2 and 3 (corresponding to minterms m_2 and m_3) of a three-variable K-map: m_2 corresponds to 010 or $\bar{A}B\bar{C}$, and m_3 corresponds to 011 or $\bar{A}BC$. The values for A and B remain the same while C is different in these adjacent blocks. This property where the two terms differ by only one variable is called *logical adjacency*. In a K-map, then, *physically adjacent blocks are also logically adjacent*. In the three-variable K-map, block 2 is physically adjacent to blocks 0, 3, and 6. Note that m_2 is also logically adjacent to m_0, m_3, and m_6. This adjacency property can be used in the simplification of Boolean functions.

Example B.6 Consider the following K-map for a four-variable function:

Blocks 8 and 12 are adjacent.

$$m_8 = 1000 = A\bar{B}\bar{C}\bar{D}.$$
$$m_{12} = 1100 = AB\bar{C}\bar{D}.$$

Also,

$$A\bar{B}\bar{C}\bar{D} + AB\bar{C}\bar{D} = A\bar{C}\bar{D}(\bar{B} + B) \qquad \text{P4b}$$
$$= A\bar{C}\bar{D}.(1) \qquad \text{P5a}$$
$$= A\bar{C}\bar{D}. \qquad \text{P1b}$$

That is, we can combine m_8 and m_{12}. This combination is shown below by the grouping of 1s on the K-map. Note that by this grouping, we eliminated the variable B because it changes in value between these two blocks.

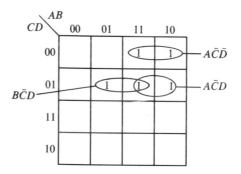

Similarly, the grouping of m_9 and m_{13} yields $A\bar{C}D$ and grouping m_5 and m_{13} yields $B\bar{C}D$.

If we combine $A\bar{C}\bar{D}$ with $A\bar{C}D$,

$$A\bar{C}\bar{D} + A\bar{C}D = A\bar{C}(D + \bar{D})$$ P4b

$$= A\bar{C}.(1)$$ P5a

$$= A\bar{C}.$$ P1b

This in effect is equivalent to grouping all *four* 1s in the top right corner of the K-map, as shown here:

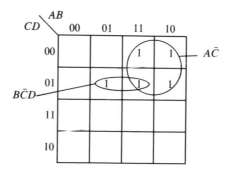

By forming a group of two adjacent 1s we eliminated 1 literal from the product term; by grouping four adjacent 1s we eliminated 2 literals. In general, if we group 2^n adjacent 1s, we can eliminate n literals. Hence, in simplifying functions it is advantageous to form as large a group of 1s as possible. The number of 1s in any group must be a power of 2; that is, 1,2,4,8, . . . , etc. Once the groups are formed, the product term corresponding to each group can be derived by the following general rules:

1. Eliminate the variable that changes in value within the group (move from block to block within the group to observe this change) from a product term containing all the variables of the function.
2. A variable that has a value of 0 in all blocks of the group should appear complemented in the product term.
3. A variable that has a value of 1 in all blocks of the group should appear uncomplemented in the product.

For the group of four 1s in the above K-map:

ABCD Start with all the variables.
ABCD A remains 1 in all four blocks.
ABCD B changes in value.
AB$\overline{C}$D C remains at 0.
AB$\overline{C}$D D changes in value.

So the product term corresponding to this grouping is $A\overline{C}$.

We can summarize all of the above observations in the following procedure for simplifying functions:

1. Form groups of adjacent 1s.
2. Form each group to be as large as possible. (The number of 1s in each group must be a power of 2).
3. Cover each 1 on the K-map at least once. Same 1 can be included in several groups if necessary.
4. Select the least number of groups so as to cover all the 1s on the map.
5. Translate each group into a product term.
6. OR the product terms, to obtain the minimized function.

To recognize the adjacencies, on a three-variable map the right-hand edge is considered to be the same as the left-hand edge, thus making block 0 adjacent to block 4, and 1 adjacent to 5. Similarly, on a four-variable map, the top and bottom edges can be brought together to form a cylinder. The two ends of the cylinder are brought together to form a toroid (like a donut). The following examples illustrate the grouping on the K-maps and corresponding simplifications.

Example B.7 $F(X,Y,Z) = \Sigma m(1,2,3,6,7)$.

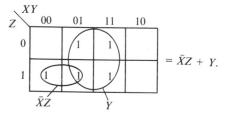

$= \bar{X}Z + Y.$

Example B.8 $F(A,B,C,D) = \Sigma m(2,4,8,9,10,11,13,15)$.

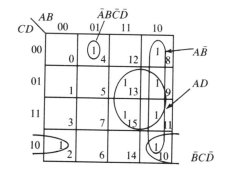

$$F(A,B,C,D) = A\bar{B} + AD + \bar{B}C\bar{D} + \bar{A}B\bar{C}\bar{D}.$$

Example B.9 $F(X,Y,Z,W) = \Sigma m(0,4,5,8,12,13)$.

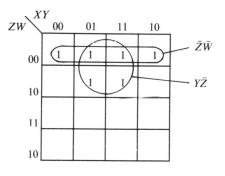

$$F(X,Y,Z,W) = Y\bar{Z} + \bar{Z}\bar{W}.$$

Example B.10 $F(A,B,C,D) = \Sigma m(0,1,2,7,8,9,10)$.

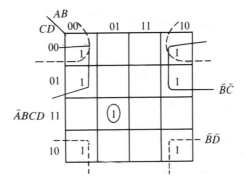

$$F(A,B,C,D) = \bar{A}BCD + \bar{B}\bar{D} + \bar{B}\bar{C}.$$

Example B.11 $F(A,B,C,D) = AB\bar{C} + ABC + BC\bar{D} + BCD + A\bar{B}\bar{D} + \bar{A}\bar{B}\bar{D} + \bar{A}B\bar{C}D$.

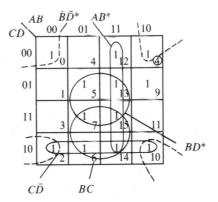

1. Groupings marked by an "*" are "essential." m_{12} is covered only by (AB); m_0, m_8 are covered only by $(\bar{B}\bar{D})$; m_5 is covered only by (BD).
2. Once the above three groups are chosen, the only minterms left uncovered are m_6 and m_{14}. To cover these, we can either choose (BC) or $(C\bar{D})$. Hence, there are two simplified forms:

$$F(A,B,C,D) = AB + \bar{B}\bar{D} + BD + BC$$
$$= AB + \bar{B}\bar{D} + BD + C\bar{D}.$$

Either of the above is a satisfactory form, since each contains the same number of literals.

B.2.5   Simplified Function in POS Form

To obtain the simplified function in POS form,

1. Plot the function F on the K-map.
2. Derive the K-map for $\bar{F}$ (by changing 1 to 0 and 0 to 1).
3. Simplify the K-map for $\bar{F}$ to obtain $\bar{F}$ in SOP form.
4. Use De Morgan's laws to obtain F.

Example B.12 $F(P,Q,R,S) = \bar{P}\bar{Q}\bar{R} + \bar{P}\bar{Q}RS + \bar{P}R\bar{S} + PQR\bar{S} + P\bar{Q}\bar{R}$.

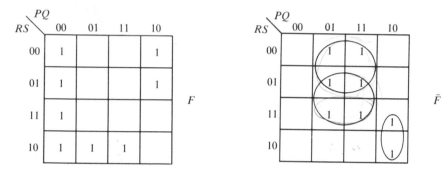

$$\bar{F} = Q\bar{R} + QS + P\bar{Q}R$$
$$F = \bar{\bar{F}} = \overline{(Q\bar{R} + QS + P\bar{Q}R)}$$
$$= \overline{(Q\bar{R})} \cdot \overline{(QS)} \cdot \overline{(P\bar{Q}R)} \qquad \text{T5a}$$
$$= (\bar{Q} + R)(\bar{Q} + \bar{S})(\bar{P} + Q + \bar{R}) \qquad \text{T5b}$$

B.2.6   Minimization Using Don't Cares

Don't cares are indicated by a "*d*" on the K-map. Each can be treated as either a 1 or a 0. It is not necessary to cover all the don't cares while grouping; that is, don't cares not covered are treated as 0s.

Example B.13   The BCD-to-Excess-3 decoder discussed in Chapter 1 expects as inputs only the combinations corresponding to decimals 0 through 9. The other six inputs will never occur. Hence, the output corresponding to each of these six inputs is a don't care.

The maps at the top of page 445 illustrate the use of don't cares in simplifying the output functions of the decoder (refer to the truth table in Chapter 1).

K-maps are useful for functions with up to four or five variables. Figure B.7 shows a five-variable K-map. Since the number of blocks doubles for

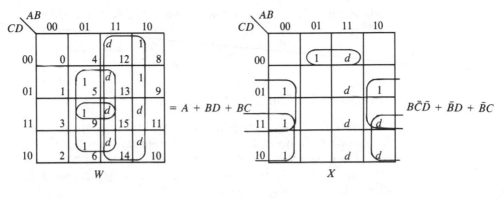

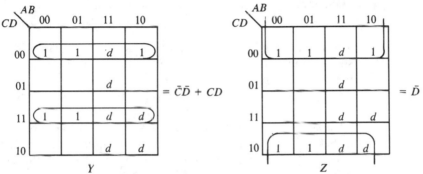

Figure B.7 Five-variable Karnaugh map

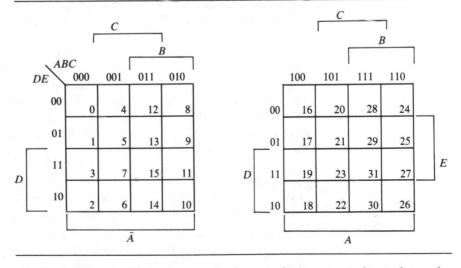

Note: The two parts of the map are treated as two planes, one superimposed over the other. The blocks at the same position on each plane are also logically adjacent.

each additional variable, minimization using K-maps becomes complex for functions with more than five variables. The Quine-McCluskey procedure described in the next section is useful in such cases.

B.3   The Quine-McCluskey Procedure

The Quine-McCluskey procedure also uses the logical adjacency property to reduce the Boolean function. Two minterms are logically adjacent if they differ in one position only; that is, if one of the variables is in uncomplemented form in one minterm and complemented form in the other. Such a variable is eliminated by combining the two minterms. The Quine-McCluskey procedure compares each minterm with all the others and combines them is possible. The procedure uses the following steps:

1. Classify the minterms (and don't cares) of the function into groups such that each term in a group contains the same number of 1s in the binary representation of the term.
2. Arrange the groups formed in step 1 in the increasing order of number of 1s. Let the number of groups be n.
3. Compare each minterm in group $i (i = 1$ to $n - 1)$ with those in group $(i + 1)$; if the two terms are adjacent, form a combined term. The variable thus eliminated is represented as "$-$" in the combined term.
4. Repeat the matching operation of step 3 on the combined terms until no more combinations can be done. Each combined term in the final list is called a *prime implicant* (PI). A prime implicant is a product term that cannot be combined with others to yield a term with fewer literals.
5. Construct a *prime implicant chart* in which there is one column for each minterm (only minterms; don't cares are not listed) and one row for each PI. An "X" in a row-column intersection indicates that the prime implicant corresponding to the row covers the minterm corresponding to the column.
6. Find all the essential prime implicants (i.e., the prime implicants that each cover at least one minterm that is not covered by any other PI).
7. Select a minimum number of prime implicants from the remaining, to cover those minterms not covered by the essential PIs.
8. The set of prime implicants thus selected forms the minimum function.

This procedure is illustrated by Example B.14.

Example B.14

$$F(A,B,C,D) = \Sigma m\underbrace{(0,2,4,5,6,9,10)}_{\text{Minterms}} + \Sigma_d \underbrace{(7,11,12,13,14,15)}_{\text{Don't cares}}.$$

Steps 1 and 2

√ 0	0000	Group 0: Terms with no 1s.
√ 2	0010	— only 1 "ones"
√ 4	0100	Group 1: Terms with 1.
√ 5	0101	
√ 6	0110	2 "ones"
√ 9	1001	Group 2: Terms with two 1s.
√10	1010	
√12	1100	
√ 7	0111	3 "ones"
√11	1011	
√13	1101	Group 3: Terms with three 1s.
√14	1110	
√15	1111	Group 4: Terms with four 1s.

The "√" indicates that the term is used in forming a combined term at least once.

Step 3

√(0,2)	00-0	Obtained by matching groups 0 and 1.
√(0,4)	0-00	
√(2,6)	0-10	
√(2,10)	-010	
√(4,5)	010-	Obtained by matching groups 1 and 2.
√(4,6)	01-0	
√(4,12)	-100	

(continued)

Step 3   (continued)

√(5,7)	01−1
√(5,13)	−101
√(6,7)	011−
√(6,14)	−110
√(9,11)	10−1
√(9,13)	1−01
√(10,11)	101−
√(10,14)	1−10
√(12,13)	110−
√(12,14)	11−0

Obtained by matching groups 2 and 3.

√(7,15)	−111
√(11,15)	1−11
√(13,15)	11−1
√(14,15)	11−

Obtained by matching groups 3 and 4.

Step 4

(0,2,4,6)	0−−0	Same as (0,4,2,6).
(2,6,10,14)	−−10	Same as (2,10,6,4).
√ (4,5,6,7)	01−−	Same as (4,6,5,7).
√ (4,5,12,13)	−10−	Same as (4,12,5,13).
√ (4,6,12,14)	−1−0	Same as (4,12,6,14).
√ (5,7,13,15)	−1−1	
√ (6,7,10,15)	−11−	
(9,11,13,15)	1−−1	
(10,11,14,15)	1−1−	
√ (12,13,14,15)	11−−	
(0,2,4,6)	0—0	PI_1
(2,6,10,14)	−−10	PI_2
(4,5,6,7,12,13,14,15)	−1−−	PI_3 Prime implicants.
(9,11,13,15)	1−−1	PI_4
(10,11,14,15)	1−1−	PI_5

No further reduction possible.

Step 5   Prime implicant chart

Minterms

	√ 0	√ 2	√ 4	√ 5	√ 6	√ 9	√ 10
PI_1	⊗	×	×		×		
PI_2		×			×		×
PI_3			×	⊗	×		
PI_4						⊗	
PI_5							×

Step 6 PI_1, PI_3, and PI_4 are "essential" since minterms 0, 5, and 9, respectively, are covered by only these PIs. These PIs together also cover minterms 2, 4, and 6.

Step 7   To cover the remaining minterm 10, we can select either PI_2 or PI_5.

Step 8   The reduced function is

$$F(A,B,C,D) = PI_1 + PI_3 + PI_4 + PI_2 \text{ or } PI_5$$
$$= 0{-}{-}0 + {-}1{-}{-} + 1{-}{-}1 + {-}{-}10 \text{ or } 1{-}1{-}$$
$$= (\bar{A}\bar{D} + B + AD + C\bar{D}) \text{ or } (\bar{A}\bar{D} + B + AD + AC).$$

The Quine-McCluskey procedure can be programmed on a computer and is efficient for functions of any number of variables.

B.4   Conclusions

Several other techniques to simplify Boolean functions have been devised. The interested reader is referred to the books listed under references. The automation of Boolean function minimization has been an active research area over the seventies. The advent of LSI and VLSI has contributed to a decline of interest in the minimization of Boolean functions. The minimization of the number of ICs and the efficient interconnection between them is of more significance than the saving of a few gates in the present-day design environment.

References

Mano, M. *Digital Logic and Computer Design.* Englewood Cliffs, N.J.: Prentice-Hall, 1979.

Nagle, H. T., J. D. Irwin, and B. D. Carroll. *Introduction to Computer Logic.* Englewood Cliffs, N.J.: Prentice-Hall, 1975.

Prather, R. E. *Introduction to Switching Theory: A Mathematical Approach.* Boston, Mass.: Allyn & Bacon, 1967.

Roth, C. H. *Fundamentals of Logic Design.* St. Paul, Minn.: West, 1979.

Shiva, S. G., and H. T. Nagle. A series of three articles on computer-aided logic design. *Electronic Design,* October 11, October 25, and November 8, 1974.

Appendix C

Hardware Description Languages (HDL)

A digital system can be described in six levels of complexity:

1. Algorithmic level, which specifies only the algorithm used by the hardware for the problem solution.
2. Processor, memory, and switch (PMS) level, which describes the system in terms of processing units, memory components, peripherals, and switching networks.
3. Instructional level (programming level), where the instructions and their interpretation rules are specified.
4. Register-transfer level, where the registers are system elements and the data transfer between these registers are specified according to some rule.
5. Switching-circuit level, where the system structure consists of an interconnection of gates and flip-flops and the behavior is given by a set of Boolean equations.
6. Circuit level, where the gates and flip-flops are replaced by circuit elements such as transistors, diodes, and resistors.

Logic diagrams and Boolean equations have been used as media for hardware description. The complexity of these media increases rapidly as system complexity increases and they are not convenient to use as we move into the higher levels from the switching-circuit level. Hardware description languages (HDL) evolved as a solution. Although the use of computer-oriented languages to describe system design can be traced back to Shannon's work on switching circuits in the late thirties, Aiken's work on switching theory in the forties, the logic diagrams at the Massachusetts Institute of Technology and the National Bureau of Standards in late forties, and the flip-flop equations in the fifties, Iverson's work on a

451

formal HDL in the sixties probably initiated the contemporary interest in this area. An HDL is similar to any other high-level programming language (HLL) and provides a means of

1. Precise yet concise description of the system.
2. Convenient documentation to generate users manuals, service manuals, and the like.
3. Inputting the system description into a computer for simulation and design verification at various levels of detail.
4. Software generation at the preprototype level, thus bridging the hardware-software development time gap.
5. Incorporating design changes and corresponding changes in documentation efficiently.
6. Designer-user (or teacher-student) communication interface at the desired level of complexity.

HDLs are capable of describing the parallelism, nonrecursive nature, and timing issues of the hardware more naturally and thus differ from the purely sequential nature of a general HLL. An HDL can be classified as either a *procedural* or a *nonprocedural* language. Each statement in a nonprocedural HDL description contains a "label" that describes the condition under which the activities described by the statement are to be performed. Thus, the sequential ordering of the statements does not dictate the ordering of the activities. In a procedural HDL description, the activities are performed according to the sequential ordering of the statements.

Several HDLs have been developed since Iverson's proposal of an HDL. Translators to convert the description into an intermediate executable code and simulators to execute this code have been written for some of these languages. No single HDL has met all the characteristics desired by a hardware design environment. The tendency has been to invent a new HDL to suit a particular design environment, basically due to the difficulty in transferring the translators and simulators to the new computing systems and extending them to accommodate the requirements of the new design environment. We will next discuss the utility of HDLs in system design and provide the details of one popular HDL, the Computer Design Language (CDL).

C.1   HDLs in System Design

Figure C.1 illustrates the utility of an HDL in a digital system design environment. The designer uses the HDL to describe his design. This description is translated into a computer-executable data base, which serves as the source for various other operations. The design can be

Figure C.1 Digital system design automation process

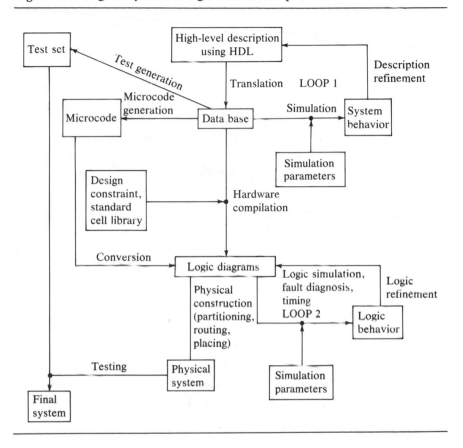

refined by simulating at the description level (loop 1) before proceeding to be a more detailed simulation (loop 2) at the logic level. The data base also serves as a source for logic diagram generation, microcode, and test-set generation. The physical construction of the system follows the simulation and refinement at the logic level.

C.2   Computer Design Language (CDL)

CDL was proposed originally by Professor Y. Chu at the University of Maryland in 1965. Several extensions to the language have been proposed since then. We will discuss a version of the language for which a translator and a simulator are available. These programs have been written in FORTRAN for UNIVAC 1100 series machines by J. Bara at the Michigan

Technological University. The translator converts a CDL description into an intermediate reverse polish notation. The simulator enables a register-transfer-level simulation of the translated description. The language and details of translator and simulator options are described in this section.

CDL describes the structural and functional parts of a digital system. The structural components such as memory, registers, clocks, and switches are described explicitly at the beginning of the description. The functional behavior of the element is described by the commonly used operators and user-defined operators. Valid data paths are declared whenever there is a data transfer. Both parallel and sequential operations are allowed. Synchronous operations require a conditional test of an appropriate signal. The language is easy to understand and is highly readable.

All the variables in a CDL description are global. The system description can be only at one level, and there is no subroutine facility in CDL making it unsuitable for describing hardware in a modular fashion. It is not possible to include special hardware components like integrated circuits in a description. However, its simplicity of structure and its portability resulting from the FORTRAN implementation have made CDL a popular language. A description of CDL syntax and semantics as accepted by the CDL translator and simulator is given below.

C.2.1   Syntax Rules

Reserved Names.   The character strings IF, ELSE, DO, RETURN, and END may not be used as variable names. The above words serve a special purpose that is discussed in detail elsewhere in this section.

Structure.   A valid CDL structure is any variable name, a variable being of one of the fifteen declarative types (e.g., CLOCK, REGISTER, MEMORY). A variable name may be alphanumeric but must begin with an alphabetic character. Only the first six characters are significant.

Constant.   A valid CDL constant is a number, be it binary, hexadecimal, octal, or one of the other possible radices, whose binary equivalent does not exceed 36 bits in length. Exception: a constant that is used in a subscript must have a binary equivalent that does not exceed 35 bits in length. (This is due to the implementation on a 36-bit UNIVAC 1100).

Delimiters.   Valid CDL delimiters are

> Comma
> Apostrophe
> Slash

Minus sign	−
Plus sign	+
Asterisk	*
Period	.
Left parenthesis	(
Right parenthesis	)
Equal sign	=

C.2.2 Operators

There are twenty built-in operators in CDL. The four categories are

1. Relational.
2. Logical.
3. Arithmetic.
4. Manipulatory.

Several operators have the format

$$\cdot oper \cdot$$

These operators have the distinction of being special operators. The basic format of an operator, however, when referenced, is described as:

1. Binary operators: Str_1 op Str_2.
2. Unary operators: Str_1 op or op Str_1.

Exception: In the case of the invert operator, the form must be

$$Str_1 \ op.$$

The parameters Str_1 and Str_2 are structures, subscripted or unsubscripted, to be operated upon, "op" being the operator in question.

Relational Operators.   All six operators have a logical value of 1 if the respective contingency is satisfied; otherwise, a logical value of 0 results.

Operator	Contingency
.EQ.	Str_1 is equal to Str_2.
.NE.	Str_1 is not equal to Str_2.
.GT.	Str_1 is greater than Str_2.
.LT.	Str_1 is less than Str_2.
.GE.	Str_1 is greater than or equal to Str_2.
.LE.	Str_1 is less than or equal to Str_2.

Logical Operators. The four logical operators perform, in parallel, the following bit manipulations.

Operator	Bit manipulation
.AND.	Performs the logical AND between Str_1 and Str_2.
*	Same as .AND. above.
.OR.	Performs the logical OR between Str_1 and Str_2.
+	Same as .OR. above.
.ERA.	Forms the EXCLUSIVE-OR between Str_1 and Str_2.
	Forms the COMPLEMENT of Str_1.

Arithmetic Operators. The four arithmetic operators are listed below.

Operator	Functional description
.ADD.	Str_1 is ADDed to Str_2.
.SUB.	Str_2 is SUBTRACTed from Str_1.
.CNTUP.	Str_1 is incremented by one.
.CNTDN.	Str_1 is decremented by one.

Manipulatory Operators. The six manipulatory operators are enumerated below.

Operator	Functional Description
.SHR.	Shifts Str_1 right one bit position; the most significant bit carried in is 0.
.SHL.	Shifts Str_1 left one bit position; the least significant bit carried in is 0.
.CIR.	Circulates Str_1 right one bit position; the least significant bit carried out is carried in to the most significant position.
.CIL.	Circulates Str_1 left one bit position, the most significant bit carried out is carried in to the least significant position.
.SHRA.	Shifts Str_1 right arithmetically one bit position; the most significant bit carried in is identical to the most significant bit before the operation was initiated.
—	Cascades, or concatenates, Str_1 with Str_2.

C.2.3 Declaration Statements

Declarations enable the logic designer to specify hardware descriptions of various logic elements. The designer may work with twelve different components in addition to three software aids—yielding fifteen different declarative types.

Register. A register declaration declares registers with the required number of bits.

REGISTER, $A(0-2), R, F\ (6-1), G(0-5)$.

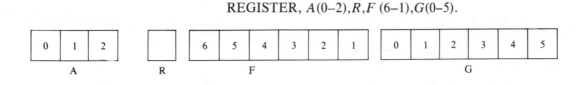

Subregister. The subregister is always used with a register name, and it refers to a part of that register. All referenced registers must have been previously declared.

SUBREGISTER, $G(OP) = G(0-2), F(OR) = F(6-4)$.

Caution: A general tendency is to give two subregisters the same name. For example,

SUBREGISTER, $R(OP) = R(0-3), A(OP) = A(0-3)$.

This is incorrect! A correct statement of the above would be

SUBREGISTER, $R(OPR) = R(0-3), A(OP) = A(0-3)$.

Encoder. In the succeeding context an encoder is a combinational network whose output is the position of a register's most significant (leftmost) 1 bit. The declaration

ENCODER, ENC(1–3) = ADDR(7–0),
1   CN (3–0) = BUFFER

defines the following hardware (ADDR and BUFFER having been previously declared). The 1 in the above declaration is a continuation flag.

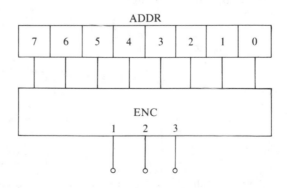

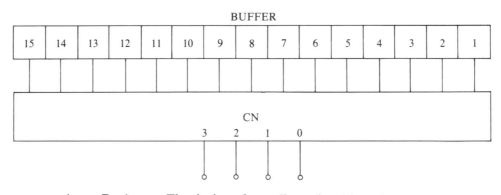

Array Register. The design of two-dimensional iterative circuits may be greatly enhanced where the array register structure is employed. The declaration

ARRAY REGISTER, ARRAY(0–2, 1–4)

defines the following register:

ARRAY

	1	2	3	4
0	1	2	3	4
1	1	2	3	4
2	1	2	3	4

Decoder. A decoder is a logic network that translates each value of the contents of register to one and only one of the outputs. The declaration

DECODER, $K(0–1) = R, L(0–15) = G(2–5)$

declares the following:

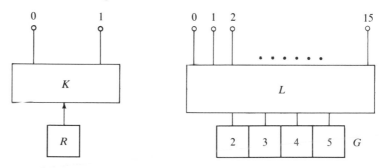

where R and G have been previously declared.

Data Selector. A data selector is a combinational network that, through an external control, selects one set of input lines from many possible inputs. An example follows. The declarations

> REGISTER, *A,B*
>
> TERMINAL, *T0* = 0,
>
> 1 $T1 = A * B,$
>
> 1 $T2 = A . ERA. B,$
>
> 1 $T3 = A + B$
>
> REGISTER, SELECT(0–1)
>
> DATA SELECTOR, DTA(SELECT) = DTA(*T0*–*T3*)

define the following topography:

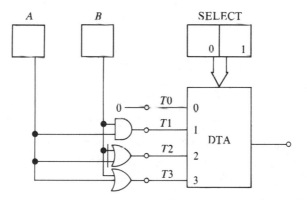

Stack Memory. The stack memory declaration facilitates the description of a random-access store similar to a memory, except that each stack memory word is, in fact, a stack that may be allocated, freed, and accessed. The declarations

> REGISTER, *MAR* (1–2)
>
> STACK MEMORY, *STK*(3,*MAR*) = *STK*(0–3,0–2)

define the following stack memory with an associated address register:

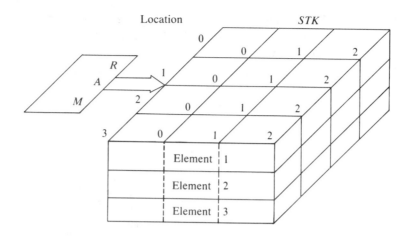

Clock.   A clock may be specified for event synchronization. The declaration

$$\text{CLOCK, } P(2)$$

defines three clocks, $P(0), P(1), P(2)$. The impulse diagrams are assumed to be the following:

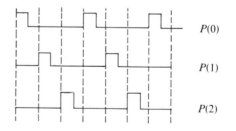

The time intervals between the impulses given by the clocks are the same. A clock may be referenced only in the expression of the label. During execution, a clock cycle is designated on the simulation results as clock time.

Switch.   The switch names are STRT and SENS. The positions for STRT are OFF and ON and for SENS they are $P1$, $P2$, and $P3$ where OFF and $P1$ are the respective initial positions.

$$\text{SWITCH, STRT(OFF,ON),SENS}(P1,P2,P3)$$

In later references, a switch is either checked for one of its positions, or set to one of its positions. When a switch is checked for a position, it has the form

$$\text{NAME}(POS) \qquad \text{as in} \qquad \text{SENS}(P2).$$

When setting a switch to a position:

$$\text{NAME} = \text{POS} \qquad \text{as in} \qquad \text{SENS} = P2.$$

Note: A maximum of ten switch positions is permitted.

Terminal. A terminal statement can simply rename a device or a part of a device or describe a logic network. All referenced devices must have been previously declared. The declarations are

REGISTER,	$A(0-2)$
TERMINAL,	$B0 = A(0)', B1 = A(1)',$
	$B2 = A(2)'$

or using subscripted terminals,

REGISTER,	$A(0-2)$
TERMINAL,	$B(0-2) = A(0-2)'$

Both of these describe the following:

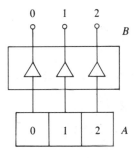

Referring to the decoder example,

$$\text{TERMINAL, ADD} = L(0),$$
$$\text{SUB} = L(1),$$
$$\text{JUM} = L(2), \text{ etc.}$$

Caution: Do not try to use a ripple (iterative) method with the terminal statement. This type of method does not work. For example,

$$\text{TERMINAL, CARRY}(1-3) = (\text{CARRY}(0-2)*(A(0-2).ERA.B(0-2))).$$

The new CARRY(1), which is equal to $(\text{CARRY}(0)*(A(0).ERA.B(0)) + (A(0)*B(0)))$, will not be used when calculating CARRY(2). Instead, the previous values of the carry bits will be used.

Bus.

$$\text{BUS, INTERNAL}(15-0), \text{DATA}(7-0).$$

This declares INTERNAL and DATA as buses consisting of sixteen and eight lines, respectively.

Block.   In order to avoid the repeated writing of a group of microstatements, the BLOCK statement and DO/statements are created. The block statement declares the name for a group of microstatements. Whenever these microstatements are required in an execution statement, a DO statement is used to call them. The formats of these declarations are

$$\text{BLOCK, name (microstatements)}$$
$$\text{DO/name}$$

A serial complementer (SERCOM) is declared:

REGISTER,	$T(1-5), A(5-1)$
SWITCH,	START(ON)
CLOCK,	P
BLOCK,	SERCOM($A = A(1)' -A(5-2)$).

The following statements call SERCOM repeatedly. The expressions between slashes (/) are labels. A statement is activated only when the label expression has a value of 1. Register T is used to control the complementation. Since A is a 5-bit register, SERCOM is used five times to completely complement it.

/START(ON)/	$T = 16$
/$T(1)$*P/	DO/SERCOM, $T(1,2) = 01$.
/$T(2)$*P/	DO/SERCOM, $T(2,3) = 01$.
/$T(3)$*P/	DO/SERCOM, $T(3,4) = 01$.
/$T(4)$*P/	DO/SERCOM, $T(4,5) = 01$.
/$T(5)$*P/	DO/SERCOM, $T(5) = 01$.

Another example of block declaration follows:

$$\text{BLOCK, PAR}(A = B, R = 0), \text{CYC}(A = A.COUNT.,$$
$$\text{IF}(A.EQ.1)\text{THEN}(R = 1)\text{ELSE}(R\ 0)).$$

All of the microstatements following the respective block names (PAR,CYC) will be executed when DO/PAR or DO/CYC are called.

Partition. The PARTITION declaration permits the logic designer to impart some significance to a particular segment of a BUS. The declarations

BUS, DATA(0–7),		
1	IO	(3–6)
PARTITION, DATA(OPCODE) = DATA(0–2),		
1	IO(DEVICE) = IO(4)	

define the following topology:

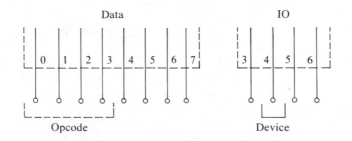

C.2.4 Continuation

All declarations start in column two. Column one thus is left blank. A declaration statement may be continued on subsequent cards by placing a 1 in column 1 on those cards. Label and switch statements (See Section C.2.8) start in column 2, but may be continued on subsequent cards by leaving column one blank, as shown by the following example:

$$\text{REGISTER } A(0\text{--}2),$$
$$1 \qquad\qquad B(0\text{--}6),$$
$$1 \qquad\qquad C(6\text{--}1),$$
$$/K*A(2)/ \quad B = B.CNTUP.,$$
$$C = C.CNTUP.$$

C.2.5 Comments

A comment may be made by placing a C in column one. The comment will be ignored by the translator. Comments are not continued in the conventional manner; rather, a C in column one of every subsequent card will continue the comment:

$$C \qquad \text{SIMULATION OF A SECOND}$$
$$C \qquad \text{GENERATION COMPUTER}$$

C.2.6 Microstatements

An *unconditional* microstatement consists of a variable representing a storage element, the replace operator, and an expression, as shown here:

$$A = 1, B(3\text{--}5) = C*D + E(0\text{--}2).$$

A given device or portion of a device must not appear on the left of a "replace by" operator more than once in any set of microstatements to be executed during a given label cycle.

A *conditional* microstatement has the following forms:

1. IF (expression) THEN (microstatements). IF (expression) has the value 1, then the operations indicated by the (microstatements) will be executed.

$$\text{IF}(A.EQ.B)\text{THEN}(R = 0).$$

2. IF (expression) THEN (microstatements) ELSE (microstatements). IF the (expression) is true then the operations indicated by the (microstatements) immediately following THEN will be executed; otherwise, the operations indicated by the (microstatements) immediately following ELSE will be executed.

$$IF(C.NE.D)THEN(R = 0)ELSE(R = 1).$$

Conditional statements may be nested in order to form a very powerful decision making capability. Note that each of the nested IFs must be enclosed in parentheses as shown in the following generalized example:

IF (exp 1) THEN (microstatements)

ELSE (IF(exp 2) THEN (microstatements))

ELSE (IF(exp 3) THEN (microstatements))

ELSE (IF . . . .)

ELSE (microstatements)))). .)

C.2.7 Labeled Statements

The label statement has the following form:

/LABEL/ microstatements

where

LABEL = expression * clock.

Restriction: The expression must not include any clock reference.

$$/K(0)*P/ A = B, B = A.$$

C.2.8 Switch Statements

The switch statement has the following form:

/NAME(POSITION)/ microstatements

where NAME corresponds to a declared switch name. In the following

SWITCH, STRT(OFF,ON), SENS(S1,S2,S3)

$$/STRT(ON)/A = 0, F = 1, SENS = S2.$$

The indicated microstatements here would not be executed since STRT(ON) is FALSE.

C.2.9   End Statement

The physical end of the description of a design is indicated by the word END.

C.2.10   IOFLAG

The IOFLAG declaration facilitates output control. The basic format for the IOFLAG declaration is

$$\text{IOFLAG, Name}$$

where "name" is the name of the declared IOFLAG. Only one IOFLAG may be declared in a given translation section; otherwise, the IOFLAG may be handled as any other single-bit register. The IOFLAG is set by storing a 1 and is cleared by storing a 0. The simulator OUTPUT routine (See Section C.4) uses the IOFLAG information. If the output "type" is ONFLAG, the following operations occur: Setting the flag at a given label cycle, output is enabled on the succeeding label cycle. When the flag is cleared, output for the following label cycles is disabled. The IOFLAG is always set prior to the initialization of a simulation.

C.3   Translator

The translator converts the CDL description into a reverse polish notation suitable for simulation. The translator is called by a special control card having $TRANSLATE punched in columns 1–10. This card is followed by the deck of cards describing the logical design using CDL. The translator remains in control until a new control card with $ in column 1 is read in. A typical deck setup should appear as follows:

$TRANSLATE	Informs the CDL executive program that the following card images, up to the $SIMULATE control card, contain a description of the design to be simulated; hence, they are to be translated into executable code.
*MAIN	Designates that all card images between itself and the first END card encountered constitute the main line.
.	
.	
.	
END	

```
*OPERATOR, . . .        Translator is in control.
       .
       .
       .
       .
       .
       .

END
$SIMULATE              Simulator is called; simulator is in control.
       .

$$                     Indicates to the CDL simulator that an end of record
                       has been encountered.
```

Declaration cards, labeled statement cards, and the end card may be punched anywhere in columns 2–72. Blanks may be used freely.

C.4   Simulator

The simulator consists of five routines: loader, output, switch, simulate, and reset. The *loader* accepts test programs from punched cards and stores them into memory or into specified registers of the designed computer. The *output* routine handles the print out of the contents of the chosen registers, memory words, buses, and position of switches and lights during the simulation. The *switch* routine simulates the operation of the manual switches. The *simulate* routine actually executes the test program. *Reset* routine reinitializes the simulator.

The execution of the test program is controlled by a loop that is called the *label cycle*. During each label cycle, the following steps are taken:

1. If a manual switch operation occurs, the corresponding executable statement for the switch operation is carried out.
2. All label values are evaluated. The activated labels, i.e., the label expressions having the value TRUE, are accounted for.
3. The microstatements of the activated labels are carried out in two steps. First, all values to be stored in various registers and memory words are evaluated and collected. Then, the collected values are stored one after the other.
4. Simulation control parameters are checked to see if the simulation should be terminated. If the simulation is terminated, the reset routine can be called and another set of data can be inserted as a test program.

Load Routine.   The loader provides the storing of test programs. The data cards should use columns 2–72; blanks may be inserted anywhere. Only declared full registers and memory words with constant addresses can be loaded with data. The format of the data cards is as follows:

Data loaded into a register: $REG = d$

Data loaded into memory words: $M(L) = d$

   or $M(L_1-L_N) = d_1,d_2, \ldots ,d_N$

   or $M(L_1-) = d_1,d_2, \ldots ,d_N,$

where REG is the name of the register whose contents must be set to the value d M is the name of the memory and L denotes word addresses. In the first case, d is loaded into memory word $M(L)$. In the second case, the words d_1-d_N are loaded into memory words with addresses L_1 to L_N consecutively. In the last case, the last address is defined by the number of numbers punched.

   A data card may contain any number of lists separated by commas. There is no provision for a continuation card; thus, each data card must start with the name of a register or a memory in column 2. An example follows:

   *LOAD

   $RI = 0,AC = 20,SEP = 72,M(0-3) = 1,2,3,4,M(77) = 345$

   $M(10-) = 70,71,72,73,74,75,76,77,100$

Output Routine.   The *OUTPUT control card has the following general form:

*OUTPUT specification = output list

where output list has the construction:

structure$_1$, structure$_2$, ..., structure$_N$

and "specification" has the format of type (contingency):

Type	Contingency
LABEL	ti (*tp)
CLOCK	ti (*tp)
ONFLAG	None allowed

The parameter ti is the initial output time, and tp is the period of outputting. Both ti and tp are integers in any one of the prescribed radices, their binary equivalents not to exceed 35 bits in length. If the period option is not specified, a period of unity is assumed. The three types of specifications are

Type	Significance
ONFLAG	Output only when the system IOFLAG is set.
LABEL	Output beginning at label cycle ti, and every tp label cycles thereafter.
CLOCK	Output beginning at clock time ti and every tp clock times thereafter. Output at each clock time is at clock phase zero.

An example output declaration is

$$*OUTPUT \qquad CLOCK(1,10) = RR, START, M(0), M(777),$$

$$AC, MQ, M(10), OVER, M(20–25)$$

The list may be continued on the next card(s) provided that column 1 is left blank on the continuation cards. The output of all listed devices is given in hexadecimal regardless of input form.

Switch Routine.   Manual switch settings are initiated by the switch routine. The necessary information is given on *SWITCH cards. For each switch setting, a separate *SWITCH card is necessary. It has the following format:

Col. 1–7	*SWITCH
Col. 11–12	L,
Col. 13–	NAME = POSITION

where L specifies the L label cycle before which the switch operation occurs. The NAME corresponds to the name of the switch with POSITION as one of its declared positions. During the simulation, an output will occur after every switch setting with a heading stating the interrupt.

Simulate Routine.   The actual simulation starts by calling the simulate routine using the control card with the following format:

Col. 1–4	*SIM
Col. 11–	n,r

where n and r are the terminating conditions, n is the maximum number of label cycles allowed, and r is the allowed maximum number of consecutive label cycles such that the same group of labels is activated in the CDL program. A command example is

$$*SIM \quad 400,3.$$

Reset Routine.   The reset routine reinitializes the simulator to its initial conditions. It is called by a control card with the following format:

Col. 1–6	*RESET.
Col. 11–	(Options).

The options may be one or more of the following terms separated by commas:

OUTPUT,	Resets the output requested previously; it is assumed that another *OUTPUT card will be given.
SWITCH,	Resets the manual switch operations requested; it is assumed that another *SWITCH card will be given.
CLOCK,	Resets the counter of the clock cycle.
CYCLE,	Resets the label cycle counter and the clock cycle counter.

A command example is given below.

$$*RESET \qquad CYCLE, OUTPUT$$

The RESET card is then followed by another OUTPUT card, possibly another LOAD card with data, and by a SIM card.

Several optional features can be invoked by the options list on the $TRANSLATE and $SIMULATE cards. The general format of these control cards is

$$\$command \qquad Optionlist$$

where

$$command = TRANSLATE \text{ or } SIMULATE \text{ and}$$

$$option \ list = option_1, \ option_2, ...$$

The available options on the $TRANSLATE and $SIMULATE control cards are

SOURCE	Lists source code generated by the translator for the appropriate simulation or translation section.
NSOURCE	Suppresses the source code listing.
TRACE	Generates a traceback of the compiler through the appropriate simulation or translation section.

NTRACE   Suppresses traceback.
DEBUG   Generates an extensive traceback.
NDEBUG   Suppresses the generation of an extensive traceback, normal traceback generated.

The following options apply only to the $TRANSLATE control card:

DECIMAL   Default radix for constants in base 10.
NONARY   Default radix for constants in base 9.
OCTAL   Default radix for constants in base 8.
QUARTIC   Default radix for constants in base 4.
TERNARY   Default radix for constants in base 3.
BINARY   Default radix for constants in base 2.
PRINT   Lists the symbol table and program segment of the polish array upon successful translation.
NLIST   Suppresses printing of the translation section.

If no radix option is present, octal is assumed.

The following options apply only to the $SIMULATE control card:

HEX   Contents of structures outputted shall be expressed in hexadecimal (base 16).
OCTAL   Contents of structures outputted shall be represented in octal (base 8).
CLEAR   Storage array shall be cleared (zeroed) prior to the next simulation (the contents of structures LOADED are not affected by this option). This option is designed primarily to clear any stack memory pointers.

If no output radix option is specified, OCTAL is assumed. The CLEAR option is always set prior to the simulation initiated by the first *SIM control card succeeding a $SIMULATE control card.

The aforementioned user-defined default radices may be overridden by use of the special character ":" (colon) in conjunction with the appropriate radix specification. To realize a radix other than the default, the following format should be used:

:specification constant.

The various radix specifications are enumerated below:

Specification	Radix of constant
B	Binary
T	Ternary
Q	Quartic
O	Octal
N	Nonary

Figure C.2 Deck organization of simple CDL run

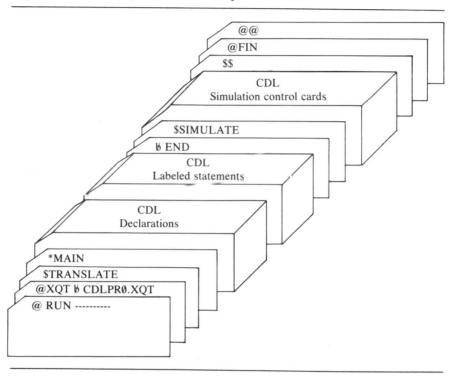

Note: ƀ indicates blank space.

The CDL software system provides an extensive set of error messages. The complete deck setup for a translation and simulation run on UNIVAC 1100 series machines is shown in Figure C.2.

C.5 Description Examples

CDL can be used to describe simple to very complex digital systems. Two descriptions are provided below to illustrate this feature.

Example C.1 *A serial 2s complementer.* A circuit to replace the contents of a 6-bit register R by its 2s complement by the copy-complement algorithm described in Chapter 2 is shown in Figure C.3 along with the CDL description. A 3-bit register C is used to count the number of shifts. Flip-flop S indicates the COPY ($S = 0$) and COMPLEMENT ($S = 1$) states. A switch SW is used to start the complementation process.

Statements 2, 3, and 5 describe these facilities. The control circuitry includes a single-phase clock P and a 1-bit state register T (statements 6 and 5). Figure C.4 shows the state diagram for the control circuitry. The controller waits in $T = 0$ state as long as the SW is off. When SW is on, the C and S are cleared, and a state change occurs (statement 8). As long as $C < 5$, the shift signal is on. Statement 9 describes the process of copying or complementing according to $S = 0$ or 1. Note that the circulation of the register R is described using the concatenation operator. When the count reaches 5, the controller goes to $T = 0$ state, thus completing the complementation.

CDL, being a nonprocedural language, evaluates labels and performs the activities corresponding to the active label. Each such evaluation is a label cycle. During simulation, the values of R, C, S, and T are requested to be OUTPUT at each label cycle (statement 11). The switch is turned on

Figure C.3 Serial 2s complementer

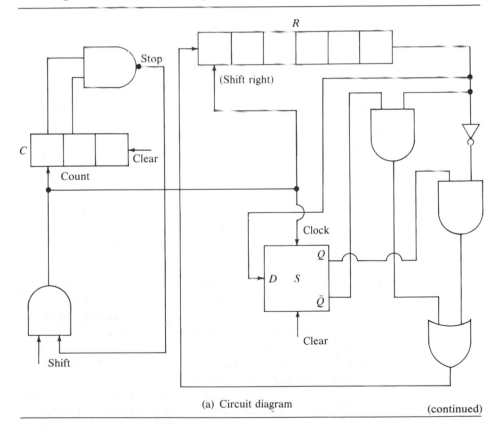

(a) Circuit diagram

(continued)

Figure C.3 (Continued)

```
$TRANSLATE

                                      T R A N S L A T I O N

   *MAIN
   C    **STORAGE**
 2  REGISTER,R(1-6),S
 3  SWITCH,SW(ON,OFF)
 4 C    **CONTROL**
 5  REGISTER,C(2-0),T
 6  CLOCK,P
 7 C    **PROCESSOR**
 8  /SW(ON)/T=1,C=0,S=0
 9  /T*P/IF(S.EQ.0)THEN(S=R(6),R=R(6)-R(1-5))ELSE
        (R=R(6)'-R(1-5)),IF(C.EQ.5)THEN(T=0)
        ELSE(C=C.CNTUP.)
10  END


   $SIMULATE



                                      S I M U L A T I O N

11 *OUTPUT    LABEL(1)=R,C,S,T
12 *SWITCH    1,SW=ON
13 *LOAD
14  R=5
15 *SIM       20,6
```

(b) Description

---

in cycle 1 (statement 12). R is loaded with $(5)_8$ (subscripts indicate the base of the number; the number is decimal if not subscripted) initially (statement 13, 14) and simulation is requested for twenty label cycles with six label-cycle evaluation repetitions to seek an active label before terminating. Figure C.5 shows the simulation results. The contents of R $(73)_8$ at the end of label cycle 6 are the 2s complement of the original contents $(05)_8$, thus indicating the validity of the design.

The clock and label cycles are RESET and R is loaded with $(21)_8$. Figure C.5(b) shows the corresponding simulation results.

Figure C.4 Controller for the 2s complementer

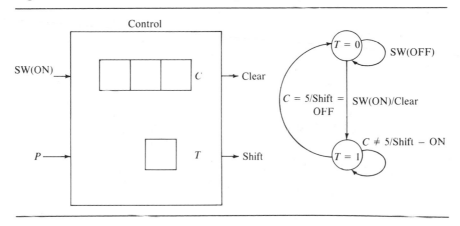

Example C.2 *A minicomputer.* Figure C.6 (page 478) shows the structural details, instruction set, and CDL description of a minicomputer. The minicomputer has a 256-word, 12-bit memory, with an 8-bit memory address register (MAR) and a 12-bit memory buffer register (MBR). There is an 8-bit program counter (PC) and an accumulator (ACC) of 12 bits. The arithmetic logic unit (ALU) receives the operands from MBR and a 12-bit X register and puts the results on to the 12-bit bus. The instructions consist of a 3-bit operation code, an indirect-address flag bit, and 8 address bits. The register-set description is provided by statements 1–3 of Figure C.6(b). The bus is not explicitly described to retain the high-level description nature.

Figure C.6(c) shows the details of the instruction set. Statement 4 describes a START switch, a RUN switch to indicate the RUN/STOP state, and a three-state switch for indicating instruction fetch (F), indirect-address computation (defer, D), and execution (E) phases. Statements 5 and 6 provide the instruction decoding details. There is a four-phase clock P (statement 7) that activates the synchronous control unit. Each major cycle consists of four minor cycles. The comments in the CDL description identify the fetch cycle, defer cycle, and execution cycle for each instruction.

Figure C.6(d) shows a program to add the four numbers in memory locations 0–3 and place the sum in location 7. The program will be located in memory locations 10–16. Location 4 is initialized to −3 and incremented by 1 each time through the loop, and tested for 0 to terminate the summing operation. The data values are accessed by an indirect reference

Figure C.5 Simulation results

```
                    OUTPUT OF SIMULATION - OCTAL

SWITCH TRANSITION AT LABEL CYCLE 1

    SW      -> ON

        R = 05      C = 0            S = 0            T = 1
****************************************************************
LABEL CYCLE 1            TRUE LABELS            CLOCK TIME 1
                         /T*P/
        R = 42      C = 1            S - 1            T = 1
****************************************************************
LABEL CYCLE 2            TRUE LABELS            CLOCK TIME 2
                         /T*P/
        R = 61      C = 2            S = 1            T = 1
****************************************************************
LABEL CYCLE 3            TRUE LABELS            CLOCK TIME 3
                         /T*P/
        R = 30      C = 3            S = 1            T = 1
****************************************************************
LABEL CYCLE 4            TRUE LABELS            CLOCK TIME 4
                         /T*P/
        R = 54      C = 4            S = 1            T = 1
****************************************************************
LABEL CYCLE 5            TRUE LABELS            CLOCK TIME 5
                         /T*P/
        R = 66      C = 5            S = 1            T = 1
****************************************************************
LABEL CYCLE 6            TRUE LABELS            CLOCK TIME 6
                         /T*P/
        R = 73      C = 5            S = 1            T = 0
****************************************************************

            SIMULATION ENDS AFTER 6 REPETITIONS
                 FINAL LABEL CYCLE IS:
                         6
*RESET      CYCLE,CLOCK

OPTIONS IN EFFECT: SOURCE=F DUMP=F HEX-F TRACE=F
DEBUG=F CLEAR=F PRINT=F RADIX=8

*LOAD
 R=21
*SIM       30,6
```

(a)

Figure C.5 (Continued)

```
                    OUTPUT OF SIMULATION - OCTAL

SWITCH TRANSITION AT LABEL CYCLE 1

    SW      -> ON

        R = 21      C = 0           S = 0           T = 1
*****************************************************************
LABEL CYCLE 1           TRUE LABELS         CLOCK TIME 1
                        /T*P/
        R = 50      C = 1           S = 1           T = 1
*****************************************************************
LABEL CYCLE 2           TRUE LABELS         CLOCK TIME 2
                        /T*P/
        R = 64      C = 2           S = 1           T = 1
*****************************************************************
LABEL CYCLE 3           TRUE LABELS         CLOCK TIME 3
                        /T*P/
        R = 72      C = 3           S = 1           T = 1
*****************************************************************
LABEL CYCLE 4           TRUE LABELS         CLOCK TIME 4
                        /T*P/
        R = 75      C = 4           S = 1           T = 1
*****************************************************************
LABEL CYCLE 5           TRUE LABELS         CLOCK TIME 5
                        /T*P/
        R = 36      C = 5           S = 1           T = 1
*****************************************************************
LABEL CYCLE 6           TRUE LABELS         CLOCK TIME 6
                        /T*P/
        R = 57      C = 5           S = 1           T = 0
*****************************************************************

            SIMULATION ENDS AFTER 6 REPETITIONS
                 FINAL LABEL CYCLE IS:
                           6


$EOJ
                              (b)
```

(*TAD** 6) to location 6, which is incremented from 0 by 1 each time through the loop. Figure C.6(d) shows the program in assembly, binary, and decimal forms. Figure C.6(e) shows the memory map just before the execution of the program. This memory map is simulated by the LOAD command of the CDL simulator [statements 43–45 in Figure C.6(b)]. The program counter is set to 10 (statement 46), the switch is turned ON (statement 42), and the simulator is requested for 200 label cycles (statement 47), outputting several register contents (statement 41) at each label cycle. The simulator results are similar to the 2s complementer example and are not shown for the sake of brevity.

Figure C.6 Minicomputer

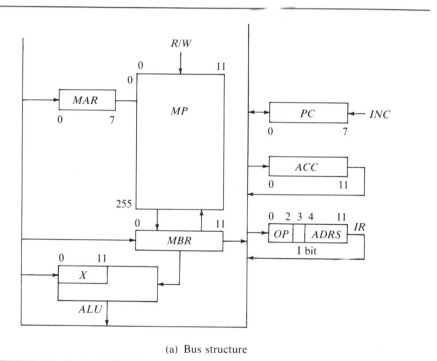

(a) Bus structure

Figure C.6 (Continued)

```
                    T R A N S L A T I O N

    *MAIN
 1  REGISTER,MAR(0-7),MBR(0-11),PC(0-7),ACC(0-11),IR(0-11),X(0-11)
 2  SUBREGISTER,IR(OP)=IR(0-2),IR(IBIT)=IR(3),IR(ADR)=IR(4-11)
 3  MEMORY,M(MAR)=M(0-225,0-11)
 4  SWITCH,START(OFF,ON),RUN(OFF,ON),STATE(F,E,D)
 5  DECODER,K(0-7)=IR(0-2)
 6  TERMINAL,AND=K(0),TAD=K(1),ISZ=K(2),DCA=K(3),JSR=K(4),JMP=K(5),
 1       RET=K(6),HLT=K(7)
 7  CLOCK,P(3)
    C
    C ****   INITIALIZATION
    C
 8  /START(ON)/ACC=0,MAR=PC,IR=0,MBR=0,X=0,START=OFF,RUN=ON,STATE=F
    C
    C ****   FIRST THREE MINOR CYCLES OF FETCH
    C
 9  /RUN(ON)*STATE(F)*P(0)/MAR=PC
10  /RUN(ON)*STATE(F)*P(1)/PC=PC.CNTUP.,MBR=M(MAR)
11  /RUN(ON)*STATE(F)*P(2)/IR=MBR
    C
    C ****   FOURTH FETCH MINOR CYCLE FOR NOT 'HALT' INSTRUCTION
    C ****   DEFER STATE IF INDIRECT, EXECUTE STATE IF NOT
    C
12  /RUN(ON)*STATE(F)*P(3)*(HLT)'/IF(IR(IBIT).EQ.1)THEN(STATE=D)
        ELSE(STATE=E)
    C
    C ****   'HALT' (SINGLE CYCLE)
    C
13  /RUN(ON)*STATE(F)*P(3)*HLT/RUN=OFF
    C
    C ****   DEFER STATE; INDIRECT ADDRESS COMPUTATIONS
    C
14  /RUN(ON)*STATE(D)*P(0)/MAR=IR(ADR)
15  /RUN(ON)*STATE(D)*P(1)/MBR=M(MAR)
16  /RUN(ON)*STATE(D)*P(2)/IR(ADR)=MBR(4-11)
17 /RUN(ON)*STATE(D)*P(3)/STATE=E
    C
    C ****   EXECUTION OF 'AND' AND 'TAD'
    C
18  /RUN(ON)*STATE(E)*P(0)*(AND+TAD)/X=ACC
19  /RUN(ON)*STATE(E)*P(1)*(AND+TAD)/MAR=IR(ADR)
20  /RUN(ON)*STATE(E)*P(2)*(AND+TAD)/MBR=M(MAR)
21  /RUN(ON)*STATE(E)*P(3)*AND/ACC=MBR*X,STATE=F
22  /RUN(ON)*STATE(E)*P(3)*TAD/ACC=MBR.ADD.X,STATE=F
```

(b) CDL description

(continued)

Figure C.6 (Continued)

```
     C
     C ****     'ISZ' EXECUTION
     C
23   /RUN(ON)*STATE(E)*P(0)*ISZ/MAR=IR(ADR)
24   /RUN(ON)*STATE(E)*P(1)*ISZ/MBR=M(MAR)
25   /RUN(ON)*STATE(E)*P(2)*ISZ/MBR=MBR.CNTUP.
26   /RUN(ON)*STATE(E)*P(3)*ISZ/M(MAR)=MBR,IF(MBR.EQ.0)THEN
     (PC=PC.CNTUP.),STATE=F
     C
     C ****     'DCA' EXECUTION
     C
27   /RUN(ON)*STATE(E)*P(0)*DCA/MBR=ACC
28   /RUN(ON)*STATE(E)*P(1)/MAR=IR(ADR)
29   /RUN(ON)*STATE(E)*P(2)*DCA/ACC=0,M(MAR)=MBR
30   /RUN(ON)*STATE(E)*P(3)*DCA/STATE=F
     C
     C ****     'JSR' EXECUTION
     C
31   /RUN(ON)*STATE(E)*P(0)*JSR/MBR=:B0000-PC
32   /RUN(ON)*STATE(E)*P(1)*JSR/MAR=0
33   /RUN(ON)*STATE(E)*P(2)*JSR/M(MAR)=MBR
34   /RUN(ON)*STATE(E)*P(3)*JSR/PC=IR(ADR),STATE=F
     C
     C ****     RETURN EXECUTION
     C
35   /RUN(ON)*STATE(E)*P(0)*RET/MAR=0
36   /RUN(ON)*STATE(E)*P(1)*RET/MBR=M(MAR)
37   /RUN(ON)*STATE(E)*P(3)*RET/PC=MBR(4-11),STATE=F
     C
     C ****     'JMP' EXECUTION
     C
38   /RUN(ON)*STATE(E)*P(0)*JMP/PC=IR(ADR)
39   /RUN(ON)*STATE(E)*P(3)*JMP/STATE=F
40   END

     $SIMULATE


             S I M U L A T I O N

41   *OUTPUT    LABEL(1)=MAR,IR,PC,ACC,MBR,X,STATE,RUN,START,M(7),M(6)
42   *SWITCH    1,START=ON
43   *LOAD
44   M(0-6)=5,6,7,4,4092,0,0
45   M(10-16)=5,774,1030,1028,2571,1543,3584
46   PC=10
47   *SIM       200,5
```

(b) CDL description (continued)

Figure C.6 (Continued)

0	AND	$ACC \leftarrow ACC * M[MEM]$	AND Memory
1	TAD	$ACC \leftarrow ACC + M[MEM]$	ADD
2	ISZ	Increment memory and skip next instruction, if zero.	
3	DCA	Deposit and clear ACC.	
4	JSR	Jump to subroutine, $M[0] \leftarrow PC$.	
5	JMP	Jump.	
6	RET	Return.	
7	HLT	Halt.	

(c)   Instruction set[1]

PROGRAM

Memory location	Assembly		Binary	Decimal
10		AND 5	000 0 00000101	5
11	L1	TAD* 6	000 1 00000110	774
12		ISZ 6	010 0 00000110	1030
13		ISZ 4	010 0 00000100	1028
14		JMP L1	101 0 00001011	2571
15		DCA 7	011 0 00000111	1543
16		HLT	111 0 00000000	3584

(d)   Program to add four integers

Memory

Address	Contents	
0	5	
1	6	DATA
2	7	
3	8	
4	−3	COUNT (= 4,092 in 1s
5	0	complement 12 bits)
6	0	
7	−	RESULT
8	5	
9	774	
10	1030	
11	1028	PROGRAM
12	2571	
13	1543	
14	3584	

(e)   Memory map

[1] [ ] indicates "contents of"; *MEM* is a memory address.

481

References

Bara, J. "Computer Design Language: User's Manual." Houghton, Mich.: Michigan Technological University, 1975.

Bara, J., and R. Born. "A CDL Compiler for Designing and Simulating Digital Systems at the Register Transfer Level." In *Proceedings of the International Symposium on Computer Hardware Description Languages and Applications,* 1975, pp. 96–102.

Chu, Y. "An ALGOL-like Computer Design Language." *Communications of ACM,* Vol. 8, October 1965, pp. 607–615.

Computer. Vol. 7, No. 12, December 1974. Special issue on CHDLs.

Computer. Vol. 10, No. 6, June 1977. HDL applications.

Proceedings of the International Symposium on Computer Hardware Description Languages and Applications, New York, 1975.

Shiva, S. G. "Computer Hardware Description Languages — A Tutorial," *Proceedings of IEEE,* December 1979, pp. 1605–1615.

Index